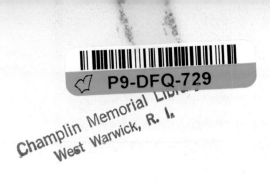

Designing Training
and Development Systems

Designing Training and Development Systems

William R. Tracey

American Management Association, Inc.

International standard book number: 0-8144-5239-6
Library of Congress catalog card number: 70-122586

Second printing

To
Kay, Bill Jr., Kevin,
Brian, Kathy, Maura, and Sean

Preface

THERE is no denying that training and development programs are expensive. They make sense only when the value of their contributions equals the costs. Since this value is often intangible, more often qualitative than quantitative, it has seldom been shown on cost-accounting sheets.

The value of a training and development program to an enterprise may take several forms. It may be stated in terms of reductions or decreases in accident rates, customer complaints, employee grievances, labor disputes, machine downtime, rejects and reworks, or work backlogs. Value may also be stated in terms of improvements or increases in production, sales, employee morale, number of promotable men, product quality, work methods, or quality of supervision. To many companies with their own training and development programs, such values more than justify the costs involved. However, few enterprises can attach a dollar definition to these values and weigh them in relation to costs. Determining a representative figure of new customers gained or old business retained as a direct result of training and development is like trying to attach a dollar value to a computer used to guide business decisions.

Regardless of the difficulties involved, however, the cost-effectiveness of training and development systems must be assessed. A necessary first step in attaining cost benefits is to design training and development systems in such a way that they maximize return on the investment of personnel, time, space, facilities, equipment, and materials.

The relationship between costs on the one hand and personnel, space, facilities, equipment, and materials on the other is readily apparent. The relationship between the dimension of time and costs is perhaps less visible, but time is a major factor in the cost-effectiveness of training and development programs.

Like profit, the concept of time in business and industry is a matter requiring constant reexamination. Each year time becomes a more important factor of cost or savings and also becomes more important in the ability of the enterprise to remain competitive. Reductions in training time, achieved by the design of more efficient training systems, result in savings.

To be competitive, an enterprise has to be aggressive and progressive and has to use to good advantage the modern systems and technologies that are now available. This applies just as much to training and development as it does to any other aspect of enterprise operations. The raison d'être of the new systems and technological innovations is, in a word, *value*.

The purpose of this book is to help training managers and others involved in training and development efforts to maximize value. The book is essentially a step-by-step guide to the *design, development,* and *validation* of training and development systems. Although the book is not intended to be completely prescriptive, it does present a systematic and practical approach to the design of training systems.

The principles and procedures presented in this book have been thoroughly and extensively tested in several different training environments with a wide range of objectives. They have proved to be both workable and effective.

To be more specific, the application of the systems approach in several training and development programs over a six-year period has resulted in positive gains. Evaluation of these systems in operation and follow-up of graduates leads to the conclusion that the new systems produce markedly better graduates than former training programs. On-the-job training requirements have been reduced 50 percent—an average of five weeks. Requirements for the direct supervision of graduates have also been cut 50 percent. As a consequence, graduates of the new systems are on the job sooner and are productively employed much earlier than graduates of the former courses.

Graduates are also more flexible and more responsive to changing requirements. They are more confident and are observably more effective in performing operational, supervisory, and management tasks. Training time has been reduced an average of 10 percent in spite of an increase of 15 to 25 percent in coverage.

In the majority of courses, academic failure has been cut by more than 50 percent. One course that consistently experienced an attrition rate of 25 percent now loses only 4 percent. In several courses academic failure is now less than 1 percent.

Trainees lacking the aptitude for a particular type of training are identified earlier (an average of four weeks as compared with the nine to twelve weeks formerly required), and they are diverted to other training or assignments that are more compatible with their aptitudes. This means that the inept are eliminated before large amounts of training time and other resources have been invested. Improvements have also been made in utilization of instructors and other resources such as equipment and materials.

Other gains include improved instructor and trainee motivation; better and more timely identification and remediation of trainee difficulties; greater and more effective attention to individual differences; better conditions and sequence of learning; easier and more timely modification of systems components (due to their modular design); improved programming for equipment, personnel, and materials; more efficient scheduling and use of facilities; and improved communication between the training activities and the operational units they support.

The impact has been overall improvement in the products of the training facility and, in turn, more effective operations.

Although the professional literature of education and training is staggering in volume, most publications are addressed to the educator rather than the trainer. In spite of the fact that a large number of "educators" are concerned with training at one level or another in both public and private enterprise, few books devoted to training are available. Admittedly, there is a rather imposing array of materials directed to the study of methods, materials, and the like as they apply to training. Unfortunately, much of this material is either unavailable to the trainer or written for an audience of scientists. In fact much of the material currently available has been written by and for behavioral scientists, human factors researchers, and engineering psychologists. For this reason, the terminology used in these publications is highly technical. Furthermore, a large percentage of even these materials is scattered among journal articles and research reports.

Of course, some books have been written for the trainer, but most of these publications are directed at a single aspect of training, such as the selection and use of training aids, the determination of training objectives, or the use of programmed instruction materials. Other published materials, obviously very useful to the trainer, deal exclusively with highly specialized training—for example, executive development, sensitivity training, case method, simulation, creativity, synectics, group process, communication, conference and discussion techniques, human relations, and T-group theory. Although valuable, these treatises do not span the programs for which the training manager is typically held responsible.

It is hoped that this book will fill the gap in the literature of training and development, for it attempts to present a complete view of the more significant aspects of the design of training systems within a framework of modern concepts of training and management.

This book is addressed primarily to the training manager, either present or future, in business, industry, government, military, and public education and training. The content should also be of interest to those who must evaluate the contributions of a training and development activity to the purposes and objectives of an enterprise. Middle- and top-level managers and executives who are not actively involved in the conduct or management of formal training and development programs should, therefore, find this book helpful.

The author recognizes that the tasks involved in designing any training system take the time, effort, and ingenuity of nonmanagerial personnel—the instructors, instructor supervisors, special training staff, psychologists, and personnel workers. This book should offer insights which will help these personnel do their jobs better.

The book has also been written with the student in mind. An attempt has been made to keep the exposition simple and straightforward, and to avoid, where possible, the special terminology of behavioral scientists and engineering psychologists. Additional references have been included at the conclusion of each chapter to permit in-depth study of the topics discussed. This book, then, could serve as either a basic or a supplementary textbook in such courses as educational psychology, supervisory and employee training, vocational education, nursing education, curriculum development, educational and training technology, job and task analysis, and principles and methods of teaching.

Thanks go to the staff, faculty, and students of the United States Army Security Agency Training Center and School at Fort Devens, Massachusetts, who have worked with me in finding workable solutions to military education and training problems. Two of my colleagues who deserve special recognition for their contributions are Dr. Edward B. Flynn, Jr., Director of the Office of Training Requirements, and Dr. C. L. John Legere, Educational Consultant and Director of the Office of Career Development Study. They are responsible for many of the ideas expressed in this book. Finally, special thanks are due to Betty M. Eaton who typed the manuscript and David N. Cantrell who prepared the illustrations.

William R. Tracey

Contents

1

The Systems Approach
to Training and Development

Since World War II, an impressive array of technologies and tools has been created to assist the manager. The new technologies include operations research, systems analysis, systems and value engineering, computer and information science, and management science. Some of the new tools are linear programming, cost-effectiveness analysis, program evaluation review technique (PERT), performance and cost evaluation (PACE), critical path method (CPM), decision theory, sensitivity analysis, simulation, and modeling.

Many of these technologies and techniques were originally designed and used in weapons systems development. More recently, however, these managerial innovations have been applied to political, economic, social, military, and industrial problems of increasingly broad scope. It is the thesis of this book that these systematic procedures can and should be employed in designing training and development systems.

The purpose of this chapter is to present a generalized, integrated, and conceptual picture of the major steps in designing, developing, and validating a *learning system*. The approach is generalized in the sense that it identifies common elements in the design and validation of training and development systems in all types of enterprise and at all levels. It is integrated in the sense that it deals with the entire process of systems design, development, and validation and describes the relationship of each sequential step to preceding and subsequent steps. The approach is conceptual in two senses: (1) fundamental principles are stressed—that is, attention is focused on the "why," "what," and "when" rather than on the "how," which is treated in the remaining chapters; and (2) neither subject matter nor methodology is discussed.

THE SYSTEMS CONCEPT

SYSTEMS DISCIPLINES

A system is any combination of human and material resources, including the organization and procedures required to coordinate their functioning, employed to achieve a mission or objective. A true *closed-loop system* has the following characteristics: (1) it is an organized and orderly whole with clearly definable boundaries, (2) it has a mission or objective, (3) it has several interdependent and interacting components, and (4) it has some type of feedback mechanism.

Systems analysis is the systems discipline that has received the greatest amount of attention. In the strict sense of the term, however, systems analysis is only *one* of a series of interrelated and interacting technologies used to analyze, evaluate, design, and engineer a total system, whether it be a vehicle, a weapon, or a training program. The relationships among the several systems disciplines are depicted in Figure 1-1.

As noted earlier, systems are created to accomplish a mission or objective and its associated functions. The left side of Figure 1-1 shows the design phase. *Systems analysis* is the process of breaking a whole into its component parts and relating these parts to each other and to the whole. The objective of systems analysis is to enable the manager to acquire a better understanding of the behavior of the whole system by studying the behavior and interactions of its parts.

Systems engineering involves a search for ways and means of satisfying the functional requirements of the system; it relates mission and system. Systems engineering translates concepts into procedures which will produce the desired systems output.

The right side of Figure 1-1 portrays the evaluation phase. *Value analysis* involves the evaluation of basic systems functions and alternative design approaches to determine which design contributes the most to overall systems value. *Value engineering* is a logical, organized method of studying hardware, software, and procedures to insure that the required systems functions are achieved at the lowest possible cost. In short, value engineering relates the system to hardware, software, and procedures.

ANALYSIS OF TRAINING SYSTEMS

Applied to training and development, systems analysis is usually considered to encompass all the systems disciplines. It is viewed as a strategy for improving decision making. The goal of the process is to enable training managers to make choices which will achieve maximum internal operating efficiency of the components of the system. More specifically, the objective of training systems analysis is to help training managers to

Figure 1-1.   The relationships among systems disciplines.

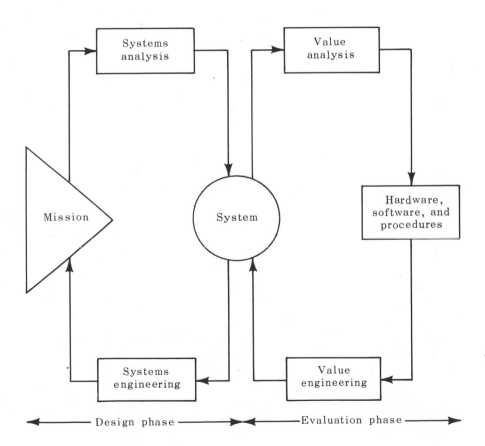

plan, organize, staff, direct, and control available resources in such a way
as to achieve enterprise training and development goals efficiently and
effectively.

The process of training systems analysis essentially involves a series
of carefully sequenced activities as follows:

1. Formulate a clear and unequivocal definition and specification of
   the system under consideration to include the need for the system
   and the delimitation of its boundaries.
2. Develop lucid and functional descriptions of the components of
   the system and the ways in which they interact.
3. Determine and define the system objectives in terms of optimal
   system operating performance and output.
4. Identify and specify the criteria to be used for evaluating the con-
   gruence of system objectives, performance, and output.
5. Identify and select alternative groupings of system components
   for evaluation in terms of practicability, desirability, and cost
   benefits, and determine the tradeoffs involved.
6. Test selected alternatives to collect data upon which decision
   makers may base their choice of the configuration of system components for implementation.

MODELS

One of the primary lessons learned in weapons systems management
is the importance of accurate and complete systems identification, including accurate specification of systems functions and the relationship of
these functions to each other and to the mission objectives.

Structure exists in training and development systems no less than it
does in weapons systems. Unfortunately, however, standardized descriptive terms and other means of identification have not been established for
training systems. Yet, such identification data are essential to the establishment of criteria for optimal systems performance; for the examination
of alternative configurations of systems elements and the determination
of their feasibility, acceptability, and cost-effectiveness; and for the
objective presentation of these alternatives, together with their supporting
data, to responsible decision makers so that they can select one of the
alternatives for design and implementation.

Not only is training a system, it is also a highly complex system; and
where there is system complexity, there is a need for a planning and
control model to permit proper management of the system.

A model is a representation of a system. The model is not the system; the model represents, in simplified form, selected features of the system under study, but the system is always more complicated and richer in detail than the model.

Mathematical models are the "in thing." They may take the form of quantitative, deterministic, or probabilistic models. There are many systems, however, which can only be partly represented by mathematical models. When this situation occurs, the analyst appears to have only three alternatives: (1) drop the analysis; (2) ignore components that do not lend themselves to mathematical representation, and construct the system from the remaining elements; or (3) arbitrarily assign values to the qualitative aspects of the system, and continue with the analysis. But there is a fourth option: use a qualitative model in the form of a flow chart to depict the total system and its interrelationships. Mathematical models of subsystems can later be constructed where such models apply.

Several components of a training system, particularly those which deal with the logistics of training, are quantifiable. However, most curriculum elements are qualitative. For this reason, it is more practical to develop the overall training systems model in the qualitative mode. Therefore, this discussion will be confined to the development of a generalized, qualitative model which portrays the total training system. The flow-chart model is shown in Figure 1-2. It depicts a closed-loop system, a continuous sequence of steps beginning with goals and functions, continuing through the other system components to evaluation of the end products of the system, and returning to goals and functions—a constantly repeating cycle of evaluation, feedback, and improvement. The system essentially consists of three major phases (1) determination of system requirements; (2) system development; and (3) system validation. Each of these phases has several steps. All components of the model will be briefly discussed in the sections that follow.[1]

GOALS AND FUNCTIONS

The boundaries and determinants of any system are prescribed by the goals to be reached and the functions to be performed. A system is appropriate only when clear-cut relationships have been established

---

[1] This material represents an expansion of the following articles: "Systems Approach Gets Results," *Training in Business and Industry* (June 1967) 4:6: 17–38. "Systems Thinking for Vocational Education," *Educate* (November 1968) 1:3; 18–24, © Gellert Publishing Corporation.

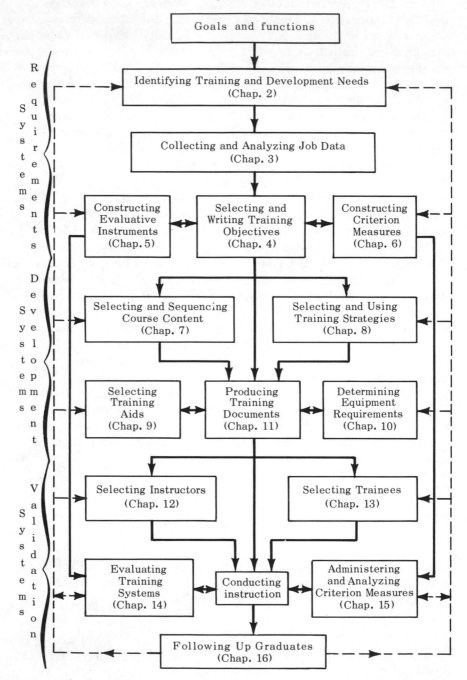

Figure 1-2. *Flow-chart model of a fifteen-step training and development system.*

between the system and its components and the goals and functions it is designed to support.

A goal originates in a recognized need, a requirement that is not being met by existing systems and organizations. Once a need has been identified, goals and functions are assigned, and the human and material resources required to meet the need are allocated.

What is the genesis of the goals of training and development activities in modern organizations? Both private and public enterprise need competent operative, supervisory, and managerial personnel. Although operators, supervisors, and managers can be developed through on-the-job training, self-study and self-development, and varied assignments, these methods are inefficient. A more practical approach is to provide formal training and development programs for selected personnel in sufficient numbers to meet current and projected requirements.

All types of enterprises have responded to the need for skilled personnel by investing in training and development programs. Too often, these programs involve what might be called the "shotgun" approach. Courses have been offered in anything and everything—from lathe operation to sensitivity training. But more and more companies are now questioning the value of such programs. Many have concluded that they are not cost-effective, that return on investment is minimal if it accrues at all.

The ineffectiveness of these programs in producing better operative employees and managers lies in the vagueness of their objectives and in their lack of job relevance. Attempts are now being made to define the objectives of training and development programs more precisely. Programs and systems are being designed to provide employees with the knowledge and skills they need to perform their jobs. The system proposed herein is designed for that express purpose.

ESTABLISHING SYSTEMS REQUIREMENTS

IDENTIFYING TRAINING AND DEVELOPMENT NEEDS

The first step in designing a complete training and development system for an enterprise is to determine precisely what training and development needs exist currently and to project future training requirements. Adequate planning for training involves consideration of many factors. Among the most critical are enterprise goals, objectives, and plans; scientific and technological change; the nature of enterprise operations; the composition of the workforce; enterprise policies; the competencies of the training and development staff; facilities for training; and costs.

When both immediate and long-range training needs have been identified for orientation, trade skills and semiskills, technical aspects, sales, safety, human relations, supervisory training, and middle-management and executive development, decisions must be made about how the training will be provided. Part of the training will be conducted by informal in-house means (on-the-job training, coaching, job rotation, or self-development). Some training may be contracted. And still other training will be conducted by means of formal in-house programs. For on-the-job training and contract training, some of the remaining steps in the design, development, and validation of training systems may be performed with enterprise resources; for example, the formulation of training objectives. In the case of in-house formal training, however, *all* the remaining steps should be performed.

COLLECTING AND ANALYZING JOB OR TASK DATA

No enterprise can afford to operate training and development programs that are not job-relevant. If the learning experiences provided for employees in company-sponsored training are not directly related to the duties and tasks job incumbents are expected to perform, return on the investment will be inadequate. Yet, often there has been little relevance in the training. Training programs have been initiated without reference to job requirements. The consequence has been wasted resources. Personnel have been trained in unneeded or obsolescent skills, and undertrained (or not trained at all) in critically needed job skills.

Training and development programs must be based on job data, not on what someone recalls that he did or thinks that a graduate should be able to do. If training systems are not based on a solid foundation of objectively collected job data, the inevitable consequence is the inclusion of irrelevant content, the omission of important content, misplaced emphasis, and, ultimately, an inadequate or overtrained product. The source of valid and realistic training objectives is the person performing the job in the plant, in the office, on the construction site, in the shop, or in the laboratory. The method of obtaining these data is job or task analysis. The form in which these data are collected is behaviorally stated performance requirements. Chapter 3 describes the procedures to be used in performing job or task analysis.

Selecting and Writing Training Objectives

The next step in the development of an instructional system is to select training objectives from the job data and formulate them in performance terms. It will be recalled that the first step in the process of systems design involves identification of the specific areas in which formal training should be provided. Job or task analysis, the immediately preceding step, provided detailed information about the duties and tasks required by the jobs. Not all these duties and tasks are appropriate for inclusion in the formal training program. Some skills and knowledge have been provided by earlier education and training—for example, basic mathematics or writing skills. Other job performance elements are not used by job incumbents until they have been on the job for some time; other elements are unique to specific enterprise settings and are best learned on the job; still others represent higher-level skills which are appropriate for intermediate-level training; and finally, there are some skills which cannot be taught because the equipment and facilities to conduct the training are not available.

Consequently, it is essential to identify job performance elements in each of these categories and to select from the total list of skills those which are most appropriate for the formal training program. This is a judgmental procedure, but it involves the application of preestablished selection criteria—for example, the difficulty of the task and the frequency with which it is performed. Qualified personnel must scrutinize all job duties, tasks, and elements and must apply criteria which will insure that all skills essential and appropriate for formal training be included in the training system. Whatever skills are not included will constitute the content of on-the-job (or other) training programs.

Once the training objectives have been selected, they must be stated in performance terms. In this form, objectives describe clearly what the individual must be able to do, the conditions under which he must be able to perform, and the standard or criterion of acceptable performance. Chapter 4 describes the procedures that should be followed in selecting and writing training performance objectives.

Constructing Evaluative Instruments

When a training or development system has been designed and developed, the systems designer needs some means of determining whether the system is appropriate and effective. One means of appraising a system and its components is to apply evaluative instruments other than tests. These devices include rating scales, questionnaires, and interviews developed in advance of the remaining components of the system so that they are uncontaminated by system content. Instruments of these types are essential to complete evaluation and validation of a training system because certain components of the learning system cannot be evaluated by tests. In other cases, these evaluative instruments are used to verify data collected by other means. Chapter 5 describes the procedures for developing rating scales, questionnaires, and standard interview forms.

Constructing Criterion Measures

Successful course completion is customarily determined by relative standings (rank in class, standard scores, or percentile scores) or by percentage or letter-grade passing scores. These measures are ineffective. Relative standings determine success by simply comparing the performance of trainees. Passing grades or scores are completely arbitrary. Neither method produces results which correlate highly with later job performance.

But with objective job and task data, such grading practices are no longer necessary. Because training objectives have been derived from detailed analysis of the tasks graduates will be required to perform, the criterion of successful completion can consist of situations which require the trainee to demonstrate the learned behavior, under appropriate conditions (simulated, if necessary) and to the standard prescribed in the objective.

To show that he has attained the objective, the trainee must meet or exceed the level of performance described in the criterion. Because all objectives are essential, unsatisfactory performance on one cannot be compensated for by superior performance on another. Under these conditions, relative grades or standings become meaningless. Standards for criterion measures, therefore, must be set in terms of levels of performance, which are identified as "minimum qualifying" or "go, no-go."

Criterion measures, then, are essential instruments in evaluating and validating instructional systems and their components. Without these instruments it is impossible to obtain objective data about the performance of the system. In addition, criterion measures are a valuable means of providing immediate knowledge of results to trainees. Procedures for constructing these measures will be found in Chapter 6. This step completes the systems requirements phase.

SYSTEMS DEVELOPMENT

SELECTING AND SEQUENCING COURSE CONTENT

The objectives of a training system represent the skeleton of the program. The content is the flesh and muscle. Content includes the subject matter to be learned, the knowledge supports, and the elements of skill which are essential to satisfactory job performance.

Content selection involves the application of judgment, but it is best performed by using predetermined selection criteria. Each behavioral objective must be carefully analyzed to identify the specific concepts, principles, facts, and elements of skill required for performance. Only that content which holds up against the criteria should be included.

Following selection, the content must be sequenced. Here again, judgment must be applied. The objective is to make certain that concepts and skills are developed in an orderly fashion and that prerequisite learnings are acquired before more advanced material is presented.

Sequence may be determined by the internal logic of the subject matter, by chronology, or by order of task performance. For example, mathematics has an inherent logic which practically dictates the learning sequence; that is, more advanced concepts are built upon prerequisite learnings. Chronological order is frequently directed by content having a historical connotation—for example, the evolution and growth of the plastics industry. Often learning order is forced by the sequence of operations in performing a task; for example, in problem solving, the progression of steps begins with the statement and clarification of the problem; continues through identifying assumptions, collecting and analyzing data, and establishing hypotheses; and terminates with a statement of conclusions and recommendations.

In sum, the selection and sequencing of content are important steps in systems development. Content must be relevant to the job and the task and must make a significant contribution to the attainment of objectives. The sequence must conform to psychological order—the best order for learning. Chapter 7 describes the procedures to be used in selecting and sequencing content.

SELECTING AND USING TRAINING STRATEGIES

Instructional strategy means the combination of methods of teaching, mediating devices, and the system of organizing trainees and instructors to accomplish an instructional objective. *Method* includes the conventional lecture, conference, and demonstration, as well as individual study, programmed instruction, case studies, and simulation. *Mediating devices* include audiovisual aids, teaching machines, closed-circuit television, trainee response systems, and computers. *Systems of organization* include conventional random groupings of trainees, homogeneous groups, and such newer systems of organization as team teaching and team learning.

Each of the alternative types of strategy elements has its advantages and limitations. These must be considered in selecting the most appropriate mix of methods, mediating devices, and system of organization. In addition, there are factors relating to the nature of training objectives, content, trainee population, instructors, time, facilities, equipment, and materials which must be carefully weighed before strategy decisions are made.

If learning conditions are to be optimal, both new and older strategies must be fully exploited; but selection of a strategy must be determined by the objectives of the instruction. To choose the best strategy requires systematic identification, testing, and comparison of the rapidly growing array of hardware, software, and conceptual developments that are the products of educational technology. However, the selection task cannot be performed in a vacuum. The preceding steps in systems development must be completed before valid strategy decisions can be made. Chapter 8 identifies the more important instructional strategies, provides a detailed list of criteria to aid in the selection of appropriate strategies, and describes the procedures to follow in arriving at strategy decisions.

Selecting Training Aids

Although concrete, direct experience is the best means of learning, use of training aids as a substitute for or a supplement to direct experience is often necessary. Sometimes a training aid must be used because of the cost involved in exposing the trainee to the "real thing," or because of the danger to personnel or equipment which would result from such action. In other cases, training aids are necessary to bridge the gap between verbalization and direct experience. Training aids, then, are essential to the provision of efficient and effective instruction.

Printed or duplicated aids, graphics, three-dimensional aids, projected materials, and auditory aids all have their place in instruction. However, judgment must be exercised in selecting aids. Chapter 9 sets forth guides to the selection of basic training aids and describes procedures for selecting appropriate aids.

DETERMINING EQUIPMENT REQUIREMENTS

Many jobs involve the operation and/or maintenance and repair of equipment. For instruction to be optimally effective, the right kind of equipment must be in the right place at the right time and in the quantities required. Careful and complete planning and coordination are required in order to determine equipment requirements and to obtain the needed items well in advance of the time they are to be used.

Because of the expense involved in using equipment for training, it is necessary to establish equipment selection standards and to monitor their application. Chapter 10 identifies the basic data needed to determine equipment requirements, describes the factors to consider in selecting training equipment, establishes standards for determining equipment needs, and prescribes procedures for procuring training equipment.

PRODUCING TRAINING DOCUMENTS

At this juncture in the design and development of an instructional system, the output has been described in terms of performance objectives, and the means of producing the desired product have been specified in terms of the instructional strategy and the supporting training aids to be used. Course content has been selected and sequenced. Equipment requirements, in terms of type and numbers of positions, have been identified, and evaluation instruments and criterion measures have been prepared. The next step is to collate these data into training documents and to establish tentative time allocations for each instructional unit.

These documents include materials for the use of instructors, training managers, and operating and staff managers. The two basic documents required are lesson plans and programs of instruction, although such items as programmed materials, guide sheets, worksheets, and other documents needed to conduct instruction and manage the training enterprise may be included. Chapter 11 describes the procedures to be used in establishing time allocations for individual lessons and for preparing and reviewing lesson plans and programs of instruction. This step concludes the systems development phase.

SYSTEMS VALIDATION

SELECTING INSTRUCTORS

The quality of any training or development program ultimately depends upon the competence of the instructional staff. The instructor is the "operator" of the training system. He is in direct contact with the trainee and all the other components of the system. To him falls the difficult task of implementing the system as designed. In addition, he must provide the guidance and assistance and the subject-matter expertise required to operate the system.

If instruction is to be planned and conducted with optimum effectiveness, instructors must be top notch. Only those best qualified in terms of experience and education should be assigned to training duties. The attainment of the training objectives hangs in the balance. Although the role of the instructor may change as training technology develops, there will always be a need for personnel to set up the learning environment; to determine the types of classroom learning activities most appropriate for the acquisition of knowledge and skill; to motivate, guide, and direct trainees as they engage in learning activities; and to provide counseling services.

For these reasons, a carefully selected list of instructor prerequisites is essential. Such a listing provides a firm basis for making selection decisions. Instructor prerequisites are established initially by judgmental procedures. Analysis of past experience will provide indicators of success which can be translated into prerequisites. During the validation stage of systems development, however, prerequisites should be checked empirically and revised as necessary.

Once instructor prerequisites have been established, the numbers and types of instructors needed must be determined. Finally, instructors must be selected and assigned responsibility for specific blocks of instruction.

The major task in instructor selection is to determine the amount and kind of subject-matter competence and teaching skill required for successful implementation of the instructional plan and to match available instructor competencies with these requirements. Chapter 12 identifies instructor capabilities needed for successful application of basic instructional methods, establishes standards for determining the number of instructors required to operate a given training program, and prescribes procedures for determining the numbers and kinds of instructors needed and for making selection decisions.

SELECTING TRAINEES

Prerequisites are the minimum qualifications required for enrollment in a training program. Essentially, prerequisites represent a prediction of the aptitudes, skills, knowledge, and experience required for successful course completion. Prerequisites are used to select or develop aptitude tests for use in screening personnel for assignment to training systems; to serve as a basis for collecting data about training systems applicants or nominees; and to assist instructors in planning. Precise selection and definition of prerequisites are essential to avoid waste of training resources and to insure that graduates of a training program will not only complete the program but will also be able to perform at an acceptable level when assigned to operating or managerial positions.

Initially, prerequisites are selected on the bases of experience and judgment. Qualified personnel, intimately familiar with the training system and its requirements, and knowledgeable about personal characteristics likely to be related to job success, establish interim standards for enrollment in specific training systems. Following the validation stage of system development, objective data are gathered and analyzed to determine the appropriateness and validity of the prerequisites and, if necessary, to revise them.

Next, the trainee input to the system must be selected. If the job of establishing prerequisites has been carefully done, this task is relatively simple and straightforward. The input to the new training program, however, should be truly representative of the trainee population for which the training system was designed. The full range of possible aptitude, ability, knowledge, and skills anticipated in future trainee groups must be represented to insure a valid trial of the system. If the group used in systems validation is not representative, any conclusion regarding the effectiveness of the system and its components would be invalid.

Chapter 13 identifies prerequisite elements for training and development systems; describes procedures for establishing, evaluating, and validating prerequisites; and recommends procedures for screening and selecting trainees.

EVALUATING TRAINING SYSTEMS

All efforts up to this point have been focused on the development of an instructional system. Now the instruction begins. The system is subjected to trial and evaluation to insure that the content, sequence, strategy, personnel, facilities, equipment, and materials are consistent with the performance objectives, are appropriate for the trainees, and actually do the intended job.

There are two basic means of accomplishing the evaluation. The first means is by observing ongoing instruction in the classrooms, shops, and laboratories. The primary purpose here is not to rate the instructor but to determine whether the instructional system is operating as intended and to determine that the objectives of instruction are being achieved.

The second means of evaluating instruction is by systematically obtaining feedback from trainees, instructors, training evaluators, training managers, and operating supervisors. Each of these functionaries has a different perspective. Full advantage of these sources of evaluative data should be taken by administering periodic surveys and conducting interviews.

Chapter 14 identifies the components of an instructional system to be evaluated, the perspectives to be represented in the evaluation, pitfalls to avoid, and the procedures to be followed in conducting the evaluation.

ADMINISTERING AND ANALYZING CRITERION MEASURES

Criterion measures provide another means for evaluating the adequacy of the instructional system. Therefore, at appropriate points in the instructional sequence, the criterion measures developed prior to the start of the tryout are administered and analyzed. The primary purpose here is not to grade the trainees. Rather, the overriding reason for using these measures is to check on system effectiveness. A secondary purpose, of course, is to provide trainees with knowledge of results. Such feedback may take the form of problem solutions, critiques of performance, ratings, and test scores.

If trainee performance on a criterion test indicates mastery of the behaviors that were the objectives of the training system, the system is an effective one. In many cases, however, the results of the administration of criterion measures must be subjected to analysis, and the resulting statistics must be reviewed to determine whether the objectives of the instruction have been achieved and specifically where, if applicable, the system requires revision. Chapter 15 describes the uses to which test results should be put, identifies the statistics which should be derived, and recommends procedures for administering, scoring, analyzing, and reporting criterion test results.

FOLLOW-UP ON GRADUATES

The final step in the validation of an instructional system is the follow-up of graduates. Follow-up provides the real proof of the effectiveness of a training or development system since measures of the quality of the graduates' performance of the job are external means of evaluation.

Follow-up may be done by interview and observation of the graduates on the job, with interviews and evaluations by their immediate superiors serving as corroborating data. Of course, this is done on a sampling basis. Follow-up can also be accomplished by questionnaire survey of graduates and their immediate supervisors. However, at least a small sample of graduates of every training system should be followed up by interview and observation because the data obtained by on-site visits are more likely to be valid and complete than data obtained solely by questionnaire.

In any event, the focal point of the follow-up should be on the quality of the performance of the graduate on the job as he evaluates himself and as he is evaluated by his immediate supervisor. In addition, the judgments should be made in terms of the behavioral objectives of the training system; that is, the same set of performance requirements used to design the system should be used in conducting follow-up. The root questions, therefore, hinge on the graduate's ability to perform his job, under the prescribed conditions, and to the standards prescribed in the objectives. Such a procedure will permit more objective judgments of the system. It also makes it possible to identify new job tasks and update the job data. This information is used to revise the instructional system when a sufficient amount of data have been collected and analyzed. Chapter 16 describes the objectives of a follow-up program, uses of follow-up data, and procedures for collecting, reporting, and using follow-up data to improve the instructional system.

SELECTED REFERENCES

"Air Force Training Technology." *Training in Business and Industry* (April 1969), 6:4: 45–48.

"Applying Systems Engineering Techniques to Education and Training." *Educational Technology* (June 1969), 9:6.

Chestnut, Harold. *Systems Engineering Methods*. New York: John Wiley & Sons, Inc., 1967, Chaps. 1, 3.

Gagné, Robert M., ed. *Psychological Principles in System Development*. New York: Holt, Rinehart and Winston, Inc., 1962.

Lehmann, Henry. "The Systems Approach to Education." *Audiovisual Instruction* (February 1968), 13:2: 144–148.

McInnis, Noel F. "Getting with Instructional Systems and Getting Instructional Systems with It." *Educational Technology* (April 1969), 9:4: 40–43.

Miller, Richard D. "A Systems Concept of Training." *Training and Development Journal* (April 1969), 23:4: 4–14.

Porter, Elias H. *Manpower Development: The System Training Concept*. New York: Harper & Row, Publishers, Incorporated, 1967.

Ramo, Simon. *Cure for Chaos.* New York: David McKay Company, Inc., 1969.

Randall, Ronald K. "Perspectives on the 'Instructional System'." *Educational Technology* (February 1969), 9:2: 8–10.

Searles, John E. *A System for Instruction.* Scranton, Pa.: International Textbook Company, 1967.

Silvern, Leonard C. *Systems Engineering of Education I: The Evolution of Systems Thinking in Education.* Los Angeles: Education and Training Consultants Company, 1968.

———. "'Systems Approach'—What Is It?" *Educational Technology* (Aug. 30, 1968), 8:6: 5–6.

Smith, Robert G., Jr. *The Design of Instructional Systems.* HumRRO Technical Report 66-18. Alexandria, Va.: George Washington University Human Resources Research Office, November 1966.

Task Group VI. "Systems Approach to Education." *Proceedings of Project ARISTOTLE Symposium.* Washington, D.C.: National Security Industrial Association, 1968.

Tracey, William R. *Evaluating Training and Development Systems.* AMA, 1968, Chap. V.

———, Edward B. Flynn, Jr., and C. L. John Legere. "A Systems Model for Instruction," *Training in Business and Industry* (June 1967), 4:6: 17–21ff.

Winston, James S. "A Systems Approach to Training and Development." *Training and Development Journal* (June 1968), 22:6: 13–20.

2

Identifying Training
and Development Needs

THE purpose of this chapter is to describe the procedures that should be used to identify the training and development needs of an enterprise. In many organizations, training and development programs are established to meet *immediate* requirements. Although current training and development needs are important, the training manager must be equally concerned with the *future* needs for trained personnel. Unless this concern results in long-range training and development plans, the training activity cannot make its expected contribution to the goals and objectives of the enterprise it serves. For this reason, both immediate and long-range training and development requirements are considered.

Upon completion of the chapter, the reader should be able to perform as follows:

Behavior   Identify and list the immediate needs of the organization for operative, supervisory, and managerial training and development programs.

Conditions   Given: the results of analyses of ongoing training programs, evaluation of the products of current training, and analyses of shortfalls in product or process.

Criterion   Lists will be complete and in accordance with the procedures described in this chapter.

Behavior   Identify and list the training and development needs of the enter-
              prise for operative, supervisory, and managerial personnel for the
              ensuing five-year period.

Conditions Given: the results of analyses of ongoing training programs,
               forecasts, authority to survey all pertinent aspects of enterprise
               operations, staff assistance, and appropriate data-gathering instru-
               ments.

Criterion   In accordance with the procedures described in this chapter.

PRELIMINARY CONSIDERATIONS

Planning is the keystone of effective and efficient management. It is
particularly crucial in training and development because, without careful
and complete planning, resources are certain to be wasted. Without sound
planning, training and development programs are not likely to support
the plans and objectives of the enterprise as a whole. On the contrary,
training and other aspects of enterprise operations are quite likely to be
competitive. Training programs will evolve without any direct relationship to enterprise needs. Often, they will take the form of emergency or
stopgap actions. They will usually be more costly than anticipated. They
may even produce products for which requirements have ceased to exist.
In short, they will not be worth the investment.

Planning is a particularly important factor in designing effective
development programs. Too often, management development programs
have reflected fads, expediency, even caprice. They have been initiated
in response to the quick sell or a desire to "keep up with the Joneses."
These get-rich-quick schemes must be replaced by more systematic
approaches.

Development programs must be based on a searching look at the
organization and on study of plans for its growth. Programs must reflect
manpower audits and inventories which identify the managerial talent
already on the payroll. They must be based on manpower forecasts,
regularly updated. And finally, they must be based on real staffing plans
and must include specific procedures for obtaining the skilled manpower
needed to meet projected job requirements. Without this kind of planning, no organization can realistically identify its manpower development
needs.

Planning, then, must precede any action to initiate training if the
training is to be relevant to enterprise needs and to have any real chance
for success. The frequency and scope of changes in modern enterprise
and the environment in which it operates demand that the future, as
well as the present, be taken into account.

FACTORS IN PLANNING

Adequate planning for training involves consideration of many factors. Some of these can be controlled; others are beyond the control of management. However, both controllable and uncontrollable factors must receive attention. A discussion of some of the factors having important implications for training and development programs follows.

Goals, objectives, and plans. It should be obvious that prevailing and projected economic conditions, both national and international, are important considerations in planning for the future operations of an enterprise. Analysis of economic trends and study of changes in the market for products and services are essential to the continued success of any enterprise.

Forecasts must be made of population growth, price levels, political environment, business cycles, tax policies, labor turnover, efficiency of production, expansion of facilities, new markets, and new products. These forecasts serve as the basis for the formulation of enterprise goals, plans, and policies. Without such projections, no enterprise can hope to remain competitive. Unfortunately, the results of these analyses, as reflected in enterprise goals and objectives, too infrequently are used as a basis for identifying training and development needs.

If training and development programs are to make the contribution to the achievement of enterprise plans, goals, and objectives that they are expected to make (and that the investment of resources in their operation would seem to indicate they will make), they must be derived from enterprise forecasts and plans.

In sum, training and development programs must be based upon enterprise goals, objectives, and plans if they are to be effective. They must be geared to enterprise planning and manpower planning in terms of the projected expansion, reduction, or diversification of operations, production, and services. Planning for training must be integrated with other types of enterprise planning.

Scientific and technological change. Changes in enterprise operations, as well as in products and services, occur rapidly and continuously. Many of these changes are caused by the growth of science and technology. No enterprise can maintain its competitive status, let alone rise to a higher position in its industry, unless it keeps abreast of new developments, replaces obsolete equipment, introduces new procedures and techniques, and makes use of all advances in behavioral, social, and physical sciences as well as the developing technology. Note, for example, the effects of automatic data processing on American industry in the

1960s. Just about every aspect of enterprise operations, from engineering to marketing, has been affected.

The impact of changes in science and technology on training and development programs should be clearly evident. When new machinery is installed or new operating techniques are introduced, employees must be trained to use them. The effects of new developments on training are not limited to operative and supervisory employees. Managerial personnel are also affected. For example, the use of computers to provide information upon which to base management decisions has created a need for manager training to insure that the full potential of such systems is realized. The relationships between scientific and technological change and employee training and development are, therefore, extremely close and vital. These changes must be reflected in training plans.

The nature of enterprise operations. Although there are similarities in the training needs of all types of enterprise—whether public or private, production or marketing, sales or service—differences in individual companies dictate the establishment of tailor-made training and development programs. No enterprise is exactly like any other; therefore, training requirements differ markedly from enterprise to enterprise.

The types of products or services produced by an organization affect training programs. The training and development needs of a sales organization, for example, differ from those of a mass production industry. Another factor is the extent to which an industry has automated its production line and its materials-handling operations. The amount and kind of skills and the technical, safety, and supervisory training will vary accordingly. Therefore, regardless of essential similarities in operator and supervisor training and in managerial development programs, each enterprise must design systems that meet its own unique requirements. Transplanted programs are inevitably unsuccessful and wasteful.

In sum, the nature of enterprise operations must be reflected in the number, types, and objectives of the training and development programs designed and operated.

The composition of the workforce. The age, sex, educational level, training, and experience of operative, supervisory, and managerial personnel, and their relative numbers, in part determine the types and levels of training required. In recent years the increased employment of high school, technical school, and college graduates has dictated changes in training programs. The presence of unions in enterprise has introduced another variable into planning for training. Some unions have their own apprenticeship programs, others cooperate with enterprise in operating training programs, and still others assume no responsibility for the training of their members. The stability and lack of mobility of the labor force in some areas create different training requirements from those in other locations where instability and mobility are characteristic. Both situations cause training problems, but they are different.

Enterprise policies. Policies often impact heavily on training and development programs. For example, if a company maintains a promote-from-within policy, appropriate and effective supervisory and management development programs must be installed and implemented to insure a continuing and adequate supply of promotable personnel.

Top management's policy with respect to support for training and development is also critical. If training is to be successful, it must have the unqualified backing of top executives. The effectiveness of the training activity in performing its functions will be directly proportional to the willingness of top management to support it and to elevate it to a position of importance in the organization structure.

The training and development staff. The numbers and types of training and development programs that can be operated depend in part upon the availability of sufficient numbers of training personnel with the required managerial, professional, and technical skills, knowledge, and experience required to plan, design, and operate the needed training systems. Therefore, the scope and intensity of local training efforts depend upon the availability of carefully selected and competent training managers and trainers. If such personnel are not available, alternative plans for conducting the required training must be identified, or plans for acquiring such personnel must be drawn up.

Facilities for training. An important consideration in planning for training and development is the availability of adequate space, equipment, and other facilities for conducting training programs. Some types of training require a replication of the operational environment; some require standard classrooms; some require laboratory and shop space; and some require only conference rooms. However, if adequate space and facilities are not available, plans for their acquisition must be made or alternative means must be found to satisfy training requirements.

Costs. Another factor that must be considered in developing plans for training is costs. The most basic questions that top executives ask about the economics of establishing or continuing a training or development program are these: What will it cost? How can the cost be reduced?

Three types of costs—fixed, variable, and total—are customarily used to account for all expenditures related to the conduct of training programs. Fixed costs are funds expended to obtain the personnel (permanent overhead), facilities, and equipment required to operate training programs. These costs are essentially constant and largely independent of the number, size, and duration of the programs offered. Variable costs are funds used to purchase instructional materials, supplies, transportation, and trainee housing. These costs are directly related to and dependent upon the number, size, and duration of programs. Total costs are simply the sum of fixed and variable costs.

The usual means by which management regulates the cost of a training program is by controlling variable costs. These costs are of considerable importance to trainers because they must be optimized. Trainers must assess the facts, compare the costs of alternative methods of providing required training, and use the results of such studies to make decisions.

Training costs are affected by both quantitative and qualitative training requirements. Quantitative training requirements are measurable in terms of the number of training programs operated and the number of trainees enrolled. The impact of these factors on costs is readily apparent. The cost implications of qualitative training requirements are less visible, but they are also present. For example, the desired level of proficiency of the products of a training system is an important factor to consider in selecting the instructional strategy to be used. Proficiency level and instructional strategy influence the length of the training program, instructor-trainee ratios, equipment-trainee ratios, and required facilities. The length of the training program and the total number of trainees, together with instructor-trainee ratios, equipment-trainee ratios, and needed facilities, determine the number of instructors and the types and amounts of equipment and facilities needed. Because training costs vary with these requirements, it is crucial that qualitative as well as quantitative training requirements be accurately identified. Procedures for doing this are described in succeeding chapters.

Up to this point, the operation of in-house training and development programs has been the focal point. It is also important that consideration be given to the costs of alternative means of providing the required training, such as contract training (either on or off the premises), tuition assistance, and self-study. However, rarely can such decisions be realistically made until detailed cost comparisons have been completed. Appendix A provides a means of calculating the costs of designing and operating training systems.

In summary, costs are an important consideration in drawing up plans for training and development programs. Because training decisions result in the expenditure of resources the attainment of cost benefits, if not cost-effectiveness, must be a primary objective in meeting the training needs of an organization.

TYPES OF TRAINING AND DEVELOPMENT PROGRAMS

Variations in the number and types of training programs operated by modern American enterprise are virtually endless. Small companies, of course, may have only limited types of training, often of the apprenticeship or on-the-job variety. However, as organizations expand and their personnel problems become more complex, a greater variety of training programs becomes necessary. Some of these programs are conducted on the job; others are conducted in classrooms, shops, and laboratories; others are operated off the premises; and still others are carried out by a combination of approaches. Some are *ad hoc* programs designed to meet a specific need and then dropped, and others are conducted on a continuing basis. Although no single organization needs all the types of programs used in American business, a description of some of the major types currently in operation may be useful.

GENERAL CATEGORIES

In most large-scale organizations there are likely to be four categories of training programs, each with a distinct purpose. These categories are as follows:

1. Induction, orientation, and job-skills programs for newly hired or assigned personnel. These programs are designed and operated to provide the new employee with the company knowledge, basic attitudes, and skills required for satisfactory initial performance on the job.
2. Remedial and retraining programs designed to correct observed deficiencies in employee knowledge, skills, or attitudes.
3. Upgrading programs designed to improve, enlarge, or increase job skills and knowledge.
4. Development programs designed to enhance the educational backgrounds of employees or to prepare them for supervisory, managerial, or other positions calling for the assumption of broader responsibilities.

FORMAL IN-HOUSE TRAINING

Formal in-house training may be defined as training and development programs conducted with enterprise-organic resources. Figure 2-1 shows a training and development progression chart. Descriptions of these formal training programs follow.

Orientation of new employees. One of the most common and widely used training programs has the objective of orienting new employees. Regardless of whether there is a formal orientation program, new employees need to be introduced to the enterprise environment. Because such programs can be more economically operated for groups, most large companies conduct at least a part of the orientation by means of formal group sessions. Such programs are designed to provide the new employee with as much information about the enterprise in as short a time as possible so that he can readily adjust to the environment and become productive.

Figure 2-1.   A training and development progression system.

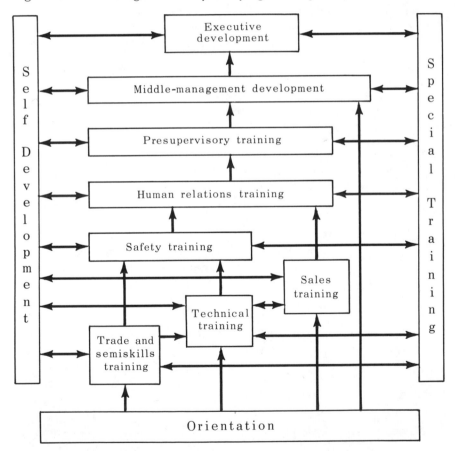

The nature and content of these programs vary with the size and type of enterprise and the type of employee. Inevitably, such subjects as working hours, company vacations, holidays, leaves, insurance and pension plans, overtime, fringe benefits, promotion, transfer, policies, rules, grievance procedures, and the like find their way into these programs.

In most companies, lower-level operative employees receive their initial orientation from a representative of the personnel department. They are then turned over to their immediate supervisor or to an older employee for further orientation.

In large companies, management trainees go through a much more extensive program. Executives brief them on company plans and policies. They are conducted on plant and office tours and then may be assigned to a manager for further orientation.

Safety training. Although safety training must be an integral part of the on-the-job training program, the importance of safety often makes it necessary to supplement on-the-job instruction with a formal safety training program. In these programs, designed for either operative or supervisory personnel, correct safety procedures are demonstrated and discussed. Many organizations develop their own instructional materials for such programs. However, much useful material may be obtained from insurance brokers that carry the company's policies.

Trade and semiskills training. Shortfalls in the training given to clerks, typists, and other people from high schools, trade, and technical schools create a need for additional company-sponsored training. Unique equipment, procedures, and techniques used by a company also create special training needs. For this reason, many enterprises have established vestibule training programs to bring new employees up to the standards required for acceptable performance of company jobs. Clerks are often trained in typing, filing, telephone courtesy, English, and the like. Other employees are taught handwriting and customer relations. Shopworkers are taught to use equipment, machines, and materials which they have not used before. Office workers are taught to use typewriters, duplicating machines, adding machines, copying machines, and dictating machines.

Technical training. Again because of shortfalls in the technical skills brought to the job by the typical new employee or because of differences in procedures, equipment, and techniques used by the company, graduates of technical schools may be given additional training. This type of training may be given at several levels of complexity or difficulty. Secretarial and stenographic personnel may be given instruction in stenography, stenotypy, and the operation of more complex office machines. At the other extreme are programs for graduates of college-level technical schools. This sort of training often involves short courses in particular technical areas; for example, production control, work simplification, and time and motion study. Other programs may be concerned with computer programming, operations research, systems analysis, scientific programming and numerical analysis, and critical path scheduling. Some programs may even lead to a master's degree in electrical or mechanical engineering.

Sales and dealer training. It should be evident that if products and services are to be marketed successfully, the sales force must be properly trained. Changes in products, as well as the complexity of today's products, make such training a continuing requirement. This type of instruction often involves training in the manufacture of products and observation of the manufacturing process. Frequently the salesman must study the equipment so that he will be able to answer the detailed and highly technical questions of potential customers. In addition, there is a need for continuing the training of sales personnel in company policies, pricing, distribution, advertising, and sales promotion.

Dealers have similar problems. They must be thoroughly knowledgeable about new products, pricing, policies, and promotion programs. Often both sales and technical training programs will be needed. Technicians must be trained so that company products can be properly installed and serviced. Automobile and appliance companies are good examples. Dealer salesmen must be trained in sales and sales promotion. To meet these requirements, a wide variety of programs exists, ranging from annual one-day meetings to comprehensive and lengthy training programs. And these programs are essential to protect the company's investment in products and services and to maintain goodwill with the consuming public.

Human relations training. Although human relations training is customarily associated with presupervisory and management development programs, many companies have found it useful to institute training programs of this type for technicians and operative employees as well. An attempt is made to change the behavior of employees in their day-to-day relationships with both enterprise personnel and customers by using conference methods, simulation, role playing, and unstructured discussion, and by using content dealing with performance ratings, employee grievances, self-development, promotion, employee problems, organizational relationships, and selection and placement of employees.

Presupervisory training. Enterprises that follow a strict policy of promotion from within are forced to train their own potential first-line supervisors. This training focuses on the development of supervisory, human relations, and leadership skills. Using the conference method and

filmed or printed cases, trainees are provided with experience in handling
employee problems. The content typically includes responsibilities of a
supervisor, work planning and scheduling, delegation, communication,
interviewing, employee training, performance rating, safety, company
policy, relations with unions and organized labor, grievance procedures,
and practical psychology.

Middle-management development. Because of shortages in qualified
middle-manager personnel, many companies have adopted the policy of
deliberately recruiting managerial candidates and developing them into
successful executives. The practice has grown in recent years because
executives have become alarmed about the gap in ages between the
junior and senior executive groups. Another contributing factor is the
rapid expansion of many industries. Their need for executives has out-
stripped the supply. Many companies have also found that they have an
excellent supply of technicians; but these technicians have had no managerial experience and hence are not ready to assume positions of greater
responsibility. The focus of such programs, therefore, is on management
theory, since graduates of the program will be required to manage managers as well as technicians. The most commonly used techniques are
lecture, discussion, simulation, business games, and case problems.

Executive development. As companies expand, a need is created for
division and plant managers—general management positions with such
titles as general manager, executive vice-president, and president. Many
companies have recognized that training and experience at middle-
manager levels cannot insure capable performance at the highest levels
of management. The question then arises: What additional skills and
knowledge are required to manage a whole enterprise (or a substantial
part of one)? Usually, what is required is broader contact with *all* the
functions performed by the enterprise. For example, a manager who has
been concerned only with controller operations needs experience in
production, marketing, and sales.

Usually, the means of providing this experience involves on-the-job
training. However, there are often aspects of the total managerial job
which can be handled in groups. Unstructured discussion, simulation,
incident process, role playing, and business games are some of the most
commonly used techniques of conducting this training.

Special training programs. From time to time, highly specialized, one-
time programs are initiated because unique training needs have been
identified. Reading improvement, effective writing, public speaking, and
zero defects are examples of such programs. Although they are not necessarily typical of any organization, when a requirement is identified for
their installation, they can loom large in importance.

INFORMAL IN-HOUSE TRAINING PROGRAMS

Too many trainers look upon a formal program as the end of training. It really represents only the beginning. Unless formal training programs are followed up with less formal types of training, full return on the initial training investment cannot be realized. Some of the most useful types of informal training are on-the-job programs for operative employees, and coaching, job rotation, understudy or assistant assignments, and committees and junior boards for supervisory training and manager development.

On-the-job training. The most common, most widely accepted, and most necessary method of training employees in the skills essential for acceptable job performance is on-the-job training. It is applicable to a wide range of semiskills, skills, and technical jobs of a nonsupervisory nature as well as to managerial development programs..

At one extreme, on-the-job training is the only type of training available to employees. This is particularly true in enterprises, both large and small, where the number of employees to be trained in a job at any given time is too small to warrant a more formal training program. However, as noted earlier, on-the-job training is also an essential follow-up activity for formal job training programs, whether conducted on or off the premises. That is, regardless of the amount and quality of the formal training programs provided for operative employees, on-the-job training is still required. This type of training raises the employee from the level at which formal training leaves off to the level of acceptable job performance. To put it another way, on-the-job training takes the employee from the entry level of job skill to the point where proficiency in performance is attained.

On-the-job training, as the title implies, is conducted at the workplace—in the shop or laboratory, on the production line, in the office, on the construction site, or behind the counter. The trainer is either a competent and highly experienced operative employee or the trainee's immediate supervisor.

If an on-the-job training program is to be effective, it must be planned and organized. Specific procedures and standards must be established, competent trainers must be assigned, and sufficient time must be allocated for the conduct of the training.

When conducted properly, on-the-job training has many advantages. The new employee gains experience in the actual environment in which he will be working. He is confronted by the same day-to-day problems he will face when he is finally on his own. He learns as he works, develops confidence as he learns, and from the beginning is productive. He can be rewarded immediately for progress, and his errors can be corrected before they become habits.

Coaching. Essentially, coaching is face-to-face counseling. It involves a close and continuing relationship between an employee and his immediate superior. Its purpose is objective analysis, by both superior and subordinate, of the subordinate's performance, so as to provide a means of developing managerial skill. Coaching may be used as a training technique at all levels of management from first-line supervisor to the vice-presidential level. It is also a valuable means of orienting managerial personnel to their jobs. It helps the subordinate to understand how his superior sees organizational functions, relationships, and personalities. When analyses are made of specific performance, both superior and subordinate are afforded an opportunity to learn why results were good or bad. In addition, particular managerial skills such as interpersonal relations and leadership can be discussed and evaluated.

Successful coaching depends upon several factors. The subordinate must have ready access to his superior since frequent face-to-face contacts are essential to the success of the technique. Both superior and subordinate must have the right combination of personal qualities. The supervisor must have the desire to develop competent managers. He must have patience and the ability to teach. He must be able to delegate. He must be confident—able to let his subordinate make mistakes. The subordinate must have confidence in his superior. He must be challenged by his job. He must like the enterprise for which he works. He must be interested in his own development. He must be objective and analytical in his approach to problems. He must have enough self-confidence to use the authority delegated to him.

Job rotation. Job rotation, in conjunction with coaching, is one of the most commonly used methods of developing managers. It may be defined as a technique whereby potential managers receive diversified training and experience under close supervision. Job rotation may take several forms:

• Rotation in *nonsupervisory jobs* to provide newly assigned or potential managers with firsthand experience in the full range of enterprise activities—for example, engineering, production, and sales.

• Rotation in *observation assignments* to enable management trainees to observe at close range the activities and performance of several different managers.

• Rotation among several managerial *training positions* to provide management trainees with actual management experience in a variety of positions.

• Rotation in middle-level *assistant positions* to broaden the experience of management trainees by having them serve as assistant managers of several departments.

• Rotation in *managerial positions* where management trainees are rotated from one department or activity to another, usually laterally, for a period of time to give them responsible and continuing experience in a variety of managerial situations.

Understudy or assistant assignments. This method of managerial training differs from job rotation in that the trainee gets experience in only one position. The objective is to broaden the trainee's perspective and develop his managerial skills by exposing him to many areas of managerial practice under the guidance of a competent and senior executive. The executive conducting this type of training can tailor the training to the needs of the assistant by providing him experiences which will enhance skill development. Tasks can be assigned which will provide certain facets of experience that need to be shored up. Leadership skills and decision-making abilities can also be tested in a variety of ways in real situations.

Committees and junior boards. This technique involves the selection of promising young employees for managerial positions. Selectees are assigned to committees or junior boards and meet regularly to consider proposals relating to the management of the enterprise. The decisions of these groups are forwarded to the responsible executive, who may adopt them, reject them, table them, refer them back for further consideration, or send them on to the board of directors. The idea is that members of such groups acquire a broader outlook, develop an understanding of enterprise goals and needs, and get realistic experience in leadership. It is also expected that trainees will acquire a sense of responsibility for the welfare of the company.

OTHER FORMS OF TRAINING

Contract training. A large number of public and private enterprises use outside facilities and trainers to provide training programs for operative, supervisory, and managerial personnel. Yearly the list of organizations offering training programs grows larger and larger. Colleges and universities, professional societies, management institutes and associations, and management and training consultants offer a wide variety of programs and courses ranging from one day to several months in length. These programs may be conducted on the premises of the contracting company, at the contractor's training facility, or at a rented facility.

Although these programs are more general in nature than most in-house programs (unless developed under contract for a specific enterprise), there are advantages to this approach. One is costs. Frequently, contract training will prove to be much less expensive than in-house programs. Another possible gain is interaction with personnel from other enterprises. The exchange of information and problems is usually one of the more valuable aspects of such programs. People not only learn that their problems are not unique, but they also learn about worthwhile solutions to these common problems.

Many universities will tailor a supervisory or management course to the needs of a given company provided that fifteen to twenty company employees are enrolled in the program. The costs of such programs vary considerably, but overall costs are moderate. Therefore, there is no reason for any enterprise today to do without supervisory management training because of size or limited resources.

Self-development. Although perhaps only indirectly related to the typical training and development programs sponsored by enterprise today, whether on or off the premises, self-development programs are not unusual. Many private and public enterprises encourage their personnel to engage in self-study or the pursuit of college degrees. Not all the areas studied are directly related to the goals, plans, or operations of the enterprise, and yet the encouragement provided is substantial. It often takes the form of time off from the job with pay (administrative or sabbatical leaves), tuition payments in whole or in part, grants and loans for study, and free books and instructional materials (often programmed) developed or purchased by the company for use in individual study. Although the return on such investments is problematic, it is apparent that a number of enterprises which support such educational efforts do have faith in an ultimate dividend.

SURVEYING TRAINING NEEDS

All too often, a decision to train is made before a problem has been fully explored. The following typical situation occurs: An operating supervisor or a manager calls the training manager and informs him that he has a training problem and wants his help. This procedure bypasses a critical step in the process: an analysis of the situation to determine what the *real* problem is.

The plain fact of the matter is that training is not always the answer to a deficiency in performance. Rather, the problem is often poor organization, inadequate supervision, unclear or ambiguous policies, poor communication, improper personnel selection policies or procedures, faulty job design, deficiencies in equipment or materials, improper work methods, or inappropriate work standards.

One of the major responsibilities of the trainer is to help operating managers and supervisors to decide whether the solution to a problem lies in better training or better management. He can do this only by analyzing the problem with the help of the manager. Together, they must find answers to the following questions: Is the discrepancy between expected performance and actual performance important? What brought the problem to light? Why is it critical? Is the performance shortfall a skill deficiency?

Mager[1] has made the point quite clear in the form of a maxim for trainers and managers: "If a man doesn't have a skill, *train.* If he has the skill but doesn't perform, *manage.*"

IDENTIFYING TRAINING REQUIREMENTS

There are several different but complementary leads to the identification of training requirements. Usually training needs manifest themselves in specific employment problems or in specific operational or employee problems on the job. In the first instance, certain technical or supervisory skills are required or forecast, and personnel with these skills are not available in the present workforce or in the sources of potential employees. Therefore, a program to train personnel in these skills is initiated either on or off the premises. In the second instance, deficiencies in the skills of operative, supervisory, or managerial personnel are brought to light by any one of several means.

Comparing job descriptions and applicant specifications with skills of employees. Job descriptions and applicant specifications identify the skills, knowledge, training, and experience required for success in particular jobs in the enterprise. By analyzing documents used in screening and selecting applicants for jobs (application forms, personal history statements, résumés, reports of employment interviews, candidate evaluation forms, and test results) and comparing them with personnel records, discrepancies between job requirements and the knowledge and skills of job incumbents and potential applicants can be identified. Of course,

[1] Robert F. Mager, "The Revolution in Training," Day Keynote Address delivered at the Twenty-fifth National Conference and Training Equipment and Services Exposition of the American Society for Training and Development, Miami Beach, Fla., May 14, 1969.

training is only one means of remedying such discrepancies, but it is an important one. Other solutions involve changes in existing job descriptions and applicant specifications, the development of new methods of doing the job (job redesign), more careful recruiting, screening, and selection procedures, and improved supervision.

Analyzing performance ratings. Most enterprises today have instituted elaborate performance rating systems as a means of insuring the attainment of minimum standards of performance and of insuring rewards for job performance that exceeds the established standards. Such ratings can provide a useful source of data for analyzing training requirements. Areas of substandard performance can be isolated and analyzed. Relationships among certain personal characteristics, background of education and experience, test scores, and the like can be investigated to determine whether training and development programs can provide a remedy for substandard performance.

Analyzing personnel records. Study of employee personnel records can be a big help in identifying specific training and development needs. Analyses of requests for transfers, demotions, promotions, terminations, and exit interviews may indicate deficiencies in skills or in supervision which can be remedied by training. Study of the number and types of employee grievances may reveal the need for supervisory training or a change in emphasis in the training currently offered. Analysis of the types of self-study assistance given or undertaken by employees under a tuition assistance program may reveal that an in-house program could meet requirements better and more cheaply.

Analyzing other types of enterprise records. There are many other enterprise records where useful information with possible training implications may be found. Records of absenteeism, accidents, break-in time for new hires, customer complaints, employee errors, employee suggestions, grievances, labor disputes, lost time, machine damage, machine downtime, misinterpretations of company policy, morale studies, number of promotable men, projections of position vacancies, operating costs, production bottlenecks, production records, rejects and reworks, overtime, sick leave, tardiness, time required to introduce new products or processes, return on investment, quality control, sales records, training audits, turnover, unit costs, violations of company rules and regulations, waste and spoilage of materials, and work backlogs are all useful in identifying training and development needs. They may indicate a need for additional orientation, trade and semiskills, technical, sales and dealer, safety, and supervisory training and management development programs.

Analyzing operating problems. Line managers and supervisors frequently observe operating problems which sometimes have training implications. Usually, the most worthwhile approach to the solution of these problems involves the application of carefully designed research procedures. By means of such techniques as tests, observation, interview, questionnaires, group conferences, and the collection and analysis of records and data of all types, the operating problem can be analyzed and a determination of the real problem can be made. Such problems arise frequently in most organizations. If training can provide a part of the solution, the result will be the installation of a remedial training program designed to prevent or minimize future recurrences of the problem. This is the easiest type of training program to sell to top management because the need is so obvious and line managers are so anxious to have the problem solved. In addition, the results are readily seen after the program has been implemented. This is the origin of most skills and technical training programs.

Analyzing long-range plans and forecasts. Although there is little doubt that in most enterprises management is concerned with immediate problems and their solution, competent managers are equally concerned about the future. This concern is reflected in enterprise long-range plans and programs based upon projections and forecasts of the environment of the future. Economic trends, markets, new products, and scientific and technological trends and developments are all a part of this environment. To be fully effective and make its contribution to the attainment of enterprise plans and programs, training and development activities must also be concerned with long-range planning. Unless this concern results in realistic training and development plans which support overall enterprise plans, the enterprise is likely to find itself with all kinds of skill shortages. The net result will be the implementation of expedient solutions in terms of staffing and training, often at a cost far in excess of the potential return. For this reason, training and development programs must be designed in terms of long-range plans.

What is required, then, is a comprehensive survey of the training and development needs of the enterprise in light of enterprise forecasts. Otherwise training and development programs are likely to be piecemeal and wasteful. But, if an overall survey is made, prevention of problems, rather than cure of staffing ills, will be the result. Of course, such an approach involves immediate expense for later long-term return. It means that some personnel will be trained in advance of need. This fact may make it difficult for the trainer to sell his program to top management. It is important, therefore, to gather data from as many sources as are available, to tie the information to enterprise plans and forecasts, and to present realistic alternatives in the form of training plans.

PROCEDURES FOR IDENTIFYING TRAINING
AND DEVELOPMENT REQUIREMENTS

1. Determine immediate needs.
    a. Evaluate current training and development programs to determine whether the training produces the desired behavioral changes.
        (1) Evaluate ongoing training programs.
            (a) Review training documents for adequacy.
            (b) Observe trainers and trainees in the learning environment of the classroom, shop, or laboratory.
            (c) Analyze in-course and end-of-course test results.
            (d) Interview trainers and trainees.
        (2) Evaluate the *products* of the training system.
            (a) Interview line supervisors.
            (b) Interview and observe trainees at the workplace.
            (c) Review personnel records and performance ratings.
            (d) Administer questionnaires to line supervisors and trainees, and analyze the questionnaires.
            (e) Analyze work samples.
    b. List and analyze shortfalls in process or product. Determine whether they are due to:
        (1) Poor organization.
        (2) Inadequate supervision.
        (3) Unclear policies.
        (4) Poor communications.
        (5) Improper personnel selection policies or procedures.
        (6) Poor job design.
        (7) Equipment or material problems.
        (8) Work methods.
        (9) Inappropriate work standards.
        (10) Inadequate operator or supervisor training.
    c. Survey all aspects of enterprise operations to determine areas where additional training is required.
        (1) Compare job descriptions and applicant specifications with personnel records.
        (2) Analyze performance ratings.
        (3) Analyze all enterprise records for areas of possible deficiency.
        (4) Identify and analyze operating problems.
        (5) Use interviews, questionnaires, group conferences, tests, and work samples to determine training problems.
        (6) Subject each problem to careful analysis to determine whether the problem is due to:
            (a) Poor organization.
            (b) Inadequate supervision.
            (c) Unclear or ambiguous policies.

Figure 2-2. Training and development needs, 19___ to 19___.
(See page 40, point 4.)

Type of training	Number to be trained									
	19___		19___		19___		19___		19___	
	IP*	OP†	IP	OP	IP	OP	IP	OP	IP	OP
Orientation										
Operative employees										
Supervisory employees										
Managers										
Safety										
Operative employees										
Supervisory employees										
Trade and semiskills (list specific programs)										
_____										
_____										
_____										
_____										
Technical training (list specific programs)										
_____										
_____										
_____										

Number to be trained

Type of training	19__		19__		19__		19__		19__	
	IP*	OP†	IP	OP	IP	OP	IP	OP	IP	OP
Sales										
Dealer										
Presupervisory										
Human relations										
Operative employees										
Supervisory employees										
Managers										
Middle-management development (identify specific jobs)										
_____										
_____										
_____										
Executive development (identify specific jobs)										
_____										
_____										
_____										

* In-house program.   † Out-of-enterprise program.

        (d) Poor communications.
        (e) Improper personnel selection policies or procedures.
        (f) Poor job design.
        (g) Equipment or material deficiencies.
        (h) Improper work methods.
        (i) Inappropriate work standards.
        (j) Training deficits.

2. Determine long-range training needs.
   a. Analyze enterprise plans, policies, and forecasts to determine their potential impact on staffing needs.
   b. Identify and analyze future systems, equipment, techniques, and procedures to determine their impact on personnel requirements.
   c. Determine whether current training systems will support future personnel requirements in terms of
      (1) Operative personnel.
      (2) Supervisory personnel.
      (3) Managerial personnel.
   d. Identify training system shortfalls.
3. For each training requirement, determine whether the training should be provided on or off the premises, and whether it should be formal or on-the-job. Consider:
   a. Comparative costs (see Appendix A).
   b. Availability of in-house personnel, equipment, and facilities resources.
4. Summarize training needs (see Fig. 2-2).
5. For off-the-premises programs, develop objectives, prepare contract specifications, solicit and evaluate proposals (see Appendix B), and select a contractor.
6. For in-house programs, develop objectives and guidelines following the procedures described in the remaining chapters of this book.

SELECTED REFERENCES

Byham, William C. *The Uses of Personnel Research,* AMA Research Study 91. AMA, 1968, Chap. 7.

Cantalanello, Ralph F., and Donald L. Kirkpatrick. "Evaluating Training Programs—The State of the Art." *Training and Development Journal* (May 1968), 22:5: 2–9.

Chartrand, P. J. "Progressive Skill Training." *Training and Development Journal* (September 1966), 20:8: 38–44.

DePhillips, Frank A., William M. Berliner, and James J. Cribbin. *Management of Training Programs.* Homewood, Ill.: Richard D. Irwin, Inc., 1960, Chaps. 6, 11, 12, 13, 14, 15.

Frankel, Harold. "On-the-job Training—A Permanent Solution." *Training and Development Journal* (March 1969), 23:3: 28–32.

Gill, Thomas W. "The Training Forecast: How to Make It—How to Use It." *Training in Business and Industry* (November 1966), 3:11: 34–35ff.

Goodman, Steven E. *National Directory of Adult and Continuing Education: A Guide to Programs, Materials, and Services.* Rochester, N.Y.: Education and Training Associates, 1968.

Graves, George P. "Initial Sales Training." *Training and Development Journal* (August 1968), 22:8: 26–30.

Johnson, Richard B. "Determining Training Needs." In Robert L. Craig and Lester R. Bittel, eds. *Training and Development Handbook.* New York: McGraw-Hill Book Company, 1967, Chap. 2.

Manske, Fred A. "Supervisory Training: An Evaluation of On-the-job Methods." *Training and Development Journal* (October 1966), 20:9: 44–51.

Miraglia, Joseph F. "Human Relations Training." *Training and Development Journal* (September 1966), 20:8: 18–26.

O'Donnell, Cyril J. "Managerial Training." *Training and Development Journal* (January 1968), 22:1: 2–11.

Randall, Lyman K. and Ernest M. Schuttenberg. "Participative Managerial Learning." *Making the Most of Training Opportunities,* Management Bulletin 73. AMA, 1965.

Rose, Homer C. "A Plan for Training Evaluation." *Training and Development Journal* (May 1968), 22:5: 38–51.

Sheer, Wilbert E. "A Practical Approach to Supervisory Training." *Personnel Journal* (May 1969), 48:5: 369–371.

Singer, Henry A. "ECL: A Dynamic Approach to Group Executive Training." *Personnel Journal* (May 1969), 48:5: 372–374.

Tracey, William R. *Evaluating Training and Development Systems.* AMA, 1968.

Wheeler, E. A. "Economic Considerations for Industrial Training." *Training and Development Journal* (January 1969), 21:1: 14–19.

3

Collecting and Analyzing
Job Data

I<small>F</small> training and development programs are to provide an adequate return on investment, they must be job-relevant. That is, the learning experiences provided for trainees must be directly and explicitly related to the duties and tasks they will be required to perform in their assignments.

Too often, training systems have been constructed with little more than a passing thought about what should be taught, or even why a program should exist. Millions of dollars are wasted every year because objective job data have not been collected. The result has been under-training in critical skills and overtraining in less significant areas. If these blunders are to be avoided, training and development programs must be based upon job data. The source of valid and reliable job data is job analysis.

The purpose of this chapter is to describe methods of collecting data that accurately describe the details of activities performed by operative or supervisory personnel on the job. Upon completing the chapter, the reader should be able to perform as follows:

Behavior   Select the appropriate job analysis procedure; prepare for and conduct a job analysis interview and observation; record, process, and analyze job data; and prepare end-product reports.

Conditions   Given: guides for the selection of job analysis procedures and for the conduct of job analysis; basic data-collection formats; an adequate number of job incumbents; access to work areas; and clerical support.

Criterion   In accordance with the standards and procedures defined in this chapter.

NATURE, PURPOSE, AND IMPORTANCE

The area of job and task analysis suffers from a great deal of confusion with respect to terminology. To overcome this problem and to serve as a basis for the ensuing discussion of job analysis, the following definitions are provided.

Job analysis. Job analysis is the process of collecting, tabulating, grouping, analyzing, interpreting, and reporting data pertaining to the work performed by individuals who fill operative or supervisory positions. The process of job analysis consists of a sequence of preplanned and tested procedures designed to accomplish the following:

1. Collect, record, tabulate, analyze, and interpret the duties and tasks performed by individuals in specific jobs.
2. Describe the conditions surrounding the performance of these duties and tasks.
3. Identify the skills, knowledge, and abilities required to perform the duties and tasks.
4. Determine acceptable standards for the performance of these duties and tasks.

Job analysis is conducted within the context of a functional breakdown of the activities performed by an incumbent in doing a total job. The interrelationships of the several levels of job breakdown are illustrated in Figure 3-1.

Job. The term job is used to describe a specific unit in the hierarchy of work done to produce goods and services. The job, then, consists of the duties and tasks a single worker performs. There may be several jobs within any functional area of operations or management. A job is the basic unit used in carrying out the personnel actions of screening, selection, training, classification, assignment, and promotion. Examples of jobs are electronic equipment repairman, lathe operator, shop foreman, plant superintendent, or vice-president.

Duty. A job is made up of one or more duties. A duty is one of the major subdivisions of the work performed by one individual. It has several distinguishing characteristics: (1) it is one of the job incumbent's principal responsibilities; (2) it occupies a reasonable portion of the incumbent's worktime; (3) it occurs with reasonable frequency during the work cycle; (4) it involves work operations which use closely related skills, knowledge, and abilities; and (5) it is performed for some purpose, by some method, according to some standard with respect to speed, accuracy, quality, or quantity. In addition, a duty has one or more of the following characteristics: (1) it is used to determine initial job assignments; (2) it is used as a determinant for preassignment or postassignment training; and (3) it is used to determine the qualifications required to perform a job. For example, the duties of an electronic equipment repairman usually include inspecting, adjusting, aligning, troubleshooting, servicing, and repairing. The duties of a plant manager include planning, organizing, staffing, directing, and controlling.

Task. Each duty is made up of one or more tasks, and a task has the same relationship to a duty as a duty has to a job. In other words, a cluster of tasks constitutes a duty. A task is one of the work operations that is a logical and essential step in the performance of a duty. It is the work unit that deals with the methods, procedures, and techniques by which duties are carried out. Each task has the following characteristics: (1) it occupies a reasonable portion of the worktime spent in performing a duty; (2) it occurs with reasonable frequency in the work cycle of a duty; (3) it involves *very* closely related skills, knowledge, and abilities;

Figure 3-1. Interrelationships of job, duties, tasks, and elements.

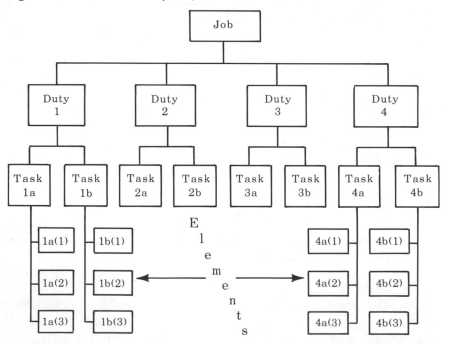

and (4) it is performed according to some standard. For example, tasks subsumed under the "servicing" duty of an electronic equipment repairman might include cleaning, lubricating, replacing tubes, and filling reservoirs with hydraulic fluid. Tasks included in the duty of staffing for a plant manager might include recruiting, screening, selecting, and assigning subordinate personnel.

Element. Tasks are made up of elements. The element is the most detailed level of work activity described in job analysis. Elements are the smallest steps into which it is practicable to subdivide any work operation without analyzing separate motions, movements, and mental processes; they are meaningful and useful groupings of the basic work units. The element is the work unit that deals with the details of how the methods, procedures, and techniques involved in a task are carried out. For example, elements performed by an electronic equipment repairman would include soldering and unsoldering connections, activating controls and switches, and tightening screws. Elements performed by a plant manager might include observing, questioning, completing forms, and signing requisitions.

OBJECTIVES

There are two objectives of job and task analysis; the first is to provide various staff elements of the enterprise with the amount and kind of information needed to carry out functions which involve jobs and job incumbents—for example, recruiting, screening, selection, classification, training, assignment, and promotion. Specific uses of job analysis data are as follows:

1. To identify and organize job content for writing and revising job descriptions and applicant specifications.
2. To establish objective information for job evaluation and to provide guidance in making decisions relating to pay, promotion, upgrading, transfer, on-the-job training, and reorganization of the enterprise.
3. To provide detailed information about current jobs which can be used to identify changes in personnel requirements resulting from installation of new equipment, tools, or work methods.
4. To improve utilization of manpower and to project future manpower requirements.
5. To aid in the development of more effective recruiting, selection, and classification instruments and procedures.
6. To establish measurable job performance standards.

7. To identify factors which induce job satisfaction, raise morale, and improve the effectiveness of individual employees.
8. To locate health and accident hazards.

The second objective of job and task analysis is to provide the training and development staff with detailed information about each enterprise job; what it consists of, how and why it is performed, how it relates to other jobs, the conditions under which it is performed, the standards of acceptable performance, the frequency and criticality of specific tasks, and the equipment, materials, and work aids used. These data are used in determining the objectives, content, sequence, emphasis, and means of conducting and evaluating training and development systems. More specifically, job data are used as follows:

1. To establish objectives and standards for training.
2. To identify the skills, knowledge, and personal attributes required for enterprise jobs.
3. To establish prerequisites for entrance into training programs.
4. To serve as the basis for the design of performance tests used in the training program.

IMPORTANCE

Job analysis is the first and most critical step in the development of an instructional system. The data collected by job analysts provide the foundation for the system. Regardless of how well the subsequent steps in system design, development, and validation are carried out, if job data are not complete, valid, and reliable, the resulting system will fail to produce personnel who are capable of performing their duties at an acceptable level of proficiency.

Job analysis, then, is not an end in itself. Information about jobs is collected because the enterprise needs the data to keep its organization functional and to accomplish necessary personnel actions and training activities in an efficient and effective manner.

THE NEED FOR TOP-LEVEL COORDINATION,
SUPERVISION, AND CONTROL

Although job data are collected at the lowest level of organization (the operator or supervisor), the procedures must be coordinated and controlled by top-level management. If this is not done, training programs will reflect "what exists" and not "what should be." Without top-level direction, support, and authority to implement more wide-sweeping changes, there is the risk of stopgap solutions being applied to training problems. Job data, therefore, must be collected under the supervision and control of top-level management, and the resulting conclusions and recommendations for changes must be reviewed and approved by a top manager. When this is done, the data used in developing instructional systems will be officially sanctioned. Of equal importance is the fact that this procedure enables coordination of related actions such as recruitment, selection, and assignment, and such as equipment research, development, and procurement.

METHODS OF JOB ANALYSIS

As noted earlier, job analysis provides the foundation for all the remaining steps in the design, development, and validation of training systems. To be of maximum use to systems designers, procedures for collecting and analyzing job data must meet several standards:

1. The procedures must provide *current* data in quantified form which clearly and completely describe the work performed by enterprise personnel.
2. They must provide objective, accurate, reliable, and valid data reflecting changes in job structure and career patterns.
3. They must be flexible so that they can be applied as often as required to the full range of operative, supervisory, and managerial jobs and to jobs with both large and relatively small inputs.
4. Establishing, applying, and maintaining them must be economical.
5. They must provide for the collection of data from all knowledgeable persons, including incumbents, supervisors, staff, and managerial personnel.
6. Insofar as possible, job data collected should be in a form that permits processing by machine.
7. The data obtained and the procedures themselves must be adaptable to changes dictated by operating requirements.
8. The data must be verifiable in terms of estimates of validity and reliability.

The method of job analysis recommended here meets all these criteria to a degree. It is essentially a composite of several basic methods. To present the background from which the method evolved, brief descriptions of some of the more common methods of job analysis, together with evaluative comments, are presented in the immediately following paragraphs.

QUESTIONNAIRE

Both the open and the closed forms of the questionnaire (see Chap. 5) have been used to collect job data. Essentially the questionnaire asks the respondent to furnish identifying information, and then provides some means for him to describe his job. Frequently, the respondent is asked to list and describe the duties and tasks he performs and the tools, job aids, and equipment he uses on the job. Estimates of frequency of performance of each task, or the percentage of on-the-job time consumed by each task, are also called for. Usually the incumbent is asked to complete the questionnaire on his own; sometimes, however, his immediate supervisor is required to assist or to verify the responses.

Most systems designers have little confidence in the questionnaire method when it is used alone. The percentage of returns is often too low to provide reliable data. Responses may be incomplete or may lack sufficient detail to be usable. Tabulation and interpretation of responses are difficult under the best conditions; with open forms, the problems are multiplied. Considerable subjectivity in interpretation is the inevitable result. Although the questionnaire method is among the least expensive to apply, it is inefficient and subjective when used as the primary means of collecting job data. In a supporting or corroborating role, it can be extremely useful.

CHECKLIST

The checklist is a special form of the questionnaire. It consists of a list of task descriptions for a job. The incumbent is asked to check the items he performs (and often to indicate the frequency of performance or time consumed in performance). The checklist is the product of some other means of collecting job data—such as the questionnaire or the observation-interview method—applied to a small sample of personnel.

The checklist is subject to many of the problems inherent in the questionnaire. Terminology, ambiguity in the task statements, overlapping tasks, length, and the like often result in data that are difficult to tabulate and interpret. In addition, the checklist does not provide information about the sequence in which tasks are performed. The effectiveness of the checklist depends upon the quality of the sample, the thoroughness of the preliminary analysis, and the expertise of the checklist designer.

In spite of these shortcomings, the checklist has certain advantages. It calls for recognition rather than recall of job tasks, and it can be administered quickly and easily to large groups of job incumbents. Responses are adaptable to machine tabulation and statistical treatment.

INDIVIDUAL INTERVIEW

With this method, trained job analysts interview selected job incumbents using a standard interview form. Data are collected on duties and tasks performed, frequency and duration of performance, sequence of tasks, importance and difficulty of tasks, supervision received, and tools and equipment used.

The interview has the advantages of encouraging rapport between interviewer and respondent, flexibility in getting the data required, and the opportunity to evaluate the credibility of responses. The interview, however, is a time-consuming process. It does not lend itself to the collection of data from large samples of the population. Its effectiveness is also largely dependent upon the skill of the job analyst as an interviewer.

OBSERVATION INTERVIEW

This method is essentially the same as the interview method except that the incumbent is observed in the job environment performing all or a substantial part of the job. The analyst may also question the incumbent as he performs the tasks to obtain more complete information.

The observation-interview method is the approach most favored by system designers, as it produces more complete information than any other single method and is more reliable. However, only expert job analysts can do an adequate job, and it is a time-consuming process and one of the most expensive to apply.

GROUP INTERVIEW

In this method, a large number of job incumbents are called together to provide information about their jobs. A trained job analyst asks questions designed to elicit job performance data. In some cases, incumbents are asked to complete standard forms. Following the interview, the job analyst combines the data into a single composite job schedule.

The group interview has one of the lowest price tags of all approaches to the collection of job data. However, it has proved to be among the least effective in getting accurate data about work performed. Because it involves recall, rather than recognition, the group interview often provides data that are incomplete or inaccurate.

JURY OF EXPERTS

With this approach, a group of personnel, selected for their experience, expertise, and knowledge of the job, are brought together to record the duties and tasks that make up the job. The data are organized and recorded under the direction of a trained job analyst, and in a predetermined and standardized format.

The jury-of-experts method has proved to be one of the most reliable methods of collecting job data, and the information collected is typically complete and thorough. Sometimes, however, experts either underestimate or overestimate requirements. Experts who underestimate have so much expertise that they cannot put themselves into the place of the neophyte, with the result that what is really difficult seems simple to them. On the other hand, experts who overestimate allow the completeness of their knowledge to influence them to require everyone to match their own knowledge and skill in order to be considered qualified.

The jury-of-experts method is probably the most expensive of all methods of job analysis because of the personnel involved and the time required. However, it is the only feasible method of collecting certain types of job data. This is particularly true of managerial and supervisory positions where many of the most critical behaviors are covert and therefore not directly observable. For this reason the jury-of-experts method is frequently used to prestructure data-gathering forms or as a supplement to interview and observation.

DAILY WORK RECORD

This method, sometimes called the work-participation method, in-plan, is a variation of the daily diary. Incumbents are required to fill out daily records of tasks performed over a period of weeks or months. Its advantages are that the method is self-administering and reasonably adaptable to machine processing. It is limited, however, by the conscientiousness of the respondents and by their understanding of the task listings and coding. It works best when closely monitored by the immediate supervisors of respondents and when logs are checked before processing.

WORK PERFORMANCE

This method, sometimes called the work-participation method, involves performance of job tasks by the job analyst. Simpler job operations may be performed without prior instruction. More complex job activities require some training and supervision until learned. The analyst then performs the job in the regular work environment. Either concurrently or afterwards, he develops written task descriptions.

The method has the advantage of providing complete and accurate job data. However, the time and expense involved are typically so exorbitant that the method is usually impractical.

CRITICAL INCIDENT

This method involves collecting statements based on direct observation by supervisory personnel or analysts, or on recall of job behavior by incumbents, which "typify" both competent and unsatisfactory performance of a job or task. Usually a great number of incidents are collected which emphasize the behavioral aspects of the job. The technique has value inasmuch as it underscores or calls attention to critical job behaviors. However, it does not in and of itself cover *all* job behaviors, and hence it is limited in usefulness.

ANALYSIS OF TECHNICAL PUBLICATIONS

The contents of technical publications, particularly operator and maintenance and repair manuals, are carefully examined to identify specific tasks and to find out how they are performed. The major limitation is that since these publications are usually written by the manufacturer, they do not always describe the optimum method of task performance. In addition, experience with manuals reveals that they often contain errors. The method is also limited to analysis of operator and maintenance jobs.

PLANNING FOR JOB ANALYSIS

Prior to the actual collection of job data, a great deal of preliminary planning and training must be done. During the planning and training phase, the functional area of operations or management to be analyzed is selected, members of the job analysis teams are chosen, administrative arrangements are made, fiscal approvals are sought, job analysts are trained, and data-gathering forms are developed.

SELECTING JOB ANALYSTS

Job analyses, regardless of the method used, should be performed only by carefully selected personnel. Although members of a job analysis team may be drawn from any operating or staff element of the enterprise, certain traits and abilities are essential to success. Foremost among these traits is the desire to participate in job analysis. Personnel drafted as analysts against their will cannot do a creditable job. Analysts should have a general knowledge of the job categories to be studied, and should be capable of avoiding bias. They should have the mental ability and insight required to probe and elicit information in a systematic manner, and to recognize commonalities and variations in specific jobs. In addition, job analysts should be articulate and methodical; should be able to write reasonably well, to observe astutely, and to attend to detail for relatively long periods of time; and of course, should be interested in people and jobs.

The team should be headed by an experienced job analyst, preferably a member of the staff of the training and development activity. Members of the team should represent a balance between individuals with considerable expertise in the functional area to be analyzed and individuals with only a general knowledge of that area. The former are included to insure a sufficient amount of technical competence and background to provide a thorough analysis, and the latter to overcome the problems of bias and overfamiliarity with the jobs being studied.

SELECTING UNITS TO BE SURVEYED

When the interview-observation method of job analysis is to be used, the units to be surveyed must be selected early in the planning phase so that applicable documents can be obtained and used in the training of analysts. Units selected for survey should meet the following criteria:

1. Positions must be authorized and filled for the jobs and functional areas to be analyzed.
2. For operative and first-line supervisory jobs, there must be at least five job incumbents who meet the selection criteria identified in a later paragraph of this chapter.
3. Units selected must be truly representative of all "using" units for the job to be analyzed.
4. Units must be representative in terms of functions, products, or services.
5. Units must reflect "typical" (as distinguished from unique) requirements for the jobs to be analyzed.
6. Units must be geographically and environmentally representative of all organizational elements of the enterprise.

TRAINING JOB ANALYSTS

Regardless of intelligence or background, no one is a born job analyst. All analysts must complete a formal training program before they are allowed to participate in job analysis. An outline program of instruction for training job analysts is shown in Figure 3-2. It should be noted that techniques of interview and observation and the prestructuring of data-gathering forms are emphasized in the recommended training program. In addition, as a part of their training, job analysts should:

1. Study documents relating to the mission, functions, organization, products, and services of the enterprise units to be surveyed.
2. Review equipment lists.
3. Study current job descriptions for the jobs to be analyzed.
4. Examine existing job analysis schedules for the jobs to be analyzed (if available).
5. Prepare and rehearse standard briefings for managers, staff, supervisory personnel, and job incumbents of the units to be visited.
6. Develop a schedule for the conduct of the analysts. (A sample schedule is shown in Figure 3-3.)

PREPARING DATA-GATHERING INSTRUMENTS

As a part of their training, job analysts should prepare the forms they will use in collecting job data. Essentially, these prestructured forms have four parts: (1) identifying information, (2) details of duties, tasks,

Figure 3-2. Outline program of instruction for training job analysts.

Subject	Scope	Time allocation (hours)
Introduction	Greetings; course objectives and requirements; source materials; administrative matters.	1
Introduction to job analysis	Mission and functions of job analysis teams; definitions of job analysis, job, duty, task, element, and job description; purposes of job analysis; uses of job analysis data.	2
Overview of the process of job analysis	Steps in planning, conducting, consolidating, and reporting job analysis data.	1
Planning for job analysis	Criteria for selecting units; previsit coordination; study of organization documents, equipment lists, and job description; preparing standard briefings; establishing procedures; scheduling.	8
Analyzing a job	Use of job analysis schedules and related forms; recording information; breaking a job into duties, tasks, and elements; identifying environmental conditions and contingencies; use of importance codes and levels of supervision.	8
Techniques of the interview	Purpose of the interview; environment; time frame; establishing and maintaining rapport; attitude and actions of the interviewer; dos and don'ts; concluding the interview; practice interviews and critiques.	8
Techniques of observation	Purpose of observation; environment; establishing and maintaining rapport; making notes; dos and don'ts; practice observation and critiques.	8
Consolidating job data	Tabulating and consolidating data; importance indexes; preparing a consolidated job schedule; format for the final report.	2
Prestructuring data-gathering forms	Preparation of prestructured forms to the task level for all jobs to be analyzed.	40

Figure 3-3.   Sample schedule for job analysis teams.

First Day	Second (and Third) Day	Fourth Day

1. Brief manager of unit on purpose, procedures, and requirements.
2. Study the mission, organization, and functions of the unit.
3. Make a preliminary survey of worksites.
4. Brief supervisory personnel on the purposes and procedures of the analysis.
5. Select job incumbents for interview and observation.
6. Review records of job incumbents and complete appropriate items on job analysis forms.
7. Brief incumbents on the purpose and procedures of interview and observation.
	1. Interview the first (and second) job incumbent.
	  a. Identify duties and tasks performed.
	  b. Collate a job analysis form.
	  c. Make outline notes of key words and phrases which describe duties and tasks.
	  d. Record and classify technical terminology.
	  e. Arrange a time for observation of the job incumbent.
	2. Observe the job incumbent performing the duties and tasks of his job.
	  a. Make notes of the observation.
	  b. Describe environmental conditions and contingencies.
	3. Complete the draft job analysis schedule.
		1. Check and validate the draft job analysis schedule with job incumbents and supervisory personnel.
		2. Provide exit briefing for manager of unit.

and elements, (3) equipment information, and (4) general information. These parts will be described and illustrated in a later section.

Data collected to describe the jobs, duties, tasks, and elements of positions for which training will be provided must describe all aspects of the job. The most complete and meaningful description of a job, duty, task, or element is a statement that identifies the basic *behavior* required of the job incumbent, the *conditions* under which he must perform, and the *standard* of acceptable performance. The following format is therefore recommended for reporting job, duty, task, and element descriptions.

Behavior   This should be a statement of what the incumbent does or must do. Usually, this will be something directly observable. The description of the behavior should begin with a verb—for example, calibrates, solders, actuates, plans, counsels, inspects.

Conditions   The condition describes the factors directly affecting performance. It consists of a statement of what the incumbent has available in doing the job or task, or what he cannot use in doing it. Tools, equipment, job aids, and amount and kind of supervision or assistance are defined here.

Criterion   The criterion identifies the standard used to judge performance of the job, duty, task, or element. It may be expressed in terms of quality (accuracy, tolerances, completeness, format, sequence, clarity, neatness, number of errors); quantity (number of work units produced per unit of time, or total number of work units required; and time (speed of performance).

To save time and effort during the data-gathering phase of interview-observation analysis, data-collection forms should be prestructured. This means that the forms should contain tentative and open-ended statements of behavior for duties and tasks. If the analyst finds during an interview or observation that the duty or task described on a certain page is not performed, he simply discards that page of the prestructured form. If the description or any part of it is inaccurate, he makes the needed changes to bring it into line with the realities of the job. If a new duty or task is identified, he merely adds a new page.

Elements, however, are not prestructured. They are so procedural, so detailed, and so subject to variation that prestructuring would be a waste of time. All element descriptions, therefore, are collected during interview and observation in the work environment.

COORDINATION AND ADMINISTRATIVE ARRANGEMENTS

All units to be visited by job analysis teams should be informed in writing of the purpose, time, and duration of the visit well in advance of the proposed date of arrival of the team. Travel arrangements must be completed and hotel reservations made, and for overseas travel, passports and visas must be obtained and inoculations administered.

CONDUCTING JOB ANALYSIS

Upon arrival at each enterprise unit, the top manager and his staff should be briefed on the purposes of the analysis, the procedures to be used, the uses to be made of the data, and the assistance the team requires. Before the team begins to collect job data, a tour of facilities and particularly of the worksites to be surveyed should be made. In addition, the team should spend as much time as necessary in reviewing organization documents (organization and functions manuals, procedures manuals, equipment lists, and job descriptions) before starting the interviews.

SELECTING JOB INCUMBENTS

Supervisory personnel should be asked to nominate subordinates for interview and observation. The following guidelines should govern these nominations:

1. Incumbents should perform duties typical of the functional area under study.
2. Incumbents should perform their duties with average, satisfactory proficiency.
3. Incumbents should have been working in the job for a long enough time to be adjusted to it, but not for such a long period of time that their awareness of steps in the job and degrees of difficulty have been dimmed.
4. Incumbents should not possess unusually extensive or limited educational backgrounds, or unusually varied or limited prior work experience for the jobs they hold.

Records of nominees should be reviewed by members of the team to eliminate personnel who do not match the specifications. Pertinent data for those selected for analysis should be entered on the forms. Tentative times for interview and observation should then be scheduled by the supervisors of job incumbents to be surveyed.

INTERVIEWING INCUMBENTS

In general, the usual rules for conducting other types of interviews apply to the job analysis interview (see Chap. 5). Job incumbents should be informed of the purpose and procedures of job analysis and the uses to which the information will be put. It is especially important to emphasize the nonevaluative context of job analysis.

In conducting the interview, the job analyst should observe the following rules:

1. Establish rapport before attempting to collect job data.
2. Let the incumbent describe his job (do not tell him what he does).
3. Get at the specifics of job performance—the what, when, where, why, and how.
4. Record all data; make outline notes of key words and phrases that describe duties and tasks, including technical terminology, immediately and carefully.
5. End the interview when it becomes apparent that the incumbent can no longer give pertinent and useful information.
6. Schedule a time for observation of performance and a recheck of data collected.

OBSERVING JOB INCUMBENTS

Ideally, job incumbents should be observed at work long enough to witness performance of all major duties. If this is impossible, it is important that performance of the primary duty be observed in its entirety (all tasks and elements). The observer should position himself so that he can see all actions, but so that he is not in the way. Questions should be asked only when absolutely necessary. Careful and complete notes on the observation, including environmental conditions, should be made on the spot.

RECORDING JOB DATA

Job, duty, task, and element data should be recorded on prestructured Job Analysis Report forms similar to the one shown in Figure 3-4. The procedures for completing each section are described in the following paragraphs.

COVER PAGE

The "Approvals" section of the cover page is completed *after* the entire form has been filled out. The approvals establish the fact that the job data contained in the report have been reviewed and approved by the analyst and supervisory or managerial officials.

Figure 3-4. *A sample prestructured job analysis form.*

Job Analysis Report for
Electronic-Equipment Repair Supervisor

Part A.   Identifying Information

Part B.   Details of Duties, Tasks, and Elements

Part C.   Equipment Information

Part D.   General Information

Approvals

Job analyst_____ Date _____

Incumbent's supervisor_____ Date _____

Department or section manager_____ Date _____

Part A. Identifying information

1. Name of incumbent_____

2. Job title of incumbent_____

3. Training of incumbent

    a. Highest level of schooling_____

    b. Schools or training courses attended:

4. Experience of incumbent

    a. Number of months in present position_____

    b. Positions held:

5. Name of organization_____

6. Address of organization_____

7. Title of subdivision_____

8. Functions of job incumbent's section:

9. Date of observation or interview_____

10. Organization of subdivision:

11. Personnel composition of the division

Job code and title	Number		Remarks
	Authorized	Actual	

Part B. Details of duties, tasks, and elements

Job: Electronic equipment repair supervisor

Partial outline of duties and tasks:

Duty 01 Plans

        Task 0101 Drafts budget estimates

        Task 0103 Recommends revisions to policies

        Task 0105 Determines personnel requirements

        Task 0107 Establishes work priorities

        Task 0109 Plans workflow

Duty 03 Staffs

        Task 0301 Drafts job descriptions

        Task 0302 Orients new personnel

        Task 0304 Assigns personnel to duty positions

        Task 0306 Conducts on-the-job training

        Task 0308 Recommends individuals for training

Duty 04 Directs

        Task 0401 Supervises subordinate foremen

        Task 0403 Directs utilization of resources

        Task 0405 Demonstrates equipment and procedures

        Task 0408 Supervises conduct of inventories

Duty 06 Controls

        Task 0601 Establishes performance standards

        Task 0603 Evaluates performance of subordinates

        Task 0605 Supervises the preparation of reports

        Task 0607 Evaluates quality control procedures

        Task 0610 Recommends corrective action for recurring problems

Title: 01 Plans

Behavior: Plans for the use of resources of all types (men, money, material, equipment, space, and time)

Importance code: 1 2 3

Percentage of time_____ Actual time_____

Conditions:

Supervision: A B C D

Tools and materials:

Equipment:

References:

Not given:

Criterion

1. Procedures must be in accordance with_____

2. Work activity must be accomplished in_____

_____ (min/hr/days)

3. Work product must be in accordance with specifications outlined in

_____

4.

_____

Duty Continuation Sheet

This work activity is performed on or with the following equipment:

		Criterion Document	
Equipment	Condition	Procedure	Characteristics

Title: 0101 Drafts

Behavior: Drafts budget estimates

Importance code: 1 2 3

Percentage of time_____ Actual time_____

Conditions:

Supervision: A B C D

Tools and materials:

Equipment:

References:

Not given:

Criterion

1. Procedures must be in accordance with_____

2. Work activity must be accomplished in_____

_____ (min/hr/days)

3. Work product must be in accordance with specifications outlined in

_____

4.

_____

Element Description Sheet

Duty title and number: Plans 01

Task title and number   Drafts budget estimates 0101

Element behavior	Condition	Criterion

Part C. Equipment information

Equipment number and nomenclature	Reference document	Involvement (check one)		Percentage of work time
		Operate or repair	Supervise	
Crystal unit test set TS-268E/U				
Digital counter CP-772/U				
Digital pattern generator TS-1671/G				
Electronic voltmeter AN/URM-145				
Fairchild model 767 oscilloscope				
Frequency meter TS-186/UP				
Multimeter TS-585/U				
Noise figure meter HP-340B				
Noise generator HP-X347A				
Pulse generator AN/UPM-15				

Part D. General information

Definitions: (list and define terms used by job incumbents which may not be understood by personnel unfamiliar with the job):

Environmental conditions (describe the work environment of the incumbent; include *all* factors affecting performance):

General comments (record all comments relating to job activities of the incumbent offered by supervisory personnel; include both positive and negative comments, and, if possible, include the recommended solution to problems identified):

PART A. IDENTIFYING INFORMATION

All information needed to identify the enterprise unit in which the job data were collected and all information about the incumbent are recorded here (see Figure 3-4 Part A). One copy should be completed for each job incumbent interviewed. Explanations for items that are not self-explanatory follow:

Item 3a. Record the highest level of schooling attained by the incumbent—for example, technical school, grade 14, A.A. in industrial management.

Item 3b. Record the names of schools and training courses attended beyond high school. Do not include locally operated courses which are unrelated to the positions the incumbent has held.

Item 4b. Record by position title and time in months all the positions to which the incumbent has been assigned starting with his first full-time job.

Item 5. Enter the exact official designation of the unit in which the position is located.

Item 7. Enter the division, branch, section, unit, team, or crew in which the position occurs—for example, maintenance section.

Item 8. Record the specific responsibilities or functions of the sub-division in which the incumbent works.

Item 10. Draw a simple organization chart, indicating by an asterisk the position being analyzed and also indicating the immediately higher supervisory position, immediately subordinate positions (if any), and other positions closely related to the job being analyzed. Insert the names of people who currently fill the positions.

Item 11. Enter the position titles, job codes, and authorized and actual number of people assigned to the subdivision.

PART B. DETAILS OF DUTIES, TASKS, AND ELEMENTS

The first task with each interviewee is to determine which major duties he performs. An outline of duties and tasks, such as the one shown in Figure 3-4 Part B, is used for this purpose. Each duty and its associated tasks are checked with the job incumbent. Duties and tasks not performed are crossed out, and additional duties and their associated tasks are added. The resulting outline of duties and tasks is used to collate a job analysis form for the individual being analyzed. Therefore, for each duty that is a responsibility of the incumbent, the following pages are collated from the kit of forms: a Duty Description Sheet for each duty, a Duty

Continuation Sheet for each duty, a Task Description Sheet for each task, and an Element Description Sheet for each task. These forms are completed as follows:

Duty description sheets. These forms (Fig. 3-4 Part B) are used by the analyst to record the results of his interview of the incumbent and of his observation of performance of work activities that meet the criteria for identification as a duty.

Importance code. Circle *one* of the following numbers on the Duty Description Sheet:

1   The duty is not one of the incumbent's principal responsibilities. It occupies a minor portion of his total work activity (or in the case of a task, a minor portion of the duty). It occurs infrequently in the workcycle of the position (or duty).

2   The duty is recognized as one of the incumbent's principal responsibilities. It occupies a reasonable part of the incumbent's worktime (or, in the case of a task, duty time) and occurs with reasonable frequency in the workcycle (or duty cycle).

3   The duty is recognized as one of the incumbent's principal responsibilities. It occupies a major portion of his worktime (or duty time, in the case of a task), and occurs frequently in the work cycle (or duty cycle).

Percentage of time. The percentage of time the duty occupies in the work cycle (or duty cycle, for a task) is entered in this space. If a work cycle requires three hours and a man spends one hour performing the duty, then 33⅓ percent would be entered in the "Percentage of time" section.

Actual time. Because the lengths of work cycles (and duty cycles) vary considerably, the actual time required for performance of the work cycle (or duty cycle) must be recorded. This provides a validity index for the "Percentage of time" section and allows for flexibility in the consolidation and treatment of the data.

Supervision. Circle the appropriate letter on the Duty Description Sheet:

A   The most detailed level of supervision. The supervisor provides detailed instructions concerning which work activity the incumbent is to perform and how he is to perform it. The job incumbent is not permitted to proceed to any new work activity until further instructions have been given. The supervisor provides all necessary tools, materials, work aids, and references, or specifies which ones will be used for a given job. The incumbent is not permitted to make judgments concerning additional requirements and is not permitted to proceed independently.

B   A less detailed level of supervision than level A. The supervisor provides specific instructions about which task or duty to perform, but allows the incumbent to determine how the work is to be done. The incumbent selects his own tools, materials, job aids, and references. The supervisor is available for consultation about how to do the work.

C   A broad, permissive level of supervision. The supervisor assigns to the incumbent a broad area of work activity and permits the individual to decide which specific activities, within the broad area, must be performed, and in what priority they must be performed. The incumbent also decides how to perform the activities and selects his own tools, materials, job aids, and references. The supervisor is available for consultation concerning which job to do.

D   An independent level of operation. The incumbent is assigned to a broad, all-encompassing area of functional responsibility, and he determines which jobs must be performed and how they should be performed. The incumbent is subject to ordinary regulatory controls, but is independently responsible for the activity within his functional area. At this level, responsibilities of the incumbent usually include the supervision of others.

Tools and materials. List all tools, materials, and job aids used by the incumbent in performing the duty (or task).

Equipment. List all the equipment used by the incumbent in performing the duty (or task).

References. List all documents, manuals, and the like used by the incumbent in performing the duty (or task).

Not given. List any items the incumbent is specifically denied in performing this duty (or task).

Criterion. Select the most appropriate partial statement and complete it. If none of the statements is applicable, formulate a statement that specifies the standard (quality, quantity, or time) used to judge the performance of the duty (or task).

Duty continuation sheet. On the Duty Continuation Sheet (Fig. 3-4 Part B), identify other items of equipment which the same job incumbent uses in performing this duty. Any changes in conditions and criteria should also be recorded to make them applicable to the different items of equipment.

Task description sheet. Separate Task Description Sheets (Fig. 3-4 Part B) should be completed for each task checked or added to the duty outline. These task sheets should be filled out in the same way as the Duty Description Sheets, using the same coding for importance and level of supervision. Note that the term "duty" is substituted for "work activity" in the code descriptions for tasks. It is important, too, to check the behavioral descriptions for accuracy.

Element description sheets. Separate Element Description Sheets (Fig.

3-4 Part B) should be completed for each task. Each list of elements must present a clear, concise picture of the behavior necessary to perform the elements of the task, their conditions of performance, and the criterion of acceptability.

PART C. EQUIPMENT INFORMATION

The job incumbent should be asked to review the equipment list (Fig. 3-4 Part C) in light of his job and to indicate the items of equipment with which he is involved, the kind of involvement (operate and repair, or supervise), the manuals or documents he uses when working with the equipment, and the percentage of his worktime spent with the equipment. Items of equipment not included in the prestructured listing should be added, and the same information should be provided on involvement and time.

PART D. GENERAL INFORMATION

This portion of the form has space for definitions, environmental conditions, and general comments (Fig. 3-4 Part D).

Definitions. Job Analysis Reports contain many references to technical terminology and jargon which must be understood if the data are to be properly analyzed and used. These terms and their definitions should be given in this section.

Environmental conditions. The environment in which the job incumbent works is a very important factor to consider in analyzing a job. The environment includes the physical setting, physiological factors, noise and nuisances, lighting, the position of the worker, and any other factors which bear on job performance. The supervision which the incumbent gives or receives is also a part of the picture. If the level of supervision is inadequately described by the coding system, it should be explained here.

General comments. The comments which the incumbent, his supervisor, or other members of the staff make about the position should be included in this section. Although this sort of information is likely to be subjective, it does have some value; at the very least it provides these functionaries with the opportunity to have their feelings recorded—and recorded in such a way as to separate them from the factual data contained in other sections of the report.

PROCESSING JOB DATA

CONSOLIDATING JOB DATA

When the job data have been collected and the job analysis team has returned to headquarters, the third phase of job analysis, the consolidation of data, begins. During this phase, the individual job analysis reports completed at the worksites are consolidated into one report or job schedule which describes the division of jobs, duties, and tasks within the functional area analyzed. More specifically, during the consolidation phase the following is done:

1. Average indexes describing the criticality or importance of each duty and task are developed for each job.
2. The frequency with which each item of equipment is used is determined.
3. Duties, tasks, and elements performed are consolidated for each job, and a statement of the overall job, in terms of behavior, conditions, and criterion, is developed.
4. Duties judged to be not significant, and their accompanying task and element descriptions, are listed separately.

ANALYZING JOB DATA

In this phase, the consolidated job analysis reports, together with individual job schedules, are analyzed to determine the requirements for new jobs, revised job descriptions, new training systems, changes in existing training programs, new equipment requirements, organizational changes, and the like.

It should be noted that a completed job analysis report describes the duties, tasks, and elements performed by incumbents of a job at the time the job analysis is made. For this reason, a job analysis presents a picture of a job as it *exists*, not as it *should be* or *may become*. If a training program is based exclusively on data derived from periodic job analyses, it may include instruction that will be unnecessary or obsolete by the time the trainee is assigned to the job. Similarly, the training will not include instruction in new duties and tasks or changes in equipment, procedures, or techniques that have occurred since the last job analysis was performed (unless a follow-up program is in effect).

Therefore, in addition to the data derived from job analysis, careful consideration must be given by analysts to the probable impact of evolving organizational systems; new concepts of operations; new products and services; and new equipment, materials, and techniques. These new developments must be identified and assessed by the analysts and, where appropriate, incorporated into the data. However, it is critically important that these items be clearly identified as projections. The primary sources of these data are short- and long-range company forecasts, and research and development reports.

REPORTING JOB DATA

The final step in processing job analysis data is the preparation of a formal written report. This report informs all interested personnel of the conclusions reached by the team and the supporting facts. In addition, the report serves as a permanent record of findings and as a basis for following up recommendations. The format of the report may take several forms. However, the format recommended for follow-up reports in Chapter 16 is well suited for the job.

CHECKLIST

PLANNING

1. Do the specific units selected for survey:
   a. Have spaces authorized and filled for the jobs under study?
   b. Have assigned a minimum of five job incumbents who match the selection criteria?
   c. Represent all types of using units?
   d. Reflect "typical" job requirements in the occupational areas studied?
   e. Represent the enterprise geographically and environmentally?
2. Have units been notified of the purpose, time, and length of the visit?
3. Have members of job analysis teams received formal training? Have the following documents relating to the mission, organization, and functions of the units to be visited been studied:
   a. Organization and functions manual?
   b. Equipment listings?
   c. Current job descriptions?
   d. Existing job analyses, if any?
4. Have standard briefings been prepared and rehearsed for presentation to:
   a. Managers of activities to be visited?

b. Supervisory personnel?

c. Job incumbents?

5. Have detailed procedures for the conduct of job analysis been developed and dry-run?

6. Have administrative arrangements been made to include:

a. Travel and hotel reservations?

b. Passports, visas, and inoculations (for overseas travel)?

CONDUCTING JOB ANALYSIS

1. Are managers of units briefed immediately on:

a. The purposes, procedures, and requirements of job analysis?

b. Why the analyses are being performed?

c. What the team requires in the way of assistance and support?

d. How the team plans to conduct the analyses?

e. How the job analysis reports will be used?

f. The fact that analyses are not investigative but rather are a means of gathering data to serve as a basis for improving training?

2. Does the team spend some time reviewing the mission, organization, and functions of the unit, including:

a. Organization charts?

b. Organization and functions manual?

c. Standard operating procedures?

d. Job descriptions?

e. Workflow?

f. Overages and shortages of personnel, and other unique conditions?

3. Is a preliminary survey made of worksites to note types of equipment used, workflow, and the organization of the unit under operating conditions?

4. Are supervisory personnel briefed on the purpose and procedures of the analysis?

5. Do job incumbents selected for interview and observation meet these standards:

a. Perform the typical duties of the job?

b. Perform duties with average, satisfactory proficiency?

c. Been working in the job long enough to master it but not so long that perception of the difficulties of the job is dimmed?

d. Possess neither unusually high nor unusually low educational background, nor unusually varied or unusually limited prior work experience?

6. Are the records of personnel to be interviewed and observed reviewed and pertinent data entered on the job analysis forms?

7. Are job incumbents briefed on the purposes and procedures of the interview and observation, including:

     a.   Pertinent items from the standard briefing?

     b.   Emphasis on the fact that the analysis is not investigative or evaluative?

     c.   Setting a time and place for interview and observation?

  8. In conducting interviews,

     a.   Is a place chosen that is private, comfortable, and free from distractions?

     b.   Is rapport established before any attempt is made to collect job data?

     c.   Is the incumbent encouraged to explain his own duties?

     d.   Does the analyst make outline notes of key words and phrases?

     e.   Does the analyst get at the specifics of job performance?

     f.   Does the analyst end the interview when the incumbent no longer can provide pertinent and usable information?

  9. In conducting observation,

     a.   Does the analyst observe long enough to see performance of all major duties?

     b.   Does he avoid getting in the way?

     c.   Does he ask questions only when necessary?

     d.   Does he make careful notes of his observations?

10. Are job analysis forms checked and validated by the incumbent and his immediate supervisor?

CONSOLIDATING, ANALYZING, AND REPORTING

1. Are individual job analysis reports consolidated into one report?

2. Are the consolidated job analysis reports analyzed to determine the requirements for new jobs, revised job descriptions, new training systems, changes in existing training programs, new equipment requirements, and organizational changes?

3. Is consideration given by analysts to the probable impact of evolving organizational systems, new concepts of operations, new products and services, and new equipment, material, and techniques?

4. Are the factors in question 3 reported?

5. Is a final, comprehensive report of findings and recommendations prepared and distributed for review, comment, and concurrence?

SELECTED REFERENCES

Chenzoff, Andrew P. *A Review of the Literature on Task Analysis.* Technical Report: NAVTRADEVCEN 1218-3. Port Washington, N.Y.: U.S. Naval Training Device Center, June 22, 1964.

Cummings, Roy J. "Removing Intuition from Course Development." *Training and Development Journal* (January 1968), 22:1: 18–30.

Department of the Army. *Army Job Analysis Manual I,* SDB Report 1-60-OR.

Washington, D.C.: Systems Development Branch, Research and Development Division, Adjutant General's Office, March 1960.

Dunnette, Marvin D., and George W. England. "A Checklist for Differentiating Engineering Jobs." *Personnel Psychology* (Summer 1957), 10:2: 191–198.

————, and Wayne K. Kirchner. "A Checklist for Differentiating Different Kinds of Sales Jobs." *Personnel Psychology* (Autumn 1959), 12:3: 421–430.

Folley, John D., Jr. *Guidelines for Task Analysis.* Technical Report: NAV-TRADEVCEN 1218-2. Port Washington, N.Y.: U.S. Naval Training Device Center, June 22, 1964.

————. *Development of an Improved Method of Task Analysis and Beginnings of a Theory of Training.* Technical Report: NAVTRADEVCEN 1218-1. Port Washington, N.Y.: U.S. Naval Training Device Center, June 22, 1964.

Hemphill, John K. "Job Descriptions for Executives." *Harvard Business Review* (May 1959), 37:5: 55–67.

Johnson, Richard B. "Determining Training Needs." In Robert L. Craig and Lester R. Bittel, eds. *Training and Development Handbook.* New York: McGraw-Hill Book Company, 1967, Chap. 2.

Legere, C. L. John. *USASA Command Job Analysis System: Job Analysis Handbook and Guide,* 2d ed. Fort Devens, Mass.: HQ USASATC&S, January 1966.

Melching, William H., Robert G. Smith, Jr., Jesse C. Rupe, and John A. Cox. *A Handbook for Programmers of Automated Instruction.* Alexandria, Va.: George Washington University Human Resources Research Office, September 1963, Chap. 2.

Miller, Robert B. *A Method for Man-Machine Task Analysis.* WADC Technical Report 53-137. Wright-Patterson Air Force Base, Ohio: Wright Air Development Center, Air Research and Development Command, June 1953.

————. *A Suggested Guide to Position-Task Description.* ASPRL TM-56-6. Lowry Air Force Base, Colo.: Air Force Personnel and Training Research Center, Air Research and Development Command, April 1956.

————. "Task Description and Analysis." In Robert Glaser, ed. *Psychological Principles in System Development.* Pittsburgh: University of Pittsburgh Press, 1962, pp. 31–62.

Morsh, Joseph E., Joseph M. Madden, and Raymond E. Cristal. *Job Analysis in the United States Air Force.* WADD-TR-61-113. Lackland Air Force Base, Tex.: Personnel Laboratory, Wright Air Development Division, Air Research and Development Command, February 1961.

————. "The Analysis of Jobs: Use of the Task Inventory Method of Job Analysis." In Edwin A. Fleishman, ed. *Studies in Personnel and Industrial Psychology.* rev. ed. Homewood, Ill.: The Dorsey Press, 1967, pp. 4–11.

Smith, Robert G., Jr. *The Development of Training Objectives.* Research Bulletin 11. Alexandria, Va.: George Washington University Human Resources Research Office, June 1964, Chaps. 3, 5.

Tracey, William R. *Evaluating Training and Development Systems.* AMA, 1968, pp. 123–126.

4

Selecting and Writing
Training Objectives

T<small>HIS</small> chapter deals with the problems of selecting, writing, and organizing training objectives. Although course outlines, programs of instruction, or instructor guides may be available to the trainer, most of these documents are of limited help in planning training activities. Furthermore, as emphasized earlier, the only source of valid training objectives is systematically collected and objective job or task data. The effectiveness of the instructional system depends upon the efficiency of the trainer in selecting and writing meaningful objectives. The purpose of this chapter is to provide the trainer with general principles, criteria, and procedures that can function as guides to the selection and writing of appropriate and usable training and development objectives.

After completing the chapter, the reader should be able to perform as follows:

Behavior   Select appropriate objectives for formal training and development programs.
Conditions   Given: complete job or task analysis data, criteria for selection, appropriate forms, and clerical assistance.
Criterion   To the standards defined in this chapter.

Behavior   Write training and development objectives in performance (behavioral) terms.

Conditions   Given: complete job or task analysis data for a specific job, procedural guides, appropriate forms, and clerical assistance.

Criterion   Objectives will be complete, realistic, grammatically correct, and consistent with the standards defined in this chapter.

Behavior   Review draft statements of performance (behavioral) objectives for adequacy.

Conditions   Given: complete job or task analysis data for a specific job, criteria for selection, completed Training Objectives Worksheets, and criteria for reviewing objectives.

Criterion   To the standards defined in this chapter.

DEFICIENCIES IN STATEMENTS OF OBJECTIVES

SELECTION

The selection of objectives is a judgmental procedure which involves close scrutiny by qualified personnel of the full range of job duties, tasks, and elements performed by incumbents in a particular job and detailed in job analysis schedules. The criteria used by the trainer as a basis for selection must insure that the skills which are appropriate for formal training are formulated as objectives for specific training programs or courses of instruction.

Job analysis schedules detail the full dimensions of a particular job with all its variations, caused by enterprise, geographical, product, procedural, or environmental conditions. It would be extravagant, in terms of time, personnel, money, and other resources, to provide the amount and kind of training required to equip every graduate of a training program to perform any job task associated with a particular occupation or skill in any position anywhere. For the same reason, it is often impractical to train personnel to the level of proficiency required in some positions. Some training is more realistically and more practically conducted on the job. Consequently, it is essential for the trainer to select from the total list of job performances those which are most appropriate and feasible for formal training and to decide what standards or level of proficiency will be required for successful course completion.

Training priorities for specific job duties and tasks must also be assigned to insure that the most critical skills are taught even if reductions in the length of the training program are necessary. That is, if business or other conditions require the implementation of an austerity program, training in essential skills will still be possible without revamping the entire training program. The cut can come at the end of specified segments of the program, and whatever is left over can become the sum and substance of the on-the-job training program. These requirements can be easily passed on to supervisors of operating activities in a form which will tell them precisely how much of the needed training has been provided and what remains for them to accomplish.

FORMULATION

Part of the waste that occurs in training is directly due to the fact that objectives, even if valid, have not been stated in terms which permit the development of optimally effective training programs. Too often, the objectives of training have been stated vaguely. Typically, statements of objectives have been worded in such ways as "to provide the student with a general knowledge of . . . ," "a working knowledge of . . . ," "an understanding and appreciation of . . ."; or "to develop the ability to. . . ." Statements like these are ambiguous; they can be, and inevitably are, interpreted differently by staff, trainees, and instructors. They are imprecise: they do not provide the direction and guidance needed to select instructional methods, to develop instructional materials, or to construct valid evaluation instruments and devices. Objectives must be understood by both the instructor and the trainees, and therefore, if precise and efficient training is to be provided, objectives must be stated in behavioral terms. This means that they must describe clearly and unambiguously what the trainee must be able to do, the conditions under which he must be able to perform, and the standard or criterion of acceptable performance, both at critical points during the development of job skills and at the end of the training program.

Admittedly, the formulation of behavioral objectives is a difficult task. Yet, if objectives are not stated in this form, the likelihood of achieving the purposes of the training is extremely small. Unquestionably, even with vaguely stated objectives the trainee will learn something; but what he learns may bear little resemblance to what was intended.

If it is argued that there are learning outcomes that defy precise description, it must also be admitted that determining whether they have been attained is equally impossible. The premise must be rejected. If behavior exists, it can be observed and described. By definition, learning is a goal-directed change in behavior. Therefore, it should be possible to

set up situations which require the learner to demonstrate newly acquired behavior. Behaviorally stated objectives provide for this.

USES OF OBJECTIVES

Training objectives provide the basis for all the remaining steps in
the development of an instructional system. They constitute the real heart
of a training program. The quality of other instructional decisions rests
heavily on the adequacy of statements of objectives. In addition, training
objectives serve certain administrative purposes. Some of the more important uses of training objectives follow.

CONSISTENCY IN THE DESIGN OF THE TRAINING SYSTEM

Training systems are composed of several interacting and integrated
subsystems. There are the human elements—the instructors and the
trainees. There are the material elements—the equipment, training aids,
texts, handouts, and the like. And there are the organizational and strategy elements—the methods, techniques, systems of trainee and instructor
organization, and media. To make sure that all these elements dovetail
and support each other, they must be selected and used on the basis of
a set of objectives that are common to all subsystems.

EFFECTIVE COMMUNICATION

The main function of statements of objectives is communication.
Instructional objectives that are sent clearly by the sender and received
ungarbled by the receiver are more likely to be achieved than objectives
that are not clearly communicated. In short, with clearly stated objectives,
instructors can do a better job of instructing and trainees can do a better
job of learning. The instructor knows precisely what he is attempting to
do, and trainees know what is expected of them in terms of behavior or
performance as a result of training. Statements of objectives are therefore
useful to the instructor to develop means of checking on his and the
trainees' performance. The instructor may also use objectives to inform
his colleagues, substitute instructors, department heads, training supervisors, managers, and executives about the content of his program and

to tell them how trainees will be able to perform when they have completed the training system.

SELECTING APPROPRIATE COURSE CONTENT

Well-stated objectives provide a practical and objective means of determining the specific facts, principles, concepts, and skills that must be included in a training program. They take much of the guesswork out of deciding what content is pertinent and what is extraneous. Objectives represent the skeleton or framework of a training program. The flesh and muscle consist of the course content. Judicious choice of objectives permits the selection of the right kind and amount of content and helps avoid the dangers of both undertraining and overtraining.

SELECT THE MOST SUITABLE INSTRUCTIONAL STRATEGY

Well-stated objectives provide a clear description of job requirements. Because objectives can be written in a fashion that avoids equivocation and ambiguity, the process of selecting the optimum method, medium, and system of organization is greatly simplified. If the instructor knows precisely what the trainee must be able to do upon completion of the instructional block or unit, he can be more objective about selecting the strategy which will accomplish the goal.

CLEAR-CUT INSTRUCTOR AND TRAINEE GOALS

Training objectives permit both the instructor and the trainees to know precisely what is required of the student at the end of any instructional unit or complete course. This knowledge provides the trainee with a sense of direction, and enables him to determine for himself what progress he is making toward the attainment of the goal. Such knowledge is, in itself, a strong motivating factor. Knowledge of goals helps the instructor to avoid gaps and unnecessary duplication in instruction. In short, well-stated objectives make learning more effective and more efficient.

BASIS FOR DEVELOPING CRITERION MEASURES

Training objectives are essential to the construction of valid and reliable criterion tests. Valid tests are difficult to construct under any conditions, but without well-stated objectives to serve as a foundation, the validity of criterion tests and measures is likely to be questionable.

Go, No-Go Standards

Precisely stated objectives make it relatively easy to determine at what points in a course or program a trainee must demonstrate that he has acquired the knowledge and skills needed to progress further in the program. Such actions as analysis of trainee difficulties, provision of remedial instruction, and elimination from the program are more easily and more objectively accomplished when well-stated objectives are available.

Objective Evaluation of Instruction

Precisely stated objectives provide the ingredient that has been missing in instructor evaluation programs—agreement between the evaluator and the one evaluated about what the instructon should accomplish. With well-stated objectives both the instructor and the evaluator know what the outcome of the instruction should be. This permits objective evaluation of the instructional program in action—and acceptance by the instructor of the validity of the comments of his evaluator.

On-the-Job Evaluation of Graduates of the Training Program

It is practically impossible to obtain reliable judgments of the effectiveness of trained men in performing their jobs unless there are firm and objective standards for evaluation. Well-stated objectives provide these basic standards.

Requirements for On-the-job Training Programs

With well-stated objectives available to them, supervisors have a clear picture of the knowledge and skills that graduates of a training program bring to the job. This facilitates the development of realistic on-the-job training programs which will dovetail with the formal training program.

Last, precisely stated training objectives can be used to define training requirements to contract trainers if the training is to be conducted either in-house with out-of-enterprise resources or out-of-house. Behaviorally stated objectives make it possible to communicate to contractors exactly what the output of the training must be able to do. Such a step means not only that there will be a better chance of getting the required training product but also that the danger of wasting funds will be minimized. In short, with behavioral objectives, contractor performance is more easily monitored.

TYPES OF OBJECTIVES

Training objectives are statements describing the changes in behavior or performance that are the desired outcomes of trainee and instructor activity and interaction. They may also be referred to as goals, purposes, aims, or outcomes. Changes in behavior include new, modified, or improved skills (manual, manipulative, verbal, problem-solving, supervisory, and managerial); abilities involving the application of facts, principles, concepts, or ideas; and emotionalized controls (attitudes, interests, ideals, and appreciations). Therefore, a statement of objectives expresses the skills, abilities, knowledge, attitudes, and the like that are the desired outcomes of specific training activities. This applies whether the objectives are statements for a total training program or for an individual lesson.

CLASSIFICATION OF OBJECTIVES

Objectives may be classified in many different ways. For purposes of this discussion, however, they will be divided into two categories: primary and derived.

Primary objectives. A primary objective is one of the core learnings of a training program or a major unit of that program. It is an objective of central and dominant importance in an instructional system. It gives meaning, clarity, and unity to all learning activities in the training program. A primary objective may deal with the development of a manipulative skill, such as the repair of equipment; it may involve the acquisition of a special ability, such as employment interviewing; or it may involve the development of complex problem-solving skills in a managerial role.

Derived objectives. The attainment of the primary objective often hinges on the development of contributory knowledge and skills. Certain fundamental understandings, concepts, principles, or elements of skill are often required to support the attainment of the primary objectives. These are not mere steps toward the primary objective; they are integral or closely related elements of the primary objectives.

Usually, derived objectives are the heart of an individual lesson. For example, if the development of skill in repairing equipment is the primary objective, derived objectives might involve the skill of soldering, the use of mathematical equations, the use of test equipment, and a host of other integral skills, abilities, and knowledge supports. In employment interviewing, derived objectives might involve the ability to use probes, to prepare a rating scale, to establish rapport, and the like.

FORMS OF STATEMENTS OF OBJECTIVES

Both primary and derived objectives should be stated in a form that will make them most useful in selecting methods and materials, in guiding training activities, and in evaluating results. Objectives can be stated in many ways, but few of the approaches to objective statements currently in use meet the requirements of effective and efficient instruction. Four of the most common forms are instructor-centered, subject-matter-centered, trainee activity-centered, and trainee performance-centered. Only the latter form provides the precision required for adequate planning, conduct, and evaluation of instruction.

INSTRUCTOR-CENTERED OBJECTIVES

Objectives can be stated in the form of activities which the instructor is to perform. Here are some examples of instructor-centered objectives.

- To demonstrate the operation of a turret lathe.
- To discuss the need for identifying gaps in the work history of a job applicant prior to the conduct of an employment interview.
- To develop in the trainee an appreciation of the need for teamwork.
- To demonstrate the proper method of inserting a hypodermic syringe.

These are statements of what the *instructor* does, but they really are not statements of training objectives or of the desired changes in the behavior or performance of the trainees. For this reason, they are totally inadequate as guides for planning, conducting, or evaluating instruction.

SUBJECT-MATTER-CENTERED OBJECTIVES

Objectives can also be stated in the form of topics, concepts, principles, or other elements of the *content* to be taught in a training program. Here are a few samples of objectives stated in terms of the subject matter to be taught concerning the operation of the 10 kw power generator:

- Nomenclature.
- Preventive maintenance.
- Starting and warm-up procedures.
- Refueling procedures.
- Emergency procedures.
- Close-down procedures.
- Safety precautions.

This form of objective statement identifies the area of *content* to be taught and learned, but it does not indicate what the trainees are to be able to do following the training. What are they to be required to do with power generators? Memorize the content of the lessons? Apply principles? Operate the equipment? Operate it how well? Operate it under what conditions? The objectives as stated do not provide the answers to these or to a lot of other critical questions.

TRAINEE ACTIVITY-CENTERED OBJECTIVES

Objectives can also be stated in terms of what the *trainee* is to do during the training period; that is, the objectives describe trainee activities. For example, the following objectives are set forth in terms of trainee activity:

- To learn to operate a forklift.
- To learn company cost-accounting procedures.
- To learn to adapt procedures and routines to the needs of operative employees.
- To learn the principles of magnetism.
- To disassemble a carburetor.
- To learn PERT.

Here again, the form of the objective statement does not specify very clearly what the trainee is to be able to do following the training, nor does it establish a criterion or standard of acceptable performance.

TRAINEE PERFORMANCE-CENTERED OBJECTIVES

Last, training objectives can be stated in terms of what the trainee is to be able to do upon completion of training—or at any point during his training—including how well he is to be able to perform. This form is illustrated as follows:

The trainee will be able to calculate the square roots of 6-digit numbers, including decimals, with complete accuracy, without using tables of square roots or a slide rule.

The trainee will be able to operate a key punch at the rate of 40 words per minute with less than 1 percent error for a period of 10 minutes.

The trainee will be able to identify, locate, and repair any one of 10 common malfunctions in the radio receiver R 390/URR within a period of 60 minutes.

The trainee will be able to read, interpret, and use IBM 360/40 runs as a basis for scheduling and controlling production.

This form of statement of objectives expresses the desired changes in behavior—the learning outcomes—in terms of skills and abilities. The trainee is required to perform or do something at a certain level of proficiency before he is considered to have achieved the goal.

This is the form that is most useful in any type of training program because it is the form which lends itself best to objective evaluation of results. The performance element of this type of training objective is readily recognizable: to calculate, to operate, to record, to repair, and so forth.

Examination of these abbreviated objectives will reveal that they include both the performance aspect and the content aspect. In other words, they indicate what the trainee is to be able to do with what. Further study of these objectives will indicate the necessity for the formulation of derived or contributory objectives needed to attain the primary objective. For example, take the first objective stated above, namely, "will be able to calculate the square roots of 6-digit numbers. . . ." To reach this objective, more specific objectives relating to the knowledge supports, and the elements of skill necessary for the attainment of this objective must be delineated. This can be done either through a statement of the derived objective or through a statement of the content and learning activities essential to the attainment of the primary objective. Obviously, the former course is eminently preferable.

CRITERIA FOR SELECTING TRAINING OBJECTIVES

The following criteria are offered as guides for the selection of appropriate objectives for training. It is not essential for all criteria to be met if any single item is to be included in the list of training objectives of a course or program. In some cases, the meeting of one criterion alone may be sufficient justification for the inclusion of a job element in a list of training objectives.

UNIVERSALITY

Emphasis should be placed on the development of skills and associated knowledge supports and emotionalized controls (ideals, attitudes, interests, and appreciations) that are used by personnel in occupations or typical positions regardless of where they occur. That is, the job element is required no matter where or when the trainee works. Regardless of the unit, department, or plant to which the employees may be assigned, the shift that he works, or the product he works with, the skill or knowledge is required for adequate performance of the job.

For example, a computer console operator should be taught the functions and skills which apply to all computer applications regardless of the type of problem involved or the application—be it in cost-accounting, inventory, scheduling, or sales forecasting. In the case of basic management skills, emphasis in a training and development program should be on those skills which are usable by managerial personnel regardless of department, branch, or location.

In essence, then, the criterion of universality asks the questions: Where is this skill or knowledge used? In which positions? Does it have wide or narrow application? Is it so unique that it is infrequently found in the job descriptions of incumbents of positions with this title? If it is truly unique, the likelihood is that the skill should be taught on the job, rather than as a part of the formal training program.

DIFFICULTY

Emphasis should be placed on content or skills which are so difficult to learn that it highly unlikely that job incumbents will or can acquire them on their own, or on skills that are so difficult to learn that they require intensive formal training, conducted by competent instructors, in order that the trainee may acquire the desired level of proficiency.

For example, although it is conceivable that an individual could learn to read blueprints without assistance, the process would be a lengthy, trial-and-error one. The same thing might be said for computer programming, accounting, equipment repair, and a host of other skills. Added to the difficulty of the skill is the danger to men or the hazard to equipment which could result from the unguided efforts of a neophyte to learn on his own.

Therefore, the difficulty criterion asks the trainer the questions: Is the skill or concept difficult to acquire? Are people likely to learn this skill on their own and with minimum danger to themselves, to equipment, or to materials? If the answer is "no," and if the item meets at least one other criterion, it probably should be included in the list of training objectives.

CRUCIALITY

Skills and knowledge supports should be selected which are critically essential to satisfactory job performance *when needed,* even though the tasks may not be performed frequently. In other words, although the specific skill may not be needed often, when it is needed, it is critical to adequate performance of the job.

For example, more and more equipment is being produced which has high reliability. In the field of electronic equipment, solid-state devices are less subject to breakdown than their vacuum-tube predecessors. This should reduce the amount of maintenance training that an operator would ordinarily require. However, there may be a number of malfunctions which, although they occur very infrequently, would be extremely critical if immediate corrective action were not taken by the operator. Severe damage to the equipment, or to materials or products, might be the result. Under such circumstances, the criticality of the infrequently used skill is so great that training should be provided.

In summary, the criterion of criticality asks the questions: How important is the skill when practice of it is called for? What happens if the job incumbent does not possess the required knowledge or skill? What is the impact of this deficiency on the operation, the product, the equipment, or the image of the industry?

FREQUENCY

The skills and knowledge supports which are used often on the job should be emphasized. A skill that is used frequently may warrant special training under formal conditions, even though acquiring it on the job may be possible. It is often more economical of time and materials to teach the skill correctly in the beginning than to allow workers to learn by trial and error. It is also true that teaching the best way of doing something results in more efficient performance and greater consistency in the quality of the product or service produced.

The criterion of frequency, then, asks the questions: How often must the incumbent perform this task? Is there a known best way of handling it? Can a standard way of doing this task be taught? Is there any real benefit in teaching it?

PRACTICABILITY

Whether the time, effort, money, and other resources required to develop the skill or knowledge are commensurate with the gains in job proficiency must be determined. This criterion asks: Is the training really worthwhile? People can be trained to do any job-related function, and yet, the question often arises of whether the costs of the training will be repaid in terms of improved performance.

If, for example, the proficiency of a formally trained man is only slightly higher than the proficiency of an individual trained on the job (or self-taught), then the practicability of the training may be open to serious question. Realistically, from the standpoint of costs, training should result in a significantly higher level of job performance or a measurably greater degree of skill in performing some task than can be acquired without the formal training.

For example, training in typing is usually accepted as a suitable skill for formal instruction. However, it is undoubtedly true that there is a rather definite break-even point in typing training—a point at which further investments in training result in smaller and smaller incremental improvements in typing speed. Probably there is a level of skill, which might be stated in the number of words per minute with a maximum allowable number of errors, which could be justified in terms of costs. But to continue training beyond this level would be to invest proportionately more than the gains are worth. Attaining proficiency beyond this level might be a proper goal for on-the-job training.

In summary, this criterion asks the questions: Will the investment in training yield proportional increases in skill? Is a formally trained person a measurably better performer than someone who has learned the skill on his own or on the job?

ACHIEVABILITY

It must be considered whether an objective is attainable in terms of the level of skill or proficiency required, the aptitude and intelligence of the input to the training program, and the resources available. Objectives must be compatible with the abilities and aptitudes of the trainees, as well as with their needs and the requirements of the job. To set standards of accomplishment which are beyond the reach of any sizable percentage of the trainee group is unrealistic—and expensive in terms of attrition from the training program or loss of the employee. (They may quit if they become frustrated enough.)

For example, a trainer may decide that production could be speeded up and efficiency in offices could be improved if typists were able to type at a rate of 150 words per minute. Yet, this level of proficiency is undoubtedly unrealistic. Very few people would be able to achieve the standard; it is truly unattainable for the great majority of typists.

To take another example, the training director may be persuaded that equipment repairmen need a solid foundation in electronic theory. This may be true, but if the input to the training program does not possess a high level of intelligence (and perhaps a rather good grounding in basic mathematics) the instruction is likely to be way over the heads of the trainees. They will not be able to achieve the desired level of accomplishment.

In summary, the criterion of achievability asks the questions: Can the majority of enrollees meet the standard described in the objective? Do they have the aptitude, the intelligence, the maturity, the motivation, and the educational and experience background required to deal with the content and to attain the desired standard?

QUALITY

The skills and knowledge which are more useful to men of "average" proficiency than to those of "mediocre" or "outstanding" proficiency should be selected. In other words, objectives should be selected which reflect acceptable skills and standards, rather than those which either fall short of acceptability or plainly exceed job requirements. To train individuals at a level of achievement which is less than that required on the job is to place an unnecessary burden on supervisory personnel for on-the-job training. In this case, the training program is not serving the enterprise as it should. On the other hand, it is wasteful to train individuals, or attempt to train them, in skills and at levels of achievement which are characteristic of only the best performers. The investment will be heavy, and the number of individuals who complete the training successfully will be few.

In sum, this criterion asks the questions: Are the skills to be acquired most useful to average-acceptable workers? Does the program result in either overtraining or undertraining?

DEFICIENCY

Training should be given in the essential job skills and knowledge in which job incumbents consistently or frequently demonstrate inadequate proficiency or knowledge. In any job, there are tasks that are more difficult or easier to "muff" than other aspects of total performance. An inventory of these can be easily produced by tabulating the judgments of supervisory personnel. These items, regardless of their difficulty or criticality, might well appear as points of emphasis in a listing of objectives.

For example, if rejection rates in a production operation are caused by faulty soldering or improper inspection, these items might well be emphasized in the list of training objectives for the training of operators.

In sum, this criterion asks the questions: What is it that people in this job frequently do poorly or not at all? What aspects of the job need to be emphasized because a sizable number of job incumbents make mistakes or display an unacceptable level of proficiency?

RETAINABILITY

The time interval between completion of training and use of the skill on the job should be considered. The factor involved is the amount of deterioration of skill that is likely to take place during that time interval. The degree to which a skill deteriorates through disuse, and the time over which the deterioration takes place, should play a large part in determining the level of achievement in performance of the skill required for successful completion of formal training. In turn, the desired level of attainment will determine the amount of time and emphasis given to the development of the skill. Some skills deteriorate rapidly; others deteriorate slowly or not at all. Of course, this criterion relates to a few others, notably frequency and criticality. Judgment must be exercised first in arriving at a determination of whether the skill should be taught until it is likely to be used. If a decision is made to teach the skill, then the amount of emphasis, practice, and maintenance training required are critical to the retention of the skill.

For example, the ability to take shorthand is a relatively difficult skill to acquire. If the skill is not used, a certain amount of deterioration is certain to occur. If the skill is only rarely needed by secretarial personnel, it may be wise to train only a few stenographers. However, if the decision is made to train all secretarial personnel in this skill, a higher level of initial proficiency will be required to absorb the deterioration of the skill which is certain to accompany disuse, thereby providing an acceptable level of proficiency if and when exercise of the skill is called for.

In short, the criterion of retainability asks the questions: How long will it be before the trainee uses this skill on the job? How susceptible to deterioration is this skill or knowledge? Does it require maintenance training to retain it? What level of accomplishment is required at the conclusion of initial training to insure a sufficient residue of the skill to handle tasks involving it some time later on the job?

Follow-on Training

Both the kind and the amount of training which are customarily given to personnel following completion of training must be considered. Follow-on training may take the form of advanced formal training or on-the-job training. A training program must be so set up that it will dovetail with any training that may follow. Trainees must be brought to the level of proficiency required to undertake either advanced training or on-the-job training with reasonably good promise of success. Those who plan the advanced training or the on-the-job training must know the minimum level of accomplishment they can expect of the input to their programs. This is the starting point for their planning and the development of the objectives for their programs. In short, initial training programs and following training programs must mesh. Otherwise, unnecessary costs will be incurred.

This criterion, then, raises the questions: What level of proficiency is needed for a graduate of this program to undertake a program of advanced or on-the-job training? What should the planner of the following training be able to count on in the way of prior knowledge and level of skill?

PROCEDURES FOR SELECTING OBJECTIVES

The completed job analysis report provides a basis for decisions with regard to whether a specific skill or knowledge will be taught and the levels of training required. Although the data indicate such facts as the percentage of job incumbents performing each duty and task, the frequency with which they are performed, and an index of their criticality, other important criteria require the application of judgment by qualified personnel. Such judgments must be made by fully qualified personnel using a standard rating scale to arrive at decisions on training objectives and their priorities.

The following procedure for selecting objectives is recommended.

Step 1. On the Training Objectives Worksheet shown in Figure 4-1, list all the duties and tasks contained in section B of the Job Analysis Report (Fig. 3-4).

Step 2. Rate each of the items in the list of duties and tasks in terms of each of the ten criteria discussed earlier. Values for each criterion are described in the Criterion Scoring Guide in Figure 4-2.

Step 3. Sum the scores for each duty and task, and enter the total in column 12 of the Training Objectives Worksheet.

Step 4. Establish the training priority for each task. Indicate this priority by assigning a priority number in column 13 of the Training Objectives Worksheet. A range of scores for each priority is included at the bottom of the worksheet.

The meanings of the priorities are as follows:

0   The task will not be taught at all.

1   Complete and thorough training will be provided; all trainees must demonstrate mastery of the task; they must be able to perform at the level of speed and accuracy required on the job.

2   Some training will be provided all trainees; trainees must demonstrate that they can perform the task, but not with the speed and accuracy required on the job.

3   All trainees will be introduced to the task; they will not be expected to be able to perform the task upon completion of training, but it has been described and demonstrated to them.

4   If time permits, trainees will be introduced to the task, but they will not be expected to be able to perform the task upon completion of training.

FINAL SELECTION

The completed Training Objectives Worksheets should be submitted to at least three qualified supervisors for review of task ratings and priorities. Reviewers should have the complete Job Analysis Report (Fig. 3-4) when making this review. When the forms have been reviewed, all

Figure 4-1.   Training Objectives Worksheet.

Tasks	Criteria											
	Universality	Difficulty	Cruciality	Frequency	Practicability	Achievability	Quality	Deficiency	Retainability	Follow-on training	Total score	Priority
1	2	3	4	5	6	7	8	9	10	11	12	13

Total score	Priority
0 - 10	0
11 - 20	4
21 - 30	3
31 - 40	2
41 - 50	1

Figure 4-2. Criterion Scoring Guide.

Criterion	Score					
	0	1	2	3	4	5
	0–10	11–25	26–50	51–75	76–90	90–100
• Universality: What percentage of incumbents perform the task?						
• Difficulty: Can the task be learned on the job?	Very easily	Practical	Minor problems	Many problems	Major problems	Practically impossible
• Cruciality: Is the task critical to job performance?	Not critical	Rarely critical	Sometimes critical	Often critical	Very often critical	Always very critical
• Frequency: How often is the task performed?	Less than quarterly	Quarterly	Monthly	Weekly	Daily	Several times per day
• Practicability: How does the proficiency of a formally trained man compare with those who learned on the job?	Much less proficient	Somewhat less proficient	About the same	Somewhat higher	Much higher	Very much higher
• Achievability: Can the task be learned to the degree required in a reasonable time frame?	Practically impossible	Major problems	Many problems	Minor problems	Practical	Very easily
• Quality: To which type of incumbent is the skill most useful?	Poor performer	Outstanding performer		Below average performer	Above average performer	Average performer
• Deficiency: How frequently are deficiencies noted in job incumbents?	Never	Rarely	Sometimes	Often	Very often	Always
• Retainability: What is the time interval between training and use of the skill?	Used immediately	Used within first month	Used within 1–3 months	Used within 4–6 months	Used within 7–12 months	Used after 12 months
• Follow-on training: What type of training is given on the skill following initial formal training?	Immediate advanced formal training	Thorough and complete on-the-job training	Some formal on-the-job training		Occasional informal on-the-job training	No additional training

people involved should meet face-to-face to iron out differences in the ratings and assignment of priorities. The objective of the meeting is to reach a consensus on the inclusion of specific duties and tasks in the training system and their respective priorities.

WRITING PERFORMANCE-CENTERED OBJECTIVES

A meaningful and useful objective clearly and unambiguously pictures what the trainee will be doing when he demonstrates a specific desired behavior or behavior pattern. The picture presented must be one that will be interpreted in exactly the same way by all personnel involved in the training or development program. The general rules for good expository writing apply to the writing of objectives. The overriding consideration is to be certain to use plain, generally understood English, since the basic purpose is to communicate the instructional intent.

To communicate clearly and get ideas across correctly, these five rules must be followed:

1. *Avoid unfamiliar words.* Consider the reader's comfort, interest, and capacity to understand. Unfamiliar words make no mental impression, so use only words which you are certain the reader of the objective will understand.

2. *Do not confuse or misuse words.* It is easy to make mistakes in usage, but errors can be avoided if you develop a writing conscience. An old admonition that applies is: "When in doubt, look it up or leave it out."

3. *Be terse.* Brevity makes written communication easier to understand. Long and involved sentences make it difficult to comprehend the intended meaning. Use only one idea in a sentence.

4. *Seek simplicity.* Use simple, short words, phrases, and sentences to keep the "fog count" down. Economize on adjectives and language flourishes. Make every word count.

5. *Read what you write.* After following all the preceding rules in writing objectives, there is more to be done. You must read the objectives to ascertain whether the words you have used are the right ones, saying what you wish to convey. The first word that occurred to you in drafting your objectives may not be the best one. Find the one that says what you want to say.

VAGUE TERMS VERSUS PRECISE TERMS

As pointed out earlier, personnel engaged in education and training have customarily used words and phrases in writing objectives which have no universal meaning. Their products deserve the label "pedagese." Consider the following examples of vague pedagogical terms and the clearer expressions of learning goals in the two listings that follow.

Vague terms	*Precise terms*
To provide a general knowledge of	To calculate
To provide a working knowledge of	To repair
To qualify	To adjust
To know about	To classify
To understand	To install
To develop an appreciation for	To construct
To be familiar with	To select
To perceive	To differentiate
To be aware of	To assemble
To comprehend	To operate
	To organize
	To state
	To list
	To demonstrate
	To solve

CHARACTERISTICS OF PERFORMANCE-CENTERED OBJECTIVES

A performance-centered objective is a statement that clearly communicates an instructional intent; that is, it describes precisely a desired change in the behavior of a trainee. Mager[1] has identified three essential characteristics of performance objectives as follows:

1. *They identify the terminal behavior.* The statement of an objective must identify exactly what the trainee must be able to do at the end of an instructional unit or complete course of instruction to demonstrate that he has achieved the desired behavior. The learned behavior may involve the application of knowledge or the demonstration of a specific skill or constellation skills.

2. *They describe the conditions of performance.* The statement of a performance objective must describe clearly and completely the conditions under which the trainee must be able to demonstrate the behavior. That is, the conditions of the objective identify what the trainee will be given to use in doing the job (tools, equipment, job aids, references, materials), what he will be denied (tools, equipment, and the like), what assistance he will have (if any), what supervision will be provided, and

---

[1] Robert F. Mager, *Preparing Objectives for Programmed Instruction.* Palo Alto, Calif.: Fearon Publishers, 1962, p. 12.

the physical environment in which he must perform (climate, space, light, and the like).

3. *They set a criterion of acceptable performance.* The statement of a performance objective must describe how well the trainee must be able to perform. The criterion or standard establishes the minimum performance requirements for a duty, task, or job element. To do this, the objective statement must prescribe the quality of the work product or service produced (accuracy, completeness, clarity, tolerances, and the like); the *quantity* of work products produced (the number of work units completed); the *time* allowed to complete the job, duty, task, or element; or any combination of quality, quantity, and time standards.

WRITING PERFORMANCE-CENTERED OBJECTIVES

Step 1. Identify the desired behavior. The essence of a performance objective is found in the description of observable, end-product behavior. Although several other ingredients contribute to the acquisition of any behavior (for example, knowledge, elements of skill, attitudes, and ideals), it is extremely important that these elements be recognized for what they really are: components of the instructional situation or prerequisites to desired behavior rather than the end behavior itself. By definition, performance objectives are statements that describe behaviors which are to become established either during or at the end of a sequence of instruction. They can be seen and measured. Statements of desired behavior that meet this standard will provide a firm foundation for planning instruction and will ultimately be the criterion for determining whether the instruction has been successful.

To meet this standard, the behavioral statement must begin with a verb, completely describe the performance, describe a meaningful unit of performance, be highly relevant to the job or task, be accurate and precise, and avoid overlapping other behaviors.

Here is an example of an inadequate behavioral statement: *To develop an understanding of the 407 accounting machine.* This statement is difficult to interpret because it does not picture the trainee displaying learned behavior. Rather than describing the learner *doing* something, it sketches an abstract state of mind which in some way or another relates to an accounting machine. Although many learning outcomes are by nature abstract, it is also true that these learnings have some outward manifestation which makes the understanding or appreciation observable. If an attempt were made to determine the behavioral requirement hidden in the objective as stated, it might be established that the trainee really must be able to *identify by name each of the controls on the front panel of the 407 accounting machine,* or *construct an operational flow chart of the 407 accounting machine,* or *troubleshoot and locate specific malfunctions in the 407 accounting machine.* It should be apparent that these statements are eminently more precise in communicating the desired behavior the trainee is really expected to acquire.

Another relatively common approach to the statement of training objectives is found in the use of the term "working knowledge"—for example, *the trainee must have a working knowledge of the radio receiver R-390/URR.* Although the phrase "working knowledge" contains a strong implication that some definite actions are to be performed with the receiver, the statement does not provide information about what these actions are. Is the working knowledge equated to an ability to operate the receiver? Or does it mean that the trainee can list the operational characteristics of the receiver, or diagram signal flow through the components? Whatever the case, the objective must picture the trainee doing something with or to the receiver as a result of training, as opposed to leading him to some vague intellectual state.

Some examples of acceptable statements of behavior follow:

- Translate any decimal number into its binary equivalent.
- Locate any malfunctioning component in a standard superheterodyne radio receiver.
- Identify and select all defective line bearings from a mixed sample of line bearings.
- Connect and solder a wire to a terminal lug.
- Energize a radar.
- Code a message.
- Test an inductor.
- Plan a lesson.
- Calculate a value.
- Identify the windings on a multicap transformer.
- Calculate the magnetic azimuth between any two map points.
- Adjust head bolts.
- Construct an organization chart.

Step 2. State the required conditions under which the behavior will be performed. Another essential part of a complete and explicit statement of an objective is the specification of the conditions which will ordinarily be present in the situation and which are, in fact, directly associated with the desired behavior. The conditions are the environmental factors surrounding the behavior or the resources the learner must use in performing. The environment encompasses such elements as climatic or geographic conditions—for example, temperature, humidity, light, location, terrain, distances, time of day, and presence of precipitation. Resources include hardware and software, such as tools, equipment, references, and work aids, and the critical element of supervision or assistance received during the performance.

To measure up, the conditions portion of the statement of the objective must meet these standards:

- Specify exactly what the trainee will be given or provided when he demonstrates the behavior.
- Specify restrictions or limitations imposed (if any).
- Identify the tools, equipment, and clothing used (where applicable).
- List the references and job aids to be used (if any).
- Describe special physical or environmental conditions (if applicable).

Here is an example of a poorly stated condition. *Given an operable radio receiver power supply and appropriate tools, the trainee must be able to calculate resistance, current, and voltage at selected points in the . . . circuit of a superheterodyne radio receiver.* Examination of this statement reveals that the trainee is pictured doing something, with particular end products desired, and in relation to a specific item of equipment. However, the statement leaves many unanswered questions: Is the trainee to perform these calculations with or without references? With or without formulas? Will the calculations be made with test equipment on an actual circuit, or will they be merely paper and pencil calculations? If a circuit is involved, will the condition of the circuit be static or dynamic? What are appropriate tools? These questions indicate that the statement of conditions must be amplified. The following rewritten statement serves the purpose much more effectively: *Given ten operating superheterodyne receivers, preadjusted to represent variable circuit conditions, a power supply, a standard set of tools to include a voltmeter and an ammeter, and a handout containing Ohm's law and resister color codes, the trainee must be able to calculate resistance, current, and voltage at preselected points in a superheterodyne circuit.*

Another example is: *The trainee must be able to list in writing the ten basic components of the radio receiver R-390/URR.* Must the trainee provide this information from memory, or will he be able to use notes, a chart, or a technical manual? The statement is not clear because here the conditions have not been specified. Consider these improved statements: *From memory, the trainee must be able to list in writing the five technical characteristics of the radio receiver R-390/URR.* Or, *When shown a radio receiver R-390/URR, the trainee will be able to identify*

*by name each of its twenty-six operational controls without the aid of notes
or references. Or, Given a properly functioning radio receiver R-390/
URR and a set of operating instructions, the trainee must be able to tune
to any specified frequency within the receiver's range.*

Other examples of acceptable statements of conditions follow:

- Given a 1:25,000 scale map, a compass, and a protractor . . .
- Given access to IBM 360/40 computer runs . . .
- Given a standard tool kit, a multimeter, and schematics . . .
- Given a field compass and a specified magnetic azimuth, and placed on a surveyed course . . .
- Given standard reference 3-69 . . .
- Given an electronic scope and standard test kit . . .
- Given a fluctuating temperature range of 60° to 105° F . . .
- Given an altitude of 2,000 feet, mean atmospheric pressures of . . .
- Under continuous supervision . . .
- Without supervision . . .
- Over dirt roads or open fields, under dry, wet, icy, or snow conditions . . .
- In a prone position . . .
- In temperatures from —35° to 115°F . . .

Step 3. State the criterion of acceptable performance. When the required behavior and conditions of performance have been specified, the ability of the objective to communicate can be increased by stating how well the trainee must be able to perform. This is done by defining the criterion or standard of acceptable performance. The criterion consists of words that describe minimum acceptable performance, set a time limit where appropriate, or define quality and/or quantity standards for the work product or service produced. To be completely usable, criterion statements must

- Be realistic and attainable.
- Be relevant to the job or task.
- Specify clearly the minimum acceptable level of achievement.
- Avoid the use of imprecise words such as "effective," "acceptable," "proper," and "average."
- Be measurable.

Here is an example of a statement of objectives without a properly stated criterion: *From memory, the trainee must be able to list and define in writing the technical characteristics of the radio receiver R-390/URR.* What is acceptable performance here? How many technical characteristics are there? How many must the trainee list and define? How is the adequacy or accuracy of the definitions checked? The objective as stated does not answer these questions. Consider these improved statements: *From memory, the trainee must be able to list in writing four of the five technical characteristics of the radio receiver R-390/URR and define these characteristics as set forth in pages 5 and 6 of TM. . . .* Or, *When shown a radio receiver R-390/URR, from memory the trainee must be able to identify orally by name, each of the twenty-six operational controls within five minutes and with complete accuracy. Nomenclature used must conform with standard terms used in the operating manual.* Note that the trainee must be able to identify *all twenty-six controls, within five minutes,* and *with complete accuracy.* No interpretation is needed to identify the exact standard required.

Here is another example: *The trainee must have a working knowledge of resistor color coding.* What must the trainee "know" about resistor color coding? How can acceptable performance be determined? This objective leaves many unanswered questions. Consider this revised statement: *Given a schematic diagram of a five-resistor series parallel circuit with the values of the resistors marked, an assortment of fifteen resistors including five with values corresponding to those on the diagram, a circuit board, and wiring, the trainee must be able to select the correct resistors and construct a circuit electrically equivalent to the diagrammed circuit within a time limit of ten minutes.* In this example the criterion is clearly specified.

Here is still another example: *The trainee must be able to use an ammeter and a voltmeter to determine capacitive reactance and capacitance.* Here, the behavior is clear, but the conditions and criterion are not specified. An improved statement follows: *Given a working two-component series RC circuit connected to a variable frequency source, an ammeter, a voltmeter, slide rule, pencil, and paper, the trainee must be able to determine the capacitive reactance and capacitance to two significant figures and within 5 percent of preestablished values within five minutes. The values of the resistor and capacitor in the circuit will be illegible, but the settings of the power source will be visible.* Note that in this example both a quality and a time criterion are specified.

Other examples of acceptable statements of criteria are as follows:

- Arrive at the destination within half an hour of the scheduled time.
- Azimuth must be correct within one degree.
- Within two minutes . . .
- Without error . . .
- 100 percent correct . . .
- At least nine out of ten . . .

- Each of the five principles . . .
- All of the following . . .
- To a tolerance of . . .
- The exact techniques of . . .
- Accurate to the nearest tenth . . .
- Within ±2 degrees . . .
- Within 1,600 meters . . .
- To conform to a template . . .
- In accordance with procedures defined in . . .
- To the standards defined in . . .
- Accurate to two significant figures . . .

FORMAT AND PROCEDURES

Although by far the most common method of writing behavioral objectives is to combine the three components into a single sentence or paragraph, experience has convincingly demonstrated the desirability of *physically separating* the behavior, condition, and criterion. This format permits the writer to approach the task of drafting an objective one part at a time, insures that all three parts are included, and simplifies the process of reviewing statements of objectives. Therefore, regardless of whether the objective is written for a job, duty, task, element, or supporting skill, a format similar to that used to state objectives at the beginning of each chapter of this book should be used.

Behavior   The trainee must be able to . . .
Conditions Given: . . .
Criterion   To the standards defined in . . .

Performance objectives should be drafted on a form similar to the sample shown in Figure 4-3. Using the final priority list on the Training Objectives Worksheet (Fig. 4-1), a separate Performance Objective Workcard should be prepared for each job duty, task, and element. The procedures for completing these cards is as follows:

Step 1. Enter on each card the title of the major duty, the title of the task, and the numbers of elements—for example, "1 of 3 elements."

Step 2. Using the steps defined under "Writing Performance-centered Objectives," make separate entries to describe the behavior, conditions, and criterion of performance for each job duty, task, and element.

Step 3. Enter under "Major References" the primary source document relating to the duty, task, or element.

CHECKLIST

PERFORMANCE-CENTERED OBJECTIVES

Draft objectives should be subjected to a final, rigid check prior to their publication, distribution, and use. The items listed below are some of the most important standards to apply in checking the adequacy of performance-centered objectives.

1. General.
   a. Are the statements free from grammatical, spelling, and typographical errors?
   b. Has the writer avoided the use of unfamiliar words?
   c. Is the sentence structure clear, concise, simple, and straightforward?
   d. Is the use of punctuation, abbreviations, and hyphenation correct and uniform?
   e. Do the statements avoid ambiguity?
   f. Is extraneous or confusing information excluded?
2. Behavior
   a. Does the statement clearly and precisely describe what the trainee will be doing when he demonstrates what he has learned?
   b. Does the statement avoid the use of "loaded words"?
   c. Does the statement describe a complete action?
   d. Does the statement begin with a verb?
   e. Does the statement describe a meaningful unit of performance?
   f. Is the behavior clearly relevant to the job or task?

Figure 4-3. Performance Objective Workcard.

Major duty: Task:
Major references: _____ of _____ elements

Behavior	Condition	Criterion

3. Conditions
   a. Does the statement clearly and completely describe the conditions under which the trainee must demonstrate the required behavior?
   b. Does the statement begin with the word "given"?
   c. Does the statement identify what the trainee will be given to do the job or task (tools, equipment, job aids, or materials)?
   d. Does the statement clearly identify what tools, equipment, job aids, or materials the trainee will be denied (when this is pertinent)?
   e. Does the statement describe the physical environment (space, climatic conditions, lighting conditions, and the like) when these are significant?
   f. Does the statement describe the assistance the trainee will receive (if any)?
   g. Does the statement describe the amount and kind of supervision (if any) the trainee will receive during job performance?
4. Criterion
   a. Does the statement clearly describe how well the trainee must perform?
   b. Is the minimum level for acceptable performance clearly defined?
   c. Is the quality of the work products or services defined in terms of standards of accuracy, completeness, format, sequence, clarity, neatness, tolerances, or number of errors permitted?
   d. Is the quantity of the work products or services defined in terms of the number of units to be completed per unit of time or in terms of the total number of units required?
   e. Are time standards clearly defined in terms of duration of performance, speed of performance, or total time allowed for performance?
   f. Are the standards realistic and attainable?
   g. Are the standards relevant to the job or task?
   h. Are the standards measurable?
   i. Do the standards avoid the use of such imprecise words as "effective," "acceptable," "proper," and "average"?

SELECTED REFERENCES

Ammerman, Harry L., and William H. Melching. *The Derivation, Analysis, and Classification of Instructional Objectives*. Alexandria, Va.: George Washington University Human Resources Research Office, May 1966.

Bloom, Benjamin S., ed. *Taxonomy of Educational Objectives: The Classification of Educational Goals, Handbook I: Cognitive Domain*. London: Longmans, Green & Co., Ltd., 1956.

Burns, Richard W. "Objectives and Classroom Instruction." *Educational Technology* (Sept. 15, 1967), 7:17: 1–3.

———. "The Theory of Expressing Objectives." *Educational Technology* (Oct. 30, 1967), 7:20: 1–3.

———. "Objectives Involving Attitudes, Interests, and Appreciations." *Educational Technology* (Apr. 30, 1968), 8:8: 14–15.

Canfield, Albert A. "A Rationale for Performance Objectives." *Audiovisual Instruction* (February 1968), 13:2: 127–129.

Craik, Mary B. "Writing Objectives for Programmed Instruction—Or Any Instruction." *Educational Technology* (Feb. 28, 1966), 6:4: 15–21.

Harmon, Paul. "A Classification of Performance Objectives in Job Training Programs." *Educational Technology* (January 1969), 9:1: 5–12.

Herriott, W. Phil. "Training: Do You Know Your Goals?" *Supervisory Management* (June 1964), 9:6: 10–12.

Hoover, W. F. "Specification of Objectives." *Audiovisual Instruction* (June 1967), 12:6: 597.

Jones, Edna M., and Jean B. Fairman. "Identification and Analysis of Human Performance Requirements." In John D. Folley, Jr., ed. *Human Factors Methods for System Design*. Pittsburgh, Pa.: American Institutes for Research, 1960, pp. 43–62.

Kapfer, Philip G. "Behavioral Objectives in the Cognitive and Affective Domains." *Educational Technology* (June 15, 1968), 8:11: 11–13.

Krathwohl, D. R., B. S. Bloom, and B. B. Masia. *Taxonomy of Educational Objectives, Handbook II: Affective Domain*. New York: David McKay Company, Inc., 1964.

Mager, Robert F. *Preparing Objectives for Programmed Instruction*. Palo Alto, Calif.: Fearon Publishers, Inc., 1962.

Miller, Robert B., and Harold P. VanCott. *The Determination of Knowledge Content for Complex Man-Machine Jobs*. Pittsburgh: American Institutes for Research, December 1955.

Smith, Robert G., Jr. *The Development of Training Objectives*. Alexandria, Va.: George Washington University Human Resources Research Office, June 1964.

————. *The Design of Instructional Systems*. Alexandria, Va.: George Washington University Human Resources Research Office, November 1966.

Tracey, William R. *Evaluating Training and Development Systems*. AMA, 1968, Chap. V.

5

Constructing Evaluative Instruments

Training systems are designed to produce the job performance described by the training objectives. If the training objectives are realistic and the other components of the training system are appropriate and effective, the system will operate as intended and produce the desired results. But how can the trainer determine whether the system is appropriate and effective? He needs evaluative tools—a means of appraising the components of the system and their interaction so that (1) the system can be validated, (2) needed modifications can be introduced as soon as deficiencies have been identified, and (3) required quality controls can be applied.

One of the means of accomplishing these objectives is the administration of criterion measures—tests of one kind or another. A complementary means involves systematic application of evaluative instruments other than tests. These devices must be developed in advance of the instructional system so that they are uncontaminated by the content of the system and unaffected by the biases of personnel who developed the system and therefore have a vested interest in its success.

The purpose of this chapter is to describe the procedures used in designing the evaluative instruments that should be applied during the system validation stage to prove and modify the system and during the operational phase to maintain quality control of the system. Criterion tests will be the subject of the immediately following chapter.

Upon completion of the chapter, the reader should be able to perform as follows:

Behavior   Construct instruments, including rating scales, questionnaires, and standard interview forms, for use in evaluating training and development systems.

Conditions   Given: behaviorally stated objectives for the system, guides for the construction of evaluation instruments, clerical assistance, and opportunity to use the instruments on trial populations.

Criterion   Instruments will meet the standards described in this chapter.

THE NATURE AND PURPOSES OF EVALUATIVE INSTRUMENTS

Three general types of evaluative instruments will be considered in the discussion that follows: rating scales, questionnaires, and standard interview forms.

A rating scale is an instrument designed to transform observation of behavior or conditions into objective evaluations. Rating scales may be designed to evaluate performance, personal characteristics, materials and aids, equipment, or learning conditions. They are used either during or immediately following observation.

A questionnaire is an instrument designed to elicit objective judgments with regard to programs, conditions, or practices about which respondents are presumed to have knowledge. They may also be used to inquire about the opinions or attitudes of a group. They may be designed to evaluate systems, courses, persons, equipment, or conditions. They are customarily completed without the supervision of the designer; hence, they must be constructed carefully and tested prior to use to make certain that the needed data are collected.

A standard interview form or schedule is a device used by an interviewer to guide the conduct of the interview, insure standardized coverage of elements, and insofar as possible, objectify the recording, tabulation, evaluation, and interpretation of data.

PURPOSES OF EVALUATIVE INSTRUMENTS

Evaluative instruments are used to obtain evidence or measures of the effectiveness of elements of a training system. Sometimes they represent the only means of obtaining an objective and reasonably unbiased human judgment about the effectiveness and deficiencies of the components of the system. Other times they are used to verify data obtained by other means.

Fundamentally, these evaluations are used to serve three different but complementary purposes: system validation, system modification, and system quality control.

In system validation, evaluation instruments are used (1) to determine whether the components of the training or development system are working as intended, (2) to insure that all components are interacting with each other as envisioned by the designers, and (3) to make certain that the system produces the results intended.

In terms of system modification, analyses of findings derived from the administration of evaluative instruments are used to make needed changes in various system components to improve the effectiveness and efficiency of the total system.

From a quality control standpoint, evaluative instruments are administered at critical points in the operating system (following validation and implementation) to insure that the system continues to operate as it did initially and to call attention to defects or deterioration in system components that might otherwise escape notice. Their purpose, then, is to prevent breakdown of the system.

RATING METHODS

The process of evaluating by judgment is called rating. Judgment involves the collection, correlation, and interpretation of facts and impressions to arrive at an estimate or an opinion about a person, trait, object, or situation. In other words, the facts do not "speak for themselves," and human interpretation of the facts is essential. Since rating is judgment, and judgment is saturated with opinion, rating is always subjective to some degree. Because of this fact, many people oppose ratings and would like to do away with them altogether. But there will always be rating whether people want it or not. People in all walks of life are rated daily by their peers, subordinates, and superiors, whether they know it or not. Sometimes these ratings are formal; other times they are informal. They are ratings nonetheless.

There is a stronger reason, however, for designing and using rating systems. Ratings are necessary in many situations to measure characteristics for which tests are either unavailable or completely impractical. Because there are aspects of a training system which should be evaluated and for which tests cannot be designed, ratings of one type or another provide the only means of measurement. Since they are necessary, every effort must be made to make ratings as objective as possible.

VALIDITY AND RELIABILITY OF RATINGS

In all types of evaluation the source of unreliability and invalidity is poor judgment. An evaluation is reliable when it describes and measures traits, abilities, or conditions consistently. An evaluation is valid when it describes and measures the traits, abilities, or conditions it is supposed to measure, and not something else.

The reliability of ratings is relatively simple to determine. If, for example, a group of qualified evaluators rate the performance of the same instructor at the same time, and the ratings they assign agree on the quality of his performance, the rating is reliable. If the raters disagree on the quality of his performance, the rating is unreliable. The degree to which the raters agree on the rating, then, is a measure of the reliability of the rating.

Determining the validity of these same ratings poses quite a different and more difficult problem. The fact that the evaluators are rating the instructor in a classroom environment lends a certain amount of face validity to the rating, but this is often deceiving. The question might well be asked: Did the evaluators rate what they were supposed to rate? If all the raters were qualified as instructors, and if it were assumed that they are equally competent raters, theoretically they would agree completely on the elements to be used in arriving at a final rating. But they may not agree. However, if the ratings do agree perfectly regardless of the rating bases, it is often assumed that the rating is perfectly valid. Since there is no evidence to the contrary, the reliability of the rating becomes the measure of its validity. But this assumption too can be, and often is, misleading.

It is possible for several raters to give the same adjectival or numerical rating to an instructor, but it is likely that all are using different criteria. For example, if there are five raters, one may be using appearance as the standard; another, control of trainees, another, voice and speech; another, use of training aids; and still another, knowledge of the subject. Their ratings reflect the priorities they assign to various elements of the learning situation.

Actually, it is a rare occasion when several evaluators agree perfectly on the adjective that best describes an instructor's performance even if they agree on priorities. Semantic difficulties provide a part of the reason for the problem. For example, one evaluator may describe a performance as "excellent," while another describes the same performance as "superior." Even numerical scores are no more likely than adjectives to mean the same thing to raters.

The solution to the problem lies in the selection of situations in which ratings are appropriate, and in the construction of scales that will reduce subjectivity and bias. This applies whether the raters are trainees, instructors, training managers, or operating supervisors.

CLASSES OF RATING METHODS

There are two general classes of rating methods: relative and absolute. Rating scales may apply either method exclusively, or they may combine the best features of both.

Relative rating methods. Relative methods of rating are often used when several persons or situations are being rated. Each person or situation is rated only in comparison with others. With purely relative ratings, no attempt is made to assign meaningful values. A description of some of the more common methods of relative rating follows.

Rank order. The rank order or ranking method involves the comparison of traits or characteristics of members of a group with each other and the assignment of a rank to each within the group. The result is that the members of the group are arranged in order from highest to lowest or from best to worst.

The best way to construct a rank order rating is to select the highest, most important, or most effective in the group, and the lowest, least important, or least effective. Then the second most effective and the second least effective are chosen. The process is continued until all members of the group have been ranked.

To make the ranking more objective, an average may be obtained. The group is ranked by several raters, individual ranks are summed, and the sum is divided by the number of raters.

The rank order method has certain advantages. Because someone or something must be at the top of the scale and someone or something at the bottom, the maximum spread of scores is obtained. Any logical (or illogical) connection between traits is also severed because the rater deals with only one trait at a time and tends to disregard the ranks he assigned to previous traits.

There are also several weaknesses in rank order, however. One limitation is that the rater is forced to give extreme ratings; someone or something must be placed at the bottom of the group. This may be interpreted to mean that the person or trait is unsatisfactory or unimportant. What it really means is that the person or trait is the lowest or the least important *in the group being rated.*

Ranking also does not portray the magnitude of differences between the items or persons rated. For example, as Figure 5-1 shows, if five persons were rated on a 10-point scale in terms of proficiency as instructors, and these ratings were translated into rank order, important differences in ability among the group would be lost. The five appear to have equal differences in ability.

Of course, for some purposes, the distance between persons or traits is unimportant—for example, when the objective is to select the best two persons for a job, eliminate the two poorest from consideration, or identify the two or three most important traits. In such cases only the extremes are important.

Still another limitation rests in the difficulty of making meaningful differentiations among the members of a large group. Most evaluators cannot rank more than ten persons or items with acceptable accuracy or reliability.

One final problem is that rankings of one group cannot be meaningfully compared with those of another group. The top man in a group, for example, is simply the best man *in that group,* but his rank does not tell how he compares with the top man in another group. This fact is demonstrated in Figure 5-2.

If rank in class is used, a trainee's performance in a conference leadership seminar cannot be meaningfully compared with the performance of other trainees who have completed the training unless a composite scale is available. For example, trainee a's performance (rank 9 of 9) in class X can be described as the poorest in a relatively poor class, and trainee

Figure 5-1. Comparison between rating on 10-point scale and rating by rank order.

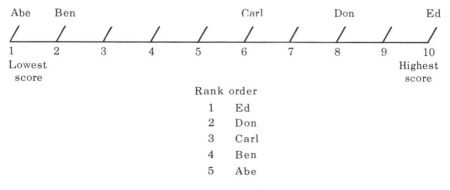

Figure 5-2. *Comparison of the performance of twenty-five trainees (a to y) in three conference leadership seminars.*

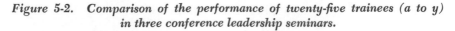
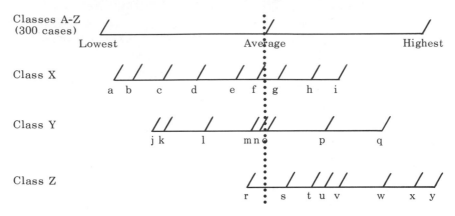

i's as highest (1 of 9) in a relatively poor class. Trainee r's performance in class Z can be described as poorest (8 of 8) and trainee y's as best (1 of 8) in a relatively good class. Note that trainees a, j, and r rank last in their own classes and trainees i, q, and y rank first in their classes. However, in no case is the performance equal. Trainee a's performance is considerably lower than that of trainees j or r.

Equal intervals. This method is a variation of the ranking technique. It is used when many persons or traits are to be ranked. Instead of ranking everyone in order, the rater places them in groupings which seem to be equally spaced. Those who appear to be alike with respect to the trait or ability are then placed in the same grouping. Figure 5-3 shows how a rater ranked twenty-four men in speaking ability.

Paired comparisons. This method requires the rater to compare each member of a group with every other member. Because it requires the maximum possible number of comparisons, it usually produces the most reliable results. To be most dependable, only one trait or variable should be compared at a time.

The technique is applied as follows: Five individuals are to be rated on leadership. Their names are placed on a matrix as shown in Figure 5-4. The rater begins by comparing Abe and Ben on leadership ability. He decides that Ben is a better leader than Abe, so he places a plus sign in Ben's column beside Abe and a minus sign in Abe's column beside Ben.

The rater then compares Abe and Carl. He decides that Carl is a better leader than Abe; therefore, he places a plus sign in Carl's column beside Abe and a minus sign in Abe's column beside Carl. The rater then goes on to compare Abe and Don, Abe and Ed, and Abe and Fred. The

Figure 5-3. Rank on speaking ability given to twenty-four persons by the method of equal intervals.

		Walt		
		Vince		
		Tom		
	Xavier	Quentin		
	Ray	Ollie	Upson	
	Pete	Luke	Ned	
	Mike	Harry	Ike	Sam
	Ed	Fred	Don	Ken
Joe	Carl	Abe	Bob	George

Group 5 (poorest)	Group 4	Group 3	Group 2	Group 1 (best)

process is continued until all 15 comparisons have been made, and all blocks of the matrix have been filled in.

When the matrix is complete, the number of plus signs in each column is added. The total identifies reverse rank order in the group for each person rated. That is, the person with the highest number of pluses (in this case, Don) ranks first, the one with second highest (Carl) ranks second, and so on.

The principal weakness of the paired comparison technique is that ratings tend to be influenced by the rater's overall impression of the individuals being compared. A second limitation lies in the fact that the

Figure 5-4. Matrix for rating six workers on leadership by the method of paired comparisons.

	Men rated					
Compared with:	Abe	Ben	Carl	Don	Ed	Fred
Abe		+	+	+	+	−
Ben	−		+	+	−	−
Carl	−	−		+	−	−
Don	−	−	−		−	−
Ed	−	+	+	+		−
Fred	+	+	+	+	+	
Total	1	3	4	5	2	0

technique is extremely cumbersome if more than ten persons or traits are to be rated.

The formula $n(n-1)/2$ expresses the number of comparisons required, where n is the number of persons or traits in the group. It can be seen that for a group of ten persons 45 comparisons must be made; for a group of twenty-five, 300 comparisons.

Absolute rating methods. Absolute methods of rating require the rater to assign an absolute value to the trait or performance being measured without any reference to the traits or performance of any other person. In other words, the rater places the person, trait, or performance on a fixed scale. There are six types of absolute scales. Each will be described in turn.

Numerical. The numerical scale is the simplest form of scale. Although any number of points can be used, an odd number is usually selected so that the middle number represents the average. The number of points on the scale depends upon the number of observable differentiations, the use to which the ratings are to be put, and the ability of the raters to discriminate accurately. For example, a training manager may want to find out which of his trainers are below-average instructors so that he can give them further training. A 3-point scale may provide the amount of differentiation required. But suppose the training manager wants to select the five top instructors to present a special development program to a group of executives. A 3-point scale would not permit fine enough differentiation. He would have to use a scale with more points.

Most people can make at least five differentiations. A 5-point scale divides a group into highest, above average, average, below average, and lowest. Few evaluators, no matter how highly trained, can make more than nine differentiations. For this reason, most rating scales contain 5 to 9 points.

Descriptive Scales. Descriptive scales use adjectives or phrases to rate levels of ability or proficiency. Figure 5-5 shows a descriptive scale for rating writing ability. Five levels of ability are described. Descriptive

Figure 5-5.   A descriptive scale for rating writing ability.

Instructions: Place a check mark in the scale below the word that most accurately describes the writing ability of the person being rated.

Unsatisfactory	Satisfactory	Good	Excellent	Outstanding

Figure 5-6. A descriptive scale for rating instructor ability.

Instructions: Place a check mark in the scale below the word that best describes the instructor being rated.

Instructor	Acceptable	Fair	Good	Excellent	Superior
Armstrong, J.					
Baker, C.					
Collins, D.					
Dorin, L.					
Franklin, P.					

scales are more versatile than numerical scales because the adjectives or phrases can be varied to suit the situation.

For example, suppose that a training manager wants to evaluate the ability of his instructors. He feels that all members of his instructional staff are satisfactory, but he wants to know how much better than adequate they are. He could use a numerical scale, but substandard performance is usually associated with the lower numbers on a scale. If he uses a scale like the one shown in Figure 5-6, the raters are given a frame of reference. The lowest possible rating is "acceptable."

Careful selection of adjectives or descriptive phrases without extremes at the ends tends to make all points of the scale usable. The major disadvantage is semantic. An "excellent" instructor does not mean the same thing to all raters; some might describe the same instructor as "superior."

A further problem is that it is difficult to select adjectives or phrases that describe equally spaced degrees of performance. When the scale in Figure 5-6 is used, most raters feel that there is less distance between "excellent" and "superior" than between "fair" and "good."

Graphic scale. The graphic scale combines the numerical and descriptive scales. It contains both a numerical scale and adjectives or descriptive phrases placed below a horizontal line. The length of the line represents the full range of the ability, performance, or trait to be rated. The rater must consider both the numerical scale and the descriptive phrases.

Three common forms of the graphic scale are shown in Figure 5-7. In

Figure 5-7.   Typical forms of the graphic scale.

Example A. Appearance: consider appearance on the job day in and day out

1	2	3	4	5
Slovenly	Careless	Generally satisfactory	Good model and standard	A nearly perfect model and standard

Example B. Trainee participation

1	2	3	4	5
Unable to obtain participation; fails to generate interest	Trainee interest and participation marginal; only the more aggressive trainees participate	Real interest in participating aroused in most trainees; only timid and weaker trainees not responding	Almost all trainees interested and participating; a few must be cajoled into taking part	Participation spontaneous; all trainees eager to take part

Example C. Knowledge of subject matter

1	2	3	4	5
Fundamental knowledge lacking; devoid of allied information; frequent errors of fact		Knowledge limited to specific area of instructional responsibility, but clearly adequate for present duties		Demonstrates mastery of subject; genuine scholarship; rich store of information; wide knowledge of related fields

example A, the rater is asked to judge appearance. He is directed to mark the scale after considering the appearance of the person to be rated on a day-in, day-out basis. These instructions encourage the raters to consider the same traits about each person, but they allow errors because the rater must both judge and evaluate. Points at the extremes of the scale are unlikely to be used. They could be made more attractive by strengthening the words at the lower end of the scale and weakening those at the higher end. For example, point 1 might be labeled "untidy," point 2 "somewhat careless," point 3 "moderately neat and well groomed," point 4 "a good model and standard," and point 5 "an excellent model and standard."

Such changes as these would be likely to produce a greater spread of ratings and therefore can be justified. In any event, the rater knows that he is giving the lowest rating whether the term is "slovenly" or "untidy," and whether the highest is "nearly perfect" or "an excellent model and standard."

Example B in Figure 5-7 shows a graphic scale in which a certain trait is described at five different levels. With most scales, the rater must not only observe but also evaluate his observation and translate it into a rating. People can *observe* more accurately than they can *evaluate* what they have observed. Therefore, whenever ratings can be based on observation alone, reliability is greatly improved. With the scale in example B, the rater does not have to evaluate the instructor. He merely records his observations of the trainee group, and hence his rating is more objective.

One caution: in preparing this type of scale, care must be taken to insure that the behavior described for each point is actually an improvement over that for the behavior immediately below it. In each instance, distances between points should be about equal.

The scale in example C is similar to that in example B except that descriptive phrases are not provided for all points of the scale. Frequently raters feel that the rating should fall somewhere between two points. Such ratings are made possible by this type of scale.

Checklist. Although the checklist is sometimes considered a separate rating method, it is actually a 2-point rating scale. A checklist is useful for rating performance of set procedures. It also provides a simple method of rating skills when the objective of the rating is to find out if trainees have reached a certain minimum performance level. Figure 5-8 shows a portion of a checklist used for evaluating oral presentations. In using this scale, the evaluator indicates whether each item is satisfactory or unsatisfactory.

The reliability of a checklist is usually high because the range of decisions is reduced to two. However, only a limited amount of information can be obtained from a checklist. The scale in Figure 5-8, for

Figure 5-8. A portion of a checklist for evaluating oral presentations.

Instructions: If the item is satisfactory, place a plus sign in the space provided. If the item is unsatisfactory, place a minus sign in the space.

1. Did the speaker gain and hold the interest of the audience?   _____
2. Did the speaker communicate facts and ideas clearly and
   convincingly?   _____
3. Was the presentation coherent and understandable?   _____
4. Did the presentation reflect originality?   _____
5. Were examples and illustrations used effectively?   _____

---

example, does not indicate how successful the speaker was in gaining the interest of his listeners, to what extent the presentation was clear and convincing, or how appropriate the examples and illustrations were.

Product scale. Sometimes the product of a performance is to be rated rather than the performance itself. This poses quite a different problem from rating performance. Take the case of an automobile mechanic trainee who takes two days to repair a malfunctioning carburetor. When repaired, the carburetor is in top-notch condition. The end product is excellent, but the performance is poor because an experienced mechanic might have done the same job to the same standards in less than two hours.

Because the product, unlike the performance, is usually a tangible thing, product rating is more reliable than performance rating. Even bias is eliminated because it is not necessary for the rater to know who made the product.

Forced choice. The forced-choice method of rating uses two to five descriptions of behavior in each section. Both favorable and unfavorable statements may be included in a section. Most forced-choice instruments contain twenty-five to thirty sections. Figure 5-9 shows a single section containing four descriptions, two favorable and two unfavorable. The rater is asked to select the statement that is most characteristic and the one that is least characteristic.

Although it is easy to distinguish between the favorable and unfavorable statements, the rater does not know whether statement 1 or statement 2 is more desirable. The differentiation required is subtle, and therefore, the rater must ignore his general impression and recall specific instances of behavior. Because the rater reports behavior without being permitted to judge the quality of the behavior, reliability is greatly improved.

One objection to the forced-choice technique is that a large amount

Figure 5-9.   A single block of a forced-choice instrument.

	Most characteristic	Least characteristic
1. Perseveres in the face of difficulty		
2. Possesses an outgoing personality		
3. Often procrastinates		
4. Reluctant to make decisions		

of research is necessary to produce a scale for any given purpose and to devise a fair method of keying the responses.

STEPS IN CONSTRUCTING A RATING DEVICE

Rating devices must be constructed systematically, which involves the following specific steps:

Step 1. Determine the objectives of the rating and carefully define them in terms of observable behavior or characteristics. Be sure to consider how the rating is to be used; the use must be compatible with the objective.

Step 2. Select the traits or factors which determine success or failure, adequacy or inadequacy, satisfactory or unsatisfactory performance. When selecting factors observe these rules:

a. Select only factors or items that are relevant and important. For example, if speed of performance is not necessary to determine degree of proficiency, do not include it.

b. Select factors or items that are specific.

c. Select factors or items that have the same meaning for all observers.

d. Use approximately seven items or factors, but do not use fewer than three or more than twelve.

Step 3. Define the factors or items in precise terms. Where possible, definitions should be phrased in terms of specific observable behavior.

Step 4. Establish from five to nine degrees of success or achievement for each factor or item. Insure that the phrases describing degrees of the item to be rated are arranged in ascending or descending order.

Step 5. Determine how important each factor is, and weigh it accordingly. It is not likely that all factors are of equal importance. Weights can be determined by pooling the judgments of several qualified observers.

Step 6. Select the form for the rating instrument that is best for the situation.

Step 7. Use the rating scale on a trial basis with ten to twenty-five people and revise the scale as indicated by the results of the tryout.

CHECKLIST

REVIEWING RATING SCALES

Rating scales should be reviewed before use, and periodically they should be critically examined. The following checklist is designed to assist in conducting this review:

1. Are the objectives clearly defined?
2. Are the factors included essential in the performance of the job or in the evaluation of the situation?
3. Have enough factors been included to describe completely the performance or situation?
4. Is each factor defined in terms of specific, observable behavior and not in terms of general traits?
5. Have the initial weights for each factor been carefully determined by pooling the judgments of several qualified observers?
6. Do all factors on the scale differentiate between successful and unsuccessful performance, adequate and inadequate conditions, and the like?

QUESTIONNAIRE METHODS

Questionnaires are used to extend an investigator's or an evaluator's powers of observation by standardizing and objectifying the observations of many other persons. A questionnaire also isolates and defines elements of a situation for observation and reporting. It calls attention to particular aspects of a situation for observation and evaluation. A well-constructed questionnaire specifies the units and terminology to be used in reporting observations, and insures responses to the same items from all respondents. It is used to secure information from varied and widely scattered sources; it is a particularly useful method of data collection when the investigator cannot readily see personally all the people from whom he wishes to obtain evaluations.

LIMITATIONS

The questionnaire has value as a means of gathering data. However, it is a difficult technique to use and requires a rather large investment of time for construction of the instrument and for tabulating, summarizing, and interpreting the data. Often, the questionnaire yields disappointing results. Either respondents fail to return the questionnaire, or the returns are incomplete, indefinite, or uninterpretable and hence unusable.

CLASSES OF QUESTIONNAIRES

There are two general classes of questionnaires, closed form and open form. The open form is often referred to as "open-end" or "free-response." Either of these forms may be used exclusively, or they may be combined in the same questionnaire.

Closed form. The closed form of the questionnaire contains a list of categories or items to be checked, a list of alternative answers to be selected, or blanks to be filled in with words or numbers. Figure 5-10 shows a part of a closed-form questionnaire designed to collect data with regard to the frequency with which supervisory personnel perform certain tasks.

The closed form of the questionnaire has certain advantages. It is likely to take the respondent a minimum amount of time to complete and therefore increases the chances that responses will be obtained from all persons surveyed. The processes of tabulating and summarizing responses to the questionnaire are also simpler and less time-consuming than the open form. However, the closed form is particularly dependent upon completeness of all of the categories or lists. The respondent tends to depend on the list as written for completeness and is unlikely to write in additional items even if space is provided. He may, therefore, omit items he would have included had there been no list.

The closed form is also more difficult to construct since the designer must be careful to make provisions for all possible responses in advance. This is extremely difficult because no individual is likely to think of all

Figure 5-10. Part of a closed-form questionnaire used to determine the frequency of performance of supervisory tasks.

Instructions: Place a check mark beside each task in the column that best describes how frequently you perform the task.

Tasks	Frequency					
	Several times per day	Once daily	Once weekly	Once monthly	Less than monthly	Do not perform
Develop work schedules						
Assign employees						
Order material						
Keep work records						
Confer with superior						
Check on work						
Orient new employees						

the ways in which a group may respond, nor is he able to anticipate the interpretations respondents may assign to items or terms. Tryout and revision of the form in advance of use is therefore a critically important step in the construction of closed-form questionnaires.

Open form. The open or free-response form offers the respondent an opportunity to present a more complete view of a situation. It may invite him to go beyond the factual material or statistical data and get into the area of attitudes, the background of answers, or the reasons for particular preferences or decisions. Part of an open form designed to gather data about participants' observations of the effectiveness of a management seminar is shown in Figure 5-11.

The advantages of the open form are that it is less rigid and restrictive and permits more complete answers to questions. It is also less demanding on the designer because the danger of overlooking additional responses is greatly minimized. However, the open form requires more of the respondent's time to complete, and appealing to his interest and attention and winning his cooperation are therefore necessary. The open form also presents great difficulties in tabulating and summarizing the responses; they are complex and time-consuming tasks.

VALIDITY AND RELIABILITY OF QUESTIONNAIRES

A questionnaire is valid to the extent that it covers the aspects of the subject of study and excludes irrelevant materials from the response. Although part of the answer to the question of validity is provided by study and analysis of the individual *questions,* it is mainly determined by study and analysis of the *responses.* To be valid, a reasonably large proportion of the people surveyed must respond. Their responses must have depth and reality, show a reasonable range of variation, and be complete in terms of the inclusion of the desired elements in each response.

Reliability of questionnaires may be determined by preliminary tryout of the materials. Tryout should show that questions are clear and unambiguous, that their implications are understood, and that the questions address something stable, nonsuperficial, and typical of the situation. Furthermore, the information obtained must be consistent and must agree with what is known; if it departs from expected responses, it must do so in a believable direction. It must not controvert other information, and it must correlate with evidence obtained by other means.

Figure 5-11. Part of an open-form questionnaire used to collect participant reactions to a management seminar.

Instructor _____   Date _____

Subject _____   Time _____

Directions: Provide brief answers to the questions that follow. Do not pull your punches, but be as objective as you can.

1. In general, how would you describe the level of interest of seminar participants in the subject?

2. How do you feel about the organization of the material? What changes do you recommend?

3. How would you describe the quality of the instruction presented? What were its strengths? Weaknesses?

4. How useful do you believe the subject will be to you in your job? How can it be made more useful?

5. In what other ways could this presentation be improved?

The production of a valid and reliable questionnaire does not occur by accident. It involves systematic coverage of a sequence of carefully defined steps. These steps follow:

Step 1. Determine the objectives of the questionnaire, and carefully define them. Give careful consideration to the characteristics of the group to whom the questionnaire is to be addressed, as well as to how the results will be used.

Step 2. Select the topics or factors to be covered in the questionnaire. When selecting these factors, observe the following rules.

    a. Select only factors or items that are relevant. For example, if the age of the respondent is immaterial, do not include it.

    b. Select items or factors that are specific rather than general.

    c. Select items or factors that can be defined or described in terms that will be understood by all respondents.

Step 3. Develop an outline that groups similar or related items and establishes a logical sequence.

Step 4. Draft the questions and observe the following rules:

    a. Use standard terms and definitions.

    b. Keep questions clear, direct, and short; use checklists whenever possible.

    c. Avoid questions that can be answered with "yes," "no," "depends," or other single words.

    d. Avoid questions that are likely to be embarrassing to the respondent.

Step 5. Select the format for the questionnaire; be sure that it is attractive and easy to follow, and that it provides enough space for responses.

Step 6. Draft the directions to the respondent.

Step 7. Draft a cover letter to respondents; include the purpose, the identity of the group to which the form is to be sent, the approximate amount of time required to complete it, when and how the form should be returned, and what use is to be made of the data collected.

Step 8. Prepare a final draft of the questionnaire, the instructions, and the cover letter, and reproduce them in several copies.

Step 9. Select three or more qualified persons to review and comment on the questionnaire.

Step 10. Revise the questionnaire and supporting materials as indicated by the review.

Step 11. Administer the revised questionnaire to a small sample of the population (six to twelve persons) for which it is intended.

Step 12. Analyze the returns from the preliminary form and make such revisions as seem to be needed.

CHECKLIST

REVIEWING QUESTIONNAIRES

As noted in step 9, questionnaires should be reviewed by qualified personnel prior to use. The checklist that follows is designed to assist personnel in making such reviews.

1. Are the objectives clearly defined?
2. Is the cover letter complete and convincing?
3. Does the questionnaire deal with items that respondents are likely to feel are genuinely important?
4. Is the time required for completion of the form reasonable?
5. Are the directions for completing the form clear and unambiguous?
6. Is the questionnaire attractive and well-designed?
7. Is sufficient space allowed for answers to all questions?
8. Have trivial and irrelevant questions been avoided?
9. Are responses simple to make; for example, have checklists been used where appropriate?
10. Do questions avoid unnecessary details or specifications?
11. Are the questions clear and unambiguous?
12. Do the questions fit the respondent's situation?
13. Do the questions avoid putting words in the mouth of the respondent?
14. Do the questions encourage the respondent to be definite without forcing decisions where definiteness does not exist?
15. Do the questions elicit responses of sufficient depth to avoid superficiality?
16. Are questions that can be answered by "yes," "no," "depends," or other single words avoided?
17. Are questions asked in such a way that the respondent will not be embarrassed?
18. Are questions asked in such a way that the respondent will not feel that there is a hidden purpose in the questionnaire?
19. Do the questions avoid unnecessary narrowness or restrictiveness in the scope of responses?
20. Do the questions permit the respondent to present his point of view or frame of reference?
21. Is the questionnaire complete?
22. Are the questions phrased so that responses can be readily tabulated and summarized?
23. Has the questionnaire been tried out?

INTERVIEW METHODS

Many of the concepts, principles, and techniques presented in discussing questionnaires are applicable to the preparation of standard interview forms. Although its specific purpose, form, or content may differ, the interview is basically a method of collecting information directly from others in face-to-face contacts. The nature of the information sought may be a description of events (what happened in a situation in which the interviewee was a participant or an observer); it may involve description of behavior, past, present, or intended (of the respondent or another he observed); or it may involve descriptions of attitudes, values, habits, or perceptions (again of the respondent or someone else).

In certain situations, the interview is the only feasible method of acquiring the needed information. More often the interview is an alternative means of getting the information. Sometimes it is the most effective method of gathering data that could also be obtained by observation, questionnaire, tests, records, or other means. Most often, however, the interview is used to complement other data-gathering techniques.

ADVANTAGES OF THE INTERVIEW

One special value of the interview as a data-collection method is that respondents may provide information in face-to-face contacts that they would not put in writing. Frequently, respondents are suspicious about the use to which information will be put; these anxieties can be allayed by the interviewer. At other times respondents are simply reluctant to commit to writing something that they might be willing to say directly to another person.

A second advantage is that the interview offers an opportunity to draw out information. In an interview, the investigator can follow up leads and take advantage of small clues, including nonverbal ones, which would be impossible to exploit with a questionnaire.

Still another advantage is that the interview permits the investigator to form an impression of the respondent. Completed questionnaires do not permit the investigator to make judgments about the respondent to gauge the truth of answers. There are also limitations on ability to determine the internal consistency of related answers to questions. In the interview situation, the investigator has an opportunity to "read between the lines," to watch facial expression, to ask for clarification or elaboration of responses.

LIMITATIONS OF THE INTERVIEW

Advantages are always counterbalanced by limitations, and interviewing as a data-gathering method is no exception. One important limiting factor in the use of the interview is costs. Interviews take a considerable amount of time in terms of forethought, planning, development, and actual data collection. The time of personnel qualified in the use of the interview technique is directly translatable into costs.

Another limitation is the danger of distortion. Although the interviewer may form judgments about the responses of an interviewee, he is no oracle. The respondent may have a faulty memory or may distort reports unconsciously. He may even deliberately mislead the interviewer.

A third limitation of the interview pertains to relevance. The data obtained by interview often contain much unrelated and therefore useless information. This material must be carefully separated from the relevant and useful information.

Last, the interview is limited by the qualifications, background, values, and skills of the interviewer—his age, sex, ethnic background, personal values, perceptions, training, and experience.

VALIDITY AND RELIABILITY OF THE INTERVIEW

Essentially the same considerations apply to interview validity and reliability as to questionnaire validity and reliability. Validity is governed by the relevance of the questions to the purpose of the interview, but even more by the relevance of the responses to the issues being investigated. The responses of the interviewee must be complete, and must show depth, truthfulness, and a reasonable degree of variation. Similarly, the reliability of the interview is ascertained by preliminary tryout of the structured materials with representatives of the population with whom the technique is to be used. The results of the trial should prove that questions are clear, that their implications are understood, and that they are concerned with items that are reasonably stable, important, and typical of the situation under study. And the information collected must be consistent, must agree with what is known, and must correlate with data and evidence collected by other means.

FORMS OF THE INTERVIEW

Basically, there are two categories of interview. The first is the *standardized* or *structured interview*. This form is used when the same information is to be collected from each interviewee. Because the standardized interview is designed to get the same information from each respondent, the answers of all interviewees to all questions must be comparable and classifiable; that is, they must deal with exactly the same subject matter. Differences or similarities between responses must reflect actual differences or similarities between interviewees and not differences that can be attributed to the questions they were asked or the meanings they attached to the questions.

The second broad category is the *nonstandardized interview*. The user of the nonstandardized interview makes no attempt to obtain the same information from every respondent. Generally, this type of interview is used to explore broad problems or to find an explanation for an unexpected situation. It is used much less frequently than the standardized interview, and its methodology is therefore varied, complex, and difficult to describe. For this reason, discussion will be limited to the standardized interview.

The standardized interview has two forms, the *schedule interview* and the *nonschedule standardized interview*. In the schedule interview, every respondent is asked for precisely the same information, and the interviewer reads the questions from a prepared schedule. The wording and sequence of questions are determined in advance, and the questions are asked of all respondents in exactly the same way and in the same sequence.

In the nonschedule interview, standardization is achieved without the use of a prepared schedule. Instead, the interviewer is thoroughly briefed on what information is required and then is allowed to vary the wording and the sequence of the questions for maximum effectiveness with individual respondents. Obviously, the nonschedule interview is much more demanding on the interviewer, and results are more subject to question with respect to reliability. Since most investigators believe that standardization is most effectively achieved with the schedule interview, this is the type that is herein recommended. An excerpt from a typical schedule interview is shown in Figure 5-12.

As can be seen, from a systems evaluation standpoint, the interview can be a significant means of gathering data. The persons interviewed—the instructors, trainees, training supervisors, and operating managers—have been either directly or indirectly involved in a concrete training situation or an operating situation in which the training has been put to use. The hypothetically significant elements and total structure of the training or operating situation can be described and analyzed, and a set of significant hypotheses concerning the meaning and effects of specific aspects of the situation can be established. On the basis of this analysis,

Figure 5-12. **Excerpt from a schedule used by supervisors to evaluate training.**

Name of trainee _____   Interviewed by _____

Position _____   Date _____

Department _____

1. How long have you been a supervisor in this department?
   a. Less than six months
   b. Six to twelve months
   c. One to two years
   d. Over two years

2. How long have you been (trainee's name) supervisor?
   a. Less than six months
   b. Six to twelve months
   c. One to two years
   d. Over two years

3. Did (trainee) attend (training program) while you were his supervisor?
   a. Yes
   b. No (skip to item 10)

4. Did you recommend him for the training?
   a. Yes
   b. No (skip to item 6)

5. Why did you recommend him?
   _____
   _____

6. How was he selected for the training? By whom?
   _____
   _____

7. How would you have rated his performance before he entered the training program?
   a. Unsatisfactory
   b. Below average
   c. Average
   d. Above average
   e. Superior

8. What specific deficiencies did you note in his performance prior to the training?
   _____
   _____

9. Have these deficiencies been remedied by the training?
   a. Yes
   b. No

10. How would you rate his overall performance as of today?
    a. Unsatisfactory
    b. Below average
    c. Average
    d. Above average
    e. Superior

11. What are his specific deficiencies?
    _____
    _____

an investigator can develop a standardized interview guide or schedule which outlines the major areas of inquiry and the specific data to be obtained in the interview. The interview can then be focused on the experiences and perceptions of the people exposed to the situation or its effects. Their recorded responses can be tabulated and analyzed and used to test the validity of the hypotheses and to determine the reasons for unanticipated responses to the situation. They can also be used to verify conclusions drawn from analyses of other data-collection means regarding the training system and its components.

STEPS IN CONSTRUCTING A SCHEDULE

The steps in developing a standardized interview schedule are similar to the steps used in constructing a questionnaire.

Step 1. Determine the objectives of the interview and carefully define them. Consider the characteristics of the group with which the schedule is to be used.

Step 2. Select the topics or factors to be covered in the interview. In selecting these factors, observe these rules:

a. Select only factors or items that are relevant.

b. Select items or factors that are specific.

c. Select items or factors that can be defined or described in terms that will be understood by all respondents.

Step 3. Develop an outline which groups similar or related items and establishes a logical sequence.

Step 4. Draft the questions, observing these rules:

a. Use standard terms and definitions.

b. Keep questions clear, direct, and short.

c. Avoid embarrassing questions.

d. Key vocabulary and sentence structure to the group.

Step 5. Draft the opening statement. Be sure to include the purpose of the interview, the identity of the respondent group (not the individuals), and the use to be made of the data collected.

Step 6. Prepare a final draft of the schedule.

Step 7. Select three or more qualified persons and have them review the schedule.

Step 8. Revise the schedule as indicated by the comments of the reviewers.

Step 9. Interview a small sample of the intended population on a trial basis.

Step 10. Analyze the responses of the trial population and make such revisions to the schedule as seem to be needed.

CHECKLIST

REVIEWING INTERVIEW SCHEDULES

The following checklist is provided to assist personnel in reviewing interview schedules:

1. Are the objectives clearly defined?
2. Is the introductory statement complete and convincing?
3. Does the schedule deal with items that respondents are likely to feel are genuinely important?
4. Have trivial and irrelevant questions been avoided?
5. Do the questions avoid unnecessary details or specifications?
6. Are the questions clear and unambiguous?
7. Do the questions fit the respondent's situation?
8. Are leading questions avoided?
9. Do the questions encourage the respondent to be definite in his answers without forcing definiteness where it is inappropriate?
10. Do the questions elicit responses of sufficient depth to avoid superficiality?
11. Are questions asked in such a way that the respondent will not be embarrassed?
12. Are questions asked in such a way that the respondent will not feel that there is a hidden purpose in the interview?
13. Do the questions permit the respondent to present his own point of view or frame of reference?
14. Is the schedule complete?

SELECTED REFERENCES

Adams, Georgia Sachs. *Measurement and Evaluation.* New York: Holt, Rinehart and Winston, Inc., 1964, Pt. II.

Cenci, Louis. *Skill Training for the Job.* New York: Pitman Publishing Corporation, 1966, Chap. 9.

Cronbach, Lee J. *Essentials of Psychological Testing.* 2d ed. New York: Harper & Brothers, 1960, Chap. 17.

Dooher, M. J., and Vivienne Marquis, eds. *Rating Employee and Supervisory Performance.* AMA, 1950.

Horst, Paul. *Psychological Measurement and Prediction.* Belmont, Calif.: Wadsworth Publishing Company, Inc., 1966.

Kirkpatrick, Donald L. "Evaluation of Training." In Robert L. Craig and Lester R. Bittel, eds. *Training and Development Handbook.* New York: McGraw-Hill Book Company, 1967, Chap. 5.

Kleinmuntz, Benjamin. *Personality Measurement: An Introduction.* Homewood, Ill.: The Dorsey Press, 1967, Chaps. 4–7.

Noll, Victor H. *Introduction to Educational Measurement.* Boston: Houghton Mifflin Company, 1965, Chap. 13.

Nunnally, Jum C., Jr. *Tests and Measurement: Assessment and Prediction.* New York: McGraw-Hill Book Company, 1959, Chap. 13.

Remmers, H. H., N. L. Gage, and J. Francis Rummel. *A Practical Introduction to Measurement and Evaluation.* New York: Harper & Row, Publishers, Incorporated, 1965, Chap. 11.

Richardson, Stephen A., Barbara Snell Dohrenwend, and David Klein. *Interviewing: Its Forms and Functions.* New York: Basic Books, Inc., Publishers, 1965, Chap. 2.

Rose, Homer C. *The Development and Supervision of Training Programs.* New York: American Technical Society, 1964, Pt. I., Chaps. 5–8.

Smith, Patricia Cain, and L. M. Kendall. "Retranslation of Expectations: An Approach to the Construction of Unambiguous Anchors for Rating Scales." In W. Leslie Barnette, Jr., ed. *Readings in Psychological Tests and Measurements,* rev. ed. Homewood, Ill.: The Dorsey Press, 1968, pp. 192–200.

Stanley, Julian C. *Measurement in Today's Schools,* 4th ed. Englewood Cliffs, N.J.: Prentice-Hall, Inc., 1964, Chap. 9.

Stufflebeam, Daniel L. "Toward A Science of Educational Evaluation," *Educational Technology* (July 30, 1968), 8:14: 5–12.

Thorndike, Robert C., and Elizabeth Hagen. *Measurement and Evaluation in Psychology and Education.* New York: John Wiley & Sons, Inc., 1961, Chap. 13.

Worthen, Blaine R. "Toward a Taxonomy of Evaluation Designs." *Educational Technology* (Aug. 15, 1968), 8:15: 3–9.

6

Constructing Criterion Measures

C HAPTER 5 dealt with one aspect of internal evaluation of training and development systems—the construction of evaluative instruments other than tests. The construction of criterion measures is the subject of this chapter. Criterion measures are specialized tests that provide the system designer with another means of determining whether the training system is appropriate and effective.

The purpose of this chapter is to describe the procedures for designing criterion measures used to validate the system and later to maintain quality control over the output of the system. The discussion of tests is limited to achievement tests; intelligence, aptitude, and personality measures are not considered.

After reading the chapter, the reader should be able to perform as follows:

Behavior   Construct criterion measures, including performance tests, for use in evaluating and controlling the quality of training and development systems.

Conditions   Given: behaviorally stated objectives for the system, guides for the construction of criterion measures, clerical assistance, and opportunity to try out the measures with a sample group from the intended trainee population.

Criterion   Tests will be constructed in accordance with the procedures defined in this chapter, and will meet the standards of validity, reliability, objectivity, administrability, comprehensiveness, and economy defined in this chapter.

Behavior   Perform rudimentary statistical analyses of test results.
Conditions   Given: raw scores, graphic item count (GIC), calculator, formulas, and clerical assistance.
Criterion   In accordance with the procedures and standards described in this chapter.

THE NATURE AND PURPOSES OF TESTS

Tests are critically important in a training setting for many reasons. Although tests may not be popular with trainees or instructors, they can and do serve very essential functions. It is true that trainees often think of tests as barriers to surmount, rather than as a means of finding out where they stand and where they might improve. To instructors, tests may mean the arduous job of thinking up test situations and test items, the dull business of proctoring examinations, or the time-consuming tasks of scoring tests and making entries in trainee records. Tests may also induce anxiety in instructors who often feel that evaluation of their job performance is based on their trainees' performance on tests.

Yet, tests are necessary if trainees are to be classified and grouped properly for instruction; if training systems designers are to have a reliable means of determining the effectiveness and quality of the instructional system; if trainees are to be provided the guidance, remedial assistance, and training suited to their individual needs; and if management is to be informed about the kind and amount of progress employees are making and the degree of proficiency they bring to the job. Obviously, a well-conceived testing program is needed to serve these purposes.

The Need for Tailor-made Tests

The question of greatest importance from the standpoint of evaluating the outcomes of custom-built in-house training and development programs is this: Can the tests commonly used to evaluate trainee achievement be used to evaluate the outcomes of a carefully designed and validated training system? Or, more specifically, can commercial standardized tests or off-the-shelf evaluative instruments be used to determine the amount and kind of learning trainees have acquired by exposure to the system? Can the system itself be validated by these tests? Can the ordinary, garden variety of instructor-made tests be used for these purposes? To these questions, the answer must be a resounding "No!"

Commercial standardized tests or tests constructed for earlier training programs are unlikely to be appropriate measures of achievement for a new training system. The problem is one of test validity. It is a well-known (but frequently ignored) fact that the title of a test tells little about what the test actually measures. The standardized test may include content that has not been included in the training system. Conversely, it is also likely that the training system contains content that is not included in the standardized test. Under either set of conditions, the test is invalid.

The obvious solution is to be certain that the test matches the training system. However, for several reasons, matching a test with a training program is a very difficult task. The form of statements of objectives for training systems described in an earlier chapter requires precise definition of what the trainee is to be able to do rather than what he is to know. This fact dictates the use of a far greater number of performance tests than have been used heretofore. The kind of mental process involved in answering test items, even the *form* of the response the testee is to make, also has a bearing. If the behaviors taught by the system do not match the behaviors measured by the test, the validity of the test may well be questioned.

Essentially the same problem exists with off-the-shelf instructor-made tests. They are typically highly unreliable, but what is even more important, they are invalid measures of the products of a training system. It would be an error to assume that ordinary instructor-made tests can provide an accurate and consistent picture of trainee achievement, and If the tests are to be used to validate an instructional system, the inadequacies of such tests are even more critical.

In sum, the selection of valid tests from among the great array of available standardized tests and off-the-shelf in-house tests is an impossible task. Specially designed tests are the only answer.

THE MEANING OF MEASUREMENT

Measurement is the use of numbers to describe behavior. Observations of the way people behave are assigned numerical values, and these numbers are then used to obtain new information or to describe relationships among the people observed. Measurement is obtained by tests. A test is a means of observing and describing how people perform in a specific, controlled situation. In a training program, therefore, a test is a standardized situation in which trainees are required to demonstrate mastery of one or more of the objectives of the training system. The test sets the tasks, and words or numbers are used to report different kinds of information about the people who take the tests.

CHARACTERISTICS OF AN ACCEPTABLE TEST

Tests used as criterion measures in a training or development situation must meet certain standards. Specifically, every test must be valid, reliable, objective, administrable, standard, comprehensive, and economical. All tests meet these requirements to greater or lesser degrees, but no test is completely valid or invalid, nor is any test completely reliable or completely unreliable. Figure 6-1 shows an evaluation of the essential characteristics of one test used in a training situation.

VALIDITY

A test is valid if it measures what it is supposed to measure and nothing else. For example, a test designed to measure ability to use equipment block diagrams which actually measures reading speed and comprehension is not a valid test. If a test is intended to measure the ability of trainees to apply knowledge, it must measure application and not merely the ability to recall facts and write the facts on paper. Test validity has implications for both the form of the test (oral, written, or performance) and its coverage. The form must be appropriate to the required performance, and the test items must cover each individual objective.

Figure 6-1.   Rating of a test on seven essential features.

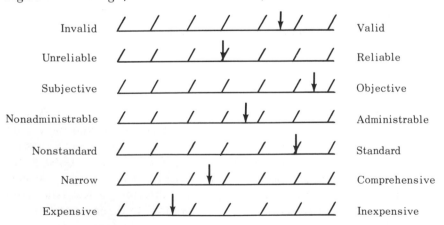

RELIABILITY

A test is reliable when it yields consistent results. If identical measurements are obtained every time the instrument is used, the test may be considered to be very reliable. However, no instrument is perfectly reliable. For example, a rough measure of the reliability of an odometer can be obtained by taking several readings of the distance recorded by the instrument over a measured mile. Except for the errors made by the person taking the readings, the amount of scatter in the readings may be considered as the degree of unreliability of the odometer.

To obtain a measure of the reliability of a test is a very complex problem because the things measured by tests do not remain constant. If the same test is readministered, the trainee can be expected to change from one administration of the test to another because he learns some things by taking the test the first time (and he may even remember some of the answers). But if the same test is administered on two occasions to the same group of trainees, and they have had no additional training on the test subjects, the relative standings of the group should not change appreciably. If they do, the test is unreliable. Sources of unreliability include failure to standardize test directions, errors in scoring, nonstandard testing conditions, guessing by testees, errors in content sampling, and chance fluctuations in testees' attention, attitude, or physical condition. Usually, carefully established standards for administration, machine scoring, and lengthening the test will increase reliability.

OBJECTIVITY

A test is objective when the judgment or bias of the scorer is eliminated from the scoring. If a test is completely objective—the ideal—different persons scoring the same performance or test paper at different times will arrive at the same score. That is, if ten scorers independently graded the same test and they all arrived at the same score, the test would be considered objective.

ADMINISTRABILITY

A test is administrable when it can be given to a group with relative ease and with excellent possibilities of communicating clearly to the test administrator and testees what is to be done. Some tests are very difficult to administer and require professional training. Other tests are practically self-administering; they merely require distributing tests and answer sheets, giving starting and stopping signals, and collecting the materials. Administrability is insured by preparing written directions for the administration of the test and requiring either that the examiner read them verbatim to the group or that the testees read them. Administrability is also increased by using separate answer sheets for testees' responses.

STANDARDABILITY

A test is standard when a systematic sample of performance has been obtained under prescribed conditions and scored according to definite rules. Factors in standardization include equipment, tools and working aids, materials, arrangement, difficulty of problems, and the testing environment. All conditions must be identical for all testees. In addition, to insure standardization, the items of a standardized test should be experimentally evaluated to obtain evidence of their validity and reliability.

COMPREHENSIVENESS

A test is comprehensive when it takes liberal and complete samples from whatever it is measuring. In training and development situations, a test must adequately sample the objectives of the training system. At best, however, any single test is only a sample of the behaviors taught by the system, and test planners must make certain that each test is a representative and comprehensive sample of the objectives.

ECONOMY

A test is economical to use when a minimum of time, equipment, materials, and personnel is required in administering and scoring it. Obviously, economy is the one factor that is most difficult to keep within acceptable bounds if the other essential characteristics of a test are to be maximized.

CRITERION MEASURES

A criterion test is a test designed to assist instructors and training system designers in arriving at reliable judgments about the adequacy of trainee performance on job-related tasks, under either authentic or simulated working conditions, and with predetermined go, no-go standards of acceptability.

A criterion test is administered to test the trainee's mastery of the skills taught in the training program. But ability to perform today is of little usefulness or consequence unless the trainee can perform tomorrow also. Therefore, a criterion test, like all other achievement tests, must also predict the future performance of the trainee.

Criterion measures are derived directly from the performance objectives for the training or development program and not from lesson plans or other instructional materials. They are, in fact, developed *prior to* and *independently of* other training materials to insure that they are uncontaminated by unessential or extraneous content.

TYPES OF CRITERION MEASURES

Although all criterion measures establish go, no-go testing situations, they may be administered at different points in the training system. Some are administered at critical points *during* the training; others are administered at the *conclusion* of training to establish qualification. A more detailed description of each type of criterion measure follows.

Internal criterion tests. At carefully selected points during the conduct of a training system, internal evaluation tests should be administered. Usually, these tests cover a single major task of a job; however, these tests may also cover clusters of related tasks. Occasionally, even job elements may be of sufficient importance and complexity to warrant the development and administration of separate tests.

The primary source of data for the construction of internal criterion measures is the Job Performance Workcard. However, these materials may be supplemented by references to course content found in content outlines or in the program of instruction when academic prerequisites (knowledge supports) are of sufficient importance to justify separate testing.

Performance standards for internal tests must be consistent with criteria specified in the Performance Objective Workcards (see Fig. 4-3). If an internal test has been constructed to measure job knowledge, rather than job skill, absolute standards, at or near mastery of the material (that is, 90 percent) should be established. These tests should be used to prove the readiness of trainees to progress to the next unit of instruction (on a go, no-go basis), as well as to identify deficiencies for remedial instruction, recycling, or elimination from the training or development program.

End-of-course qualification tests. For each training or development system, a qualification test should be constructed. This test should be administered to trainees at the completion of the training. Where possible, the test should be a comprehensive measure of the trainee's ability to perform the full range of job duties and tasks for which training has been provided. The tests should replicate, as realistically as possible, the conditions under which the trainee will be expected to perform his duties when assigned to an operating or managerial position.

The standards of performance for qualification tests should be those required for acceptable beginning job proficiency. The Job Performance Workcards are the source of data for the identification of job skills, performance conditions, and performance criteria. Successful performance on this type of test, where applicable, should be required for graduation from the training or development program.

USES OF CRITERION MEASURES

Criterion tests can be used for several purposes. Their major uses can be cataloged under four headings: system validation, system quality control, instructional uses, and experimental uses. These applications, although not completely separate and distinct in practice, are described and discussed separately to develop a clearer understanding of each.

System validation. System designers need specific information with regard to the effectiveness of the various elements of the training or development system. Therefore, during the system development phase, criterion measures are constructed and validated so that they can be used during the systems validation phase as one means of proving the effectiveness of the system. Its basic use—the one with the highest priority—is to examine the performance of trainees to see if the instructional system works as intended. Analysis of criterion test results should provide system designers with leads to the identification of deficiencies in any of the components of the system, including content, sequence, strategy, equipment, aids, and materials.

System quality control. Once a training system has been validated and put into operation on a regular basis, quality controls must be applied, to insure that the system continues to operate as originally designed and that the quality of the products continues to be acceptable. Criterion measures can meet this requirement admirably. Group and individual proficiency can be monitored by systematically testing trainees during the conduct of the training and at the completion of the course. Criterion test scores will identify not only individual trainee deficiencies, but also trainee groups among which proficiency is below the acceptable standard. Such a finding may raise questions about the aptitudes or motivation of that group. It may also make certain elements of the system suspect—for example, the quality of the instruction. Continuing analysis of criterion test results is therefore important to identify and correct deterioration in any system component.

Instructional uses. When a training system has been validated and its instructional adequacy has been demonstrated, criterion test results can be used for more conventional purposes. Some of the more important instructional uses are as follows:

1. *To diagnose learning difficulties.* Careful analysis of individual and group performance on criterion measures often reveals learning difficulties that can be remedied. That is, tests help the instructor to identify gaps in trainee knowledge and skills to help determine needs for remedial work. This type of analysis involves study of the responses of individual trainees to test items and test situations. The goal is to identify deficiencies in performance so that appropriate remedial instruction can be provided.

2. *To assess the amount and kind of behavioral change attributable to the training or development system.* The concern is not how the trainee group stands in relation to other trainee groups; rather, the objective is to compare the trainee group *before* exposure to the system with the trainee group *after* instruction. In addition, it is possible to compare the amounts of change between different trainees or trainee groups.

3. *To provide feedback to instructors.* Analysis of test results, particularly from the standpoint of overall group performance, can provide the instructor with a means of identifying deficiencies in his own performance. If he knows specifically where trainees fell short of the standard, he can review his strategy and make the needed changes to overcome the deficiency.

4. *To motivate trainees.* Criterion tests can be effective motivational devices. Knowing that they will be tested and that tests establish job qualification usually encourages trainees to be as well prepared for the test as they possibly can be. In addition, tests are reinforcing to trainees. When trainees find that they can perform at the required level, they are rewarded. Such intrinsic reward tends to cause them to increase their efforts.

5. *To counsel trainees.* The results of criterion test administration are

extremely useful as a basis for providing individual counseling and guidance to trainees. Instead of generalities, the instructor or class advisor can review specific data with the trainee, thereby making such counseling sessions more productive.

Administrative uses. Criterion measures provide a sound basis for taking certain administrative actions. To some degree, these uses overlap those applications described in the immediately preceding paragraphs; however, the perspective is somewhat different. From an administrative standpoint, criterion measures have the following uses:

1. *To eliminate inept trainees.* Criterion measures are the most valid bases for judging whether a trainee should be eliminated from a training program or be graduated. The go, no-go standards make such decisions relatively straightforward. Even in the case of paper and pencil objective tests, cut scores can be established after experience has been accumulated with relatively large numbers of trainees.

2. *To grade and rank trainees.* Sometimes grades and ranks must be determined so as to meet the requirements of other programs. Where possible, for example, personnel records should indicate the degree to which the trainee exceeded the established standards of training. In addition, special recognition for outstanding performance in a training program is desirable. Criterion measures can serve these purposes.

3. *To recycle trainees.* Analysis of the performance of trainees on criterion measures is the best means of determining whether a deficient trainee can be salvaged. Usually, this involves an investment of additional training time. The decision can be reached by determining the distance between the trainee's performance on the test and the standard and then translating this distance into an estimate of the time required to get the trainee to the required level of performance. Well-constructed criterion measures provide information upon which to make such determinations.

4. *To pretest trainees.* Pretesting is done before trainees are enrolled in a training system. The results of the administration of pretests furnish information about the repertoires of beginning trainees as compared with trainees who have completed the training program. This information provides system designers with an inventory of the skills and abilities of the average entering trainee. Having such information available reduces errors in training system design. In addition, designers are provided with a measure of the amount and kind of behavioral change that is attributable to the training system simply by comparing pretest and criterion test scores. Pretests can also be used to place trainees at different stages in the training program based on their demonstrated abilities (remedial for low scorers and bypass or advanced for high scorers). This application is particularly useful in job-skills programs where there is a strong

element of continuity—where later skills depend heavily on the acquisition of earlier ones.

5. *To determine trainees' assignments.* Few jobs are identical. Although they may have the same titles and the same descriptions, and may require the same skills, some jobs are more demanding than others. Criterion test performance can sometimes be used as a basis for determining the exact position to which a graduate of a training program should be assigned.

6. *To establish readiness for advanced training.* In some cases, criterion tests can be used as a basis for selecting individuals for advanced training. This is possible if the test distinguishes among satisfactory, better than average, and outstanding performers.

7. *To inform line managers and supervisors about the accomplishments of their subordinates.* Performance of trainees should be a matter of interest and concern to their immediate supervisors. Beyond the matter of personal interest, there is the requirement for on-the-job training to consider. On-the-job training programs must dovetail with formal training. To accomplish this, the supervisor needs to know the level of skill his subordinates bring to the job. The results of criterion measures can provide this information.

Experimental uses. Criterion measures can be used experimentally to good advantage. Some of these uses are as follows:

1. *To pretest system components.* Sometimes the complexity of a system component is so great and the investment in the development of the component is so heavy that it is desirable to try out the component before it is incorporated into the system, to insure that it will operate as intended before large amounts of resources are committed. Criterion tests are one measure of the effectiveness and efficiency of such components.

2. *To perform comparative cost analyses.* Criterion measures are invaluable as a means of comparing the effectiveness and efficiency of alternative instructional strategies designed to accomplish the same instructional objectives. The performance of the trainees exposed to alternative system components is compared on the basis of analysis of their performance on the criterion measures. This comparison provides a reliable and valid basis for decision making.

3. *To determine system prerequisites.* Analysis of the performance of randomly selected personnel on criterion measures can give leads for the establishment of realistic prerequisites for enrollment in a training program. This procedure takes much of the judgment out of the process of establishing prerequisites and goes a long way toward guaranteeing that the input will be capable of completing the training satisfactorily.

TYPES OF TESTS

PAPER AND PENCIL OBJECTIVE TESTS

These tests consist of carefully constructed test items in the form of true-false, matching, completion, multiple-choice, or arrangement items. Test items of these types are printed or duplicated for each trainee. The testee either marks his answers directly on the test, on a separate answer page, or on a card or sheet which can be scored by an electrical or mechanical machine. The questions may be all written, or printed numbers, diagrams, pictures, or other material may accompany test items.

Paper and pencil objective tests have several advantages: (1) scoring is quick and easy, (2) objectivity in scoring is insured, (3) the tests can be administered to large groups simultaneously, and (4) the tests can be designed to be essentially self-administering. But there are also limitations to paper and pencil objective tests: (1) they cannot validly measure all types of behavior, (2) they are difficult and time-consuming to construct, and (3) they are restrictive in terms of trainee response.

ORAL OBJECTIVE TESTS

These tests are quite similar to paper and pencil objective tests in their content and format except that the testee responds orally instead of in writing. Their advantages are that (1) they are easy to administer, (2) they allow the testee to qualify and clarify his answers, and (3) they offer the examiner an opportunity to clarify the questions. The limitations of oral objective tests are that (1) they are difficult to construct, (2) they must be administered to one trainee at a time, (3) they are difficult to score unless they are short-answer type, and (4) they may turn out to be less objective than desired because examiners may give more assistance to the testee than was intended by the designer.

RATINGS

Ratings, as described in the immediately preceding chapter, may be adjectival or numerical. They may be based on judgments made with or without a scale which describes behavior at several levels. Their advantages include (1) ease of administration, (2) ease of scoring, and (3) high reliability (provided that five or more raters evaluate the behavior or trait and the ratings are averaged). Their limitations are as follows: (1) individual ratings are usually highly unreliable, (2) valid and reliable rating scales are difficult to construct, (3) raters require training in the use of scales, and (4) rating procedures are time-consuming and therefore expensive.

ESSAY TESTS

An essay test is an instrument that calls for written responses to questions or problem situations, in that the testee is asked to discuss, compare, recall, classify, analyze, explain, criticize, organize, apply, describe, evaluate, solve, or the like. These tests have the following advantages: (1) they are relatively easy to construct; (2) they provide an opportunity to evaluate effectiveness in writing; and (3) they offer the trainee an opportunity to select, organize, and integrate facts. The limitations of essay tests far outweigh their advantages. The main disadvantages are as follows: (1) the content validity is low, due to the limited subject-matter sampling allowed by the test; (2) the reliability is low, due to the small number of test items and the subjectivity involved in scoring (neatness, grammar, spelling, expression, legibility of handwriting, and the personal-emotional feelings of the grader at the time of scoring may affect the grade assigned); and (3) they are time-consuming to administer and score.

PERFORMANCE TESTS

Performance tests are instruments which require the trainee to demonstrate some practical application, skill, or operation which is an essential part of a job or task. Sometimes some kind of apparatus or equipment or material is involved. The performance of the testee is observed and evaluated in accordance with a predetermined standard of performance and/or product of performance. These standards are defined in the training objectives.

Performance tests, then, require the testee to *do* something. Usually what is required is a sample of the work associated with a particular job duty or task. Scores may be based on completion time, accuracy of the work done, quantity of work completed, or quality of the work product. Usually, a performance test requires the trainee to use tools, equipment, and materials which he will use on the job. Occasionally, a performance test uses simulated tools, equipment, or materials. In rare instances, special training equipment must be fabricated for performance tests. Performance tests may be any one of three types:

1. *Identification.* This type of test measures the ability of the testee to identify essential characteristics of equipment, procedures, or techniques, and/or to identify objects; for example, troubleshooting in repair of electronic equipment.

2. *Simulation.* This type of test involves the use of simulated conditions because of the impracticality of using the actual equipment due to unavailability, costs, size, safety, control, or other factors; for example, the Link trainer in flight training, or practice bombs in bomb disposal.

3. *Work sample.* This type of test involves the completion of sample tasks, representative of a job, where the procedures, work products, or results are evaluated; for example, writing a short computer program, or repairing a specific equipment malfunction.

Performance tests have several advantages: (1) they have face validity in that they cover in a realistic way a job duty or task, (2) they are job-relevant, (3) they are usually highly reliable. Among the major limitations of the performance test are the following: (1) they usually cover only a part or sample of the job; (2) they require more time to administer per item than most other types of tests; (3) they are usually administered individually; (4) they often require tools, equipment, and materials which add to the problems and expense of administration; and (5) they are difficult to design.

DESIGNING CRITERION MEASURES

Constructing good tests is not easy. It is an art which involves elements of originality and creativity as well as knowledge of test construction theory. The purpose of this section is to define the procedures used by test development specialists in constructing tests. It does not pretend to provide the reader with mastery of the art of test construction because such competence comes only from practice, criticism, tryout, analysis, and more practice. Therefore, the most scrupulous attention to the cautions, principles, and procedures discussed in this section will not *guarantee* good tests, but it will certainly do much to prevent the production of poor ones.

STAGES IN BUILDING A TEST

Specific stages in test construction vary somewhat according to the special nature and purpose of each test. However, the typical sequence followed in building a test to be used to validate and control the quality of a training system is as follows: (1) plan the test; (2) construct the test items or situations, and assemble the test; (3) try out the test under realistic conditions; and (4) analyze the results and revise the test.

STEPS IN PLANNING A TEST

To make a good test, the test writer must have clearly in mind what he is testing for and how the results of the test will be used. A carefully planned instructional system deserves a carefully planned test covering the job behaviors taught. Good tests are not made by simply throwing together items or situations more or less related to a job until enough items have been written to keep testees busy for an hour or two. A test prepared in a haphazard manner will not really tell anyone how much men have learned or how well they perform elements of a job. Development of a test plan should overcome these obstacles to the construction of an acceptable test. The steps in test planning are as follows:

Step 1. Prepare a master plan for all criterion measures to be used (see Fig. 6-2).

Step 2. Define the purposes of each test.

Step 3. Identify the specific job tasks or elements of skill to be evaluated. In reaching these decisions, consider these factors:

    a. The importance of the tasks to the total job.

    b. Practical limitations of time, space, personnel, equipment, and materials.

Step 4. Determine the type of measure to be used in evaluating each task performance. Selection of types of measures should be based on consideration of the following:

    a. The probable validity and reliability of the measure.

    b. The administrability and comprehensiveness of the measure.

    c. The costs of construction, administration, and scoring.

Step 5. Set the standard of performance for each task according to the following:

    a. For paper and pencil or oral objective tests, state the criterion as a percentage of items correct; for example, 90 percent.

    b. For ratings, state the criterion as an absolute score; for example, 30 out of a possible 32 points, or satisfactory or higher on all scaled items.

    c. For performance tests, restate the criterion entered on the Performance Objective Workcard (Fig. 4-3).

Figure 6-2. A master plan for criterion measures.

Training system title _____

Planner _____ Department _____ Division _____

Training objective number	Type of Measure			Testing materials and conditions	Testee's product	Criterion for passing or qualification	Method of scoring
	Paper and pencil	Oral	Rating	Performance				

Approved:

Chief, Division _____ Date _____ Training manager _____ Date _____

Chief _____ Date _____

CONSTRUCTING THE TEST

The ideal test requires the testee to apply all that he has learned in a training situation up to the time of the test. Although this ideal cannot always be reached, it is possible to build tests that sample a wide range of the skills and knowledge taught. Following are the rules that should be followed in constructing the test:

1. Select realistic and practical problems. Test items or situations should require demonstration of the knowledge or skills taught to the trainee, or should present a problem of the type he will have to solve on the job. Realism of elements in terms of probable working conditions is of great importance.

2. Select important aspects of the job for testing. Items or situations selected should not deal with trivial or unimportant details of a job. The large investment of time in test construction and administration makes it imperative that only critically important elements be tested.

3. Select items or situations which demand specific job knowledge or skills. Avoid questions or problems which can be answered or solved merely by intelligent reasoning or by the application of general knowledge.

4. Select items or elements that are objectively gradable. This means that qualified judges should be able to agree on what constitutes satisfactory performance, acceptable work products, or the correct or best solution. Insofar as possible, subjective judgment must be eliminated from the scoring.

5. Use job language. Items or situations should be phrased in the working language of the job; however, the use of unnecessary technical terms should be avoided.

6. Make each item or situation independent of other items. Test items or situations should be selected so that the solution of one item does not give away the answer to another. Nor should the test be so constructed that failure to solve an item or complete an operation makes it impossible to continue the test.

7. Fit the difficulty of the item or situation to the required level of job knowledge or performance. The purpose of the test is not to trick the testee or mislead him. Wide variability of scores is not desirable in a criterion measure.

8. Make certain that the test situation is standardized. The purpose of a test is to provide the testee with an opportunity to demonstrate his newly acquired skills under realistic conditions. If the test one trainee takes differs in any respect from the one administered to other trainees, the test situation is nonstandard. Factors to be considered in standardization are as follows:

a. Difficulty. Defects or "bugs" put into equipment or problems posed to testees must be of the same order of difficulty.
b. Equipment. The equipment used by testees must be identical in type, operating characteristics, and state of repair.
c. Tools and working aids. Identical sets of tools and working aids, in terms of number, kind, and condition, must be provided all testees.
d. Materials. Materials or stock provided testees must be identical in kind, quality, and dimensions.
e. Arrangement. Equipment, tools, and materials must be arranged in exactly the same way for each testee. This includes the physical placement of all items, the settings on equipment controls, and the arrangement of manuals, reference materials, and working aids.
f. Environment. The surroundings for the test, including the number of testees and evaluators, lighting, temperature, noise level, and traffic in the area, must be identical for all testees.

Figure 6-3. A one-way test plan for a test for maintenance shop foreman trainees.

Content areas	Number of test items
Principles of management	
1. Planning	12
2. Organizing	7
3. Staffing	6
4. Direction	10
5. Control	12
Management activities	
1. Policy formulation and interpretation	8
2. Projecting manpower requirements	5
3. Preparing budgets	10
4. Preparing correspondence	6
5. Maintaining equipment records	10
6. Ordering supplies	6
7. Conducting inventories	5
8. Preparing reports	10
9. Training subordinates	10
10. Conducting inspections	8
11. Appraising performance	10
12. Scheduling	5
Total	140

STEPS IN TEST CONSTRUCTION

The steps to be followed in constructing a test follow:

Step 1. Construct a test plan (see Figs. 6-3 and 6-4).

Step 2. Select the items or situations to be used in the test.

Step 3. Draft the items (draft more items than necessary).

Step 4. Select the final items and word them carefully.

Step 5. Place the items in an appropriate sequence and format (assemble the test).

Step 6. Review and polish the items.

Step 7. Finalize the draft test.

Figure 6-4. A two-way test plan for a test in advanced electronic-equipment repair.

	Subject-matter areas					Number of items
Objectives	Signal generators	Oscillo-scopes	Electronic counters	Power meters	Servo systems	
Knowledge						
1. Nomenclature	3	3	2	2	3	13
2. Capabilities	4	3	3	2	1	13
3. Characteristics	3	2	3	2	2	12
4. Applications	4	1	2	3	3	13
5. Principles	2	3	2	2	2	11
Subtotal	16	12	12	11	11	62
Skills						
1. Operate	1	1	1	1	1	5
2. Identify malfunctions	3	3	3	3	3	15
3. Sectionalize malfunctions	1	2	1	2	1	7
4. Repair	1	1	1	1	1	5
5. Maintain records	1	1	1	1	1	5
Subtotal	7	8	7	8	7	37
Total	23	20	19	19	18	99

DIRECTIONS FOR ADMINISTRATION

The next task is to prepare directions for administration and scoring. All directions must be specific, complete, concise, clear, and standardized. Directions for both the testee and the examiner must be prepared as follows:

Step 1. Prepare directions for the testee. Directions for the testee should be so designed that they can be read to the trainee (or he can read them himself) and that no additional explanation will be necessary for the testee to accomplish the task. Generally, these directions include the following points:

    a. What the testee is expected to do.
    b. How he is to go about doing it.
    c. The conditions under which he is to perform.
    d. How much time he has.
    e. How his performance will be graded.
    f. How to record questions or comments on the critique sheet.

Step 2. Prepare directions for the examiner. Complete instructions for the conduct of the test should be printed or duplicated, and examiners must follow these directions exactly and without deviation. Instructions should clearly identify points in the test (if any) at which it is proper for the examiner to give the testee assistance. Exactly what assistance may be given and precisely how it should be given must also be defined. If the assistance is in the form of explanations necessary to enable the testee to continue with the test, the *exact* wording of the explanation should appear in the instructions. If the examiner is permitted to perform operations which the testee is unable to perform, but which are necessary for completion of the test, these operations should be specified in the instructions. If any form of help is given during the test, the exact amount to be deducted from the testee's score should also be specified in the directions. If the testee is to be questioned as a part of the test, the exact wording of the questions should be on the grading form. In general, directions should include:

    a. The conditions under which the test is to be administered.
    b. The exact procedures to be used.
    c. The equipment and materials required.
    d. The grading considerations.
    e. The time allowed.

f. The job schedule and rotation system if different tasks are to be graded at two or more testing stations.
g. How to report faults in the test or unusual testing conditions.

CHECKLISTS

REVIEWING PERFORMANCE TESTS

1. Are the elements of the test important to the total job?
2. Are the elements realistic in terms of on-the-job requirements and working conditions?
3. Are the elements objectively gradable?
4. Are the elements independent? if not, are there provisions for continuing the test if a testee cannot perform a part of an operation?
5. Are the directions to the testee clear and direct? Do they include:
    a. What he is to do?
    b. How he is to do it?
    c. The conditions under which he is to perform (what he will be given and denied)?
    d. How he will be graded?
    e. How to ask questions or make comments on the test?
6. Are the directions to the examiner clear and complete? Do they include:
    a. The exact conditions under which the test is to be administered?
    b. The exact procedures to be used?
    c. A list of the tools, working aids, equipment, and materials to be used?
    d. When and how help can be given to the trainee (if at all)?
    e. The scoring procedures?
    f. The system of rotation if different tasks are to be performed at more than one testing station?
    g. The time limits for each part of the test?
    h. Instructions for reporting faults in the test or unusual testing conditions or problems?

REVIEWING OBJECTIVE PAPER AND PENCIL MULTIPLE-CHOICE TESTS

1. General considerations.
    a. Are the instructions to examiners clear and complete? Do they:
        (1) Describe the conditions under which the test is to be given?
        (2) Describe the exact procedures to be used?
        (3) List the materials required?
        (4) Describe grading considerations (for example, the penalty for guessing)?

(5) Identify the time allowed for the total test and its parts?
  b. Are the instructions to testees clear and complete? Do they:
    (1) Include how he is to respond to the items?
    (2) Include how much time he has?
    (3) Include how he will be graded?
    (4) Include how to record questions or comments for the test critique?
  c. Is a separate answer sheet provided to facilitate scorings?
2. Test items as a whole.
  a. Are the test items important, realistic, and truly relevant to the job?
  b. Are the knowledge and skills represented by the items critical to further progress in the training program (internal test only)?
  c. Do the items adequately sample the areas of knowledge and skill encompassed by the training?
  d. Do the items call for knowledge and skills used on the job?
  e. Do the items measure application of knowledge gained through training rather than general knowledge?
  f. Do the items deal with important and useful aspects of the job rather than with trivial details?
  g. Do the items demand specific job knowledge and avoid questions that can be answered by intelligent reasoning?
  h. Are items phrased in the working language of the job? Do they avoid unnecessarily technical terms?
  i. Is each item independent of other items so that the solution of one does not give away the answer to another?
  j. Do the items avoid unnecessarily difficult vocabulary and sentence structure?
  k. Do the items avoid weak sentence structure, grammatical errors, and irrelevant inaccuracies?
  l. Are groups of related items (based on the same map, chart, diagram, or data) preceded by a heading that indicates exactly what items belong to the group?
  m. Are the items separated by enough white space to make it clear where one item ends and another begins?
3. The item stem (question or problem).
  a. Is a single, clear, central problem identified?
  b. Does the wording avoid ambiguity?
  c. Is all the information needed for the response, including qualifications, provided?
  d. Does the problem contain only material relevant to its solution?
  e. Are negatively stated stems avoided?
  f. If a negative word appears in the stem, is it emphasized by capitalization, underscoring, or italics?
4. The distractors (alternatives).
  a. Do the items avoid distractors too subtle for testees to discriminate?
  b. Are distractors plausible and attractive? Do they avoid the trivial and absurd?

c. Do the items avoid making the correct answer so obvious that testees will be suspicious of it?
d. Are irrelevant cues to the correct answer avoided (vocabulary hints, errors in grammar, or inconsistent distractors)?
e. Are distractors stated in similar or parallel form?
f. Are overlapping or inclusive distractors avoided?
g. Are highly technical distractors avoided?
h. Are the alternatives "All of the above" and "None of the above" avoided—or balanced in use?
i. Is the position of the correct alternative randomly placed?
j. Are numerical alternatives listed in ascending or descending order?
k. Are synonymous distractors avoided?
l. Do distractors avoid cues or specific determiners such as "always," "sometimes," "never," "may," "often," "generally," and "usually"?
m. Are all distractors approximately the same length?
n. Are there at least four alternatives per item?

EVALUATING AND IMPROVING THE TEST

Tests are constructed to determine whether trainees can perform job duties and tasks, or whether they possess knowledge prerequisite to the performance of these tasks. But no test can serve this purpose unless its adequacy as a measuring instrument has been proved. The value of a test must be determined by actual tryout under realistic conditions with a sample of the population for which the training program and its criterion measures have been designed.

The root question is: How well does the test work? Faults in the test as a whole, in its parts, in individual test items, and in its materials (including directions, scoring procedures, and the like) can only be identified and remedied by actual administration of the test. The following sections describe the steps to be followed in trying out the test and in analyzing test results, including the calculation of some simple statistics to determine the worth of the test.

STEPS IN TEST TRYOUT AND ANALYSIS

Before a test is put into use as a validating or quality control instrument, it must be tried out under realistic conditions to discover potential sources of error. The following steps should be followed in tryout and analysis:

Step 1. Subject the test to examiner tryout. Since the most common source of error in tests is examiner judgment, it is important to have two or three qualified examiners administer the test to two or three trainees. In the case of a performance test, these examiners should score the same performance at the same time but work independently. This is a rough check of reliability. Elements on which the examiners fail to agree in their scoring need to be made more objective. If it is not possible to get a satisfactory degree of agreement among examiners on a particular element, the element should not be scored.

Step 2. Subject the test to trainee tryout. A second tryout of the test should involve several trainees of known variability in the job skills or knowledge taught by the training program and tested by the criterion measure. In the case of performance tests, this type of tryout will prove the validity and reliability of the test. In all cases, the tryout will uncover testee problems with any aspect of the test. Once the deficiencies have been identified, the test can be revised to correct them.

Step 3. Subject the test results to statistical analysis. Statistical analysis relates primarily to the evaluation of paper and pencil objective tests of the multiple-choice variety, although performance tests can also be so analyzed. Two basic types of statistics should be considered: (1) overall test characteristics, including measures of central tendency, measures of variation, measures of reliability, and measures of difficulty; and (2) test item statistics, including graphic item counts and item difficulty. However, before the calculation of these statistical measures is discussed, an important difference between conventional tests and criterion tests must be identified.

CONVENTIONAL VERSUS CRITERION TEST DISCRIMINATION

Achievement tests customarily used in training and development programs are constructed in such a way as to detect small differences in achievement. To produce this result, tests are designed with these objectives in mind: (1) to produce a wide range of test scores, (2) to include items at all levels of difficulty from easy to hard, (3) to insure that enough difficult items are included to prevent the test from being "broken" (to prevent some trainee from achieving a perfect score), and (4) to make certain that each test item differentiates between low and high scorers on the total test.

In other words, conventional tests are constructed so as to achieve a spread of scores which is consistent with the normal bell-shaped distribution curve as shown in Figure 6-5. The "good" conventional test, therefore, clearly differentiates among all persons taking the test, including the extremes. A test with a range of performance between 40 and 80 percent is considered acceptable. To achieve this standard, the same requirement is imposed on individual test items. An item with a difficulty (percentage of trainees answering an item correctly) between 40 and 80 is considered acceptable. Such items must also discriminate; that is, they must show a difference in performance between high- and low-scoring trainees. Items that do not discriminate, or that are too easy or too difficult, are rejected.

With criterion measures of performance, however, these considerations *no longer apply.* A criterion test represents a critical job performance. Each test, each part of a test, or each test item must be completed successfully in accordance with the prescribed standard. The average difficulty of these items must be set at or near 1.00. Because all trainees must perform at the established level, discrimination indexes for criterion measures and test items have no real significance. However, the underlying basis for the concept of discrimination is adequately controlled by the go, no-go criterion.

Figure 6-5.   The normal bell-shaped distribution curve showing the approximate percentage of cases falling within certain portions of the curve.

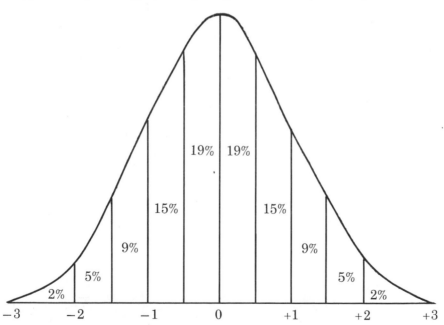

MEASURES OF CENTRAL TENDENCY

Measures of central tendency indicate how the typical testee performed on the test. These measures include the mean, the median, and the mode.

The Mean. The mean, or average score, is computed by adding the individual scores and dividing by the total number of scores, or $M = \Sigma fx/N$. Using the data depicted in Figure 6-6, the mean score is 73.52

where M = mean
$\quad\quad f$ = frequency
$\quad\quad x$ = score
$\quad\quad N$ = total number of scores

Because criterion tests are designed to test only essential knowledge and skills, the mean should be at or near the maximum possible score. Otherwise there is a fault in the test or in the instructional strategy. However, because of the inescapable matter of human error, or an occasional poorly motivated trainee, the mean score may be lowered appreciably by one or two radically low scores. For this reason, a second measure of central tendency must be calculated.

The median. This is the score that divides all scores into two equal parts; that is, the median is the middle score in a group of scores arranged in order of decreasing magnitude. This score is less affected by extremely high or low scores and provides a better measure of the effectiveness of the test. The median score must be at or near the level of mastery (a per-

Figure 6-6.   A frequency distribution of scores.

Test score	Tally	*f*	*fx*
86	/	1	86
84	//	2	168
80	/	1	80
78	///	3	234
74	//// ///	8	592
70	////	5	350
69	/	1	69
67	//	2	134
65	/	1	65
60	/	1	60
Total		25	1,838

fect score) for the same reasons that the mean should be nearly perfect. For the score distribution shown in Figure 6-6, the median is 74 (the thirteenth score).

The mode. The mode is the most common score; the score most frequently attained by testees. In Figure 6-6, the mode is 74. This measure is not particularly useful unless the number of scores is very large.

MEASURES OF VARIATION

Knowing the typical score on a test is not enough, because two groups of trainees may have the same or similar means or medians, but the spread, scatter, variability, or deviation of the scores around the average is usually different. The range and the standard deviation are commonly used to describe this spread.

The range. The range is the distance from the highest to the lowest scores in a series of scores. The formula usually used for its calculation is as follows:

$$r = h - l + 1$$

where $r =$ range
$h =$ highest score
$l =$ lowest score

In Figure 6-6, the range is $86 - 60 + 1 = 27$. On a criterion test the range should approach zero but can easily be much larger if only one testee fails to perform satisfactorily.

The standard deviation. This valuable statistic is derived by mathematical formula from either a frequency distribution or grouped data. It shows how the scores on the test distribute themselves around the mean score. The calculation of the standard deviation for a distribution of scores is shown in Figure 6-7. Other formulas for calculating the standard deviation from grouped data can be found in any standard measurement or statistics book.

Procedures for the calculation of the standard deviation of the distribution of scores shown in Figure 6-7 are as follows:

1. Make a frequency distribution listing scores on the test from highest to lowest (columns 1 and 2).
2. Multiply each test score by its frequency (column 1 multiplied by column 2).
3. Add the fx column (column 3) and divide by the total number of scores (column 2) to calculate the mean (in this case 1,742/20 or 87.1).

4. Find the deviation from the mean of each score by subtracting the mean from the score. Deviations of scores lower than the mean score appear as negative numbers (column 4).
5. Square each deviation (column 5).
6. Multiply each squared deviation (column 5) by the frequency (column 2) to obtain fd^2 (column 6).
7. Sum the fd^2 (column 6).
8. Divide the fd^2 sum (column 6) by the number of scores (column 2).
9. Extract the square root of the quotient obtained in step 8.

The formula corresponding to these steps is as follows:

$$\text{Standard deviation } (s) = \sqrt{\frac{\Sigma fd^2}{N}}$$

where Σ = sum of
       f = frequencies
       d = deviations from the mean
       N = number of scores

Figure 6-7. *Calculation of the standard deviation from a frequency distribution.*

Test score	f	fx	d	d^2	fd^2
1	2	3	4	5	6
102	1	102	14.9	222.01	222.01
100	1	100	12.9	166.41	166.41
98	1	98	10.9	118.81	118.81
96	2	192	8.9	79.21	158.42
94	1	94	6.9	47.61	47.61
93	1	93	5.9	34.81	34.81
90	2	180	2.9	8.41	16.82
87	1	87	−0.1	.01	.01
85	1	85	−2.1	4.41	4.41
84	3	252	−3.1	9.61	28.83
83	1	83	−4.1	16.81	16.81
80	1	80	−7.1	50.41	50.41
76	2	152	−11.1	123.21	246.42
74	1	74	−13.1	171.61	171.61
70	1	70	−17.1	292.41	292.41
Total	20	1,742			1,575.80

or
$$s = \sqrt{\frac{1{,}575.80}{20}}$$

$$= \sqrt{78.79}$$

$$= \quad 8.88$$

A simplified formula[1] for finding the standard deviation, accurate enough for most purposes, is as follows:

$$\text{Standard deviation} = \frac{\text{Sum of the high sixth} - \text{sum of the low sixth}}{\text{Half the number of testees}}$$

Using the data in Figure 6-7, the calculation is as follows:

$$s = \frac{364 - 271}{10} = \frac{93}{10} = 9.3$$

[The top sixth includes the top 3⅔ scores (102 + 100 + 98 + 64 = 364). The low sixth includes the low 3⅔ scores (70 + 74 + 76 + 51 = 271).]

TEST VALIDITY

In the case of achievement measures, the validity of a test, that is, the extent to which it measures what it is supposed to measure, is a very difficult characteristic to prove. Validity is best determined by comparing test results with some outside criterion or standard. Procedures for estimating the validity of a test range from relatively straightforward comparison of the test, its parts, and individual items with the objectives of the training system to the computation of validity indexes by complex statistical procedures. However, the ultimate measure of the validity of a test of ability to perform job tasks is the graduate's ability to perform satisfactorily on the job for which he has been trained. This aspect of test validity is discussed in Chapter 16.

At this point in the development of a training system, however, it must be assumed that the tests are valid. This assumption is safe since most criterion tests are performance tests, and the standards for these tests have been taken directly from the job data.

The only real question of test validity relates to tests which involve

[1] From *Short-cut Statistics for Teacher-made Tests (Second Edition)* by Paul B. Diederich. Copyright © 1960, 1964 by Educational Testing Service. All rights reserved.

the determination of the degree to which trainees have acquired the necessary job knowledge supports—the facts, concepts, and principles that underpin job performance.

The validity of these tests must be estimated by people who are completely familiar with the job and its requirements, and who can exercise judgment about the relationship between the tests and the job knowledges the training program is designed to develop.

Reliability of the Test

Certain statistical measures are used to estimate how consistently a test measures the job ability or knowledge it is supposed to measure. No outside criterion (such as later performance on the job) is required because test reliability is not related to the nature of the things measured by the test. In any event, statistical calculations of test reliability provide systems designers with one basis for judging the worth of a test and determining how much confidence can be placed in its results. Two measures can be used to determine reliability: the coefficient of reliability and the standard error of measurement.

Coefficient of reliability. The reliability of a test depends primarily on three factors: the number of test items, the standard deviation, and the mean (average). The following formula[2] can be used to calculate the reliability of an objective test in which all items are weighted equally and in which speed of performance is not a consideration:

$$\text{Reliability} = \frac{ns^2 - M(n - M)}{ns^2} \text{ (Kuder-Richardson formula 21)}$$

where n = the number of test items
 s = the standard deviation
 M = the mean

Another method for calculating the coefficient of reliability is called the *split-half method.* The test is scored in two parts as well as in total. That is, separate scores are calculated for the total test, for odd-numbered test items, and for even-numbered test items. It is important that all items in the test be independent, that success on a test item in one half of the test does not help with items in the other half. The formula is as follows:

$$r_{tt} = 2 \left(\frac{1 - s_a^2 + s_b^2}{s_t^2} \right) \text{ (Spearman-Brown formula)}$$

[2] *Ibid.* p. 30.

where s_a = the standard deviation of the first half of the test
(odd-numbered items)
s_b = the standard deviation of the second half of the test
(even-numbered items)
s_t = the standard deviation of the total test

Ideally, the reliability coefficient should approximate +1.00 for a criterion measure. In actual practice, a reliability of over +0.85 is very acceptable.

If the test does not reach these standards, and if other sources of unreliability, such as nonstandard instructions, scoring errors, nonuniform test conditions, guessing, or individual chance fluctuations, have been investigated and found to be unlikely sources of error, the test may be lengthened (by adding test items) to increase reliability. Use of the following formula[3] will indicate the number of times the test must be lengthened to get the desired reliability:

$$\frac{(\text{The reliability you want}) \times (1 - \text{the reliability you got})}{(\text{The reliability you got}) \times (1 - \text{the reliability you want})}$$

For example, if you want a reliability of 0.95 and you get 0.80,

$$\frac{0.95 \times (1 - 0.80)}{0.80 \times (1 - 0.95)} = \frac{0.95 \times 0.20}{0.80 \times 0.05} = \frac{0.1900}{0.0400} = 4.7 \text{ or } 5 \text{ times longer}$$

The standard error of measurement. The scores that testees make on a test should never be considered exact. Measurement errors tend to move scores upward or downward from the theoretical "true" mean. Furthermore, measurement errors introduce a questionable area around each estimated "true" score. The size of this area is indicated by the standard error of measurement. Therefore, an individual's score should be considered to lie within a band of scores on the total score continuum. The width of this band depends upon the size of the standard error of measurement. It is important to note that the standard error of measurement is always expressed in the score units of the test. Therefore, this statistic can only be used in making judgments about the reliability of scores and score differences on a given test, and cannot be used to make comparisons between different tests.

The standard error of measurement is calculated by using the following formula:[4]

$$\sigma \text{ meas} = \sigma_1 \sqrt{1 - r_{11}}$$

[3] *Ibid.* p. 32.
[4] Jum C. Nunnally, Jr. *Tests and Measurements.* New York: McGraw-Hill Book Company, 1959, p. 101.

where σ meas = the standard error of measurement

$\quad\quad\quad \sigma_1$ = the standard deviation of the test

$\quad\quad\quad r_{11}$ = the reliability coefficient of the test

For example, for a test with a standard deviation of 5 and a reliability coefficient of 0.90, the standard error of measurement would be calculated as follows:

$$\begin{aligned}
\sigma \text{ meas} &= 5 \sqrt{1 - 0.90} \\
&= 5 \sqrt{0.10} \\
&= 5 \times 0.3162 \\
&= 1.5810 \text{ or } 1.58
\end{aligned}$$

The standard error of measurement ideally should approach zero. In actuality, a standard error of measurement up to 5.0 is acceptable on a test of approximately 100 items.

Mean Difficulty

The mean difficulty of a test is an index of the overall difficulty of the test items that make up the measure. It is calculated by finding the average of the percentage scores. This statistic gives the analyst an index of average testee achievement in terms of the percentage of test items answered correctly. In addition, the mean difficulty is an estimate of the difficulty of the total test.

For a criterion test, the mean difficulty of the test should be close to 1.00. However, practically, a mean difficulty of over 0.90 is acceptable.

Test Item Characteristics

The three statistical indexes customarily used to determine the worth of individual test items are the item difficulty, item discrimination, and the graphic item count. Discrimination indexes for tests and test items in criterion measures have no significance, as pointed out earlier in this chapter. Therefore, only item difficulty and the GIC will be discussed.

Item difficulty. The percentage of testees answering any given item correctly is the difficulty of the item. An item having a difficulty of 0.30 is a hard item; one having a difficulty of 0.90 or higher is an easy item. As with mean difficulty, item difficulty should be at or near 1.00, although an index of over 0.90 is considered acceptable.

The graphic item count. Where a test involves alternative answers (multiple choice), a count of the number of testees selecting each alternative may be made. The GIC can be used to analyze individual test items to determine where the test or a subgroup of testees went wrong. These data are valuable as a basis for revising the test or for providing remedial assistance. A part of a GIC for an achievement test is shown in Figure 6-8.

Figure 6-8. A graphic item count for the first nine questions on a 120-item multiple-choice test.

Item number	Alternatives				Correct answer	Item difficulty
	A	B	C	D		
1		5	19		C	79
2	23	1			A	96
3			1	23	D	96
4	1	21	2		B	88
5	5	13	5	1	A	21
6	5	13	5	1	B	54
7	8	9	4	3	A	33
8	9	7	6	2	A	38
9	1		20	3	C	83

STEPS IN ANALYZING A TEST

Following the administration of a test to a representative sample of trainees, the following analytical steps should be followed:

Step 1. Make a frequency distribution of test scores.

Step 2. Find the median and the mean scores.

Step 3. Determine the range and standard deviation.

Step 4. Calculate the reliability of the test.

Step 5. Calculate the standard error of measurement.

Step 6. Determine the mean difficulty of each item and the mean difficulty of the total test.

Step 7. Make a graphic item count.

Step 8. Revise the criterion measure as indicated by the performance of the test as a whole and individual items within it.

SELECTED REFERENCES

Adams, Georgia Sachs. *Measurement and Evaluation.* New York: Holt, Rinehart and Winston, Inc., 1964, Chap. 10.

Anastasi, Anne, ed. *Testing Problems in Perspective.* Washington, D.C.: American Council on Education, 1966, Chap. 4.

Courts, Frederick A. *Psychological Statistics: An Introduction.* Homewood, Ill.: The Dorsey Press, 1966.

Cronbach, Lee J. *Essentials of Psychological Testing,* 2d ed. New York: Harper & Brothers, 1960, Chap. 2, 5, 13.

Davis, Frederick B. *Educational Measurements and Their Interpretation.* Belmont, Calif.: Wadsworth Publishing Company, Inc., 1964, Chaps. 5 and 12.

Diederich, Paul B. *Short-cut Statistics for Teacher-made Tests,* 2d ed. Princeton, N.J.: Educational Testing Service, 1964.

Ebel, Robert L. *Measuring Educational Achievement.* Englewood Cliffs, N.J.: Prentice-Hall, Inc., 1965, Chaps. 3, 6, and 11.

Educational Testing Service. *Multiple-Choice Questions: A Close Look.* Princeton, N.J.: Educational Testing Service, 1963.

Kolstoe, Ralph H. *Introduction to Statistics for the Behavioral Sciences.* Homewood, Ill.: The Dorsey Press, 1969.

Melching, William H. et al. *A Handbook for Programmers of Automated Instruction.* Alexandria, Va.: George Washington University Human Resources Research Office (Sept. 1, 1963), Chap. 4.

Noll, Victor H. *Introduction to Educational Measurement,* 2d ed. Boston: Houghton Mifflin Company, 1965, Chaps. 6 and 7.

Nunnally, Jum C., Jr. *Educational Measurement and Evaluation.* New York: McGraw-Hill Book Company, 1964, Chaps. 1–7.

Remmers, H. H., N. L. Gage, and J. Francis Rummel. *A Practical Introduction to Measurement and Evaluation.* New York: Harper & Row, Publishers, Incorporated, 1965, Chaps. 5–8.

Smith, Robert G., Jr. *Controlling the Quality of Training.* Alexandria, Va.: George Washington University Human Resources Research Office, June 1965.

Stodola, Quentin, et al. *Making the Classroom Test,* 2d ed. Princeton, N.J.: Educational Testing Service, 1961.

Tracey, William R. *Evaluating Training and Development Systems.* AMA, 1968, Chap. V.

Wood, Dorothy Adkins. *Test Construction.* Columbus, Ohio: Charles E. Merrill Books, Inc., 1961, Chaps. 3–7.

Youmans, Charles V. "Testing for Training and Development." In Robert L. Craig and Lester R. Bittel, eds. *Training and Development Handbook.* New York: McGraw-Hill Book Company, 1967, Chap. 4.

7

Selecting and
Sequencing Course Content

T HE emphasis up to this point has been placed on how the trainee should perform following exposure to the training system. Reference to the content or learning activities per se has been deliberately avoided. Now that performance has been clearly described, the knowledge, skills, and values which support each performance objective, and the sequence in which they should be developed, can be identified. Essentially, the job is twofold: first, to examine each performance objective and identify the specific facts, concepts, principles, skills, and operations involved in each task; and second, to arrange the teaching points and learning activities in the best sequence for learning.

The purpose of this chapter is to describe these steps. Although the processes of selecting and sequencing content are closely related and interwoven, for purposes of clarity each process will be described and discussed separately.

Upon completing this chapter, the reader should be able to perform as follows:

Behavior   Select the facts, concepts, principles, skills, and operations required by trainees to perform a specific job.

Conditions   Given: Job Analysis Reports, including training objectives in performance terms, guides for the identification of knowledge supports, subject-matter reference materials, access to subject-matter experts, and clerical assistance.

Criterion   In accordance with the standards defined in this chapter.

Behavior   Place the content in the proper sequence for efficient learning.

Conditions   Given: sequencing guides and a breakdown of the training system in the form of Performance Objective Workcards and detailed content outlines; the assistance of subject-matter experts; and clerical help.

Criterion   In accordance with the standards prescribed in this chapter.

CONTENT SELECTION

The term content refers to subject matter, teaching points, or learnings that enable the trainee to perform the tasks, duties, and jobs that are the terminal objectives of training and development systems. Essentially, content comprises knowledge, habits, elements of skill, and emotionalized controls.

1. Knowledge consists of facts, concepts, principles, meanings, understandings, and ideas. Examples are nomenclature and terminology, such as those relating to equipment and processes; symbols, such as map symbols, and mathematical or scientific notation; scientific principles, such as those involved in electronics repair; concepts, such as supervisory authority and responsibility; understandings, such as safety precautions, step-by-step precedures, and enterprise rules.

2. Habits are acquired tendencies to act in a certain way when certain conditions are present in the environment. Examples include observing safety precautions and showing concern for the feelings of subordinates.

3. Skills are behaviors that require some degree of facility in the performance of part or all of a complex act. Speed and accuracy are usually required. Skills may be either mental or motor. Examples are public speaking, technical writing, typing, equipment operation, soldering, troubleshooting, repairing, communicating, leading, and problem solving.

4. Emotionalized controls are attitudes, ideals, interests, and appreciations that influence or control other types of behavior.

     a. An attitude is a person's predisposition or sentiment toward other persons, objects, institutions, practices, or ideas. Examples are respect, obedience, open-mindedness, receptiveness to change, and tolerance.

b. An ideal is a standard, often of perfection, relating to persons, traits, objects, or ideas, that is accepted by an individual or group. Examples are standards of managership, leadership, and craftsmanship.

c. An interest is an acquired concern for or about objects, persons, processes, or ideas. A degree of excitement of feeling usually accompanies attention to or perception of the object of the interest.

d. An appreciation is a recognition and comprehension of value in some person, group, trait, object, idea, or process. Examples are appreciation of work, of modern art, of national traditions, of democratic institutions.

Because habits and emotionalized controls are more likely to be concomitant learnings, rather than the direct result of instruction, only knowledge and skills will be addressed here. This should not be construed as a denial of the importance of these outcomes. Rather, it is an admission that such learnings are most likely to be acquired by trainees who have been exposed to a well-designed training system and to the example of able training and development personnel.

SUBJECT-MATTER CHARACTERISTICS

In designing an instructional system, the trainer must identify, organize, and sequence the subject matter to be taught. The area of knowledge must be divided into the specific facts, principles, concepts, and elements of skill. These learnings must then be organized into units which provide the building blocks by which the trainees acquire the knowledge, skills, and emotionalized controls required for acceptable job performance.

Each subject-matter area has intrinsic characteristics which significantly affect the way in which it can be analyzed and organized for learning. Some subjects, such as mathematics, are relatively easy to analyze and organize because they are exact, systematic, and logically ordered. Other subjects, such as the social sciences, are less precise, more difficult to define and analyze, and hence much harder to organize. Characteristics of the various types of subject matters most closely related to the content of training and development systems are defined in the paragraphs that follow.

Sciences. The sciences, both physical and biological, are among the easiest to define and organize. The content of the sciences consists of objective, empirically verifiable facts and principles. The systems designer, therefore, has a firm basis for selecting the material to be included in the training program. In training and development, subject matter in this category is often found in training programs designed for technicians, engineers, and scientists. However, almost every training and development program contains some scientific content.

Mathematics. In many ways, mathematics content is the simplest to analyze and organize. Mathematical concepts, principles, and facts are all logically related, and they have been exactly defined. The required mathematical skills and knowledge can therefore be specified with considerable precision. In addition, mathematics is not subject to frequent or radical content changes. For this reason, it can be considered a relatively stable subject matter. Mathematical content, like scientific subject matter, is likely to be a part of most training and development programs, although its greatest use is found in training programs for technicians, engineers, and scientists.

Social sciences. Except for certain aspects of psychology and economics, the social sciences lack the clear definition and precision of mathematics and the physical and biological sciences. Terminology also varies considerably in the social sciences, and there are few standard authorities. In addition, the social sciences overlap. For example, it is impossible to define where psychology and sociology end, and where supervision and management begin. Nearly every important management principle is essentially a distillation of subjective and normative judgments. For these reasons, subject matter related to the social sciences cannot be easily broken down into small component units which can then be organized and sequenced as building blocks are. This combination of characteristics poses serious problems for training and development systems designers. They must find authoritative assistance in defining the subject-matter area to be covered, the meaning of terms, and the best way of selecting the subject matter to be taught. Sales training, human relations training, supervisory training, and management and executive development are heavily weighted with social science content. However, all training programs are likely to include some content in this category.

Industrial, business, and military arts, crafts, and skills. The various subjects which make up the great bulk of training programs in business, industry, and the military can be defined and organized with relative ease. Job and task analysis provides the skeleton which is later fleshed out with the required subject matter. The theoretical portion of the subject matter typically consists of scientific and mathematical facts and principles. The elements of skill, however, make up the major part of the subject matter to be taught. It is important to note that it is easy to include theoretical knowledge that is not needed for satisfactory job performance. Great care must be taken by the systems designer to avoid including nonessential materials. This is the category of subject matter most commonly found in training and development. Trade and semiskills, safety, and technical training are examples.

Sources of Content

There are two basic sources of content for training and development systems: They are job data (Job Analysis Reports, and Performance Objective Workcards, Fig. 4-3) and documents (organization and function manuals, policy manuals, standard operating procedures, technical manuals, operator or maintenance manuals, standard reference books, textbooks, periodicals, and the like). Documentary sources are complementary and supporting sources of content, but the primary source of training system content must always be the job data.

Job data, or more specifically, job tasks, must be subjected to detailed analysis to identify the facts, principles, concepts, and elements of skill required to support acceptable performance of the job. In selecting specific training system content, the following criteria should be applied: (1) the content must be relevant to the job; that is, it must be directly related to an element of performance identified by task analysis; (2) the content must be important to the development of the required performance; that is, without the knowledge or element of skill, the trainee could not perform the task satisfactorily.

Documents used to support training and development systems must also meet certain standards: (1) they must be authoritative; (2) they must be consistent with the position and approach of the enterprise; and (3) they must not conflict with approved policies or procedures.

Types of Tasks

Job analysis produces a list of tasks essential to the performance of a job, but task descriptions alone do not provide the degree of detail needed to select the subject matter necessary to their performance.

Although there is no standard and agreed-upon classification of tasks, Smith[1] has identified types of tasks associated with three major groups of jobs: operator, maintenance, and clerical and administrative.

[1] Robert G. Smith, Jr., *The Design of Instructional Systems*, HumRRO Technical Report 66-18. Alexandria, Va.: George Washington University Human Resources Research Office, November, 1966, pp. 32–42.

But there is an additional category: supervisory and managerial tasks. Various types of tasks are listed under each of these headings in the paragraphs that follow:

Operator tasks. Operator tasks are tasks associated with the operation of equipment. (They may also include things that managers must do themselves.)

Fixed procedures. These are tasks characterized by an identical series of elements, each of which is performed in the same order each time the task is performed. Pilot preflight checks are examples of fixed procedures.

Variable procedures. These tasks are characterized at some point by choice about which of several elements to apply—for example, first-aid procedures.

Discrete tasks. These are tasks which can be divided into clearly separate elements. For example, operating a computer involves a series of separate task elements.

Continuous tasks. These are tasks which cannot be divided into separate elements when performed. Examples are flying an airplane and interviewing.

Tracking tasks. These tasks involve maintaining a directional or spatial relationship between an operator's equipment and some moving object; for example, tracking a target.

Aiming tasks. These tasks require the operator to bring equipment into linear relationship with a stationary target; for example, aligning the marker with a desired station by moving it along the frequency scale of a radio or adjusting the vernier on a micrometer or sextant.

Searching tasks. These tasks involve actively looking for cues in the work environment; for example, conducting a safety inspection.

Scanning tasks. These tasks involve searching for cues subsidiary (but related) to the activity of the moment; for example, scanning the instrument panel of a vehicle while driving.

Discrimination tasks. These tasks involve observing cues that will cause the operator to take different actions—for example, noting changes in the color of processed materials.

Noise filtering tasks. In these tasks the relevant cue is partially obscured by irrelevant cues and the task is to filter out the "noise" so that the appropriate cues may be attended to—for example, a pilot listening to the air controller through static.

Short-term remembering tasks. These tasks involve the recall of facts or procedures for short periods of time; for example, remembering the responses made by an interviewee.

Long-term remembering tasks. These tasks involve recall of facts or procedures for long periods of time; for example, remembering mathematical formulas, resistor color codes, or standing operating procedures.

Coding tasks. These are tasks that involve the use of codes and symbols; for example, map reading, blueprint reading, electronic symbols, mathematical symbols, Morse code, the phonetic alphabet, or computer codes.

Decision-making and problem-solving tasks. These tasks are performed on the basis of complex factors and involving a goal to be reached and the selection of a path to the goal. Sometimes the goal itself must be selected. In any event, the task involves identifying facts and assumptions, noting available alternatives and their implications, establishing criteria for choosing actions, applying criteria or rules for selecting a solution, and fixing priorities.

Maintenance tasks. There is no sharp division between operator and maintenance tasks. Both require procedures, problem solving, identification, the use of codes, and other similar task elements. However, mechanics, repairmen, and technicians have some unique and identifiable tasks.

Preventive maintenance tasks. These tasks involve periodic inspections of equipment, repairs, and routine servicing performed according to a time schedule or after a certain number of hours of operation. For example, dusting, cleaning, painting, lubricating, and engine changes are usually scheduled tasks.

Normal operating and checking tasks. These are similar or even identical to operator tasks involving either fixed or variable procedures of preventive maintenance, verifying operator's reports of malfunctions, and the like.

Adjustment tasks. These tasks involve making adjustments to equipment or procedures during preventive maintenance checks or troubleshooting.

Troubleshooting tasks. These tasks involve the identification of malfunctioning components in equipment or systems. In many respects these tasks are similar to problem-solving or decision-making tasks.

Repair or replacement tasks. These tasks occur when the malfunctioning component has been identified and localized. The component may have to be repaired or replaced. Fixed procedures are usually involved in these tasks.

Clerical and administrative tasks.[2] There is no sharp line of demarcation between operative and clerical and administrative tasks. In fact, much of the material pertaining to operator tasks also applies to the

[2] The author assumes full responsibility for this discussion of clerical and administrative tasks, since Smith (*op. cit.*) identified only the general group of clerical and administrative tasks and not the specific tasks themselves.

present category. Some tasks involve fixed procedures; more involve variable procedures.

Typing tasks. Many clerical and administrative jobs involve typing, although the standards of performance are usually lower than those established for typists, secretarial personnel, and stenographers. Examples of typing tasks include preparing routine interoffice correspondence and completing forms and records.

Filing tasks. These tasks involve cataloging, indexing, and physically placing materials in containers in accordance with an established filing system.

Recording tasks. These tasks involve making entries in various records, completing forms and simple reports, tabulating, and making relatively simple calculations in accordance with detailed instructions.

Operating tasks. These tasks involve the operation of simple office machines, including duplicators, photocopiers, stapling machines, paper punches, and the like.

Supervisory and managerial tasks. Many of the types of tasks identified as operator, maintenance, and administrative and clerical tasks have their counterparts in supervisory and managerial jobs. Of course, the degree of difficulty and complexity in the performance of supervisory and managerial tasks is considerably greater. Generally, these tasks can be cataloged under the five functions of supervisors and managers. It should be noted that, in addition to the tasks listed below, all the functions of the manager or supervisor involve decision-making tasks.

Planning tasks. Planning tasks involve assessing the status of an activity, predicting the environment of the future, establishing goals, anticipating obstacles, and designing strategies to overcome obstacles to the achievement of the desired results. Examples are establishing objectives, policies, plans, procedures, rules, and programs; preparing budgets; and making personnel, product, or other types of forecasts.

Organizing tasks. These tasks involve identifying the activities and skills required to perform needed enterprise functions, grouping these activities into logical subdivisions, delegating authority, and clarifying authority relationships. Examples are establishing or changing the organization structure, preparing an organization and functions manual, and developing job descriptions and applicant specifications.

Staffing tasks. These tasks involve actions relating to the acquisition, training, and assignment of personnel, including recruiting, selecting, training, promoting, retiring, and terminating employees. Examples are employment interviewing, counseling, and coaching.

Directing tasks. These tasks involve various means of getting maximum performance from employees. Examples are delegating, motivating, guiding, and communicating.

Controlling tasks. These are tasks that aim to insure that performance conforms with plans. They apply to persons, equipment, and processes. Examples are establishing standards (cost, time, quantity, or quality), appraising performance, reviewing and acting on reports, and preventing (or remedying) deficiencies.

GUIDELINES FOR IDENTIFYING KNOWLEDGE REQUIREMENTS

As noted earlier, items of knowledge to be included in training and development programs must be derived from the task and element descriptions prepared after job analysis. These knowledges must help the trainee to perform the task. They should not be taught simply because they have been traditionally included in training programs. The following guidelines[3] should be applied by the systems designer in identifying the knowledge supports for task elements, tasks, and duties.

1. *When nomenclature and locations of objects must be known.* If the trainee is to be able to relate symbols to ideas, or symbols to action, he must have a vocabulary of terms. For this reason, practice in naming and locating work objects, tools, or cues is essential.

2. *When the trainee must know what to search for in the job environment.* By learning the cues, objects, indicators, controls, and aids he must search for, the trainee can actively take part in learning the job. For example, in electronic equipment repair, the trainee must be taught what manuals, test equipment, and other aids will help him to perform a particular task. In management development, the trainee must be taught to identify barriers to communication.

3. *When precautions are necessary.* A precaution warns the trainee to inhibit, take, or avoid some action which might be a hazard to himself, to others, or to equipment and material. For example, safety precautions to observe in operating cutting tools and statements and questions to avoid in employment interviewing should be identified and taught.

4. *When interpretation of symbols or signals is necessary.* In many tasks, the trainee must use and interpret standard codes or sets of symbols or signals. Map symbols and resistor color codes are examples, as

[3] Robert B. Miller and Harold P. Van Cott. *The Determination of Knowledge Content for Complex Man-Machine Jobs.* Pittsburgh, Pa.: American Institutes for Research, December, 1955.

are certain verbal and nonverbal cues in employee counseling. These must be identified as knowledges.

5. *When procedures must be learned for emergency situations not feasible to simulate.* Although the most effective way to acquire a skill is to practice the actual response required by the situation, there are circumstances when reproducing the actual conditions is not feasible. At other times providing enough practice to make the response automatic is not practical. In such cases verbal descriptions of the required response are necessary substitutes. For example, bail-out procedures for aviators, learned as statements of actions to be performed, are essential substitutes for practice of the procedures.

6. *When calculations have to be performed.* Performing calculations is a special form of problem solving. Training requirements identified as computations should be specified as precise problems trainees must be able to solve. For example, it has long been assumed that an electronic equipment repairman must "know" algebra. But, in many cases it is sufficient for him to be able to remember and use the precise formulas needed on the job. These formulas should be taught.

7. *When problem solving, diagnosis, and troubleshooting are required.* These activities consist of a series of decisions, such as the series of checks to make in localizing a trouble from symptoms. Each activity involves a choice from among several alternative responses. The alternatives available must be recalled, as well as the consequences of choosing each of the alternatives. General rules or principles concerning the efficiency of alternatives are important items of knowledge. An analysis of a problem-solving situation should focus on the following factors:

a. What cues will the trainee use to identify the problem as being of a particular type that calls for a given method of solution?
b. What are the criteria or standards for an acceptable solution?
c. What are the principal factors in the problem to consider? These variables will be related to, or identical with, the criterion variables of an acceptable solution. Usually some criteria will be more important than others.
d. What are the principal alternatives available?
e. What series of steps can the trainee take to increase the amount of information he has? This implies a series of decisions and the development of tentative solutions, rather than a single complete plan of action. The trainee must be taught how to explore for information relevant to a given situation. He should be taught to do this in a way that will provide him with the maximum of useful information for each successive action he takes.

f. What errors should the trainee especially guard against? These will tend to be irreversible errors, such as actions leading to burning out of equipment, the quitting of an employee, or the unnecessary commitment of equipment or personnel to a job.

8. *When the operator or mechanic must anticipate later conditions from earlier conditions.* Some forms of anticipation are an important kind of knowledge. The nature of present circumstances often helps the trainee to decide what to do later. These cause-and-effect relationships may help to anticipate a future effect from various present conditions, or conversely, to deduce a probable cause from a given effect. For example, when a helicopter pilot can anticipate that his descent on a patch of desert at noon will be more rapid than a similar descent on a green area (due to differences in air density), we have an example of a knowledge.

9. *When planning is required in position activities.* Planning usually is advance preparation to insure that people, equipment, and materials are in the right place at the right time. Examples are laying out tools and materials in an efficient work arrangement, and laying out parts in such a way as to avoid confusion or loss. How to make such plans is a knowledge requirement.

10. *When strategies are required.* A strategy is a series of maneuvers based in part on one's own capability and in part on the capabilities and responses of an adversary. The essential knowledges consist of one's own capabilities with respect to the adversary at any given time, and the procedures by which the adversary's capabilities and options can be reduced (or at least reveal his intentions). For example, in marketing new products the advertising strategy to be applied is critical. The elements of the strategy are knowledges.

11. *When the operator or mechanic must act in accordance with briefing instructions.* Many of the knowledges previously discussed have operational significance in understanding briefing information and carrying out instructions. Briefing on mission or assignments is a phase of operations that may be neglected in the identification of training requirements. Operators must frequently make individual plans, anticipations, calculations, interpretations, and decisions that are consistent with statements of objectives, procedures, and conditions. Types and forms of briefing data, and their contents, should therefore be examined for clues to knowledge content.

12. *When inventions and improvisations are required.* An improvisation is the adaptation of an object or technique commonly used for one purpose to serve another purpose. An invention is the construction of some "new" object, contrivance, or procedure to fulfill the requirements

of some purpose. The need to invent and improvise is rarely identified as a job requirement, but the development of these capabilities provides a margin of safety in job performance. The knowledge required for improvisation includes the functional requirements of equipment parts as they relate to the functional capabilities of objects likely to be available as substitutes in the work environment.

13. *When ideas and knowledge will simplify training.* The previous factors have generally dealt with knowledge which would be of use to personnel working on the job. There may also be some ideas, concepts, and knowledge which will help trainees to learn the job. These are statements which permit many ideas and actions to be associated with each other, so that what seems complex becomes simple. An example is an organization chart which helps trainees to learn the interrelationships of authority and responsibility in an organization.

14. *When identification and recognition of objects and complex signals are required.* Recognition of certain types of objects and signals is often necessarily taught separately. Examples are aircraft recognition and radarscope interpretation. The defining characteristics of these objects and signals are required knowledge.

15. *When use of tools and general test instruments is required.* If a tool is to be used in only one task, it is best taught as an integral part of that task. However, many tools are employed in a variety of tasks. In this case trainees can be taught generalized skills in using tools instead of being taught use of the same tools over and over as they are needed in each task. There are many tricks of the trade in the use of common tools. There are also abuses to avoid. These knowledges and manipulative skills can be identified and taught.

The Process of Content Selection

The act of identifying the facts, concepts, principles, and skills that support a performance is comparable to the process of outlining the "points to be taught" in a conventional lesson plan. The essential difference is that the content selector has a list of specific statements of required performance rather than such vague guides as "to provide a working knowledge" of some subject. That the systems designer has a set of performance objectives permits him to focus on training outcomes and identify the content of each lesson more precisely. This does not mean, however, that the presence of performance objectives makes content selection a mechanical process, but it does simplify the job and removes most of the guesswork.

OUTLINING COURSE CONTENT

The usual procedure is to prepare a rough draft of the outline, indicating the major subject-matter areas to be covered, and then gradually expanding the outline until a detailed statement of content is produced. Some designers prepare a two-dimensional matrix in which training objectives are listed on one axis and the content categories are listed on the other axis. In the resulting cells the specific facts, concepts, principles, and skills needed to achieve the objectives are inserted.

PITFALLS

In developing content outlines, care must be taken to avoid the following:
1. Leaving out important parts of the subject matter.
2. Overemphasizing topics that do not merit detailed treatment.
3. Allowing unnecessary duplication or overlapping in the material presented.

These pitfalls can be avoided by consulting with subject-matter experts and by studying documentary materials. Periodic review of outlines during development will also help to indicate omissions, duplication, and overlap.

STEPS IN CONTENT SELECTION

The following steps should be followed in selecting training system content:

Step 1. Using the fifteen guidelines for identifying knowledge requirements presented in an earlier part of this chapter, examine each performance objective and develop separate topical outlines for each task. Include all the major knowledge and skills required to achieve the specified performance. The product of this step is a complete outline of the required learnings for each job task. That is, every major concept, principle, skill, or value required for demonstration of each objective is listed, regardless of the fact that duplicate items may appear under two or more objectives.

Step 2. Submit the topical outline to subject-matter experts for a check of completeness and accuracy. The purpose of this step is not to review for detail, but rather to insure that major items of content required for performance have been included and that nonessential content has been omitted.

Step 3. Revise the topical outline in accordance with the recommendations of the subject-matter experts.

Step 4. Develop a detailed content outline for each topical outline or performance objective. Each item in the preliminary topical outline should be analyzed, and the teaching points should be formulated in declarative statements, using appropriate references.

Step 5. Eliminate unnecessary duplication within the detailed points to be taught. If a teaching point essential to the development of a concept or skill later in the sequence duplicates a teaching point developed earlier, identify it as a review item of content.

Step 6. Compare the refined content outlines with the Performance Objective Workcards. Make whatever final adjustments seem to be indicated.

Step 7. Submit the detailed content outlines to subject-matter experts for final review.

Step 8. Revise the content outlines as indicated by the reports of the reviewers.

SEQUENCING

Sequencing is the process by which the content and learning experiences are placed in the configuration which will produce the most learning in the shortest possible time. Adequate sequencing insures that component and supporting knowledge and skills have been developed before the complete behavior is demonstrated. Proper sequencing guarantees that prerequisite knowledge and skills have been acquired by the trainees prior to the introduction of advanced content or skills.

APPROACHES TO ORGANIZATION

Should the material or content be treated analytically or synthetically? This problem must be faced by all systems designers. The analytic or deductive approach to organization begins with the statement of a concept or principle. Its meaning, operation, and application are then revealed by gradually reducing it to its component parts. The synthetic approach to organization is the converse. It begins with illustrations, applications, and examination of the parts, and ends with the generalization or whole. Which method should be used in training and development programs? Probably both, each in its proper place.

Organizing and Sequencing Subject Matter

Some subjects, such as mathematics, lend themselves easily to organization and sequencing because they are already divided into fundamentals which must be taught first, and principles and applications, which are built on the fundamentals. Organization and sequencing in such subjects are relatively simple. In other content areas, however, the approach to organization and sequencing is not so apparent.

The social sciences and their derivatives, such as management development, may be approached as problem-centered expositions of material or as logically arranged bodies of facts and principles. The form or organization chosen depends upon the objectives of the training system, the place of the program within the overall training structure, or the customary divisions of materials among the subject-matter disciplines involved. Each factor warrants careful study.

Types of Sequencing

The primary criterion in sequencing is that the order of presentation make sense to the trainees. The instructional sequence, therefore, will often differ from the order in which the trainee will use the skills and knowledge taught by the system. The sequence of learning experiences can be established on one or a combination of several bases as follows.

Logical order. With logical sequence, materials are presented either in order of difficulty or in accordance with a logical arrangement of the subject matter. When it is evident that logical order must be preserved in presenting the content, the systems designer need only determine the best means of presentation; the sequence is already established. It must be remembered, however, that with logical order the trainee may not see why he should learn the material, nor will he be able to make immediate use of the newly acquired knowledge or skill.

Problem-centered organization and sequencing. Sometimes it is desirable to pose a general problem and then describe the various means of solving it; or where no solution exists, it is possible to identify the factors involved in the problem and develop alternative solutions. Problem-solving approaches are, of course, widely used in many types of training and management development programs. To be successful, problems should be presented in increasing order of difficulty and complexity. Adequate sampling of representative problems must also be insured.

Descriptive order. Many content areas are highly descriptive or taxonomic. For example, programming and budgeting, data-handling and information systems, and quality control procedures involve carefully prescribed sequential operations; descriptions of methodology, equipment, and the like; and terminology. In this case the problem is to determine the best approach to clear and concise description. Adequate descriptions of the equipment, processes, and procedures must be provided. Often it is necessary to describe the systems from several different perspectives to insure that trainees obtain the required information.

Job performance order. This is a sequence based on the sequence in which a job, duty, or task is actually performed. For example, in teaching operation or repair of equipment, it is often desirable to organize and sequence the instruction in the exact order in which each task is completed by the operator or repairman. Often, however, adjustments in the sequence must be made because of the need for practice of difficult elements prior to their insertion into the total job sequence.

Psychological order. This is an ordering of content and learning experiences based on ease of learning. For this reason it may take any one of the prior forms or a combination of all. In general, it means that older learnings serve as the basis for new learnings; that, when possible, the trainee moves from the simple to the complex, from the near to the far, from the familiar to the unknown, from the concrete to the abstract.

In actual practice, all types of sequencing have their place in systems design. All types should be used. However, sequencing decisions must be based upon the actual objectives and content involved in the development of specific job and task performances.

SEQUENCING GUIDES

The following guides should be used in determining the sequence of tasks and their supporting knowledge and skills:

1. Place easily learned tasks early in the sequence.
2. Introduce early in the sequence broad concepts and technical terms which have application throughout the training system.
3. Place practical application of concepts and principles close to the point of initial development.
4. Place prerequisite knowledge and skills in the sequence prior to the points where they must be combined with subsequent knowledge and skills and applied.
5. Provide for practice and review of skills and knowledge which are essential parts of later tasks.
6. Introduce a concept or skill in the task in which it is most frequently used.

7. Do not overload any task with elements that are difficult to learn.
8. Provide for practice of required skills and review of concepts and principles in areas where transfer of identical or related skills is not likely to occur unaided.
9. Place complex or cumulative skills late in the sequence.

Steps in Sequencing

The following steps should be followed in sequencing skills and knowledge supports:[4]

Step 1. Using the general guidelines set forth in the immediately preceding section, lay out the task-level Performance Objective Workcards and their supporting content outlines (see Fig. 7-1). Note that in the figure there are duplicate numbers representing the required skills in the content outlines for each task. This is explained by the fact that a basic set of required skills often appears under two or more tasks. Identifying these duplications permits optimum sequencing.

Step 2. Code items in the content outline (see Fig. 7-2). Determine

Figure 7-1.　Step 1 in sequencing.

Task A	Task B	Task C
Content outline:	Content outline:	Content outline:
Skill 1	Skill 1	Skill 1
Skill 2	Skill 3	Skill 3
Skill 3	Skill 5	Skill 4
	Skill 4	

Figure 7-2.　Step 2 in sequencing.

Task A	Task B	Task C
Content outline:	Content outline:	Content outline:
Skill 1　ID*	Skill 1	Skill 1
Skill 2	Skill 3	Skill 3　ID
Skill 3	Skill 5　ID	Skill 4　ID
	Skill 4	

* Initial development.

[4] To simplify the explanation, only skills are used in the example, although in actual practice both knowledge and skills are used.

whether each item of content should be initially developed within the task where it first appears in the sequence of tasks. If so, mark the skill ID (initial development) in the outline. If the item should be initially developed in another task, annotate the outline under the proper task. Uncoded items are skills which must be developed before the total task is performed.

Step 3. Make necessary compromises where specific tasks and their supporting skills are interdependent. The decision about where in the sequence the task should be placed is made on the basis of secondary guidelines, such as difficulty in acquiring the knowledge or skill, or on the basis of an equitable distribution of difficult materials among the several tasks (see Fig. 7-3). Note that the sequence of tasks has been changed from A, B, C to A, C, B.

Step 4. Complete the coding (see Fig. 7-4).

Figure 7-3.   Step 3 in sequencing.

Task A	Task C	Task B
Content outline:	Content outline:	Content outline:
Skill 1 ID*	Skill 1	Skill 1
Skill 2	Skill 3 ID	Skill 3
Skill 3	Skill 4 ID	Skill 5 ID
		Skill 4

* Initial development.

Figure 7-4.   Step 4 in sequencing.

Task A	Task C	Task B
Content outline:	Content outline:	Content outline:
Skill 1 ID*	Skill 1	Skill 1
Skill 2 ID	Skill 3	Skill 3
Skill 3 · ID	Skill 4 ID	Skill 5 ID
		Skill 4

* Initial development.

Task A	Since there is nothing before this task, all skills must be developed initially.
Task C	Required skill 1 is developed in task A.
	Required skill 3 is developed in task A.
	Required skill 4 is initially developed.

Task B   Required skill 1 is developed in task A.
          Required skill 3 is developed in task A.
          Required skill 5 is initially developed.
          Required skill 4 is developed in task C.
The identical procedure can be used to sequence the elements within a task.

CHECKLISTS

CONTENT OUTLINES

1. Is only necessary and relevant content included?
2. Have the following categories of material been *considered* for inclusion:
    a. Nomenclature and locations of objects?
    b. Cues, indicators, and controls relevant to the work environment?
    c. Precautions to be observed?
    d. Symbols and signals?
    e. Emergency procedures?
    f. Calculations and formulas?
    g. Available alternative actions and their consequences?
    h. Criteria for acceptable decisions or solutions to problems?
    i. Errors to avoid?
    j. Cause and effect relationships?
    k. How to plan?
    l. How to arrange equipment, tools, and materials?
    m. How to develop strategies?
    n. How to invent and improvise?
    o. Aids to learning?
    p. Characteristics of objects and signals?
    q. Step-by-step procedures?
    r. Use of tools, job aids, and test equipment?
3. Are source documents current, authoritative, and consistent with enterprise policies and procedures?
4. Have draft content outlines been prepared and reviewed by subject-matter experts?
5. Have gaps in content, overemphasis and underemphasis, and unnecessary duplication and overlapping been avoided?

SEQUENCE

1. Are the materials arranged so that the trainees can see the necessity for each step in the instruction; that is, does the sequence have meaning for the learner?

2. Does the sequence start with material familiar to the trainee and proceed to new materials; that is, does the sequence move from the known to the unknown?
3. Does the material proceed from the simple to the complex, from the concrete to the abstract, when this is feasible?
4. Is a context or framework taught for the trainee to use in organizing what he is to learn?

SELECTED REFERENCES

Fry, Edward. *Teaching Machines and Programmed Instruction*. New York: McGraw-Hill Book Company, 1963, Chap. 8.

Gagné, Robert M. "The Acquisition of Knowledge," *Psychological Review* (July 1962), 69:4: 355–365.

Melching, William H., et al. *A Handbook for Programmers of Automated Instruction*. Alexandria, Va.: George Washington University Human Resources Research Office, September 1963, Chap. II.

Miller, Robert B. *Task and Part-Task Trainers and Training*, Technical Report WADD-TR-60-469. Wright-Patterson AFB, Ohio: Behavioral Sciences Laboratory, Wright Air Development Division, June 1960.

————. "Task Description and Analyses." In Robert M. Gagné, ed. *Psychological Principles in System Development*. New York: Holt, Rinehart and Winston, Inc., 1962, pp. 187–228.

————. "Analysis and Specification of Behavior for Training." In Robert Glaser, ed. *Training Research and Education*. Pittsburgh: University of Pittsburgh Press, 1962, pp. 39–78.

————, and Harold P. Van Cott. *The Determination of Knowledge Content for Complex Man-Machine Jobs*. Pittsburgh, Pa.: American Institutes for Research, December 1955.

Smith, Robert G., Jr. *The Design of Instructional Systems*. HumRRO Technical Report 66-18. Alexandria, Va.: George Washington University Human Resources Research Office, November 1966, Chap. 3.

————. *The Development of Training Objectives*, Research Bulletin 11. Alexandria, Va.: George Washington University Human Resources Research Office, June 1964, Chap. 6.

Tracey, William R. *Evaluating Training and Development Systems*. AMA, 1968, pp. 135–137.

8

Selecting and Using
Training Strategies

Lᴇᴄᴛᴜʀᴇ, conference, demonstration, and performance methods have been used in training and development from the beginning. Yet, firm criteria for the selection of the optimum method, technique, or medium to achieve training objectives have not been established. Selection of an instructional approach customarily has been dictated by expediency rather than by any other consideration. A sounder, more systematic, more objective method of making such important professional decisions must be used.

Unquestionably, the selection of approach to training is a difficult problem. The inherent complexity of the process of changing behavior, the large number of variables, and the lack of consistency in the use of terminology have been the main barriers to the identification of selection standards for instructional strategies.

The decision to use one strategy or another must be made on the basis of careful analysis of the training situation from several standpoints: training objectives, course content, trainee population, instructional staff, space, facilities, equipment, instructional materials, time, and costs.

Better understanding of how people learn and the evolution of modern aids to teaching and learning have resulted in the development of a great variety of instructional strategies, methods, mediating devices, and systems of organization. The purpose of this chapter is to identify the more important strategies, to indicate the situations in which they should be used, to note their advantages and limitations, and to describe the procedures to be followed in arriving at strategy decisions.

Upon completing the chapter, the reader should be able to perform as follows:

Behavior   Select the most appropriate strategy for achieving training or development objectives.

Conditions   Given: Performance Objective Workcards (Fig. 4-3), outlines of course content, information about the trainee input and the competence of instructors, and data relating to available space, equipment, and materials, time available for training, and cost limits.

Criterion   In accordance with the standards and procedures described in this chapter.

NATURE AND IMPORTANCE OF STRATEGY SELECTION

Although the terms "method," "technique," "approach," and "strategy" have often been used interchangeably, there are important differences among them. To clarify these terms, the definitions discussed below are offered.

Instructional strategy. An instructional strategy is a combination of teaching methods and techniques designed to accomplish an instructional job. It includes mediating devices when used, and a system for organizing instructors and trainees.

Instructional method. An instructional method is the basic approach to instruction. It may be a lecture, demonstration, conference, performance, programmed instruction, study assignment, tutoring, or a combination of two or more of these basic approaches. Methods may be cataloged under three headings:

1. *Primary.* An approach which is objectively judged to be the most effective and efficient means of attaining an instructional objective.

2. *Supporting.* An approach which is objectively judged to be an essential complement to a primary method; that is, it must be used in conjunction with the primary method to insure the attainment of the instructional goal.

3. *Alternative.* An approach which may be used as a substitute for the primary or supporting method when circumstances do not permit the use of the optimum method.

Instructional technique. An instructional technique is a means of instruction which complements a method; for example, questioning, handling student responses, and using visual and auditory aids.

System of organization. A system of organization is a means of grouping instructors and/or trainees for instruction; for example, random grouping, team teaching, and team learning.

Mediating device. A mediating device is a specialized piece of equipment, or a system, specifically designed to assist in the presentation of instruction; for example, teaching machines, classroom trainee response systems, computer-based instructional systems, and closed-circuit television systems (to include video tape and kinescope recording and playback facilities).

IMPORTANCE OF STRATEGY SELECTION

Except for the selection of training objectives, proper selection of strategy will do more to promote efficiency and effectiveness of instruction than any other measure. This fact has largely been overlooked in training and education. All too often the selection of strategy has been dictated by expediency rather than based on need. Strategy must be selected through systematic, objective means if inefficiency in attaining objectives or, worse, failure to achieve objectives, is to be avoided. Two requirements, discussed below, must be met by the strategy selected.

Compatibility. There is no single best method of teaching which applies to all learning situations or instructional objectives. The system designer must choose the strategy which is most compatible with the objectives of the instruction, the nature of the training organization, the facilities and equipment available, the background and level of the trainees, and the abilities of the instructional staff.

Variation of methods. The accomplished instructor is one who has developed skill in using a great variety of methods and techniques. For each objective to be reached, the instructor should select the specific methods which will best carry trainees to the goal. The instructor who is limited in methods often tries to reach an objective by using inappropriate techniques. The results are lack of trainee interest and attention, inefficient learning, and failure to achieve the instructional goals. Too many instructors use only one or two methods. Many instructors lecture most of the time. With the great variety of interesting and effective ways of helping trainees learn which have recently been developed, the instructor should develop a repertoire of approaches.

FACTORS IN STRATEGY SELECTION

Every instructional strategy has certain advantages and limitations. It is essential that careful consideration be given to these advantages and limitations to insure that the strategy selected for a specific instructional job is the one which will be most effective and efficient. Strategy decisions must be based on careful analysis of the training situation from several standpoints: instructional objectives; subject matter; trainee population; instructors; instructional space, facilities, equipment, and materials; time; and costs. In the following paragraphs, each of these factors is discussed.

INSTRUCTIONAL OBJECTIVES

The overriding consideration in the selection of a strategy is the objective of instruction, that is, what the trainee will be required to do either during a later stage of his training or on the job. If the objectives of a specific block of instruction deal with job knowledges as supporting elements for the development of terminal behaviors, the strategy selected may be different from the method chosen to develop job performance skills.

Objectives must also be examined to determine whether the instructional job is (1) to introduce a subject; (2) to provide remedial assistance; (3) to accelerate, enrich, or build academic skills; (4) to teach manual or manipulative skills; (5) to build concepts; (6) to teach operation and functioning of equipment; (7) to develop teamwork; (8) to stimulate interest; (9) to improve reasoning and problem-solving ability; and (10) to accomplish any one of a host of other objectives which are appropriate for formal training.

COURSE CONTENT

The nature of the content itself must be considered in selecting an instructional strategy. The stability of the content, whether it is verbal or manipulative, and its difficulty determine to a great extent the strategy which is most appropriate.

TRAINEE POPULATION

The size of the trainee group, the educational level, prior training, aptitudes, maturity, reading and speaking ability, and the teaching location must be considered in selecting a strategy. For example, optimum conditions for the application of specific methods demand establishment of maximum and minimum class sizes. Where class size exceeds or falls short of the established figure, an alternative method may be necessary.

INSTRUCTORS

The number, quality, and competencies of available instructors are important factors to consider in selecting a strategy. For example, in a given situation, if technically qualified instructors are not available in sufficient numbers to handle the trainee input, the use of programmed materials, rather than a more appropriate combination of demonstration and practical exercise, may be dictated.

SPACE, FACILITIES, EQUIPMENT, AND INSTRUCTIONAL MATERIALS

Each instructional strategy requires the use of specific types of facilities, equipment, and materials. If the required facilities are not available, an alternative method may be dictated. For example, if it has been determined that teaching machines would be the most effective medium for the presentation of a block of instruction, but the machines are not available, an alternative approach will be required.

TIME

The time available for a particular block of instruction also governs the strategy selected. Conference, performance, and special participative methods demand larger allotments of time than do the lecture and demonstration methods. If time is extremely limited, an alternative to the most effective method may be required.

COSTS

The matter of costs is of paramount importance in any training program. Criteria relating to costs are not separate and distinct from other factors. Obviously, time, facilities, personnel, and the like have price tags, but two items are important enough to warrant separate considerations. First, the cost of a strategy must be reasonable when measured against teaching effectiveness. Other factors being equal, if the expected gains in learning effectiveness of a particular strategy do not offset any additional costs incurred by the use of that strategy, a less costly, even if slightly less effective, instructional strategy may be dictated. Second, savings in time, personnel, or facilities must justify the investment in the strategy. Here, the point is that an acceptable relationship between investment in the strategy and savings in other areas must exist. In sum, the cost of the strategy, regardless of its effectiveness, must under normal circumstances be offset by savings in other aspects of the training program.

BASIC METHODS

LECTURE

A lecture is a semiformal discourse in which the instructor presents a series of events, facts, concepts, or principles; explores a problem; or explains relationships. Trainees participate in a lecture mainly as listeners. A lecture is basically a means of "telling" trainees information they need to know. This does not mean, however, that all the talking done by an instructor during a class period can be termed a lecture. The term must be reserved to describe a more formal presentation used to achieve an instructional objective.

Uses. Fundamentally, the purpose of a lecture is to inform. The instructor has information which he wishes to transmit to trainees by means of oral communication. Some of the more appropriate uses of the lecture are to (1) orient trainees to course policies, rules, procedures, purposes, and learning resources; (2) introduce a subject, indicate its importance, and present an overview of its scope; (3) give directions on procedures for use in subsequent learning activities; (4) present basic material which will provide a common background for subsequent activities; (5) set the stage for a demonstration, discussion, or performance; (6) illustrate the application of rules, principles, or concepts; and (7) review, clarify, emphasize, or summarize.

Advantages. A properly planned and skillfully delivered lecture is effective when used in appropriate situations. The lecture saves time because the instructor can present more material in a given amount of time than he can by any other method. The size of a class is limited only by the size of the classroom or the efficiency of the public-address system. The lecture can be used effectively in any type of training area, indoors or outdoors. The only requirement is that the trainees must be able to hear the lecturer. A skillful lecturer can modify or adjust his material, in terms of sequence, vocabulary, and illustrations, to meet the needs of a specific group. This makes it possible to present content which is appropriate for the educational level, training, and experience of the class. The lecture can be used for orientation, introduction, review, clarification, and summary. It can be used at any point in a course, and it can be combined easily and effectively with any other method of instruction. Because the instructor determines what is to be presented and the order of presentation, the desired coverage and sequence can be accomplished with little danger of engaging in time-consuming detours.

Disadvantages. The instructor prepares and presents the material; the trainee sits, listens, and takes notes. Most lectures therefore permit little or no interchange of ideas between the instructor and the trainees. All ideas presented to the class originate with the instructor. The lecture method is an inappropriate means of attempting to teach skills such as equipment operation. Most such learning takes place through the visual sense, but the lecture, even if supplemented by training aids, appeals mainly to the auditory sense. Unless the content is interesting and challenging enough to hold the attention of the class, the results are likely to fall short of the instructional goal. During a lecture, trainees are passive: their job is to listen. Their attention, however, is difficult to attract and retain, since outside disturbances, or mental meanderings, easily and frequently distract the trainees and render the lecture ineffective.

If an instructor is to *teach*, rather than merely present information, he must be aware of trainee reactions, misconceptions, inattention, and difficulties, and he must remedy them immediately. The lecture method makes these perceptions difficult. Most trainees have acquired the ability to *appear* attentive, although they may not even be listening. The lecturer receives very little feedback, and much of what he does receive is misleading. In a lecture, trainee interest and attention must be generated by the instructor. The instructor must make careful plans, display sincerity and enthusiasm, present his material in proper sequence, use appropriate vocabulary, employ effective speaking techniques, be sensitive to the reaction of his audience, and modify his presentation on the basis of class response. Failure to do any of these things will result in loss of trainee attention and interest, and therefore in failure to achieve the objectives of the instruction. The ultimate success of a lecture depends on the skill of the instructor.

CONFERENCE

In the conference method, group discussion techniques are used to reach instructional objectives. These techniques include questions, answers, and comments from the instructor in combination with answers, comments, and questions from the trainees, and are directed toward attainment of learning goals. Basically, there are three types of conferences: directed discussion, training conferences, and seminars. No sharp lines of demarcation exist between any of these forms. However, the objectives of the conference, and the *kind* and *amount* of trainee participation, determine when a directed discussion becomes a training conference, and when a training conference becomes a seminar. The bases for these distinctions follow.

Directed discussion. The objective in directed discussion is to help trainees acquire better understanding and the ability to apply known facts, principles, concepts, policies, or procedures, or to provide trainees with an opportunity to apply their knowledge. The function of the instructor is to guide the discussion in such a way that the facts, principles, concepts, or procedures are clearly articulated and applied.

Training conference. In a training conference, the objective is to pool the knowledge and past experience of the trainees to arrive at improved or more clearly stated principles, concepts, policies, or procedures. The topics discussed in a training conference are less likely to have pat answers than those used in a directed discussion. The task of the instructor is to elicit contributions from the group, based on past experiences, which have a bearing on the topic at hand. Balanced participation, then, is the goal.

Seminar. The purpose of the seminar is to *find* an answer to a question or a solution to a problem. The instructor does not have an answer or a solution; in fact, there is no known best or correct solution. Rather, he is seeking an answer, and he uses the group to develop one. The primary functions of the instructor are to describe the problem as he understands it and to encourage free and full participation in a discussion aimed at (1) identifying the real problem, (2) gathering and analyzing data, (3) formulating and testing hypotheses, (4) determining and evaluating alternative courses of action, (5) arriving at conclusions, and (6) making recommendations to support or arrive at a solution or a decision.

Uses. The conference method is used (1) to develop imaginative solutions to problems; (2) to stimulate interest and thinking, and to secure trainee participation in situations which would otherwise allow the class to remain passive; (3) to emphasize the main teaching points; (4) to supplement lectures, readings, or laboratory exercises; (5) to determine how well trainees understand concepts and principles, and to determine whether they are ready to proceed to new or more advanced material; (6) to prepare trainees for the application of theory or procedure to specific situations; (7) to summarize, clarify points, or review;

(8) to prepare trainees for instruction which is to follow; and (9) to determine trainee progress and the effectiveness of prior instruction.

Advantages. The opportunity to express one's own views and to hear the opinions of others is stimulating. Interest is unusually high in a well-planned and skillfully conducted conference.

Because trainees actively participate in developing the lesson, they tend to accept the importance and validity of the content and are more deeply committed to problem solutions or decisions than they would be if the content were merely presented to them. The conference method enables the instructor to make effective use of the trainees' backgrounds, previously acquired knowledge, and experiences. The entire class and the instructor benefit from the experience and thinking of all trainees. Learning takes place in direct ratio to the amount of individual participation in the learning process. The conference demands a high degree of trainee participation, thereby promoting better and more permanent learning.

Disadvantages. The most important limitation is the lack of instructors capable of conducting true discussions. The conference is more exacting in resourcefulness, initiative, and ability of the instructor. The instructor must be able to guide the discussion without appearing to do so. He must be thoroughly informed on all aspects of the subject under discussion. The instructor must also (1) keep the discussion on the track, (2) minimize debate over unimportant details, (3) relate comments to topics previously discussed, (4) avoid reopening topics already discussed, (5) encourage and get full participation, (6) prevent domination by a few trainees, and (7) summarize and clinch each topic.

Most conferences require advance preparation, in the form of reading assignments, thinking, and study, before the meeting. The thoroughness of the preparation determines the quality of the discussion and the outcome of the conference. The instructor has very little or no control at all over the quality or thoroughness of trainee preparation. This results in variation among trainees in their readiness to participate in the conference. The content appropriate for discussion is restricted. Manipulative operations, functions, procedures, or introductory material do not ordinarily provide suitable content for a conference. Relatively large blocks of time must be allocated if a discussion is to be profitable. For this reason, the conference is often ruled out as an approach, although it may be well suited to the subject and the class. The conference method cannot be used effectively with groups larger than twelve to fifteen trainees because the opportunity for individual participation is too limited. More reticent members are likely to be left out of the discussion and denied valuable learning experiences. The members of a conference group, in most cases, must possess the proper background, maturity, and motivation if the discussion is to be profitable. The desired degree of participation is difficult to obtain if the group is composed of two subgroups, one which has ample experience in the area to be discussed and another which has extremely limited experience.

DEMONSTRATION

In a demonstration, the instructor actually performs an operation or does a job, thereby showing the trainee *what* to do and *how* to do it; he then uses explanations to point out *why, where,* and *when* it is done. Usually, the trainee is expected to be able to repeat the job or operation after the demonstration. For this reason, the demonstration is often used in conjunction with another method. The most usual combinations are the lecture-demonstration and the demonstration-performance.

Uses. The basic purpose of a demonstration is to show how something is done. It should be employed wherever and whenever practicable. Some of its more important applications are to (1) teach manipulative operations 'or procedures (how something is done), (2) to teach problem-solving and analytical skills, (3) to illustrate principles (*why* something *works*), (4) to teach operation or functioning of equipment (how something works), (5) to teach teamwork (how men work together to do something), (6) to set standards of workmanship; and (7) to teach safety procedures.

Advantages. Trainees learn faster and more permanently with a demonstration, for several reasons:

1. Demonstrations make explanations concrete by giving meaning to words.

2. Demonstrations provide perspective by showing complete performance of a procedure. Relationships between steps of the procedure and accomplishment of the objective are clarified.

3. Demonstrations appeal to several senses. Not only do trainees see and hear during a demonstration, but they are often given the opportunity to touch the equipment.

4. Demonstrations have dramatic appeal. When well planned and executed, a demonstration has a dramatic quality which arouses and sustains interest and attention.

Equipment is often damaged when trainees attempt to operate it without proper guidance. It is also true that material is wasted by neophytes. Much of this damage and waste can be prevented by the use of demonstration. A properly planned demonstration takes much less trainee time than other methods. It reduces oral explanation time and at the same time prevents misunderstandings about how a system or a piece of equipment works. Class size is limited only by the ability of the group to see the object being demonstrated. The use of large-scale mock-ups or models makes it possible to teach many operations to large classes.

Disadvantages. A demonstration should set a standard of performance for trainees. The procedure must be technically correct and must be performed with a skill greater than that expected of trainees. The instructor must be sure that his equipment is in working order. Nothing fails as completely as a demonstration that does not work. The demonstration room must be set up so that all trainees can clearly see every phase of the demonstration. This requires special classroom arrangements. Since the equipment, which is often expensive, must be taken out of an operational setting, its removal must be offset by gains in training. Sometimes models or mock-ups must be purchased or constructed, which involves a rather costly investment of time, money, and other resources.

PERFORMANCE

Performance is a method in which the trainee is required to perform under controlled conditions, the operation, skill, or movement being taught. Performance is learning by doing. There are four basic types of performance: (1) independent practice, in which trainees work individually and at their own rates; (2) group performance or controlled practice, in which trainees work together at the rate set by the instructor, step by step and "by the numbers"; (3) coach and pupil, in which trainees are paired and members of each pair perform alternately as instructor and trainee; and (4) team performance, in which a group of trainees perform an operation or function involving teamwork.

Uses. In general, the performance method has the same applications as the demonstration method. It is used as follow-on instruction to teach (1) manipulative operations or procedures, (2) operation or functioning of equipment, (3) team skills, and (4) safety procedures.

Advantages. Given the opportunity to apply his knowledge in a realistic situation, the trainee develops confidence in his ability and a positive attitude toward the learning situation.

Active trainee participation is maximized. This fact, coupled with the interest and attention generated by putting theory into practice, increases both the amount and the permanence of learning. With the performance method, the instructor has an opportunity to observe the degree of learning attained by each trainee, to locate trainees who have difficulty, and to determine whether there have been weak areas in the instruction.

Because performance is guided, trainees are less likely to make mistakes which will damage equipment or waste material. Guided performance makes it possible to emphasize the proper method of performance and enables prevention of accidents.

Disadvantages. If a practical exercise is to be conducted, every trainee must participate fully. Therefore, tools and properly functioning equipment must be available in sufficient quantity for the size of the class. Setting up the room and equipment, for individual or team performance of the complete operation of a well-run practical exercise, is often time consuming. Unless the class is very small, several well-qualified instructors are required, to keep a constant check on the progress of each trainee, to give assistance when needed, and to evaluate the quality of the performance.

PROGRAMMED INSTRUCTION

Programmed instruction is a method of self-instruction in which the trainee works through a carefully sequenced and pretested series of steps leading to the acquisition of knowledge or skills representing the instructional objectives. The trainee proceeds through the program at his own rate, responds actively (or covertly) to each step in the sequence, and receives immediate feedback on the correctness of his response before proceeding to the next step. Programs are usually designed to permit the trainee to *master* the desired knowledge or skills.

Uses. Programmed instruction is used (1) to provide remedial instruction; (2) to provide makeup instructions for late arrivals, absentees, or transients; (3) to maintain previously learned skills which are not performed frequently enough to insure an acceptable level of proficiency; (4) to provide retraining on equipment and procedures which have become obsolete or have been replaced since the original training was given; (5) to upgrade production, administrative, or other types of skills and knowledge; (6) to accelerate capable trainees and thereby enable them to complete a course in less than the usual amount of time; (7) to provide a means (advance study) of insuring enough common background among trainees that they can profit from formal classroom work; (8) to provide the review and practice of knowledge and skills needed to "set" the learning; (9) to provide vertical enrichment (advanced work) or horizontal enrichment (broader contact) in a content area; and (10) to control the variables in a learning situation for experimental purposes.

Advantages. Programmed instruction reduces failure rate. Basically, this is due to the fact that programs are tested and validated before they are used. The procedure insures that the program is effective in performing the instructional job. The self-pacing feature of the material also helps because trainees are exposed to the material at a rate which is appropriate for the individual. The forced-response and immediate feedback features guarantee continuous attention to the material, provide corrections for wrong responses, prevent misinterpretation, and prevent the trainee from continuing to practice errors. The pretesting, self-pacing, forced attention, and immediate feedback features of programs result in better, more efficient, and more permanent learning. Thus, end-of-course proficiency is markedly increased by the use of programs. The rigid control over content made possible by the procedures used for developing, testing, and validating programs prevents the introduction of unnecessary content and thereby reduces the time required to learn the critical material. The self-pacing feature, along with forced attention, decreases the teaching time required and frequently results in average time savings of 30 percent or more over conventional instructional methods.

The instructional content and sequence of a program are predetermined. They are not subject to the whims, preferences, experiences, or biases of the instructor. The quality of the instruction does not vary from day to day nor from instructor to instructor. There is almost complete control over the content, the sequence, and the form of trainee response. Hence, instruction becomes standardized and can be repeated without change at any time for any individual or group. Programmed materials can be used anywhere at any time. No specially equipped rooms or facilities are necessary. Although under ordinary conditions programs are not used as substitutes for instructors, they can be so used. Programs are validated under conditions where they alone do the teaching, and therefore, they are effective instructional materials even if no qualified instructor is available. Programs can be designed to accommodate wide differences in aptitude, ability, speed of learning, prior training, and experience. The needs of individuals, whether for more or less exposure, detail, or practice, can be met. The size of a class is also unimportant. Programs can be used to achieve group or individual progress. The self-pacing feature and the handling of large or small groups make for greater efficiency and economy. In addition, programs free instructors from routine, repetitive teaching tasks, and enable them to spend a larger part of their time on more difficult or more demanding aspects of instruction.

Disadvantages. Although the number of available programs is growing rapidly, the programs which may be used locally are limited because most programs produced by commercial publishers or other sources do not match the instructional objectives of local courses. For this reason, programs must be developed locally or contracted for with commercial programming concerns. Usually only a few trained programmers are available locally, and since the training of programmers is relatively lengthy and demanding, only a small percentage of personnel exposed to training will become competent programmers. Programs, whether developed locally or contracted for, are extremely costly. For local development there must be a large investment in programmer training and an even larger one in program writing, testing, and validation. Contract program development is expensive in terms of dollar outlay, and in terms of the time required by subject-matter experts and technicians for consulting with programmers and reviewing draft materials. Programmed materials cannot be selected or developed overnight. A considerable amount of lead time is required to screen and select appropriate programs from those available. If programs are developed either by staff and faculty or by contract programmers, the lead time for production, testing, and validation is even greater. If the course content is unstable or subject to frequent and radical change, it is inappropriate for programming.

Instructors must be able to motivate trainees to complete programs. They must be able to assist any trainee at any point in the programmed sequence at any time. Mediocre instructors cannot meet these requirements. If instructors are to be able to provide the motivation, guidance, and assistance required for the optimum use of programmed materials, they must have (1) insight into the learning process; (2) a thorough understanding of the rationale, principles, construction, and use of programming skill in conducting tutorial-type instruction and individual counseling; and (3) a mastery of the subject matter of the programs used.

The use of programs requires a trainee group which is mature enough and sufficiently well motivated to work more or less independently. Furthermore, they must possess reading ability at the level required for full understanding of the program. The use of programmed materials creates unique administrative problems; foremost among these are the scheduling and assignment problems caused by the self-pacing feature of programs. This feature results in different phase and course completion times, with consequent difficulties in scheduling subsequent instruction and in assigning graduates to operating units.

STUDY ASSIGNMENT

In the study assignment method, the instructor assigns readings in books, periodicals, manuals, or handouts; requires the completion of a project or research paper; or prescribes problems and exercises for the practice of a skill. This method involves imposing a task, providing for trainee motivation, and giving general directions for carrying out the assignment. Implicit in this method are the problems of setting up worthwhile learning activities, anticipating trainee difficulties, and working out means of overcoming the difficulties. If these steps are not well handled, the objectives of the assignment are not likely to be achieved. The study assignment has two basic forms: (1) independent study, where the trainee carries out the assignment without instructor assistance or direct guidance; and (2) supervised study, where the trainee carries out the assignment with an instructor available for guidance and assistance.

Uses. The study assignment is used (1) to orient trainees to a topic prior to classroom or laboratory work; (2) to set the stage for a lecture, demonstration, or discussion, that is, to serve as advance study; (3) to provide for or capitalize on individual differences in ability, background, or experience through differentiated assignments; (4) to provide for the review of material covered in class or to give the practice essential for the development of skills and problem-solving ability, that is, to serve as homework; and (5) to provide enrichment material.

Advantages. A far greater amount of material, and detailed treatment of it, can be covered in a shorter period of time by study assignments than by any other means. Used properly, assignments can serve as a substitute for lectures; or by providing a common body of knowledge, they can make lectures, demonstrations, and conferences more meaningful and more productive. Practice is essential to the development of skills. Assignments provide a means of giving enough practice to insure mastery of the skill. Study assignments can be designed to make use of the experience, special skills, or interests of trainees, or to remedy individual deficiencies in knowledge or skill. Trainees may be referred to the original source instead of being exposed only to the instructor's interpretation. This insures that the content will be presented as intended by the originator of the material.

Disadvantages. If trainees are not well motivated, they are not likely to do a thorough job with assignments, especially those which they must do on their own. The instructor must plan and assign work in such a way that the objectives are clear, the instructions are lucid, and the motivation is present; and he must follow up assignments to insure that they have been carried out. The effectiveness of study assignments is difficult for an instructor to evaluate. Determining what went wrong with a study assignment when results are not as good as anticipated is also difficult. In skill development it is critical that the skill be practiced in the prescribed mode; with independent practice, there is a particular danger that the trainee will practice an incorrect procedure or error. When this occurs, a large expenditure of time is required for "unlearning" the skill and "relearning" it correctly. The variations in reading ability in any group and the differences in motivation produce varying degrees of learning when study assignments are used. Where standardization of learning is essential, study assignments may be inappropriate.

TUTORING

In tutoring, an instructor works directly with an individual trainee. The method may involve exposition, demonstration, questioning, coaching, or guided practice.

Uses. Tutoring is used (1) to teach highly complex skills and operations, or operations which involve considerable danger to men or hazards to expensive equipment; and (2) to provide individualized remedial assistance.

Advantages. With a competent instructor, tutoring provides the optimum in individualized instruction. The needs of the individual trainee can be diagnosed, and instruction can be tailor-made to meet his unique needs. In a tutorial setting, the highest possible degree of trainee participation can be achieved. Direct involvement in the learning, by answering and asking questions, and by performing under supervision, is guaranteed. The ability of the tutor-coach to adapt his instruction to the needs of the individual, together with the trainee's high degree of interaction and participation, make this method extremely effective in achieving instructional objectives. The one-to-one instructor-trainee ratio provides close control over performance of hazardous operations, resulting in the prevention of injury to the operator or damage to the equipment.

Disadvantages. Tutoring is one of the most demanding types of instruction to conduct, as it requires complete mastery of the content as well as skill in diagnosing and remedying learning difficulties. Tutoring is probably the most expensive method of teaching. Although only one trainee is receiving the instruction, the instructor's preparation and presentation time are essentially the same as they would be for a whole class of trainees.

COMBINATION INSTRUCTION

This method of instruction uses two or more basic instructional approaches in combination. For example, one lesson might include a study assignment, a lecture in which safety precautions in handling a piece of equipment are emphasized, a demonstration by the instructor, and finally, performance by the trainees.

Uses. Combination lessons can be used to meet almost any type of instructional objective in any training situation. However, they are most appropriate where skill development is involved.

Advantages. The variety of approaches used in a combination lesson makes for an interesting and engaging instructional period. The use of several approaches frees the instructor from the restricting aspects of any single method. He can easily adjust his approach to the needs of the class and the requirements of the situation. The combination lesson maximizes the advantages of any single method. It allows the instructor to use approaches which complement each other. This fact, plus the advantage of higher trainee interest, results in improved learning.

Disadvantages. Instructors must be able to use all methods of instruction with a high degree of skill. The use of methods in combination requires closer control by the instructor and, its concomitant, better supervision of trainee activities. To obtain the desired control, classes must be kept small.

SPECIAL PARTICIPATIVE METHODS

Case Study

The case-study method involves in-depth group discussion of real-life situations. It requires reading, study, analysis, discussion, and free exchange of ideas as well as decision making and the selling of decisions to others. A case report is distributed to trainees. The report contains a factual and accurate picture, based on firsthand observation, of a situation that portrays people acting, interacting, and reacting. Trainees study the case report and discuss it in depth.

Uses. The case method is used (1) to promote thoughtful discussion of the significant factors in a situation; (2) to develop judgment, critical thinking, and problem-solving ability; (3) to deduce principles of management or leadership; (4) to build human relations skills; and (5) to read for meaning and recognize the importance of context.

Advantages. The process of developing and presenting one's own ideas is more interesting than listening to the ideas of the trainer. The products of thinking in case studies are also more relevant to the experiences of the trainees because they must inject their own perceptions, attitudes, and feelings into the case. Ideas, concepts, and principles developed through case discussion are more likely to be retained by trainees. Participants become more aware of individual differences and gain self-understanding in terms of their ways of thinking, perceiving, talking, and listening.

Disadvantages. A considerable amount of time is required for trainees to read, digest, and discuss all the materials in a case report. The participants' level of concentration must be consistently high if good results are to be achieved. Some people find it difficult to maintain the required level of attention. Introverted trainees hesitate to say what they think. More extroverted trainees tend to monopolize. Then, too, a case is not reality. Reports are written by people, and they consist of facts as seen by people. Hence, written reports are filtered—selected, arranged, and interpreted—to some degree. In short, no case report can reproduce the evolving quality of real events. Poorly handled, the case study develops into a bull session in which participants merely share their own unexamined preconceptions or values.

INCIDENT METHOD

The incident method is a variation of the case method in which only a brief sketch of the climax of a case is presented. Trainees are given a few minutes to study the incident and attempt to determine the information they need to find out what is going on. Trainees then get these facts by asking questions of the leader. Time is usually limited, and questions must be of the type that can be answered "yes" or "no," or by a simple factual statement. The group then determines the nature of the problem and the decisions needed to solve it. Each member writes an individual decision with supporting reasons. Group discussion of the case in general and the decisions reached follows.

Uses, advantages, and disadvantages. The incident method serves the same purposes as the case method and has the same advantages and limitations. In addition it enables the case to be more realistic to trainees and enables each individual's decisions and rationale to be readily identifiable.

ROLE PLAYING

Role playing is a laboratory method of instruction that involves the spontaneous dramatization or acting out of a situation by two or more persons under the direction of a trainer. The dialog grows out of the situation developed by the trainees assigned to the parts. Each person acts his role as he feels it should be played. Other trainees serve as observers and critics. Following the enactment, the group engages in discussion.

Uses. Role playing can be used in any training situation that involves interaction between two or more persons. The method has been used successfully with all levels of employees, from operative to executive, and in a wide range of training programs. Interviewing, counseling, grievance handling, salesmanship, human relations, safety, arbitration, leadership, and contract negotiations are but a few of the content areas in which role playing has been used. Within these areas, role playing is used primarily to (1) make simulation or business games more realistic; (2) illustrate aspects of an interpersonal problem; (3) promote understanding of the viewpoints and feelings of others; (4) develop skills in problem diagnosis; (5) develop insight into personal attitudes, values, and behavior; (6) discover how trainees might react under certain conditions; and (7) develop specific interpersonal or communication skills.

Advantages. By playing the roles of others, trainees become aware of what these roles mean to other people. Role playing also underscores the difference between verbalizing about actions trainees claim they would take in a situation and what they would actually do. This results in greater understanding of personal traits, feelings, attitudes, values, and abilities. The reduction of inhibitions, the spontaneity, and the "no penalty" features of role playing allow trainees maximum opportunity to discover new modes of acting. In role playing trainees can also experiment with several approaches, while in a real situation, they can try only one. Trainees also have the chance to observe and imitate others. Finally, role playing is an attention getter from the outset. It practically guarantees the interest of the observers as well as of the participants.

Disadvantages. Role playing takes a considerable amount of time from the standpoints of trainee preparation, performance, and follow-up discussion. Unless enough time is allowed, the value of the method will be lost. Without competent leadership, role playing is a waste of time. At its worst it can be completely destructive to the personnel involved and to the training program. Trainees may become resentful when they receive feedback from the group on their portrayals. Some trainees may be too embarrassed to take part; others may grandstand. Only capable instructors can prevent these extremes in behavior. Lastly, roles played by trainees have no necessary relation to actual practice; therefore, trainees may feel no responsibility for playing their roles realistically.

SENSITIVITY (LABORATORY OR T-GROUP) TRAINING

Although sensitivity training may take any one of several forms, it is a deliberate effort to apply behavioral science to problems of motivation, communication, problem solving, and teamwork. Basically, sensitivity training is small-group interaction under stress in an unstructured group composed of learners and a trainer. The objective is behavioral change. To attain the objective, a permissive or supportive environment is established by the trainer. Participants are encouraged to act their *own* roles, receive feedback, examine their concepts of self, experiment with and practice new patterns of behavior, and learn how to maintain changed behavior back on the job.

Uses. Sensitivity training is used (1) to develop better managers, supervisors, foremen, or leaders; (2) to develop the skills and insights of effective group membership; (3) to help trainees to understand themselves and others; (4) to improve communication skills; and (5) to help trainees to be able to contribute to the work of a group.

Advantages. In addition to those advantages listed for role playing, sensitivity training allows trainees to gain new insights into their ways of perceiving, feeling, and behaving. The technique opens up the potential for trainees to change their attitudes and behavior by surfacing tendencies to resist change. Mistakes in relating to others and in behavior can be made without penalty to the trainee or to the organization.

Disadvantages. Sensitivity training is usually conducted away from the workplace. One- to three-week concentrated, continuous, residential sessions, with no interruptions, is the typical arrangement. Time away from the job as well as fees, travel and living expenses adds to the total cost. Neurotic trainees who are unable to withstand stress are likely to suffer temporary, and in some cases, severe and permanent psychological or emotional damage. Employees should not be required to participate in sensitivity training against their will. Forced participation could be considered an invasion of privacy. Indirect pressures, such as granting rewards of promotion, prestige, or status to those who have completed the training, constitute subtle coercion.

GAMES, MODELS, AND SIMULATION

Originally developed for business and military training, games, models, and simulations are used in a variety of training programs in business, educational, and government organizations. Most games focus on general management principles; however, some games aim to teach specific techniques. Game applications include human relations training, war games, research, problem solving, executive testing and selection, marketing, inventory control, and management development.

Some games are simple; others are extremely complex. Some involve manual computation; others require data-processing equipment. However, the distinguishing features of a game are that they include a set of structured decision-making tasks typical of a real-life situation and that they provide a systematic means of observing and evaluating trainees' decisions. These, then, are fed back to the trainees so that they can judge their appropriateness. Most games are played by one or more teams, each composed of from one to twenty participants. There may or may not be interaction between teams. Games are usually played in periods—an interval of time which may represent a month, a quarter, or a year. Trainees are given information in the form of reports or a scenario and allowed time to study the situation and make decisions. These decisions are processed either by a control group of judges or by a computer. The resulting data or scenario projections are returned to the team for analysis, and another decision.

Uses. Games and simulation are used (1) to develop leadership skills, (2) to improve technical performance, (3) to foster cooperation and teamwork, and (4) to improve decision-making ability.

Advantages. The fact that long periods of time can be compressed into relatively short training periods makes it possible to provide in weeks the experience that would take years to gain on the job. Participants become deeply involved in the game and undergo the stresses associated with real situations. Games can be used in an infinite variety of ways for all types of training from orientation to detailed instruction. And games can often be used more than once with the same group with additional gains.

Disadvantages. Games usually cost more in terms of personnel, equipment, and money than other approaches to training. And where a computer is involved, the cost is even greater—for programming, time on the equipment, and operating personnel. Little research has been done on the effectiveness of games as a training tool; therefore, their validity as training devices has not been proved.

In-basket Exercises

The in-basket situation is composed of a representative sample of a full year's performance in all aspects of a job. Trainees are given background materials, organization charts, policy manuals, financial statements, reports, and position papers to study before the exercise begins. Each trainee is then exposed to a structured array of memos, reports, letters, telephone calls, visits, and meetings. In his role as a manager, the trainee makes decisions on the incoming "mail." In each instance he commits himself in writing to specific courses of action. Time limits are established to introduce realism and cause stress. The decision-making phase is followed by discussion and critique of the actions taken and decisions reached. All actions are analyzed, evaluated, and fed back to participants.

Uses. In-basket exercises are primarily used in supervisory training and management development. Within this context they are used (1) to analyze trainees' decision-making abilities so that needed training can be provided, (2) to evaluate managerial skills, (3) to provide practice in decision making, and (4) to improve trainees' understanding of management theories.

Advantages. In-basket exercises are challenging and fun. They are popular with trainees because they stimulate their interest and force their involvement. Trainees are more likely to behave naturally under in-basket conditions than in other types of training situations; therefore, strengths and weaknesses in decision making can be identified and remedied. Behavior samples representing months or even years of performance can be obtained in a short period of time. Because they demand individual decision making, in-basket exercises can be appraised fairly and objectively.

Disadvantages. In-basket exercises are expensive to construct, administer, and evaluate. Materials, personnel, and time are all part of the cost to the enterprise. The matter of effectiveness in achieving training objectives has not yet been answered conclusively, or even satisfactorily.

BRAINSTORMING

With brainstorming, also called freewheeling, ideation, or creative problem solving, a small, carefully selected group is given a "how to" question or problem and is asked to produce as many ideas or solutions as they can generate. Usually a time limit is set. The technique of free association is encouraged. Quantity of ideas or solutions takes precedence over quality. Judgments about the worth of ideas or solutions are deliberately postponed until a later time. Ideas are written on a chalkboard or flip chart as fast as they are called out.

Uses. Brainstorming is used (1) to develop novel or creative solutions to problems, (2) to develop creativity, and (3) to stimulate the participation of trainees.

Advantages. Although only 10 percent of the ideas produced by a brainstorming session are likely to be usable, this represents a significant number of valuable ideas. The fast-moving pace of a brainstorming session is also inherently interesting.

Disadvantages. The leader must set the stage for a productive session. He must insure that participants understand their roles. He must keep the session moving and the ideas coming. These functions require considerable skill. Probably not more than fifteen persons can participate effectively in a brainstorming session. The productivity of the group depends upon the abilities of the participants and their understanding of the process.

"BUZZ" SESSIONS

This approach, also called "huddle" groups or "Phillips 66," is frequently used in conjunction with lectures or case problems. A larger trainee group is subdivided into units of six. Each group is given a problem and allowed six minutes to discuss it and be ready to report their conclusions to the total group.

Uses. The "buzz" session is used (1) to make possible the exchange of experience and the sharing of ideas in a large group; (2) to identify questions, issues, and problems that members of a large group may wish to have considered; (3) to obtain the contributions of reticent trainees; (4) to gather suggestions from the group for improving learning activities; and (5) to evaluate problem solutions.

Advantages. Although the trainee group may be very large, the technique permits all to participate, either as leaders of a small group or as discussants. Lectures and case discussion are more effective when the speaker or leader obtains feedback from the total group.

Disadvantages. The leader must be able to organize the groups quickly and get them working on the problem without wasting time. Leaders sometimes fail to do this. Groups often consume all the time available in selecting a leader and a recorder. Six minutes is not enough time to consider problems in any depth. Only well-defined and relatively straightforward problems or issues can be handled.

COMMITTEES

With committees, a group of trainees, ranging in size from three to seven, is given a special assignment in the form of a problem. The group is asked to investigate the problem, reach conclusions, and recommend a solution or a course of action. The committee may produce a report which is often presented orally to the larger group.

Uses. Committees are used (1) to study or explore a topic or problem, (2) to broaden trainees' knowledge and experience in a particular subject-matter area, (3) to create a new concept or product, (4) to secure trainee participation in planning learning activities, and (5) to evaluate learning activities.

Advantages. Dividing responsibility for in-depth study of various problems permits greater coverage of topics in a shorter time frame. All trainees profit from the reports of the several committees. Committee work also permits maximum utilization of the talents and special abilities of group members. Finally committees offer opportunities for trainees to assume positions of leadership which they would not otherwise get.

Disadvantages. Committees take time and money. Discussion often consumes more time than it should because of personality conflicts, domination by a few members, or the group's inability to arrive at a decision. Often watered-down solutions are proposed by committee simply because compromise was necessary to reach agreement. Sometimes committees are given inappropriate tasks. Other times the problem the group is asked to solve is one that could be solved as well, or better, by an individual.

FIELD TRIPS

A field trip is a carefully planned visit or tour to a place away from the training activity. The purpose of the trip is to provide firsthand observation of objects, processes, operations, and situations not transportable to, or reproducible in, the training facility. The field trip may take less than an hour when it involves a visit to an adjoining plant, office, or shop; or it may consume several days or weeks as would be the case with a visit to a distant plant or an overseas installation.

Uses. Field trips are used (1) to provide firsthand observation of operations, processes, or practices that cannot be readily brought into the classroom, shop, or laboratory; (2) to stimulate trainee interest and participation in discussion or other types of follow-on learning activities; (3) to gather information for later use in training activities; (4) to relate theory to actual practice; and (5) to introduce or summarize a topic.

Advantages. Information provided to trainees firsthand is real and concrete. Objects, processes, and operations are seen in their true surroundings—in three dimensions and in natural color. Because interest level is high and all the senses are used, the result is greater understanding and more permanent learning.

Disadvantages. Trainees must be prepared for the field trip. Coordination must be effected with the manager of the activity to be visited to prevent interference with operations, to insure that trainees see what is intended and in the right sequence, and to make certain that safety precautions are taken. Except for brief visits to installations close by, a considerable amount of time is consumed in travel. Added to this is the expense of transportation and living accommodations.

PANELS

Three to ten people, under the direction of a moderator, present their views on a particular subject or problem, or present assigned phases of a broad topic. Usually, panelists represent different kinds of expertise, experience, or perspectives. Often they are drawn from operating and staff elements. At times experts from outside the enterprise are invited to participate. Sometimes trainees themselves serve as members of panels. Following the presentations by the panelists, trainees are encouraged to participate through questions directed to individual panelists.

Uses. Panels are used (1) to identify and explore unsettled issues or problems; (2) to present differing points of view on an issue or problem; (3) to identify and clarify the advantages and disadvantages of a course of action; (4) to make use of special knowledge, experience, or expertise; and (5) to develop interest in a particular topic or problem.

Advantages. With large groups the panel permits a degree of trainee participation otherwise impossible to achieve. The presentation of varying points of view and the differences in the personalities of the panelists make the panel an interesting method. It introduces variety into the training program.

Disadvantages. Without expert leadership, full value cannot be obtained from the panel. The moderator must have a thorough understanding of the subject, be able to handle the panelists, and be able to stimulate group participation. Panelists must be selected with care to insure that they are effective communicators. Lack of planning often results in panelists being unprepared, superficial in their coverage, or unable to limit their remarks to the subject at hand.

GROUP INTERVIEWS

A group interview is a thirty- to fifty-minute dialog between an expert and a group of trainees. For example, a line manager might be invited to answer questions from a group of foreman trainees about union-management relations. Questions are posed to explore various aspects of the topic. Interviewees are informed in advance of the kinds of questions they will be asked.

Uses. The group interview is used (1) to clarify issues and problems; (2) to analyze problems; (3) to obtain authoritative information, opinion, and impressions on an issue or problem; and (4) to set the stage for follow-on activities.

Advantages. Having trainees ask questions insures that the material covered will be in keeping with their needs. Some persons prefer to be interviewed rather than to deliver a lecture. Advance preparation can be held to a bare minimum, since the guest is already an expert in the area to be investigated. In addition, the interview is flexible; the interviewee can be asked to expand, clarify, or give examples.

Disadvantages. The group interview does not permit detailed presentation of information. Instead, short, to-the-point answers are desired. The development of information in a readily understandable sequence cannot be guaranteed. The questions of the trainees often wander over the whole subject or concentrate on one narrow aspect of the topic.

TYPES OF TRAINEE AND INSTRUCTOR ORGANIZATION

RANDOM GROUPING AND ASSIGNMENT

Random assignment of trainees and instructors is an organizational approach in which more or less heterogeneous groups of trainees are assigned to class sections, and the responsibility for conducting instruction is shared by instructors assigned to one or more training elements. The size of the class is determined mainly by available facilities, including such considerations as seating capacity or the number of equipment positions on hand. Qualified instructors are usually assigned on a chance or duty roster basis.

Uses. Although there are relatively few situations in which random assignment should be used, it can be used under the following conditions:

1. Prerequisites for enrollment in a course are sufficiently well defined and applied to insure the assignment of trainees who possess the basic aptitudes, abilities, education, prior training or experiences essential to successful progress in the course.

2. Standards of instructor qualification, in terms of both technical knowledge and teaching skills, are set high enough to insure an acceptable level of teaching competence among all instructors.

3. The content to be presented is completely new to the trainees and is presented primarily as an orientation or introduction.

4. The accomplishment of the objectives of the instruction depends upon a great variation in the backgrounds and experience of the trainees, for example, some aspect of problem solving.

5. A wide range of abilities, aptitudes, education, training, and experience is of little consequence, for example, introductory materials or orientations.

Advantages. With this system, scheduling and assignment of trainees and instructors is relatively uncomplicated. It simply involves matching classes with instructors, training space, and equipment. Variables which must be taken into account in other forms of organization can be ignored. Although planning for any subject in a course cannot be undertaken without reference to other blocks of instruction in the same course, there is less need for cooperative planning by all instructors under the random system. Because each instructor is largely responsible for the planning and conduct of instruction in a specific content area, it is relatively easy to identify deficiencies which result in failure to achieve instructional objectives.

Disadvantages. With random organization, the length of instructional periods must be standard if scheduling difficulties are to be avoided. Sometimes, a thirty-minute period is enough to complete the instructional job; but if periods are standardized at fifty minutes, the instructor must pad the instruction to fill the time. At other times, a fifty-minute period does not allow enough time, and the instructor must compress his presentation to fit the time allotted. Regardless of the rigidity of prerequisites for enrollment in any training program, wide variations in trainee aptitude, ability, education, training, and experiences are unavoidable. Although the level of the instruction may be set in terms of the prerequisites, the instructor will be dealing with the mythical "average" trainee. The level may be too high and the pace too fast for some, or it may be just the opposite for others. Because each lesson is planned and conducted mainly by one instructor, gaps, overlaps, and duplication of instruction are inevitable. They are difficult to identify and costly to remedy. The effectiveness of instruction varies with the ability of the instructor. Even where a minimum acceptable standard of instructor competence has been established, there is a wide range of expertise involved. Yet, the effectiveness of the instructor depends mainly on his ability, acting more or less on his own, to plan and conduct the instruction. The variability of the groups complicates the problem.

Homogeneous Grouping

A homogeneous group is characterized by uniformity in achievement, ability, aptitude, background, education, training, or experience. With this type of grouping, trainees are assigned to a class on the basis of selection instruments or devices which indicate that they are alike in specific attributes, traits, or abilities. Although it cannot be assumed that they are undiversified solely on the selection factor, a narrower range of diversification is established. It should be noted that even with a group composed of trainees who have scored identically on an aptitude test, there will not only be differences among that group in that aptitude (because of errors of measurement) but there will be variations almost as great as in a randomly selected group on any other selection factor, such as ability, experience, or prior training.

Uses. Homogeneous grouping is used (1) to provide remedial assistance to trainees; (2) to provide a means of accelerating trainees who are fast learners, thus enabling them to complete a course of instruction quicker; and (3) to provide faster, more able, or more experienced trainees with more advanced work in a subject, or broader contact with a content area.

Advantages. The reduced variability of the group makes it possible for the instructor to present content and to use strategies which are most appropriate for the ability, aptitude, education, training, or experience of the group. It also enables the instructor to pitch his instruction at the proper level and pace for the group. Homogeneous groups are typically smaller than randomly selected groups. This makes it possible to obtain greater individual attention and trainee participation in learning activities. The smaller number of trainees increases instructor opportunity to evaluate progress toward learning goals. Because instruction can be given at an appropriate level for the trainees in a group, even if they are slow learners, the group can achieve the learning objectives.

Disadvantages. For homogeneous grouping there must be an investment of time and money in selecting and using screening techniques and devices. In addition, smaller classes result in smaller trainee-instructor ratios; that is, more instructors are required to handle the groups. As pointed out earlier, selection of trainees on one basis of similarity does not mean that they are similar in all other traits and abilities. If a combination of traits and abilities is needed, it is extremely difficult to achieve any realistic degree of homogeneity. The increased number of groups complicates the scheduling of classes and the assignment of students and instructors.

Team Teaching

Team teaching is a system of organization utilizing a team of instructors, two to eight in number. One member is designated as the team leader and the others, who represent a range of subject matter and teaching competencies, jointly plan, conduct, and evaluate all learning activities for a relatively large group of trainees. The total trainee group may be taught simultaneously for some lessons and divided into smaller groups for other instruction.

Uses. Team teaching can be used with any type content, at any level, and for any instructional purpose. However, it is primarily used (1) to handle large and diversified groups of trainees efficiently; (2) to maximize the use of available instructor knowledge and skills; and (3) to provide a means of dealing with individual differences in trainee achievement, ability, aptitude, educational level, prior training, and experience.

Advantages. Improved instructional effectiveness is enhanced by the cooperative planning of a team of instructors. Instruction is given by the most technically qualified instructor. The best method for reaching the objective is used. There are increased opportunities for trainee participation, and attention can be given to individual differences. Team teaching permits maximum utilization of the talents of instructors. Instructors are assigned tasks commensurate with their technical knowledge, experience, and teaching skills. Routine teaching and administrative tasks can be assigned to less skilled members of the team, thereby reserving the highly skilled instructors for more demanding instructional jobs. This system of organization permits variations in both the size of trainee groups and in the length of instructional periods. Trainees can be regrouped in accordance with their needs. The result is a degree of flexibility and responsiveness, difficult to achieve with most other approaches.

Disadvantages. The success of team teaching depends on the quality of planning. Time must be available prior to and during the course for coordination and planning by members of the team. Each instructor serving as a member of a team must be able to work effectively with the other members; he must know his job, know what other members of the team are doing, and be able to interact with them. Because team teaching has not been used to any great extent in industrial training, the roles of team members must be defined; and training in performing these roles must be provided to each member.

TEAM LEARNING

Team learning is a form of organization in which a group of trainees, under one instructor, is subdivided into smaller groups or teams for instruction. Under the supervision of the instructor, these teams engage in learning activities of a variety of types aimed at the development of verbal and manipulative skills.

Uses. Team learning can be used as a means of achieving many types of instructional objectives, for any group, and with any content. Primarily, team learning is used (1) to handle individual differences in trainee achievement, ability, aptitude, educational level, prior training, and experience; (2) to teach team skills; (3) to provide guided practice in developing verbal or manipulative skills; and (4) to develop problem-solving ability.

Advantages. Team learning enhances the effectiveness of instruction because it employs a variety of methods, emphasizes trainee activity, and provides for individual differences. This form of organization permits changes in the size and composition of subgroups to meet the needs of the individual. Time can also be allocated to activities as needed. While all activities of the group are planned with the guidance and assistance of the instructor, the group and subgroups teach themselves. There is less formal presentation by the instructor.

Disadvantages. A team-learning instructor must have mastery of the subject matter, be proficient in the skills being taught, and be accomplished in carrying out all methods and techniques of teaching. Few instructors have had the training and experience required to use this system successfully. The graduates of a course operated under the team-learning concept are likely to show a great amount of variation in terms of job knowledge and proficiency because no two trainees have been exposed to identical content or learning experiences.

MEDIATING DEVICES

TEACHING MACHINES

A teaching machine is any mechanical, electrical, or electronic device which provides instruction to a trainee without the direct participation of a human instructor. Devices of this type simulate, in one way or another, the functions normally fulfilled by a teacher. They contain instructional material, present it in steps, provide a means for the trainee to respond, and provide the trainee with immediate information regarding the correctness of his response. In addition, some machines perform the following functions:

1. Discriminate the correctness of the student's response.
2. Automatically advance the program.
3. Provide random access to teaching frames.
4. Retain those frames on which errors have been made for further presentation.
5. Record and tabulate correct and incorrect responses.
6. Select and present content based on evaluation of previous responses.
7. Permit two-way communication between trainee and machine.

The media used include printed material, projected material, visual or audio signal, or a combination thereof. The response medium may be pencil, stylus, typewriter, key, lever, push button, switch, light gun, the spoken word, or any appropriate combination.

Uses. Teaching machines are used (1) to supplement other instructional methods of teaching by providing a means of advance study, practice, remedial work, makeup instruction, review, maintenance drill, acceleration, or enrichment material; (2) to substitute for conventional teaching methods in teaching facts, concepts, principles, or skills, and thereby relieve the instructor of repetitive or routine teaching tasks; (3) to control instructional materials during the development and validation stage; and (4) to insure complete control over the sequence of instruction, the form of trainee response, and the immediate correction of errors.

Advantages. Gadgetry is extremely effective in engaging and holding trainee attention. Although prolonged use of teaching machines may result in a deterioration of trainee interest, this occurs at a slower pace than with more conventional methods. With a machine, the activity of the learner—whether writing, speaking, or manipulating levers and buttons—is insured. When the trainee stops responding, the instruction stops. Because the material in a machine is programmed and self-paced, it has the same capacity as programmed instruction for reducing failure rate, for raising end-of-course proficiency, for reducing course completion time, and for standardizing instruction. A reliable and well-designed machine with a fully validated program does not require an instructor, thus freeing instructors for more difficult and demanding types of teaching.

Disadvantages. Machines are expensive in terms of capital outlay and often in terms of maintenance. There are so many types of machines on the market, and so few programs, that it is difficult to match existing programs and machines. Frequently, it is necessary to reproduce a program in a format acceptable for an available machine. This is an expensive and time-consuming process. The problems of scheduling and assignment caused by the self-pacing feature of programmed materials are just as outstanding with teaching machines as they are with book format programs. Added to these are the unique storage, maintenance, and repair problems of machines.

STUDENT RESPONSE SYSTEM

A trainee response system is an electrical or electronic means of establishing two-way communication and interaction between an instructional program (or an instructor) and trainees. Systems of this type are designed to be used by the classroom instructor, in conjunction with mass media, such as motion pictures and television, and magnetic tape recordings, lectures, and demonstrations. Periodically throughout the presentation, each trainee in the group is simultaneously asked to respond to questions. Responses may be recorded on IBM cards or paper rolls, which are automatically advanced before the correct answer is given. Multiple-choice questions may be handled by depressing keys. In this way, response data are recorded and tabulated, and the trainee receives immediate feedback from the instructor or by means of indicator lights. Similarly, the instructor can have his teaching effectiveness immediately evaluated, at any time, by means of error counters or meters which indicate the percentage of correct responses to his questions.

Uses. Trainee response devices combined with lectures, demonstrations, audio or video tape recordings, or the mass media may be used to replace an instructor or as an aid to instruction. In the former instance the equipment is used in its preprogrammed automatic mode; it prerecords all audio and visual stimuli, including questions, and maintains control of the presentation. In the latter instance the instructor provides control over the sequence, pace, and coverage of the material.

Advantages. Because instruction is carefully planned and preprogrammed, it is more effective. In addition, when the trainee response device is used as an aid to instruction, the instructor receives immediate and specific feedback from the trainees, as necessary, throughout his lecture or demonstration. He can then improve his presentation as he proceeds by clarifying points that have been misunderstood. The requirement for periodic individual trainee responses to questions by means of the response device enhances trainee attention, provides immediate feedback, and thereby improves learning. The size of the group that can be handled is limited only by the number of response devices installed in the classroom. In its automatic programmed mode, the equipment can present the same material, in the same sequence, to many groups of trainees.

Disadvantages. The instructor must not only be a highly skilled lecturer or demonstrator, he must also ask effective diagnostic questions, and clarify, on the spot, any misunderstandings. In short, he must be fluent and flexible. Because these devices are costly, they must be used frequently and judiciously if an appropriate return on investment is to be realized. Instructors must be trained to insure that lectures and demonstrations are programmed for effective presentation, and that questions are properly framed, developed well in advance, and inserted at the proper point in the instructional sequences.

COMPUTER-BASED INSTRUCTIONAL SYSTEMS

A computer-based instructional system consists of a teaching machine and associated equipment which includes a digital computer as one of its components. The computer permits individual instruction of upwards of 200 trainees simultaneously. The stimulus may be on cathode-ray tube, typewriter printout, or audio signal. Responses may be made of typewriter, light pen, or keyboard. The computer may have the capability of regulating the difficulty of the problems, the rate of presentation, and the type of material presented based on the past performance of the individual. As the trainee progresses, the speed and difficulty of the program increase automatically; if the trainee slows down or exceeds a predetermined error rate, the computer adjusts the program accordingly. In addition, a record of responses can be maintained. The computer-based system can provide the ultimate in machine instruction by engaging the trainee in a mutually responsive conversation, communicated through a typewriter keyboard.

Uses. Computer-based systems are used (1) to teach trainees to perform complex analytical tasks; (2) to provide automated and individualized drill in manual or manipulative skills; and (3) to teach deductive inference and advanced problem-solving techniques by conversational interaction and/or simulation.

Advantages. The computer-based instructional system, because it is self-paced, has the same trainee learning advantages as programmed instruction and teaching machines. The computer has the additional advantages of speed of reaction, ability to adjust the program to the individual, and the capacity to handle relatively large groups of trainees simultaneously. Use of a computer-based system speeds learning because it presents pertinent information to the trainee without time-consuming detours.

Disadvantages. Computer-based systems are elaborate, hence require a large investment for purchase or rental and for installation and maintenance. Programs are difficult to design because of their inherent complexity. Both qualified computer programmers and programmed instruction programmers are required to develop instructional materials. Therefore, the development of a program production capability locally, or contractually, is required.

CLOSED-CIRCUIT TELEVISION SYSTEMS (CCTV)

A closed-circuit television system consists of one or more television cameras (with associated control equipment), lighting equipment; audio equipment; film chains; video tape recorders; a distribution system, which makes use of coaxial cable or microwave for the transmission of picture and sound; and receivers. Closed-circuit television, therefore, is distinguished from broadcast television by the method used to distribute the picture and sound. With broadcast TV, a transmitter distributes the signal in all directions.

Characteristics. Closed-circuit television (and video tape recordings) has several characteristics of great significance for training purposes.

1. It has the quality of indefinite extension; that is, once the cost of production has been met, instructional television can be used with as many classes, either simultaneously or sequentially, as there are receivers available.
2. It communicates sound.
3. It is a visual medium, thus ideally suited for showing objects, processes, maneuvers, and their interrelationships.
4. Television transmits action; it is a dynamic medium.
5. It has immediacy, a quality which heightens its "real world" character and adds to its impact.
6. It is an inclusive medium; it can transmit clearly all the other audiovisual materials, that is, films, slides, charts, etc.

Uses. CCTV is used (1) to teach operation and functioning of equipment; (2) to teach individual and team skills; (3) to bring live, and sometimes dangerous, demonstrations into the classroom; (4) to give close-up magnification of small equipment parts; (5) to compare objects simultaneously; (6) to integrate films, graphics, or other training aids into an instructional sequence; (7) to handle large groups at dispersed locations simultaneously; (8) to repeat instruction; and (9) to provide a means of exchanging instruction (kinescope or video tape).

Advantages. With instructional television the instructor teaches to the camera; therefore, every viewer, regardless of his location in the classroom, is being addressed personally. Research has demonstrated conclusively that such eye contact provides an effective inducement for learning. Television projects personality because of direct address and the use of close-ups. If the TV instructor has a persuasive and outgoing personality, he can imbue the content with personal meaning. The ability of TV to magnify even the smallest objects through close-ups or microscopic projection is one of its greatest advantages. With TV everyone has a front-row seat.

TV represents selective attention. It draws the trainees' attention to the screen and tends to reduce the amount of random attention so characteristic of conventional instruction. TV is also selective in that it represents *edited* reality. A carefully prepared lesson, televised skillfully, eliminates extraneous material and deals only with significant instructional points and the examples illustrating them. Because of the way in which TV productions are planned and produced, they are more efficient than conventional lessons. A presentation which takes fifty minutes by conventional means can be adequately covered in a twenty to thirty minute TV version. This is largely the result of careful planning; nonessential material is deleted, visuals are presented without wasted motion, and the instructor does not wander away from the carefully rehearsed script.

TV presentations have more impact on learners than conventional lecture or demonstration. This is due partly to the special technical capabilities of TV (magnification, amplification, superimposition, split screen, rapid changes in perspective, and the optimal integration of a variety of audiovisual aids) and partly to the fact that the instruction is presented by a recognized authority, backed up by a TV production team of technical experts. Once a TV lesson has been recorded on video tape (or kinescope), it can be replayed as frequently as necessary. Each trainee is therefore exposed to the identical instruction.

Disadvantages. The TV screen, whether large or small, can handle only the amount of detail that the number of lines and the resolution of the receiving set can convey. This, at best, is considerably less than real-life visibility. For this reason, TV primarily uses medium range and close-up shots. Long shots tend to be reserved for viewer orientation. This limitation restricts the amount of written material presented and makes necessary the use of very simple charts, diagrams, and other visuals. The TV camera has difficulty in handling strong contrasts; it produces the best pictures when it deals with a somewhat limited gray scale. This means that visuals and illustrations must be specially prepared (or treated) for TV use. Of course a color system does not have this limitation.

TV usually allows for only one-way communication. The instructor misses the immediate feedback from the trainees and the clues it provides for pacing, for increasing or lessening the amount of detail, and for repeating difficult concepts or ideas. The trainees are likely to feel cut off from personal communication with the instructor because they cannot break in with a question or ask for amplification of a point.

A TV lesson cannot be interrupted, slowed down, or accelerated. The pace is set by the TV instructor for the average trainee. This pace may be too rapid for some trainees, too slow for others. The high installation, production, and maintenance costs make it necessary to select carefully the instructional materials to be presented by TV.

PROCEDURES

Advance Preparation

The process of selecting instructional strategies cannot be set forth as a series of routine steps anyone can follow. Selecting strategies involves many variables and is, therefore, an extremely complex task. Strategy decisions must be based primarily on professional and considered judgment following a careful weighing of all factors. The systems designer must have a thorough knowledge of methods of instruction, systems of trainee and instructor organization, and mediating devices; and an understanding of the uses, advantages, and limitations of each of these elements of strategy. For this reason, the first step in the selection process is to study the preceding section of this chapter. The remainder of this chapter describes a method of arriving at a choice of strategy. It is deceptively simple. However, there are many judgments involved. For this reason, the procedures must be viewed only as guides. The appropriateness of strategies selected, even using the procedures as defined, still hinges on the quality of the judgments made.

(*text continues on page 236*)

Figure 8-1. Guide to the selection of instructional strategies.*

Criteria	Primary strategies				Alternative strategies			
1	Primary method	Supporting method	Mediating device	Organizational system	Alternative method	Supporting method	Mediating device	Organizational system
	2	3	4	5	6	7	8	9
A. *Training objectives*								
1. To orient trainees to policies, rules, course purposes, learning resources, or the like.	L	C	SRS	any	L PI SA FT	C C C C	CCTV TM none none	RG RG any any
2. To introduce a subject, indicate its importance, and present an overview of its scope.	L	C	SRS	any	L PI	C C	CCTV TM	RG RG
3. To give directions to trainees on procedures to use in subsequent learning activities.	L	C	SRS	any	SA	C	none	RG
4. To provide individualized remedial assistance.	PI	T	TM	any	T	PE	none	none
5. To illustrate the application of rules, principles, or procedures.	D	PE	none	any	D	PE	CCTV	any
6. To provide means of accelerating individual trainees.	PI	PE	TM	any	PI COM COM T	PE none none PE	CBIS none none none	any TT TL none

*Key to abbreviations at end of guide.

Figure 8-1 (Continued)

Criteria (1)	Primary strategies				Alternative strategies			
	Primary method 2	Supporting method 3	Mediating device 4	Organizational system 5	Alternative method 6	Supporting method 7	Mediating device 8	Organizational system 9
7. To provide more advanced work in a subject for faster, more able, or more experienced trainees (vertical enrichment).	PI	PE	TM	any	COM COM SA CO	none none none none	none none none none	TT TL any any
8. To provide broader contact with a content area for faster, more able, or more experienced trainees (horizontal enrichment).	PI	PE	TM	any	COM COM SA C	none none none none	none none none none	TT TL any any
9. To provide an alternate means of learning for absentees (makeup instruction).	PI	PE	TM	any	T SA	none none	none none	none none
10. To build required common background for in-class study of a subject (advance study).	PI	C	TM	any	SA FT	C C	none none	none none
11. To provide review of content or practice of skills taught in class (homework).	PI	PE	TM	any	SA	PE	none	none
12. To provide a pattern for later performance and to set standards for that practice.	D	PE	SRS	any	D	PE	CCTV	any
13. To teach manual or manipulative operations, including the use of tools and test equipment, assembly, disassembly, or repair of equipment.	PE	D	none	any	PE PE PI	PI D PE	TM none CBIS	any TL any

Figure 8-1. (Continued)

Criteria	Primary strategies				Alternative strategies			
1	Primary method 2	Supporting method 3	Mediating device 4	Organizational system 5	Alternative method 6	Supporting method 7	Mediating device 8	Organizational system 9
14. To teach principles or theories (why something works).	PI	PE	TM	any	L COM COM	D none none	CCTV none none	any any TT
15. To teach operation and functioning of equipment (how something works).	PI	PE	TM	any	L COM COM	D none none	CCTV none none	any any TT
16. To teach the execution of tactical movements or team skills.	PE	D	none	any	D COM G/S	C none RP	CCTV none none	any TL none
17. To teach use or control of the voice, balance, breath, or muscles.	PE	D	none	any	PE PE	D none	TM CBIS	any any
18. To stimulate trainee interest and thinking through group participation.	C	none	none	RG	C FT CS P L	none C RP GI BS	none none none none none	TL none none none none
19. To make use of trainees' past experience in collecting facts and ideas for the solution of a problem.	C	SA	none	RG	C L CO	SA B none	none none none	TL none none
20. To teach safety procedures.	D	PE	CCTV	any	COM T	none PE	none none	TL none

Figure 8-1. (Continued)

	Primary strategies				Alternative strategies			
Criteria	Primary method	Supporting method	Mediating device	Organizational system	Alternative method	Supporting method	Mediating device	Organizational system
1	2	3	4	5	6	7	8	9
21. To improve reasoning and problem-solving abilities.	C	SA	none	any	C PI CS IM G/S IE	SA C none C none none	none TM none none none none	TL any none none none none
22. To illustrate the application of concepts and principles.	D	C	SRS	any	D D	C C	CCTV none	any TT
23. To provide for maintenance of a skill.	PE	none	none	any	PI	none	TM	any
24. To review, clarify, emphasize, or summarize material.	L	C	SRS	any	L PI FT	C C C	CCTV TM none	any any none
25. To evaluate learning.	PE	C	SRS	any	none IM IE	none none none	none none none	none none none
26. To control learning conditions for experimental purposes.	PI	PE	TM	any	PI L	PE D	CBIS CCTV	any any
27. To build human relations skills.	CS	RP	CCTV	any	ST	none	none	none
28. To teach principles of management and leadership.	CS	RP	none	any	IM G/S IE	C C C	none CBIS none	none none none

Figure 8-1. (Continued)

Criteria	Primary strategies				Alternative strategies			
1	Primary method 2	Supporting method 3	Mediating device 4	Organizational system 5	Alternative method 6	Supporting method 7	Mediating device 8	Organizational system 9
29. To develop communication skills.	CS	RP	CCTV	any	ST IM	none C	none none	none none
30. To develop self-understanding.	ST	none	none	none	RP CS	C C	none none	none none
31. To develop managerial skills; for example decision making.	IE	C	none	none	G/S IM CS	none C RP	CBIS none none	none none none
32. To develop teamwork.	G/S	none	none	none	CO	none	none	none
33. To improve technical performance.	G/S	none	CBIS	none	GI	P	none	any
34. To develop creativity—creative solutions to problems.	B	none	none	none	CO	none	none	none
35. To gather facts or points of view on an issue or problems.	P	BS	none	none	CO FT GI	none C none	none none none	none none none
36. To stimulate interest and participation in a large group.	BS	none	none	none	P GI CO	BS none none	none none none	none none none
B. *Content*								
1. Deals mainly with concepts and principles.	PI	C	TM	any	L L COM CS P	D D none RP GI	SRS CCTV none none none	any any TT none none

227

Figure 8-1. *(Continued)*

Criteria 1	Primary strategies				Alternative strategies			
	Primary method 2	Supporting method 3	Mediating device 4	Organizational system 5	Alternative method 6	Supporting method 7	Mediating device 8	Organizational system 9
2. Deals mainly with reasoning and problem solving.	C	SA	none	any	SA PI CS IE	none C RP C	none TM none none	any any none none
3. Deals mainly with manual or manipulative operations.	PE	D	none	any	PE PE PI	PI D PE	TM none CBIS	any TL any
4. Requires intensive individual practice.	PE	D	none	any	PI PI SA	PE PE none	TM CBIS none	any any none
5. Requires intensive team practice.	PE	D	none	any	PE G/S	none none	none none	TL none
6. Deals with materials which require visual or auditory illustration.	L	D	SRS	any	L PI	D none	CCTV TM	any any
7. Requires control over performance to prevent the practice of errors.	PE	D	none	any	PI PI	PE PE	TM CBIS	any any
8. Involves hazard to men or equipment.	D	PE	CCTV	SG	T	PE	none	none
9. Requires absolute control over the sequence of presentation.	PI	PE	TM	any	L PI	D PE	CCTV/SRS CBIS	any any

Figure 8-1. (Continued)

Criteria 1	Primary strategies				Alternative strategies			
	Primary method 2	Supporting method 3	Mediating device 4	Organizational system 5	Alternative method 6	Supporting method 7	Mediating device 8	Organizational system 9
10. Demands absolute control over the form of the trainee's response.	PI	PE	TM	any	PI T	PE PE	CBIS/SRS none	any none
11. Lends itself to oral presentation.	L	D,C	SRS	any	L COM PI	D none none	CCTV none TM	any TT any
12. Is relatively stable.	PI	PE	TM	any	PI L	PE D	CBIS CCTV	any any
13. Is subject to frequent and radical change.	L	D	SRS	any	C COM COM	none none none	none none none	any TT TL
C. Trainee population								
1. Is relatively homogeneous in terms of aptitude, ability, speed of learning, prior training, or experience.	L	D	SRS	HG	L	D	CCTV	RG
2. Has wide differences in aptitude, ability, speed of learning, prior training, or experience.	PI	PE	TM	RG	PI COM COM	PE none none	CBIS none none	RG TT TL
3. Is mature enough and sufficiently motivated to work more or less independently.	PI	PE	TM	any	COM SA CO	none none none	none none none	TL any none
4. Has the level of reading ability required to deal with the instructional material.	PI	none	TM	HG	COM SA CS	none none none	none none none	TL HG none

Figure 8-1. (Continued)

Criteria	Primary strategies				Alternative strategies			
1	Primary method 2	Supporting method 3	Mediating device 4	Organizational system 5	Alternative method 6	Supporting method 7	Mediating device 8	Organizational system 9
5. Is relatively large in numbers.	PI	none	TM	RG	L L COM BS	D D none none	SRS CCTV none none	RG RG TT/TL none
6. Is relatively small in numbers.	D C PE	PE none none	none none none	any any any	COM CO CS	none none RP	none none none	TL/TT none none
7. Has experience, background, or prior training which are germane to the content.	C	none	none	HG	PE COM IM IE	D none C C	none none none none	HG TL none none
8. Has sufficient skill to put opinions, ideas, and experiences into words.	C	none	none	any	CS IE ST B	RP C none none	none none none none	none none none none
9. Has been prepared for the instruction by reading, lecture, or demonstration.	PE	none	none	any	C CS IM IE	none RP none none	none none none none	any none none none
D. Instructors 1. Technically qualified.	L D PE PI C T	D PE none PE none none	SRS SRS none TM none none	any any any any any none	COM T ST RP	none none none none	none none none none	TT none none none

Figure 8-1. (Continued)

	Primary strategies				Alternative strategies			
Criteria 1	Primary method 2	Supporting method 3	Mediating device 4	Organizational system 5	Alternative method 6	Supporting method 7	Mediating device 8	Organizational system 9
2. Pedagogically qualified.	L	D	SRS	any	L	D	CCTV	any
	D	PE	SRS	any	COM	none	none	TL
	PE	none	none	any	COM	none	none	TT
	C	none	none	any	T	none	none	none
	T	none	none	none	all SPM	none	none	none
3. Available in sufficient numbers.	L	D	SRS	any	T	none	none	none
	D	PE	SRS	any				
	PE	none	none	any				
	C	none	none	any				
	T	none	none	none				
4. In short supply or unavailable.	PI	PE	TM	any	PI	PE	CBIS/SRS	any
5. Polished speakers.	L	D	SRS	any	L	D	CCTV	any
	D	PE	SRS	any	COM	none	none	TT
6. Competent leaders of group discussion.	C	none	none	any	all SPM	none	none	none
7. Carefully rehearsed.	L	D	SRS	any	L	D	CCTV	any
	D	PE	SRS	any				
8. Skilled in the use of individual tutoring techniques.	PI	PE	TM	any	T	none	none	none
9. Have adequate time for planning.	L	D	SRS	any	L	D	CCTV	any
	D	PE	SRS	any	COM	none	none	TT
					all SPM	none	none	TL
								none

Figure 8-1. (Continued)

| Criteria | Primary strategies | | | | Alternative strategies | | | |
| | Primary method | Supporting method | Mediating device | Organizational system | Alternative method | Supporting method | Mediating device | Organizational system |
1	2	3	4	5	6	7	8	9
10. Able to work effectively as members of a team.	COM	none	none	TT	none	none	none	none
11. Masters of a variety of methods and techniques of teaching.	COM	none	none	TL	all SPM	none	none	none
E. Facilities, equipment, and materials								
1. Centralized classroom, conference room, or laboratory facilities are available.	L D PE C	D PE none none	SRS SRS none none	any any any any	COM all SPM	none none	none none	any none
2. Centralized facilities are in short supply or lacking.	PI	PE	TM	none	SA	C	none	none
3. Appropriate training aids are available.	L D	D PE	SRS SRS	any any	L COM COM	D none none	CCTV none none	any TT TL
4. Seating permits face-to-face communication.	C	none	none	any	COM all SPM	none none	none none	TL none
5. Equipment components are large enough for all trainees to see them clearly.	D	none	SRS	any	none	none	none	none
6. Equipment components are too small for all trainees to see them clearly.	D	none	none	SG	D	none	CCTV	any

Figure 8-1. (Continued)

	Primary strategies				Alternative strategies			
Criteria	Primary method	Supporting method	Mediating device	Organizational system	Alternative method	Supporting method	Mediating device	Organizational system
1	2	3	4	5	6	7	8	9
7. Expense of required mockups is justified.	D	none	none	any	COM D	none none	none CCTV	TL any
8. Equipment and materials are in adequate supply.	D PE PI	PE none PE	SRS none TM	any any any	COM	none	none	TL
9. Safety precautions are adequate.	D PE	PE none	SRS none	any any	COM COM FT	none none none	none none none	TL TT none
10. The training area is so arranged as to facilitate close supervision of the trainees.	PE	none	none	any	COM	none	none	TL
11. Each trainee has adequate working space.	PE	none	none	any	COM	none	none	TL
12. Furniture is movable.	C	none	none	any	COM all SPM	none none	none none	TL none
F. Time								
1. A large amount of material must be taught in a short period of time.	L	D	SRS	HG	PI L COM G/S	none D none none	TM CCTV none none	any any TT none
2. A minimum amount of lead time is available for the preparation of instruction and instructional materials.	L D C	D PE none	SRS SRS none	any any any	COM	none	none	TT

233

Figure 8-1. (Continued)

Criteria (1)	Primary strategies				Alternative strategies			
	Primary method (2)	Supporting method (3)	Mediating device (4)	Organizational system (5)	Alternative method (6)	Supporting method (7)	Mediating device (8)	Organizational system (9)
3. Lead time for the preparation of instruction and instructional materials is plentiful.	PI	COM	TM	any	L D COM COM all SPM	none none none none	CCTV CCTV none none none	any any TT TL none
4. Personnel must complete training at the same time.	L D PE C	D PE none none	SRS SRS none none	RG/HG RG/HG RG/HG RG/HG	L D COM COM	none none none none	CCTV CCTV none none	RG/HG RG/HG RG/HG RG/HG
5. Different course completion times are not critical to subsequent training or assignments.	PI	COM	TM	any	PI COM	none none	CBIS none	any TL
G. Other								
1. Individual and continuous trainee progress is essential.	PI	PE	TM	any	PI COM	PE none	CBIS none	any TL
2. Active trainee response is critical to learning.	PI PE	PE none	TM none	any any	PI L C all SPM	PE D none none	CBIS SRS none none	any any any none
3. Active trainee response is not critical to learning.	L D	D none	none none	any any				
4. Standardization of instruction is critical.	PI	PE	TM	any	L PI	D PE	CCTV CBIS	any any

Figure 8-1. (Concluded)

Criteria	Primary strategies				Alternative strategies			
1	Primary method 2	Supporting method 3	Mediating device 4	Organizational system 5	Alternative method 6	Supporting method 7	Mediating device 8	Organizational system 9
5. Standardization of instruction is not desired.	COM	none	none	TL	SA all SPM	C none	none none	any none
6. Mastery of a skill is critical.	PE	none	none	SG	PI PI	PE PE	TM CBIS	any any
7. An accurate record of trainee responses is needed.	PI PI	PE PE	TM CBIS	any any	L D	D none	SRS SRS	any any
8. Immediate correction of errors is critical.	PI PI PE	PE PE none	TM/SRS CBIS none	any any any	L D all SPM	D none none	SRS SRS none	any any none
9. Problems of integration with other instructional strategies are not critical.	PI PI PE	PE PE none	TM CBIS none	any any any	L all SPM	D none	CCTV none	any none

Key to Abbreviations

Basic methods:

C   Conference
COM   Combination instruction
D   Demonstration
L   Lecture
PE   Practical exercise
PI   Programmed instruction
SA   Study assignment
T   Tutoring

Special participative methods:

B   Brainstorming
BS   Buzz session
CO   Committee
CS   Case study
FT   Field trip
GI   Group interview
G/S   Games or simulation
IE   In-basket exercise
IM   Incident method
P   Panel
RP   Role playing
SPM   Special participative methods
ST   Sensitivity training

Mediating devices:

CBIS   Computer-based instructional system
CCTV   Closed-circuit television
SRS   Student response system
TM   Teaching machine

Trainee and instructor organization:

HG   Homogeneous grouping
RG   Random grouping and assignment
SG   Small group
TL   Team learning
TT   Team teaching

STEPS IN SELECTION

Step 1. Study the performance objective for the specific block of instruction as entered on the Performance Objective Workcard (see Fig. 4-3). Note carefully:

    a. What the trainee should be able *to do* following the instruction.

    b. The *conditions* under which he must perform.

    c. The *criterion* of successful performance.

Step 2. Compare the behavior described in the performance objective with the training objectives listed in Figure 8-1, section A, items 1 to 36.

When the objective has been found that most closely matches that of the instructional block, note the primary and supporting methods in columns 2 and 3 and the organizational system identified in column 5. The mediating device identified in column 4 is not essential to the use of the method.

Step 3. Check the tentative selection of method against the remaining criteria listed in Figure 8-1, sections B to G. If the item describes the type of content the instruction deals with, the type of trainee in the class, the instructor considerations that apply, as well as the facilities, equipment, materials, and time factors that bear, then look as the primary method entered in column 2. If this does not match the original selection, go back to the item and select an alternative method from column 6. Recheck this method against all applicable criteria in sections B to G.

The following is a specific example of how to carry out the three steps just mentioned.

Objective: Without using references, and with a time limit of five minutes, the student must be able to calculate the resistance of a resistor of unknown value using the Wheatstone Bridge circuit.

Step 1. The typical training objective in Figure 8-1 which most closely matches this objective is Criterion A14. The primary method recommended in column 2 is programmed instruction (PI) followed by a practical exercise (PE) in column 3. It so happens that a program is available to teach this skill. Now, check section B of the criteria, Items 1, 4, 6, 7, 9, 10, and 12 apply. Note that for each criterion, PI is either the primary or alternative method recommended.

Step 2. Now check section C. Criteria 2, 3, 4, and 5 apply. Again either the primary or alternative methods include PI. Check sections D to G in the same way.

Step 3. Suppose, however, that a programmed course is *not* available. Check column 6 for Criterion A14 to find the alternative method. The method recommended is a lecture-demonstration on closed-circuit television (kinescope or video tape recording). No such recording is available. The second alternative is a combination lecture-demonstration-practical exercise using any grouping. This is one method that could be selected. Here is where judgment again enters the picture. There are other alternatives, and all of them must be considered before a decision is made.

SELECTED REFERENCES

Boocock, Sarane S. "Simulation Games Today." *Educational Technology* (Apr. 30, 1968), 8:8: 7–10.

Craig, Robert L., and Lester R. Bittel, eds. *Training and Development Handbook*. New York: McGraw-Hill Book Company, 1967, Chaps. 8–14.

DePhillips, Frank A., William M. Berliner, and James J. Cribbin. *Management of Training Programs*. Homewood, Ill.: Richard D. Irwin, Inc., 1960, Chap. 7.

Eitington, Julius E. "T-Group Learnings for Group Effectiveness." *Training and Development Journal* (May 1969), 23:5: 44–47.

Hoover, Kenneth H. *Learning and Teaching in the Secondary School*. Boston: Allyn and Bacon, Inc., 1964, Chaps. 5–8.

Jacobs, David L., and Thomas M. Calero. "Building Stress into Case Discussions." *Training and Development Journal* (August 1966), 20:7: 48–50.

Kibbee, J. M., C. J. Craft, and B. Nanus. *Management Games: A New Technique for Executive Development*. New York: Reinhold Publishing Corporation, 1961.

Lopez, Felix M., Jr. *Evaluating Executive Decision Making: The In-basket Technique*. Research Study 75. AMA, 1966.

Merrill, Harwood F., and Elizabeth Marting, eds. *Developing Executive Skills*. AMA, 1958, Pt. II.

Miller, Harry L. *Teaching and Learning in Adult Education*. New York: The Macmillan Company, 1964.

Moore, Larry F. "Business Games Versus Cases as Tools of Learning." *Training and Development Journal* (October 1967), 21:10: 13–23.

Morgan, Barton, et al. *Methods in Adult Education*. Danville, Ill.: The Interstate Printers and Publishers, Inc., 1963, Chaps. 4–10.

Pigors, Paul, and Faith Pigors. *Case Method in Human Relations: The Incident Process*. New York: McGraw-Hill Book Company, 1961.

Randall, Lyman K., and Ernest M. Schuttenberg. "Participative Managerial Learning." *Making the Most of Training Opportunities*. Management Bulletin 73. AMA, 1965, pp. 20–31.

Rose, Homer C. *The Development and Supervision of Training Programs*. New York: American Technical Society, 1964, Pt. II, Chaps. 5, 7.

Staton, Thomas F. *How to Instruct Successfully.* New York: McGraw-Hill Book Company, 1960, Chaps. 5–8.

Tracey, William R. "Seven Crucial Tests for Programmed Instruction." *Training in Business and Industry* (January, February 1965), 2:1: 38–43ff.

————. *Evaluating Training and Development Systems.* AMA, 1968, pp. 137, 161–174.

9

Selecting Training Aids

THE basis for all learning is experience, and the most effective and permanent learning is derived from concrete, direct experience. However, it is not always possible to provide firsthand experience for trainees. Often, the instructor must resort to an economical means of communicating facts and ideas—the use of symbols, both spoken and written. But words alone cannot provide the vivid, realistic experience required for optimal learning; they must be supplemented and reinforced by other media.

The wise selection and proper use of a variety of audiovisual materials can fill the gap between verbalization and real-life, direct experience. For this reason, training aids are an essential means of increasing the efficiency and effectiveness of training. Good training aids reduce the number of words required to communicate ideas. They stimulate interest, increase attention, promote understanding, and provide experience not obtainable in other ways.

The purpose of this chapter is to set forth guides for the selection of training aids. After completing the chapter, the reader should be able to perform as follows:

Behavior Select the most appropriate training aids to complement and support a training strategy used to achieve training or development objectives.

Conditions Given: a program of instruction and its supporting lesson plans, outlines of content, basic selection guides, access to a master file

of training aids, and the assistance of a training-aids staff specialist.
Criterion   In accordance with the standards and procedures described in
this chapter.

THE NATURE AND PURPOSE OF TRAINING AIDS

In the broadest sense, training aids include almost anything that
assists the instructor in conducting training. For the purposes of this
discussion, however, the items listed below, when used for training and
development, are classified as training aids.

Printed or duplicated aids. These aids include books, manuals, pamphlets, policy and procedures manuals, financial statements, regulations,
directives, job sheets, advance sheets, and handouts.

Graphic aids. These aids include pictures, drawings, illustrations,
photographs, blueprints, templates, chalkboards, bulletin boards, easels,
magnetic placards, embossograph placards, maps, charts, diagrams, and
flip charts.

Three-dimensional aids. These aids include objects, globes, models,
cutaways, mock-ups, sand tables, synthetic trainers, and displays.

Projected Aids. These aids include slides and transparencies of all
sizes, filmstrips, microprojection, motion pictures, and kinescope and
video tape recordings.

Auditory aids. These include disk and tape recordings, and speech-compression recordings.

PURPOSE OF TRAINING AIDS

Training aids are used to facilitate communication of facts, ideas,
principles, and concepts. In many cases, the aids are a substitute for
reality but a necessary one to insure the accurate transmission of information. In other instances training aids are reality because the actual
object, tool, instrument, or organism is observed or manipulated by the
trainee. Regardless of their nature, the overriding purpose of training aids
is to help the trainee acquire the knowledge and skills that are the
objectives of training.

CRITERIA FOR SELECTING TRAINING AIDS

FUNCTIONAL CONSIDERATIONS

Judgment must be applied in the long-range and day-to-day choice
of training aids and in the ways in which they are used. The instructor

must assume the responsibility for insuring learning effectiveness and efficiency by selecting or developing training aids that complement the basic instructional strategy chosen to accomplish the training objectives. Each training medium has certain advantages and limitations. These factors must be carefully weighed before a final selection of aids is made.

BASIC SELECTION GUIDES

The following general guides should be used in selecting training aids regardless of type:

1. Select aids that fit the maturity, interest, and abilities of the trainee group. Aids that are childish or naive will alienate a mature group. Aids that are obscure or overcomplicated only serve to confuse.

2. Select aids which are most appropriate for the particular learning activity. An aid can meet all standards with respect to content, layout, or design and still be unsuitable for a specific learning situation.

3. Maintain a balance in the kinds of aids selected. Avoid repetitive use of any single kind of aid to the exclusion of others. Too many instructors use only one aid—for example, 2 by 2 inch transparencies—because it is convenient. With the variety of aids currently available, this should not happen.

4. Select aids that complement, rather than duplicate, other learning resources. Avoid senseless duplication, such as showing slides of a piece of equipment that can be seen in an adjoining shop or laboratory or of a schematic that is included in a manual or handout issued to all trainees.

5. Avoid the overuse of aids. A training session should not be a three-ring circus nor a psychedelic happening. The instructor who assails the senses of trainees with a broadside of training aids may be a good show-man, but he is not an effective instructor. Do not use an aid just because it is available.

6. The major criterion of selection is simply this: Will it advance learning; is it needed? A training aid must actually *aid* learning and not serve as mere "eyewash."

CONDITIONS FACILITATING THE USE OF AIDS

Certain factors and conditions tend to encourage the use of training aids. Some of these conditions are as follows:

1. Aids are available in sufficient variety and quantity to permit selectivity.

2. Required equipment is available in sufficient quantities and is in good repair.
3. Technical advice and assistance for the selection, fabrication, and use of aids are readily available.
4. The lead time for fabrication, procurement, or purchase of aids is minimal.
5. Aids are centrally cataloged and stored to facilitate control and use.

GUIDES TO THE SELECTION OF TRAINING AIDS

PRINTED OR DUPLICATED AIDS

Printed or duplicated aids are materials used to support instruction in the form of books, manuals, periodicals, pamphlets, regulations, directives or handouts.

Uses. Printed or duplicated aids are used (1) to provide advance assignments, that is, to serve as background information necessary for effective participation in classroom learning activities; (2) to provide reference material, that is, to serve as a basis for the preparation of reports or as source material for the solution of a problem; (3) to provide review and practice materials, in class or out of class; and (4) to evaluate or check on the effectiveness of other learning activities.

Advantages. Printed or duplicated aids can be organized carefully because they are prepared in advance of use. Large quantities of printed materials, usable in many training programs, are readily available from in-house and commercial sources. Printed or duplicated materials are among the least expensive training aids. They are also the most compact, and they can be easily and quickly duplicated in the required quantity.

Disadvantages. Unless printed materials are locally prepared, parts of the material may be unsuitable for local requirements because of the bias of the writing, the perspective represented, or the amount of detail included. Printed materials cannot provide for individual differences. They cannot be written at a level best suited to the abilities, interests, or backgrounds of all members of a trainee group. The extent to which the printed word conveys the intended meaning depends upon the clarity and comparability of the meanings the writer and reader attach to the terms used. Finally, the amount of learning derived from printed materials is a function of the reading speed and comprehension of trainees. Differences in these skills within a trainee group will result in differences in the amount of learning as well as in varying completion times for any reading or study assignments.

Criteria. Printed or duplicated materials selected or produced to support training and development must (1) emphasize content which relates to and is consistent with the training objectives; (2) be free of bias and ambiguity; (3) be presented in an interesting and readable form and format; and (4) include, where applicable, aids to the reader in the form of indexes, glossaries, references, questions, and study hints.

Incidental Graphics

Graphic aids are materials that communicate facts and ideas through a combination of pictures, drawings, symbols, and words. The term "incidental graphics" refers to the use of a chalkboard, easel, or flip chart for illustrating symbols, or words, during or immediately preceding the presentation of instruction.

Uses. Incidental graphics are used for the following: (1) Outline objectives. The chalkboard and easel are convenient media for emphasizing the objectives and scope of an instructional block. (2) Introduce technical terms. The devices offer a practical way of introducing the spelling, pronunciation, and definition of technical terminology. (3) Provide illustration. The devices offer a simple and convenient means of illustrating processes, objects, or ideas by the use of sketches or line drawings. (4) Record key points. The devices can be used effectively to record progress and evolution of ideas in problem solving and to emphasize the key points in a discussion.

Advantages. Incidental graphics are convenient. Almost all classrooms are equipped with chalkboards or easels, well-positioned for easy use by the instructor. They are also flexible. The devices allow freedom in creating materials on the spot and in rearranging existing materials.

Disadvantages. Although the devices are easy to use, this factor often results in careless use and in resultant inefficiency in learning. The background of the trainee determines the interpretation he makes of words, symbols, and even drawings. Extensive chalkboard illustrations and listings require a great amount of preparation time. Care should be taken to insure that lengthy boardwork is prepared prior to each class. The use of other media should be considered.

Criteria. Materials placed on chalboards or easels must be: (1) appropriate for the instructional objectives, (2) neatly and clearly drawn or printed so as to be clearly visible or readable to all trainees, and (3) accompanied by adequate explanation.

PREPARED GRAPHICS

Prepared graphics are printed, embossed, or photographic materials which communicate ideas clearly and forcefully in condensed form through a combination of pictures, drawings, symbols, and words. They include flat pictures, embossograph placards, charts, maps, graphs, and diagrams.

Uses. Prepared graphics are used for the following: (1) Introduce topics. Graphics can be used to introduce new topics in such a way as to capture trainee attention. (2) Stimulate interest. Well-constructed graphics add interest to a lecture or discussion and stimulate trainee questions. (3) Provide illustration. Graphics provide an effective means of illustrating objects, procedures, or ideas presented in lectures or demonstrations. (4) Effect emphasis. Carefully selected graphics focus attention on the critical or important elements in a presentation. (5) Summarize topics. Graphics are effective summarizing devices.

Advantages. Quantitative data and complex relationships can be presented simply and clearly by means of graphics. Graphics are also inherently more interesting than verbal descriptions or numerical tabulations. They are relatively inexpensive to procure or produce. Finally, graphics are easily adaptable to many learning situations.

Disadvantages. Graphics are principally abstract and symbolic; hence they must be supplemented by other methods or media. They must focus on key points and dispense with detail. In some situations this loss of detail may be critically important. They are two-dimensional. Therefore, if depth is important to the learning, graphics may be completely unsuitable; or if motion is essential, graphics may be inappropriate.

Criteria. Graphics used in instruction must (1) be large enough so that all students can see them clearly, (2) be pleasing in composition and arrangement, (3) be accurate and truthful, (4) be sharp and clear so that all details are easily distinguishable, (5) avoid too much detail or an insufficiency of detail, (6) use color judiciously, (7) employ easily identifiable symbols, and (8) include only essential data.

THREE-DIMENSIONAL (3-D) AIDS

A 3-D aid may be any one of the following: (1) real objects (such as equipment, components, or tools removed as units from their normal settings); (2) models or cutaways (recognizable 3-D representations of real things); (3) mock-ups (imitations of the real thing that are not necessarily similar in appearance).

Uses. Three-dimensional aids are used to provide illustration and to teach operation or functioning. Instead of merely talking about an object, or showing a picture of it, the actual object, or a model, is often a more effective illustration. How to operate equipment, tools, or instruments is often most effectively taught by using the actual objects, models, cutaways, or mock-ups.

Advantages. Three-dimensional aids give depth and substance to the item under study and thereby enhance learning. Nonessential elements of the item can be omitted or removed from the aid so that basic elements can be more easily observed. Models, cutaways, and mock-ups can provide interior views of objects ordinarily covered or otherwise invisible. In addition, large objects can be reduced in size, and small objects can be enlarged to convenient size for study and observation. Finally, color and texture can be added to 3-D aids to accent or emphasize important parts or features.

Disadvantages. Models, cutaways, and mock-ups are expensive to construct and maintain. Problems of clarity of communication and misunderstanding of size, function, or complexity may be created by 3-D aids. Such misunderstandings are difficult to correct. Three-dimensional aids are difficult to catalog and require a considerable amount of storage space.

Criteria. Three-dimensional aids used in instruction must be: (1) accurate, that is, true to life, (2) large enough to be clearly visible to the entire student group, (3) as uncomplicated as possible, and (4) durable.

Displays and Exhibits

A display or exhibit is a collection of graphic, photographic, or 3-D aids grouped and displayed to accomplish a specific instructional purpose.

Uses. Displays and exhibits are used to introduce a subject and to summarize a subject. A well-designed exhibit or display is an excellent means of stimulating interest and student motivation. An exhibit or display can also be an effective means of providing a summary for a specific instructional block.

Advantages. Well-designed displays and exhibits are inherently more interesting than verbal descriptions. They are flexible and lend themselves to almost any type of content.

Disadvantages. Worthwhile exhibits and displays are time consuming to design and produce. They need adequate space in a desirable location to be shown to best advantage. Trainees may not know what to look for in a particular exhibit or display; this problem, compounded with the fact that the items are not in their real-life settings, often leads to misunderstandings that are difficult to correct. Some things cannot be brought into the classroom or training area because of size, safety considerations, or expense.

Criteria. An exhibit to be effective must (1) have a single central theme; (2) occupy a place of prominence; (3) be left up only long enough to achieve its purpose; and (4) be attractively arranged, well lighted, and clearly labeled.

SLIDES, TRANSPARENCIES, AND FILMSTRIPS

Slides are single transparent pictures or drawings that can be projected onto a screen. They are usually made of photographic film, although sometimes they are etched on glass or plastic. Transparencies are large slides, usually 7 by 10 inches or 10 by 10 inches in size. Filmstrips consist of a fixed series of individual slides placed on a single strip of 35-millimeter film.

Uses. Slides, transparencies, or filmstrips can be used to present an introduction and an overview of a subject or a process. Similarly, they can provide an effective means of summarizing and reviewing content previously taught by other means. They offer a simple and convenient means of illustrating objects, processes, or ideas.

Advantages. Slides, transparencies, and filmstrips can illustrate objects, events, and ideas that are far away in time or space; enlarge difficult-to-see objects; and stop action. Given a darkened or semidarkened room and a brilliant screen, the attention of the students is focused on the instructional materials. Actual photographs lend realism to instruction—the next best thing to firsthand experience. With slides, transparencies, and filmstrips the illustration can be left on the screen for any length of time for study and discussion. Projection equipment is easy to operate. Films, transparencies, and filmstrips cost little to purchase or produce, occupy little storage space, and are easily cataloged. Projected visuals are suited for color as well as for black and white and can be used in a variety of learning situations.

Disadvantages. Sometimes the set sequence of a filmstrip, or the preplanned sequence of a series of slides, is inappropriate. In the case of the filmstrips, it is impossible to change the order of frames. Equipment in good repair may not always be readily available, and sometimes the equipment breaks down. A still medium cannot portray motion effectively. If motion is essential, the slide, transparency, or filmstrip may be inadequate.

Criteria. Slides, transparencies, or filmstrips used in instruction must (1) fit the training objective; (2) avoid the inclusion of extraneous material; (3) be well designed; (4) be accurate, that is, true to life; and (5) be accompanied by appropriate commentary.

MOTION PICTURES

Motion pictures include black and white and color with or without sound, on 8-millimeter or 16-millimeter film, directly photographed or produced by kinescope recording.

Uses. Motion pictures can be used effectively to present an introduction and an overview of a subject. They provide an excellent means of explaining processes not available for direct observation because of time, distance, or safety. They also offer a way of presenting complex materials, of slowing down or speeding up processes, and of showing applications. Motion pictures can provide an effective means of summarizing content previously presented by other means.

Advantages. Motion pictures can bring remote events into the classroom without loss of realism. Films can substitute for field trips thereby saving time. The condensed nature of a film production also results in time savings. The use of sound and motion increases interest, focuses attention on critical elements, and enhances learning.

Disadvantages. With motion pictures, trainees play a passive role. Because of the darkened room, note-taking is kept to a minimum. Motion picture projectors, while not difficult to operate, are not always available; and they are subject to mechanical or electrical failure. Trainees must be carefully prepared for film viewing, and some sort of follow up is needed to insure learning. Trainees view films in the light of their own experiences. If provisions are not made for follow-up, misunderstanding may be the result.

Criteria. Motion pictures used for instruction must (1) fit the specific instructional purpose, (2) be preceded by specific preparation for viewing the film, (3) be followed by appropriate learning activities, and (4) be current.

AUDITORY AIDS

Auditory aids include disk and tape recordings and their associated equipment.

Uses. Tape recorders can be used to record, evaluate, and improve speech habits, diction, voice, intonation, enunciation, and general speech patterns. Tape recorders and recordings are an effective means of building foreign language speech and listening skills. Recordings also provide a change of pace when more than one voice is used.

Advantages. Actual sounds can be reproduced with sufficient fidelity to foster the development of high-level discrimination skills. Recorders are easy to operate. Tape recordings are relatively inexpensive and are reusable, which further reduces costs.

Tapes can be used in a variety of learning situations, singly or in combination with other media, and by individuals as well as by groups. Contents of tapes are easily changed to suit the instructional objective.

Disadvantages. Since recorders are necessary, they must be in good working order at all times. Equipment breakdowns, however, are quite common. Particularly when used by individuals, recordings can easily be misinterpreted; this could lead to a misunderstanding of concepts and errors being carried out in practice.

Criteria. Recordings used for instruction must make a definite contribution to the achievement of the training objective and be true to life.

PROCEDURES

To analyze requirements for training aids, the following steps should be taken.

Step 1. On the Training Aids Selection Worksheet (see Fig. 9-1), enter the lesson plan number, title, the program of instruction (POI) number and title, and the recommended instructional strategy.

Step 2. Copy the performance objective from the POI in the space provided. Study the performance objective until you have clearly in mind what it is that the trainee must be able to do, the conditions under which he must perform, and the criterion of successful performance. Keep these factors before you as you select your training aids.

Step 3. Analyze the trainee group scheduled for this block of instruction in terms of previous instruction, related training and experience, acquired skills, vocabulary, level of maturity, and instruction that will follow. Keep these factors in mind when you select a training aid.

Step 4. Consider the facilities which will be used to conduct instruction in terms of class size, time available for instruction, room characteristics, and equipment available.

TENTATIVE SELECTION

Step 1. Carefully review each part of the content outline, and make appropriate entries in column 1 of the Training Aids Selection Worksheet. These entries should:

 a. Indicate the purpose and coverage of the introduction.

 b. List the major teaching points in abbreviated form.

 c. Indicate the main points of the summary of the lesson.

Step 2. For the introduction, the body of the lesson, and the summary, if appropriate, select a typical aid which will supplement, rather than supplant, the method or strategy being used. Enter the name of the aid

Figure 9-1.   Training Aids Selection Worksheet.

LP Title _____   LP No. _____

POI Title _____   POI No. _____

Performance Objective _____

Instructional Strategy _____

Content outline 1	Applicable types of aids 2	On hand 3	Requires fabrication or requisition 4
Introduction to lesson			
Body of lesson (Enter abbreviated list of major teaching points.)			
1.			
2.			
3.			
4.			
5.			
6.			
7.			
8.			
9.			
10.			
Summary			

in column 2 of the worksheet, for example, transparency, motion picture, model, or handout. Before making your decision, carefully check the uses, advantages, and disadvantages of each type of aid detailed in an earlier section of this chapter.

FINAL SELECTION AND PROCUREMENT

Step 1. Check local resources. If the type of aid desired is available, get it and study it with these questions in mind:

a. Does it meet the objectives?
b. Does it support the strategy?
c. Is it current and accurate?
d. Does it avoid extraneous detail?
e. Is it well-designed?

Step 2. If the answer to each of these questions is "yes," place a check mark in column 3 of the worksheet for each part of the outline for which a training aid is on hand. If the answer to any one of the questions is "no," arrange with the training aids division to update or redesign the fabricated type aid.

Step 3. If no suitable fabricated type aid is available, consult with a training aids specialist to determine whether a suitable aid can be fabricated. Get answers to these questions:

a. Can the teaching point be adequately visualized?
b. Can the aid be made locally?
c. Is sufficient leadtime available for fabrication of the aid?

Step 4. If the answer to each question in step 3 is "yes," place a check mark in column 4 of the worksheet. Prepare a rough sketch or sample of the required training aid; and prepare a request for procurement, duplication, purchase, or fabrication.

SELECTED REFERENCES

Blamberg, Siegmar F. "Instructional Pre-Analysis," *Training and Development Journal* (June 1969), 23:6: 50–51.
Brown, James W., and Kenneth D. Norberg. *Administering Educational Media.* New York: McGraw-Hill Book Company, 1965.
DeBernardis, Amo. *The Use of Instructional Materials.* New York: Appleton-Century-Crofts, Inc., 1960.

DeKeiffer, Robert, and Lee W. Cochran. *Manual of Audio-Visual Techniques.* Englewood Cliffs, N.J.: Prentice-Hall, Inc., 1962.

DePhillips, Frank A., William M. Berliner, and James J. Cribbin. *Management of Training Programs.* Homewood, Ill.: Richard D. Irwin, Inc., 1960, Chaps. 8, 9.

Eitington, Julius E. "Ten Ways to Use Films in Management Training Seminars." *Training Directors Journal* (May 1963), 17:5: 26–30.

Erickson, Carlton W. H. *Fundamentals of Teaching with Audio-Visual Technology.* New York: The Macmillan Company, 1965.

———. *Administering Instructional Media Programs.* New York: The Macmillan Company, 1968.

Goodman, Louis S. "Training Aids." In Robert L. Craig and Lester R. Bittel, eds. *Training and Development Handbook.* New York: McGraw-Hill Book Company, 1967, Chap. 17.

Hartsell, Horace C., and Richard A. Margoles. "Guidelines for the Selection of Instructional Materials." *Audiovisual Instruction* (January 1967), 12:1: 23–26.

Hoover, Kenneth H. *Learning and Teaching in the Secondary School.* Boston: Allyn and Bacon, Inc., 1964.

Rose, Homer C. *The Development and Supervision of Training Programs.* New York: American Technical Society, 1964, Pt. II, Chaps. 8, 12.

"Selection and Evaluation of Media." *Audiovisual Instruction* (January 1967), 12:1.

"Textbooks for Industry." *Training in Business and Industry* (June 1969), 6:6: 46–49.

Thomas, R. Murray, and Sherwin G. Swartout. *Integrated Teaching Materials.* New York: Harper & Brothers, 1957.

Tracey, William R. *Evaluating Training and Development Systems.* AMA, 1968, pp. 138, 174–180.

Weaver, Gilbert G., and Elroy W. Bollinger. *Visual Aids: Their Construction and Use.* Princeton, N.J.: D. Van Nostrand Company, Inc., 1966.

Wittich, Walter A., and Charles F. Schuller. *Audiovisual Materials: Their Nature and Use.* New York: Harper & Row, Publishers, Incorporated, 1967.

10

Determining Equipment Requirements

SEVERAL types of equipment are required to conduct training programs designed to develop job skills. If instruction is to be maximally effective, the right type of equipment in the right quantities must be available. Equipment is usually expensive, and a considerable amount of lead time is necessary for its procurement and installation. In addition, time is needed to arrange for plant support requirements—space, power, and environmental control. For these reasons, the amount and kind of equipment needed to support instruction must be precisely determined well in advance of use. As a guideline, equipment requirements should be determined accurately two to five years in advance if usable facilities are to be available when instruction begins.

Careful planning, the application of standards, and close coordination between the training activity and line and staff elements of the organization are essential to the timely and accurate determination of equipment requirements. The purpose of this chapter is to establish standards and procedures for determining the types and quantities of equipment needed to support training and development programs.

After completing this chapter, the reader should be able to perform as follows:

Behavior   Identify and list the types and quantities of equipment required to support enterprise training and development systems for the ensuing five-year period.

Conditions   Given: long- and short-range plans and forecasts of training needs, performance objectives, criteria for selecting equipment, access to logistical and procurement personnel, and clerical assistance.

Criterion   In accordance with the standards described in this chapter.

NATURE AND IMPORTANCE OF TRAINING EQUIPMENT

Several categories of equipment are used in training. The first type consists of standard classroom fixtures, such as chairs, desks, tables, and laboratory benches. Standard training aids equipment, that is, projectors, screens, tape recorders, chalkboards, and easels, comprise the second category. The third category includes specialized training equipment associated with training for a particular job. Typewriters; power tools; electronic test equipment; computers; models or mock-ups of these items; and communication, flight, and optical simulators are examples of equipment in this category. The present chapter deals exclusively with the third category.

Many formal training and development programs require equipment actually used on the job, or realistic simulators. Once a decision has been made to provide formal training (instead of on-the-job training), there is a need for replication of working conditions. An important aspect of these conditions is the equipment the employee will use on the job or, when feasible, simulators or mock-ups of the operating equipment.

Equipment, as noted earlier, is expensive, both in terms of the purchase or rental cost and in terms of the loss to production when used for training. The wrong kind of equipment, or an inadequate number of equipment training positions, will result in shortfalls in meeting training objectives. Too much equipment is an unnecessary waste of space and money, while too little is a waste of time and personnel—and money. For these reasons, calculating equipment requirements carefully, both kind and quantity, is an important aspect of training system design.

BASIC DATA REQUIREMENTS

Before a decision is made regarding the types and quantities of equipment to be procured for training, six critical questions must be answered:

1. What are the objectives of the training?
2. Should formal training on a specific item of equipment or position be provided?
3. Who should receive the training?
4. How many employees should be trained on the equipment per year?
5. Where should the training be provided?
6. What training strategy is to be used?

Types of Data Needed

To provide adequate answers to the foregoing questions, certain data must be collected and carefully analyzed. These data are as follows:

Current equipment. Information regarding equipment currently authorized, installed, and in use in operating elements of the enterprise is of first priority. Specifically, the following data must be collected:

1. By type, the equipment installed and in use in operating line or staff elements and its location by geographical area and type of operational unit.
2. The purpose of each item of equipment and the type of mission, function, or process it is designed to support or perform.
3. The job titles of personnel using, operating, maintaining, and repairing the equipment.
4. The number of positions of each type installed or programmed for installation in the immediate future throughout the enterprise.

Future equipment. Because equipment required to support training must be included in long-range procurement programs, equipment needs must be determined two to five years in advance of use. This means that forecasts of equipment must be obtained. These projections must include all the data under "Current equipment" plus the following information:

1. The time frame during which prototypes of the equipment will be available for task analysis.
2. The time frame in which the operating equipment will be installed.

Availability of equipment. For planning purposes it is essential that information be obtained pertaining to the availability of current and future equipment and positions for training. Sometimes budgetary limitations, or operational necessity, preclude the use of equipment for training purposes.

Equipment costs. Some items of highly complex equipment are so expensive that training positions cannot be justified. This is particularly true in cases where a relatively small number of employees are to be trained. A later section of this chapter recommends the establishment of cost-per-trainee limits for equipment training positions. To apply such standards, information pertaining to equipment procurement and maintenance costs must be obtained.

Trainee input. To apply the cost-per-trainee standards referred to above requires accurate forecasts of trainee input to specific training systems. In addition, the number of items of equipment or positions needed to conduct training is in part a function of the number of personnel to be trained concurrently. Therefore, planning for equipment procurement must be based upon reasonably accurate trainee input forecasts up to five years in advance. Specifically, the following information is required annually for planning purposes:

1. By quarters, the number of employees required to fill enterprise jobs in each category.
2. The number of classes that will be in session concurrently.
3. The number of trainees to be enrolled in each class.

SOURCES OF DATA

Some of the data needed to determine equipment requirements are usually available within the training activity; however, the really critical information must be obtained from other sources. This means that effective and continuous coordination and liaison with other staff and operating elements of the enterprise must be established and maintained. The sources of these data will vary with the organization of the enterprise. However, the following types of organizational elements are likely places to obtain the required information:

1. Current equipment allocations and usage.
    a. Job Analysis Report.
    b. Performance Objective Workcards (Fig. 4-3).
    c. Periodic reports from operating and staff elements.
    d. Follow-up reports of interview and observation.
    e. Questionnaires addressed to operating supervisors.
    f. Operating divisions of the enterprise; for example, manufacturing, production, sales.
    g. Maintenance department.
    h. Logistics office.
2. Future equipment.
    a. Research and development activity.

    b. Engineering division.
    c. Plans and programs division.
    d. Operating divisions.
    e. Logistics office.
3. Equipment availability and costs.
    a. Operating divisions.
    b. Logistics office.
    c. Controller.
    d. Purchasing department.
    e. Finance department.
4. Trainee input.
    a. Five-year training and development forecast.
    b. Personnel department.
    c. Office of plans and programs.
    d. Operating divisions.

SELECTING TRAINING EQUIPMENT

Primary Selection Factors

Once a decision has been made to conduct training on specific equipment or positions, the types and quantities of equipment must be determined. Several factors must be carefully weighed before requisitions for equipment are submitted. The following factors must be considered.

Training objectives. The fundamental consideration in the selection of equipment is the objective of the training. Where the objective of the instruction is to teach nomenclature or simple identification, no actual equipment may be required; a training aid may suffice. However, if the objective is to develop operator, maintenance, or repair skills, equipment of some type will be needed. Training equipment may be installed in three different configurations, depending upon the objectives of the training.

Operational configuration. In cases where performance must be developed under conditions identical to those of the job environment, actual equipment, in the configuration used in operating elements of the enterprise, must be used for training. For example, pilots and flight engineers must be able to operate in the limited space of the cockpit or flight deck of an aircraft; therefore, aircraft and mock-ups complete with simulators must be available for training.

Expanded configuration. Training is very often facilitated when an equipment position is installed in a configuration which permits either easier access to components or simultaneous training of several trainees.

In this case actual positions are used, including all ancillary equipment; but these positions occupy more space because they are spread out. Furthermore, components may not be arranged exactly as they would be in an operational setting. This type of configuration is often used in training repair and maintenance personnel because trainees must have access to subchassis of the equipment.

Rack item configuration. Where training is given only on the main components of a position, a training position may consist of the major components, complete with interconnecting cables, but without ancillary equipment installed or connected. For example, in training military communicators, the training position may consist of transmitters and receivers but without the antennas and power generators which would be a part of a tactical communications position.

Instructional strategy. The instructional strategy used to achieve the training objective has a direct bearing on the types and amounts of equipment needed. Different instructional strategies may require different types of equipment. But regardless of which strategy is used, the basic purpose of the equipment is to help achieve the training objectives. Equipment that is too simple or too sophisticated cannot support the instruction. Quantity of equipment is another factor. Individual performance may call for more equipment than team performance. Both of these performance strategies require more equipment positions than the demonstration method.

Trainee population. The number of trainees in a class and the number of classes taught concurrently determine, in part, the number of pieces of equipment needed to support the instruction. The schedule of classes provides the data necessary for determining the amount of equipment required.

Limiting factors. In an earlier section of this chapter, the basic consid-erations for determining the type and quantity of training equipment required were identified. Standards based exclusively on these factors would produce an ideal training situation. Unfortunately, compromises may often be necessary because of certain limiting factors. These constraints on equipment are as follows:

Training area. Limitations on the type and quantity of training equipment are often imposed by the size and layout of the training area or the facilities in which training is to be conducted. For example, certain types of equipment require air conditioning, exhaust systems, special power supplies, or unusual room dimensions. These factors may restrict equipment in terms of kind, number, and configuration.

In passing, it should be noted that the layout of equipment is one of the most critical tasks in shop and laboratory planning. In planning for equipment installation, a scale model of each major item should be placed on a scale plan and studied from the standpoints of relation to other equipment, working space, safety requirements, work flow, aisle space and traffic, power supplies, lighting, ventilation, and other pertinent factors. Some manufacturers of equipment and machine tools provide scale models on loan, at minimal cost, or without charge. If such models are not available, blocks of wood can be cut to shape and scaled to size to represent equipment. These models should be used with scaled floor and wall plans to select the most efficient layout.

Safety requirements. Special attention must often be given to safety requirements in determining both the kind of equipment, the number of positions, and their physical layout or arrangement. These factors are often crucial in determining trainee-equipment ratios. In addition, equipment must often be modified, or equipped with special safety devices, when used for training to protect trainees or the equipment itself.

Availability. Often there are limits on the number of items of equipment available for training. Sometimes the requirements of operating elements must be met before equipment positions can be made available for training. This has the effect of dictating higher than desirable trainee-equipment ratios; extra training shifts; changes in scheduling; rotation of trainees; simulation of equipment by the use of models and mock-ups, or by the use of older models of the equipment.

Costs. The investment in equipment often represents a very large part of the total training budget. As noted earlier, some items of equipment are so expensive that procurement of positions in the number indicated by the standards may be impossible to justify. It may sometimes be necessary to settle for fewer pieces of equipment or fewer equipment positions than the ideal trainee-equipment ratio would normally call for, in order to keep costs at a reasonable level.

STANDARDS FOR DETERMINING TRAINING EQUIPMENT REQUIREMENTS

KNOCKOUT STANDARDS

There are four factors which should be used to determine whether or not formal training will be conducted on an item of equipment. These are cost per trainee, universality of equipment allocations, trainee input, and equipment utilization. If any of these factors is below the standard, training on the equipment should in all probability be conducted on the job.

Cost per trainee. Because the cost of equipment may exceed an amount that can be justified, maximum cost standards must be established and applied in reaching a decision to train or not to train. This means that when costs exceed the established maximum, training on the equipment should be conducted at a location other than the local training facility, such as at the manufacturer's or on the job. Thinking in terms of the cost per trainee, rather than the total equipment cost, is wise because the procurement of expensive equipment may well be warranted by the total number of trainees to be trained annually on the equipment. If the number is high, trainee-output costs are thereby reduced to an acceptable level. The cost-per-trainee index is computed by dividing the actual cost of the equipment, or position, or the cost of fabricating a model, mock-up, or simulator, by the trainee input to courses in which the training equipment will be used. A training activity, therefore, should establish a maximum cost per trainee for equipment used in each training system.

Universality of equipment allocations. It would be extravagant in terms of both time and equipment costs to train all personnel in a specific job to operate, maintain, or repair sophisticated or costly equipment that is unique to a particular organizational unit or location. For this reason, it is necessary to establish an arbitrary minimum cutoff (in percentage terms) to be applied in determining whether a specific item of equipment is to be procured for formal training. This means that for the job concerned, at least the selected percentage of the organizational units to which the trainee might be assigned must have the equipment installed and in use if training is to be given. A percentage below the standard would indicate that the training should be conducted by the manufacturer or on the job.

Trainee input. Because trainee input is a function of equipment cost per trainee, and because even relatively low equipment costs cannot be justified for small trainee groups, standards based on trainee input alone must also be established. Therefore, training activities should set a standard relating to the minimum number of employees to be trained per year on specific items of equipment. This standard should then be applied in determining whether specialized training equipment should be procured.

Equipment utilization. Training equipment may meet the standards pertaining to cost per trainee, universality of allocation, and trainee input and still represent an unjustifiable cost because of extremely limited utilization for instructional purposes. Therefore, a standard should be established with respect to the utilization of equipment, in terms of the minimum number of man-hours per trainee enrolled in courses using the equipment for instructional purposes.

SELECTION STANDARDS

Once it has been determined that training on a specific item of equipment can be justified, the next consideration is to determine the types of equipment required. As noted earlier, training effectiveness and efficiency must be achieved. This can be realized only by selecting training equipment which complements the training objectives and the instructional strategy. The following general standards should be applied in selecting equipment to be used in training.

Appropriate for learning activity. The equipment used for training must be appropriate for the particular learning activity. For example, if the objective of the learning activity is to build skill in operating equipment, the actual equipment, rather than a model or mock-up, should be used.

Complements other learning resources. The equipment must complement rather than duplicate other learning resources. For example, a mock-up of an equipment position should not be fabricated if operational or training positions are available in sufficient numbers to meet requirements and if safety is not a factor.

Currently in operational use. Equipment currently in operational use in enterprise units must be selected. With few exceptions, equipment and positions which are no longer used in operating units should not be used for training. The exceptions include cases where only minor modifications have been made to equipment, modifications of the sort which would not pose problems of transfer of training.

Realistic. If simplified equipment, simulators, mock-ups, or models are used, they must be realistic. For example, if a mock-up of a piece of complex and expensive equipment is used, the layout and configuration of the mock-up, control panels, and the like must be exact representations of the real item.

Essential to training. Only that equipment essential to the conduct of proper training, and only in the amounts required to handle the trainee input efficiently, should be procured. In cases where a model or mock-up will do the training job, and the cost is less than that of the actual equipment (both for fabrication and maintenance), the substitute should be used. Of course, safety might be an overriding consideration.

QUANTITY STANDARDS (TRAINEE-EQUIPMENT RATIOS)

The number of items of equipment required to conduct training efficiently can be substantially reduced by the rotation of groups and classes and by careful scheduling. For this reason standards, such as those recommended in the paragraphs that follow, should be established as maximums.

Lecture and demonstration. For a lecture or demonstration involving only equipment recognition, nomenclature, technical characteristics, and applications, one item of equipment or position to be described or demonstrated per class in session should be procured. It should be noted that it may be possible to use some type of training aid instead of the equipment. This should be studied before the actual equipment is requisitioned.

Demonstration. For demonstration of the operation of equipment, one item of the equipment or one position per class in session should be allocated for training.

Individual performance. For performance of individual skills, one item of equipment or one position per trainee receiving instruction concurrently should be procured.

Team performance. For performance of team skills, one item of equipment or position per team receiving the instruction concurrently should be obtained.

PROCEDURES FOR CALCULATING EQUIPMENT REQUIREMENTS

CURRENT REQUIREMENTS

For jobs that have been analyzed, the following steps should be carried out in identifying current requirements for training equipment:

Step 1. Apply the knockout standards found in the immediately preceding section to determine the specific equipments or positions on which instruction will be provided. These requirements are reflected in the Performance Objective Workcards developed following job analysis.

Step 2. Match the objectives, strategy, and equipment listed on the Performance Objective Workcards with the selection standards identified earlier. This analysis will culminate in the selection of a typical configuration for the training equipment.

Step 3. Determine the quantity of equipment required by analyzing the training system, its lesson plans and criterion tests. A sample analysis is shown in Figure 10-1. The procedures are as follows:

a. In sequence, identify each lesson plan and criterion test requiring equipment, and enter the lesson plan or test number in column 1 of the form.

Figure 10-1. Sequential listing of equipment requirements per class.

Lesson plan/ test number	Time allocation, hours	Instructional strategy	Requirements
1	2	3	4
EA 0001	35	L	One 10-man classroom
EA 0103	7	LD	One 10-man classroom and one each AN/GSQ-88, AN/GSQ-77, and AN/MSC-99
EA 0104	28	PE	One room adequate to install three each AN/GSQ-88, three each AN/GSQ-77, and two each AN/MSC-99*
EA 0109	7	PE	Uses EA 0104 equipment
EA 0111	14	LD	One 10-man classroom and one mock-up each of control panels for tactical positions ABC-13, DEFG4, and MMR-37
EA 0113	14	LD	One 10-man classroom and one each AT-904, AT-903, and 5-kw generator
EA 0123	70	PE	Requires field training on two each ABC-13, two each DEFG-4, and one each MMR-37†
EA 0125	14	PE	Demonstration equipment used in phases 2 and 5 respectively on each morning of phase 8A
CT 5000	7	Test	One 10-man classroom
EA 0126	3	PE	One each ABC-13, DEFG-4, and MMR-37 classroom
CT 5002	4	Test	One 10-man classroom
CT 5004	7	Test	Two each ABC-13 and DEFG-4 and one each MMR-37 classroom

* The AN/GSQ-88 receives 50 percent of the instruction; the AN/GSQ-77 receives 33 percent of the instruction; and the AN/MSC-99 receives 17 percent of the instruction. These figures are estimates of the time required to complete each practical exercise. If this equipment were taught in separate phases, the requirement would increase to 5 each. The determination of whether groups of equipment may be taught together depends on whether a specific sequence of instruction must be followed.

† The three mobile positions used in the field problem are used in conjunction with each other. Two men operate each position; therefore, five positions are required. During the 70-hour practical exercise the students will operate all the positions by rotation.

   b. Enter the time allocation for each lesson plan and test in column 2.

   c. In column 3, enter the instructional strategy, including criterion tests, involving use of the equipment.

   d. Using the quantity standards defined in an earlier section of this chapter, enter in column 4 the number of items (or positions) required and their names (or designations).

   e. From the schedule of classes, determine the number of classes that will be in session concurrently and the number of trainees per class.

   f. Determine the total number of items of equipment of each type required. With complex course schedules, the use of equipment and space must be programmed graphically to simplify the process of determining the number of items of equipment or positions required. Figure 10-2 provides a sample graphic program. Figure 10-3 shows how the total equipment requirements for Job 000 are computed under the conditions defined in Figures 10-1 and 10-2.

Step 4. Make necessary compromises. Sometimes it will be impossible to achieve the ideal in terms of type of equipment, configuration, or quantity. Lack of space, lack of facilities, or unprogrammed increases in trainee input may dictate an arrangement which is not ideal. In such instances, the training manager should identify all alternatives, such as increased trainee-equipment ratios, shift scheduling, rotation of trainees, or use of mock-ups; and select the most advantageous alternative.

Step 5. Submit a requisition to the appropriate organizational element for acquisition and installation of the equipment. This request should include all the information available on the need for the equipment so that the procuring element can justify the purchase.

Future Requirements

The accuracy of forecasts of future requirements depends upon the completeness and accuracy of reports from staff and operating elements to the training activity and on the quality, thoroughness, and timeliness of the liaison and coordination between the training activity and the various subdivisions of the enterprise. As an absolute minimum, the following steps should be completed annually:

Step 1. Survey all staff and operating elements of the enterprise to identify future training requirements. Review and analyze periodic reports (quarterly, semiannual, or annual) from operating and staff elements to identify these requirements.

Step 2. Review forecasts of trainee inputs for each training program including new programs, for the succeeding five-year period. Update these forecasts to conform to changes in training requirements.

Step 3. Identify specific equipments for training using the knockout and selections standards described in an earlier section of this chapter.

Step 4. Initiate procurement action for needed training positions on a time-phased plan that will insure availability of the equipment at the time the training must start.

Figure 10-2.   A sample graphic analysis of equipment requirements.

Class starts Jan. 3, 19__
Class size: 10 students
Class length: 6 weeks
Class input cycle: Each week one 10-man class

Class week

1 2 3 4 5 6 7 8 9 10 11 12 13 14 15 16 17 18 19 20 21

One room and equipment adequate to install three each AN/GSQ88, three each AN/GSQ77, and two each AN MSC-99

One 10-man classroom

One 10-man classroom and one each AN/GSQ88, AN/GSQ77, AN/MSC99

One 10-man classroom, and one each AT-904, AT-903, and 5-kw generator

One 10-man classroom and one mock-up each of control panels for tactical positions ABC13, DEFG4, and MMR37

Requires field training on two each DEFG4 and one each MMR37

Figure 10-3.   Summary of equipment requirements.

Line item number	Equipment	Quantity
N/A	10-man classroom	3
N/A	10-man equipment laboratory	1
0**001	AN/GSQ-88	4
0**002	AN/GSQ-77	4
0**003	AN/MSC-99	3
0**004	AT 904, antenna	1
0**005	AT 903, antenna	1
0**006	1.5-kw generator	1
N/A	Mock control panels:	
	ABC-13	1
	DEFG-4	1
	MMR-37	1
N/A	Complete mobile positions:	
	ABC-13	4
	DEFG-4	4
	MMR-37	2

N/A: Not applicable.

CHECKLISTS

CURRENT TRAINING REQUIREMENTS

1. Have knockout standards for equipment been established in terms of the following:
   a. Cost per trainee?
   b. Universality of equipment allocations?
   c. Equipment utilization in training?
   d. Trainee input?
2. Have equipment selection standards been established with respect to the following:
   a. Appropriateness for training?
   b. Complementing rather than duplicating other learning resources?
   c. Use in operating units?
   d. Realism?
   e. Essentiality to training?
3. Have equipment quantity standards been established for each typical instructional strategy as follows:
   a. Lecture and demonstration?

    b. Demonstration?
    c. Individual performance?
    d. Team performance?

FUTURE EQUIPMENT REQUIREMENTS

1. Are annual surveys made of line and staff operating elements to identify new training requirements?
2. Are reports from operating elements analyzed to identify future training requirements?
3. Are forecasts of personnel requirements studied for their equipment implications?
4. Are specific equipments required for training identified in a timely fashion?
5. Is procurement action initiated in a timely way so as to insure availability of equipment at the time the training must begin?

SELECTED REFERENCES

Delta Power Tool Division. *School Shops for Today and Tomorrow*. Pittsburgh: Rockwell Manufacturing Company, Delta Power Tool Division, 1955.

DePhillips, Frank A., William M. Berliner, and James C. Cribbin. *Management of Training Programs*. Homewood, Ill.: Richard D. Irwin, Inc., 1960, p. 294.

Goldsmith, J. Lyman. "3-D Block Layout and School Shop Planning." *Industrial Arts and Vocational Education* (March 1955), 44:3: 69–70.

Hultgren, Ralph D. "Automation Course in 30 Hours." *Training in Business and Industry* (June 1966), 3:6: 17–21.

Johnson, Richard B. "Determining Training Needs." In Robert L. Craig and Lester R. Bittel, eds. *Training and Development Handbook*. New York: McGraw-Hill Book Company, 1967, p. 18.

McClelland, W. A. "R & D." *Training in Business and Industry* (January 1969), 6:1: 36–44ff.

Prakken Publications. *Modern School Shop Planning*, 5th ed. Ann Arbor, Mich.: Prakken Publications, Inc., 1967.

Roberts, Lewis. "$4,000,000 Training Center Pays for Itself." *Training in Business and Industry* (September 1968), 5:9: 57–62.

Scherer, Paul L. "Equipment Selection." In Ralph K. Nair, ed. *Planning Industrial Arts Facilities*. Eighth Yearbook, American Council on Industrial Arts Teacher Education. Bloomington, Ill.: McKnight and McKnight Publishing Company, 1959, Chap. 5.

Sokol, Edward A. "Train with the Optical Comparator." *Training in Business and Industry* (April 1969), 6:4: 49–53.

Tracey, William R. *Evaluating Training and Development Systems.* AMA, 1968, pp. 138–142.

Vanburgh, H. D. "When It Pays to Lease Equipment." *Supervisory Management* (May 1965), 10:5: 15–18.

Walker Turner Division. *School Shop Planning Manual.* Plainfield, N.J.: Kearney and Trecker Corporation, Walker Turner Division, 1952.

11

Producing Training Documents

Aᴛ this point in the development of an instructional system, both the input to the training program and the desired output have been described in detail. In addition, the means of producing the desired product have been specified. That is, the instructional strategy, together with its supporting training aids, has been selected; equipment requirements have been determined; and evaluation devices and criterion measures have been designed. The next step is to produce the documents which collate these data into readily usable form and to set time allocations for each instructional unit.

The purpose of this chapter is to describe the procedures for collating training objectives, content, strategy, and evaluation techniques into lesson plans and programs of instruction.

Upon completing the chapter, the reader should be able to perform as follows:

Behavior Write lesson plans for specific instructional blocks.
Conditions Given: Performance Objective Workcards and supporting content outlines, reference documents, assistance of other subject-matter experts, guides and formats for the preparation of lesson plans, and clerical assistance.
Criterion In accordance with the procedures and standards defined in this chapter.

Behavior Calculate time allocations for specific lessons.
Conditions Given: a complete lesson plan, appropriate formulas, the assistance of experienced instructors, and clerical help.
Criterion In accordance with the procedures and standards defined in this chapter.

Behavior Write programs of instruction for specific training and development systems.
Conditions Given: job performance requirements (Job Analysis Report), Performance Objective Workcards, lesson plans, guides and format for the preparation of programs of instruction, and clerical assistance.
Criterion In accordance with the procedures and standards defined in this chapter.

NATURE, PURPOSE, AND IMPORTANCE OF TRAINING DOCUMENTS

LESSON PLANS

A lesson plan is a document that sets forth the objectives to be attained in a single lesson, the content to be learned, and the means by which the objectives are to be achieved and the content acquired.

A good lesson plan, then, is more than just an outline of what trainees are to learn. It must also include *how* the facts, principles, concepts, and skills are to be taught.

The purposes served by a lesson plan are as follows:

1. To insure that the instructor has considered all factors necessary for the conduct of an effective lesson.

2. To guide the instructor in conducting learning activities; keep pertinent materials before him; insure smoothness, order, and unity in presentation; prevent the introduction of digressions, detours, and irrelevancies; and guard against the omission of essential materials.

3. To help the instructor maintain a constant check on his own activities as well as on the progress of trainees.

4. To standardize instruction for all training groups whether conducted concurrently or in different time frames.

5. To serve as a blueprint for substitute instructors.

6. To inform managerial personnel of what is being taught to trainees, and how it is to be presented.

PROGRAMS OF INSTRUCTION

A program of instruction is a document that describes all elements of a training or development system. Essentially, a program of instruction is a training system blueprint, just as a lesson plan is a lesson blueprint. Its purposes are as follows:

1. To serve as a training system quality control document.
2. To insure standardization of specific training or development systems regardless of when, where, or how often they are operated.
3. To provide a basis for the calculation of instructor requirements and the determination of requirements for other resources, such as training support personnel, equipment, space, and facilities.
4. To provide a means of reviewing the adequacy of training and development programs in meeting enterprise needs.
5. To aid line and staff supervisors in nominating their subordinates for enrollment in training and development programs.
6. To inform all supervisory personnel of the knowledge and skills taught to their subordinates.
7. To serve as the basis for the development of on-the-job training programs.

PROCEDURES FOR WRITING LESSON PLANS

GENERAL INSTRUCTIONS

Performance Objective Workcards (see Chap. 4) and their supporting content outlines (see Chap. 7) provide the basic sources of guidance for determining lesson plan content. In preparing lesson plans, the writer must be certain to coordinate with any other persons having instructional responsibility in the training system to insure that unnecessary duplication and conflicting concepts are avoided in his lesson plans. Lesson plans should be prepared in draft and reviewed by a responsible official before publication or duplication. This review should focus on format, organization, strategy, and the accuracy and currency of content and references.

TIME ALLOCATIONS

Realistic estimates of the amount of instructional time trainees require to develop necessary job performance skills cannot be made until a lesson plan has been drafted. Because experience factors are not available with a newly developed training system, initial time allocations must be calculated mathematically. To do these calculations properly, several factors must be considered, both individually and in combination; for example, factors in estimating time requirements.

Type of content involved. The nature of the content—whether a series of facts and principles or a skill—has a direct relationship to time requirements. Skills, for example, typically require more training time because they involve practice.

Amount of detail. The number of separate facts or principles, or the number of separate elements within a skill, relates to time requirements. In general, more complex skills and knowledge require more training time.

Learning difficulty. Difficulty in the learning of a specific principle, concept, or skill has a direct bearing on the time required to teach it. Obviously, the more difficult the learning, the greater the time required to teach it.

Instructional strategy. The method or medium and the system of organization used to teach the principle, concept, or skill relates to time. Practical work and participative methods usually require more time than lectures and demonstrations.

Evaluation strategy. Time requirements vary with the type of evaluation strategy used. For example, individual testing requires more time than group testing; performance tests usually require more time than paper-and-pencil tests.

Number of trainees. The factor of class size is of primary importance when coupled with other factors; for example, strategy, equipment, and instructors.

Number of instructors. The availability of assistant instructors has a direct relationship to time. For example, where individual performance of skills is the objective of the lesson, the total amount of time required is directly related to the number of instructors available to supervise the practical exercise.

Number of equipment positions. If a sufficient number of equipment positions is not available to accommodate all members of a class simultaneously, the time required will be increased materially.

Movement of trainees. If trainees must be moved or transported to a training area away from the central training facility, time requirements will increase.

Estimating time requirements. Initially, time estimates are based on judgment. Several experienced instructors should be asked to provide three estimates of the amount of time required for trainees to achieve the objectives defined in a lesson plan. Estimates should be based upon consideration of the factors defined in the immediately preceding section. The three estimates are as follows:

Longest time. This is the time it could take if the trainees were slow learners, the class were scheduled late in the day, the equipment were to break down, or some other unanticipated, but reasonable, snag were to occur.

Most likely time. This is the time necessary for the development of the concept, skill, or other learning outcome, if all conditions are normal.

Shortest time. This is the time it could take to achieve the lesson objectives, assuming that conditions are optimum; for example, all trainees are fast learners, equipment functions perfectly, and everything goes according to plan.

Calculating time requirements. To arrive at a final time estimate, the following steps should be followed:

Step 1. Find the arithmetic average of *each* of the three estimates given by instructors; that is, find the average for the longest time (EL), the most likely time (EML), and the shortest time (ES). Assuming that three instructors have provided time estimates, the formulas are as follows:

$$\frac{EL_1 + EL_2 + EL_3}{3} = \text{avg EL}$$

and

$$\frac{EML_1 + EML_2 + EML_3}{3} = \text{avg EML}$$

and

$$\frac{ES_1 + ES_2 + ES_3}{3} = \text{avg ES}$$

Step 2. Calculate the final time estimate (TE) using the following formula:

$$TE = \frac{\text{avg EL} + 4 \text{ avg EML} + \text{avg ES}}{6}$$

Refining time estimates. Time estimates computed by means of the formulas presented above are gross. However, for planning purposes in conducting the first trial of a new training or development system, they are useful. These estimates should be entered on the lesson plans and used. During the validation phase of system development, these time estimates can be revised as experience with trainees indicates a need for such change.

LESSON PLAN FORMAT

Although there are many ways in which lesson plans can be written, a standard format should be adopted by any training activity. The format shown in Figure 11-1 has proved to be useful and easy to follow.

Identifying information (see Fig. 11-1).

Heading: Enter the name and location of the training activity and the title of the job training program the lesson plan supports.

File number: Enter the lesson plan number. (A numbering system should be adopted for all lesson plans used by a training activity.)

Date: Enter the date the lesson plan was approved by the approving authority.

Time allocation: Enter the number of minutes allocated to the lesson.

Duty and task identification: Enter the duty and task numbers or letters found on the Performance Objective Workcards the lesson plan supports.

Title of lesson: Enter the title of the lesson plan.

Instructional strategy: Enter the primary and, if applicable, supporting instructional strategy to be used. For example, Primary: demonstration; Supporting: performance. Or, Primary: lecture using trainee response system; Supporting: performance.

Classroom or area requirements: Specify the facilities, such as type, size, arrangement, and location, required for the lesson.

Evaluation strategy: Describe the means to be used to check trainee performance on the task or collection of elements.

Instructors: List the number of instructors and assistant instructors required. If highly specialized skills or knowledge are required of instructors, describe them here.

Training aids and equipment: List all required training aids and equpiment by type and number.

References: List by author, title, publisher, and page or paragraph numbers all references needed by trainees and instructors.

Trainee supplies required: List supplies the trainee needs to bring to class; for example, pen, pencil, notebook, or slide rule.

Trainee handouts: List by title and number all types of handouts (outlines, advance sheets, programmed materials, illustrations, bibliographies) to be given to trainees during the lesson.

Transportation: List transportation requirements, including mode of travel, times, and places.

Authentication page (see Fig. 11-1, Part A). Each lesson plan should contain the signature blocks of the preparer, reviewer, approving author-

Figure 11-1.   Lesson plan format.

Organization _____ Date _____

Location _____ File number _____

Job title _____ Time allocation _____

Duty number _____ Task and element number _____

Title of lesson plan: _____

Instructional strategy

   1. Primary _____

   2. Supporting (if applicable) _____

Classroom or area requirements _____

Evaluation strategy _____

Instructors _____

Training aids and equipment _____

References

   1. For the trainee _____

   2. For the instructor _____

Trainee supplies required _____

Trainee handouts _____

Transportation _____

Part A. Lesson plan authentication page

Authentication

   1. Prepared by   _____
                             (signature)

                                   _____
                            (typed name)

                                   _____
                            (typed title)

                Date _____

---

2. Reviewed by _____
(signature)

_____
(typed name)

_____
(typed title)

Date _____

3. Approved by _____
(signature)

_____
(typed name)

_____
(typed title)

Date _____

Editorial approval

Approved by _____
(signature)

_____
(typed name)

_____
(typed title)

Date _____

Annual review

Date _____ Name _____ Title _____

Posted on date _____ By _____

Date _____ Name _____ Title _____

Posted on date _____ By _____

Date _____ Name _____ Title _____

Posted on date _____ By _____

1. Introduction
   a. Objective
      (1) Trainee behavior
      (2) Conditions of performance
      (3) Criterion of performance
   b. Importance
2. Explanation
   a. First increment of content
      (1) Subobjective
         (a) Trainee behavior
         (b) Conditions of performance
         (c) Criterion of performance
      (2) Content
         (a) Fact, principle, or element of skill
         (b) Fact, principle, or element of skill
         (c) Fact, principle, or element of skill
         (d) Fact, principle, or element of skill
      (3) Evaluation
   b. Second increment of content
      (1) Subobjective
         (a) Trainee behavior
         (b) Conditions of performance
         (c) Criterion of performance
      (2) Content
         (a) Fact, principle, or element of skill
         (b) Fact, principle, or element of skill
         (c) Fact, principle, or element of skill
         (d) Fact, principle, or element of skill
      (3) Evaluation
   c. Third increment of content
      (1) Subobjective
         (a) Trainee behavior
         (b) Conditions of performance
         (c) Criterion of performance
      (2) Content
         (a) Fact, principle, or element of skill
         (b) Fact, principle, or element of skill
         (c) Fact, principle, or element of skill
         (d) Fact, principle, or element of skill
      (3) Evaluation
3. Summary
   a. Recapitulation
   b. Performance evaluation
   c. Reemphasis
   d. Closing statement

ity, and editor. In addition, each lesson plan should include three blocks for recording annual reviews.

Body Format (see Fig. 11-1, Part B). The three parts of a lesson should be typed in accordance with the following format:

1. Introduction. The introduction sets the stage for the lesson. Contact is established between the instructor and the class; trainee interest is aroused and trainee attention secured. Also, at this time the nature of the subject is disclosed, and objectives are clarified.
   a. Objectives. The lesson plan objectives should be stated under each of the following headings:
   (1) Trainee behavior
   (2) Conditions of performance
   (3) Criterion of performance
   b. Importance. This item should consist of a statement defining the reason for learning the content of the lesson, and underscoring the importance of the material to the individual, and its relationship to a particular job duty, task, or element.
2. Explanation. The explanation should consist of the content materials and teaching points required to support the lesson plan objectives. Here, the subject matter is explained, performance is developed, understanding is acquired, and skills are built. The explanation is a breakdown, in terms of specific facts, principles, or skills, of the content required to achieve the objectives. Each group of learnings for each objective and subobjective should be followed by a description of the technique of evaluation to be applied in determining whether the performance standard (criterion) has been met.

   Normally, a lesson plan will include in the explanation section all training objectives for a specific set of learnings. However, some performance objectives may involve content of such complexity and detail as to produce an oversized document. In such cases, separate lesson plans may be prepared for subdivisions of the particular subject matter. All lesson plans will not necessarily contain separate subobjectives for teaching points. The format shown here is a guide and is not intended to connote that every heading used is always required.
   a. Lecture method. With this method, the explanation consists of a series of statements which logically develop the material to be learned.
   b. Conference and other participative methods. Here the explanation consists of a series of key questions and answers that cover the facts, principles, and concepts to be developed in the lesson.
   c. Demonstration method. With this method, the explanation consists of a series of steps which, when demonstrated by the instructor, will present a visual image of how an operation should be performed.
   d. Performance method. The explanation here consists of a series of steps which, when practiced by the trainees, will result in the desired skills at the required level of performance.

    e. Programmed instruction method. With this method, the explanation consists of an outline of the content covered by the programmed materials.

3. Summary. The summary is a brief review of the complete presentation. It contains the following elements:

    a. Recapitulation. This section contains a brief repetition or restatement of the main teaching points of the lesson.

    b. Performance evaluation. In this section, the means of determining whether the trainees' performance is go or no-go is described.

    c. Reemphasis. Here, important ideas selected from the teaching points, steps of procedures, or safety precautions are reviewed for special emphasis.

    d. Closing statement. This section consists of a strong concluding statement designed to leave with the trainees a lasting impression of the importance of the content of the lesson.

Enclosures. Each lesson plan should contain a complete package of all graphic materials required to conduct the lesson. Therefore, the enclosures should consist of a copy of each trainee handout, worksheet, standard form, instructor quiz, and graphic training aid used in the instruction. The original art work used to produce overhead or 35-millimeter transparencies can be reproduced in sufficient copies to meet this requirement.

Program of Instruction (POI) Format

The format shown in Figure 11-2 has proved to be useful as a system blueprint and for the guidance of line supervisors in planning on-the-job training programs.

Title page (see Fig. 11-2).
Heading: Self-explanatory.
Date of publication: Self-explanatory.
POI title: Self-explanatory.
Job title and job code: Self-explanatory.
Table of contents: List each section of the POI by title in sequence.
Length: Enter course length in weeks and days.
Approval: Self-explanatory.

Part A. Preface (see Fig. 11-2 Part A).
1. Course: Enter the POI number and job title.
2. Purpose: State the overall job performance requirements the sys-

tem was designed to meet in the objective terms of behavior, conditions, and criterion.

3. Prerequisites: List here all requirements that must be met prior to enrollment in the course; for example, educational attainment, previous training, aptitude scores, and special physical requirements.

4. Length: Enter the total number of hours in the POI.

5. Training location: Enter the name of the training activity and its location.

6. Type of academic instruction: Enter the number of hours of each type of instruction given in the course.

7. Manpower factors: Enter the instructor and platform factors for each type of instruction conducted in the training system (see Chap. 12).

Figure 11-2. Format for program of instruction.

Patton Electronics, Inc.
Notown, Nostate

Jan. 15, 1970

Program of Instruction
for
106-E8
Electronics Repair Supervisor
Job code: SOI-20

Part A. Preface
Part B. Job performance requirements
Part C. Training performance objectives
Part D. Performance evaluation
Part E. Sequence of instruction and classroom requirements
Part F. Master list of skills
Part G. Degree of training matrix

Length: 16 weeks, 3 days

Approved by: I. M. Smart
Manager, Shop Maintenance

This document supersedes POI for Electronics Repair Supervisor Course dated Dec. 2, 1968

Part A. Preface

1. Course: 106-E8, Electronics Repair Supervisor
2. Purpose
   a. Job performance objective:
      (1) Behavior: The trainee must be able to manage an electronic-equipment repair activity.
      (2) Conditions: Given a manned and equipped electronic-equipment repair activity, supervisory authority, enterprise plans and policies, and technical publications and directives.
      (3) Criterion: Activities must be in accordance with enterprise plans and policies, technical publications and directives, and sound management principles and procedures.
   b. Job for which trained: Electronics repair supervisor
3. Prerequisites: Employed by Patton Electronics, Inc. or one of its subsidiaries. Is a graduate of one of the following training programs: Receiving Systems Repairman; Recording Systems Repairman; Demultiplex Systems Repairman. Has a minimum of two years experience in that specialty.
4. Length: 674 hours.
5. Training location: Patton Electronics, Inc., Notown, Nostate.
6. Type of academic instruction

	Hours
a. Lecture	221.2
b. Conference or participative methods	55.5
c. Demonstration	36.0
d. Training film	17.8
e. Performance	123.0
f. Criterion evaluation	151.5
Total	605.0

7. Manpower factors

	Instructor factors	*Platform factors*
a. Lecture	2.00	1.26
b. Conference or participative methods	2.00	1.00
c. Demonstration	2.00	1.26
d. Training film	1.30	1.00
e. Performance	1.30	3.00
f. Criterion evaluation	2.00	3.00

8. Summary

	Hours
a. Academic time	605.0
b. Nonacademic time	
(1) Study time	57.0
(2) In-processing	8.0
(3) Out-processing	4.0
Total	674.0

Part B. Job performance requirements

Duty I: *Plans.* The supervisor must be able to prepare plans for an electronics repair activity.

Task A: Drafts budget estimates
Task B: Prepares standing operating procedures
Task C: Prepares work schedules
Task D: Recommends revisions to policies
Task E: Determines personnel requirements
Task F: Establishes work priorities
Task G: Plans workflow

Duty II: *Organizes.* The supervisor must be able to organize an electronics repair activity.

Task A: Subdivides the repair activity into logical and manageable organizational units
Task B: Prepares and maintains an organization chart
Task C: Reviews job descriptions and applicant specifications for the positions in his unit

Duty III: *Staffs.* The supervisor must be able to perform the staffing function for his unit.

Task A: Recommends personnel for employment
Task B: Orients new personnel
Task C: Assigns personnel to duty positions
Task D: Conducts on-the-job training
Task E: Recommends subordinates for additional training

Duty IV: *Directs.* The supervisor must be able to motivate, guide, and lead subordinate personnel.

Task A: Delegates authority
Task B: Supervises subordinate foremen
Task C: Holds individual conferences with subordinates
Task D: Holds regular staff meetings
Task E: Prepares notices and memoranda for the guidance of subordinates
Task F: Prepares recommendations for awards for subordinates

Duty V: *Controls.* The supervisor must be able to establish and apply appropriate standards, assess performance in terms of these standards, and apply corrective measures.

Task A: Establishes performance standards for each job
Task B: Evaluates performance of subordinates
Task C: Supervises the preparation of reports
Task D: Reviews production reports
Task E: Establishes quality-control standards
Task F: Evaluates quality-control procedures
Task G: Conducts inspections

Part C. Training performance objectives

Lesson plan file number	Lesson plan time and type	Lesson plan title and performance objectives	Job references	Content references
0-730	30.0 hrs 5.5 L* 6.0 D† 14.0 PE‡ 4.5 CE§	Recording systems Behavior: Must be able to operate recording systems through all their modes and capabilities, recognize when equipment is malfunctioning, sectionalize a malfunction, and prescribe corrective action. Conditions: Given Graphic Pulse Recorder AN/GSH-25A, Recorder-Reproducer CM-114, Sound Recorder-Reproducer AN/UXH-4, Multimeter ME-26/U, Multimeter ME-30U, Oscilloscope Tektronix Model 545, Recorder Test Set ME-254/U, Sierra Model 125B Waveform Analyzer, Signal Generator SG-299/U, Signal Generator TS-382/U, Spectrum Analyzer TS-723/U, Wow and Flutter Meter ME-254/U, Ampex Manual for VR-1000, Mincom Manual for CM-100U, no other references, no supervision. Criterion: Procedures followed must be in accordance with referenced technical publications.	Duty VI Task B	Ampex Corporation, Operation and Maintenance Manual for VR-1000 Video Tape Television Recorder, 1964; Mincom Div of 3M Co, Instruction Manual for CM-100U Recorder-Reproducer, Dec. 64; Manual for Graphic Recorder Set; Manual ASP-50 Magnetic Tape Recording, Jan. 68; TM 11-489.

Subobjective: Advanced magnetic recording techniques:

Behavior: Must be able to identify, interpret, and apply to the maintenance of recording systems, advanced magnetic recording techniques.

Conditions: No references; no supervision.

Criterion: Techniques must be identified, interpreted and applied correctly; time—20 minutes.

Supply Procedures

Behavior: Must be able to supervise supply activities.

Conditions: Given Patton Electronics, Inc., Supply Policies and Standing Operating Procedures.

Criterion: Procedures used must be in accordance with reference publication.

Duty V
Task C

Patton Electronics, Inc., Supply Policies and Standing Operating Procedures

N-380   8.0 hrs
4.0 L
3.0 PE
1.0 CE

* Lecture.
† Demonstration.
‡ Practical exercise.
§ Criterion evaluation.

Part D. Performance evaluations

Evaluation identification	Strategy	Coverage	Time, hours	Week
0-702	Multiple choice	0-702	1.0	1
0-705	Multiple choice	0-705	2.0	2
0-710	Multiple choice and performance	0-710	21.0	5
0-720	Multiple choice and performance	0-720	4.0	6
.				
.				
.				
0-840	Performance	0-840	8.0	12
0-845	Multiple choice and performance	0-845	4.0	12
0-850	Performance	0-850	8.0	13
0-855	Performance	0-855	7.0	14
0-860	Performance	0-860	13.0	15
0-865	Performance	0-865	2.0	15

Part E. Sequence of instruction and classroom requirements

Lesson plan file number	Lesson plan title	Classroom requirements
0-700	Introduction to the course	A*
0-705	State-of-the-art electronic devices	A
0-710	Receiving systems	A and B† with IRN1/2/ 3/4 and EDL-81
0-730	Recording systems	A and B with DCN2/3/5
.		
.		
.		
0-840	Principles of management	A
0-845	Maintenance concepts	A
0-850	Resources management	A
0-860	Supply management	A
0-865	Maintenance management reports	A
0-875	Training management	A
0-885	Inspections	A and B
0-890	Maintenance management	A

* Type A. Standard lecture room with chairs and tables for 12 trainees.
† Type B. Standard electronics laboratory with benches, stools, and test equipment for 12 trainees.

Part F. Sample items from a master list of skills

The electronics repair supervisor must be able to:

1. Identify the fundamental characteristics of state-of-the-art electronic devices.

2. Operate receivers, recorders, and associated test equipment in all modes; recognize when the equipment is malfunctioning; sectionalize the malfunction; and prescribe corrective action.

4. Supervise the installation of electronic equipment.

10. Determine manpower requirements for an electronics repair activity.

12. Determine space requirements for an electronics repair activity.

15. Establish and maintain work schedules in accordance with enterprise requirements and capabilities of assigned personnel.

18. Prepare correspondence.

20. Establish and maintain a functional filing system.

25. Conduct inspections.

30. Conduct inventories, prepare applicable reports, and make necessary adjustments to records.

36. Establish on-the-job training objectives and priorities.

37. Prepare and present instruction.

Please turn page for Part G.

Part G. Degree of training matrix

Skill number	Degree of training			Equipment							
	1	2	3	CU-872/U	R-390A	R-1555	RA-6369	AN/TNH-5	AN/FRA-12	RD-62/U	Not applicable
72			X				X		X		
73			X						X		
74			X			X			X		
75		X				X	X				
76			X								X
77			X				X				
78			X	X	X	X	X	X	X	X	
79			X			X					
80			X			X					
81			X			X	X				
82			X			X			X		
83	X			X	X			X	X	X	
84	X					X	X				
85			X	X	X				X		
86			X			X					
87			X						X		
88			X								X
89		X		X	X	X		X	X	X	
90	X										X
91			X								X
92		X									X
93			X		X	X		X	X	X	
94			X					X			

286

8. Summary:

    a. Academic time. Enter only time (in hours) utilized in an instructional mode.

    b. Nonacademic time. Enter separately the number of hours required for study, in-processing (registering), and out-processing (checking out).

Part B. Job performance requirements (see Fig. 11-2 Part B). The duties and tasks (and sometimes elements) of the overall job requirements are enumerated here in behavioral terms. The source of the information for this section is the Job Analysis Report which was developed from job analysis data. Duties are identified by Roman numerals, tasks by capital letters, and elements, when they are present, by Arabic numbers; for example, Duty I, Task B, Element 3.

Part C. Training performance objectives (see Fig. 11-2 Part C). This section is a consolidation of the performance objectives as expressed in each of the lesson plans in the sequence in which they will appear in the operating training system. The source of this information is the Performance Objective Workcards. A columnar arrangement should be used as follows:

Column 1: Lesson plan file number.

Column 2: Lesson plan time and type of instruction. The lesson plan time may be shown in hours or minutes as appropriate for the particular POI. However, time references should be consistent. If time is reflected in minutes for one lesson plan, then all lesson plan time allocations should be expressed in minutes.

Column 3: Lesson plan title and performance objectives. This section describes what the trainee must be able to do as a result of the instruction, the conditions of performance, and the criterion.

Column 4: Job References. Each lesson plan should be cross-referenced to the job requirements that are supported by the plan. References are made by using the duty, task, and element identification as contained in Part B; for example, Duty II, Task D, Element 6.

Column 5: Content References. Self-explanatory.

Part D. Performance evaluations (see Fig. 11-2 Part D). This section shows the type and coverage of measuring instruments used as the basis for determining trainee progress and level of proficiency. These instruments are administered at critical junctures during and at the end of the training, and are used as go, no-go standards. The individual lesson plan evaluations (developed by instructors) need not be included in this listing. The arrangement of this section is also columnar.

Column 1: Evaluation identification. Enter the file number of the instrument.

Column 2: Strategy. Enter multiple-choice, oral test, performance test, or other as appropriate.

Column 3: Coverage. Enter the lesson plan file numbers, the contents of which are included in the evaluation.

Column 4: Time. Enter the time required to administer each evaluation.

Column 5: Week. Enter the week of training during which the evaluation instrument is administered.

Part E. Sequence of instruction and classroom requirements (see Fig. 11-2 Part E). List the lesson plan file numbers and titles in the order in which they are introduced in the training system. It is recognized that some lesson plans will cover large blocks of hours and must be interspersed throughout the course. Such lesson plans may be entered each time they are used. The classroom or training area requirements for each lesson plan should be included and should identify any special requirements. For example, an equipment lesson may require the use of a laboratory that has a minimum number of a particular type of equipment positions installed; this should be noted.

Part F. Master list of skills (see Fig. 11-2 Part F). List here all skills required to perform the job.

Part G. Degree of training matrix (see Fig. 11-2 Part G). In the spaces provided, enter the nomenclature of any equipment used as a training vehicle in the system. Next, enter the numbers of all skills in the extreme lefthand column. Place an X in the appropriate column to indicate the degree of training achieved for each skill, and additional X's in the appropriate columns under each item of equipment to which the particular skill applies. Definitions of the three degrees of training follow.

Degree of training 1. The primary training vehicle (usually equipment), means, or material was not available; the individual has had extremely limited contact with the subject-matter area. In the case of equipment, he has been taught the principles involved using block diagrams and schematics. Extensive applicatory experience is required to bring the individual to the point where he is job proficient.

Degree of training 2. The individual has had only limited practical experience with the subject-matter area or equipment due to limitations of time, personnel, or equipment. Additional applicatory experience is required to achieve job proficiency.

Degree of training 3. The individual is job proficient. He has had sufficient applicatory practical experience, and no additional training is required.

Master List of Skills and the Degree of Training Matrix

Parts F and G of a program of instruction, the master list of skills and degree of training matrix, are designed to assist line supervisors and staff officials in developing on-the-job training programs for their subordinates. By referring to these parts of a POI, shortfalls in training, due to lack of time, equipment, or other resources, can be easily identified and remedies provided.

For example, it can be seen from Figure 11-2 Part G that the electronics repair supervisor is not job proficient on skills 75, 83, 84, 89, 90, and 92. In the case of skills 75, 89, and 92, all he needs is opportunity to practice the skill. In the remaining cases, he needs both instruction and practice. With these data, the supervisor can identify the training needs of his subordinates and design an on-the-job training program which picks up where the formal training program stopped.

CHECKLISTS

Reviewing Lesson Plans

1. General
   a. Is the plan written in accordance with an approved standard format?
   b. Is the plan numbered in accordance with a standard numbering system?
   c. Is a complete packet of all graphic materials used to support the lesson attached?
2. Identifying information. Does the plan include.
   a. The name and location of the training activity?
   b. The title of the job the plan supports?
   c. File number?
   d. Date of approval?
   e. Duty and task identification numbers?
   f. Time allocation in minutes?
   g. Lesson title?
   h. Primary and supporting strategies?
   i. Classroom and training area requirements?
   j. Evaluation strategy?
   k. Instructor requirements?
   l. List of required training aids and equipment?
   m. List of instructor and trainee references?
   n. Trainee supplies required?
   o. List of trainee handouts?
   p. Transportation requirements?

3. Authentication page. Have the following blocks been signed and dated:
   a. Preparer?
   b. Reviewer?
   c. Approving authority?
   d. Editor?
4. Introduction.
   a. Is it designed to secure trainees' attention and arouse their interest?
   b. Does it include a statement of objectives in behavioral (performance) terms?
   c. Does it tie the lesson in with previous lessons?
   d. Does it provide for review when needed?
   e. Does it show the importance and value of the content to the individual?
   f. Does it show the relationship of the lesson to particular duties, tasks, or elements of the job?
5. Explanation.
   a. Are the facts, principles, concepts, and skills to be learned arranged in the best order for learning?
   b. If the lecture method is used, does the explanation consist of a series of statements that develop the material in a logical way?
   c. If a conference (or other participative method) is used, does the explanation consist of a series of questions and desired answers?
   d. If a demonstration is used, does the explanation consist of a series of steps for the instructor to follow?
   e. If a performance is used, does the explanation consist of a series of steps for the trainees to follow?
   f. If programmed instruction is used, does the explanation consist of an outline of the content covered by the program?
   g. Does the explanation section provide for internal checks of trainee learning?
6. Summary.
   a. Are the major teaching points recapped?
   b. Has evaluation of learning been provided for?
   c. Are critically important points reemphasized?
   d. Has a strong closing statement been formulated?

REVIEWING PROGRAMS OF INSTRUCTION

1. General.
   a. Is the document written in accordance with an approved standard format?
   b. Does the document contain as a minimum:
      (1) Title page?
      (2) Preface?
      (3) Job performance requirements?

        (4) Training performance objectives?
        (5) Performance evaluations?
        (6) Sequence of instruction and classroom requirements?
        (7) Master list of skills?
        (8) Degree of training matrix?

2. Title page. Does the title page contain:
    a. The name and location of the training activity?
    b. Date of publication of the document?
    c. Title of the program of instruction?
    d. Job title and job code which the document supports?
    e. Length of the training in weeks and days?
    f. The name and title of the approving authority?

3. Preface. Does the preface contain:
    a. The POI number and title?
    b. The purpose of the training stated in overall performance requirements for the job?
    c. Prerequisites for enrollment?
    d. Length of the training program in hours?
    e. The training location?
    f. The types of instruction?
    g. Manpower factors?
    h. A summary of academic and nonacademic time?

4. Job performance requirements.
    a. Are job performance requirements stated in terms of duties and tasks?
    b. Do they include the behavior, conditions, and criterion for each duty and task?

5. Training performance objectives.
    a. Are they identified in terms of behavior, conditions, and criterion?
    b. Are lesson plan file numbers identified?
    c. Are times and types of instruction identified?
    d. Are job references identified?
    e. Are content references provided?

6. Performance evaluations.
    a. Are file numbers assigned for each performance evaluation?
    b. Is the type of evaluation strategy clearly described?
    c. Are the lesson plans covered by each evaluation identified?
    d. Is the time for administration specified?
    e. Is the week during which the evaluation is administered identified?

7. Sequence of instruction and classroom requirements.
    a. Is the sequence of instruction listed?
    b. Are classroom requirements identified for each lesson?

8. Master list of skills.
    a. Are all skills required by the job identified and listed?
    b. Are the skills set forth in behavioral terms?

9. Degree of training matrix.

a. Is the level of training identified for each skill listed in the master list of skills?
b. Are the equipments (if applicable) to which the skills apply identified?

SELECTED REFERENCES

Bergevin, Paul, Dwight Morris, and Robert M. Smith. *Adult Education Procedures*. Greenwich, Conn.: The Seabury Press, 1963, Chap. 2.

Cenci, Louis. *Skill Training for the Job*. New York: Pitman Publishing Corporation, 1966, Chap. 5.

Clark, Leonard H., and Irving Starr. *Secondary School Teaching Methods*, 2d ed. New York: The Macmillan Company, 1967, Chap. 5.

DePhillips, Frank A., William M. Berliner, and James J. Cribbin. *Management of Training Programs*. Homewood, Ill.: Richard D. Irwin, Inc., 1960, pp. 156–163.

Hoover, Kenneth H. *Learning and Teaching in the Secondary School*. Boston: Allyn & Bacon, Inc., 1964, pp. 53–80.

Rose, Homer C. *The Development and Supervision of Training Programs*. New York: American Technical Society, 1964, Pt. II, Chap. 9.

Smith, Robert G., Jr. *The Design of Instructional Systems*. HumRRO Technical Report 66-18. Alexandria, Va.: George Washington University Human Resources Research Office, November 1966, Chap. 8.

Staton, Thomas F. *How to Instruct Successfully*. New York: McGraw-Hill Book Company, 1960, Chap. 4.

Tracey, William R. *Evaluating Training and Development Systems*. AMA, 1968, pp. 145–149.

12

Selecting Instructors

NEXT to the trainee, the instructor is the most important component of an instructional system. He sets the pace, provides the guidance and assistance, and furnishes the subject-matter expertise. He also plays an important role in evaluating the instructional system during the validation phase of system design. Therefore, the quality of the total training system depends largely upon the competence of the instructional staff. For the foregoing reasons, the task of selecting instructors and establishing standards for their employment represents an important step in the design of instructional systems.

The purpose of this chapter is to discuss some of the more important factors in instructor selection, to identify sources of instructor personnel, to describe the skills required by different instructional strategies, and to propose standards and procedures for determining instructor requirements in terms of both kind and numbers.

After completing the chapter, the reader should be able to perform as follows:

Behavior   Identify and list instructor prerequisites for a specific instructional system.

Conditions   Given: the program of instruction, training objectives, outline of content, list of strategies to be applied, and the assistance of staff specialists.

Criterion   In accordance with the standards and procedures defined in this chapter.

Behavior   Calculate total instructor requirements for a training and development activity.

Conditions   Given: programs of instruction, standards for platform hours, platform-preparation time ratios, instructor-trainee ratios; formulas, forms, and directions; and clerical assistance.

Criterion   In accordance with the standards and procedures defined in this chapter.

Behavior   Select personnel to conduct instruction in a specific training or development system.

Conditions   Given: a program of instruction, instructor prerequisites, personal data sheets of assigned instructors, and guides for selection.

Criterion   In accordance with the standards and procedures defined in this chapter.

ESTABLISHING PREREQUISITES

If instruction is to be planned and conducted with optimum effectiveness, instructor personnel must be top-notch. Only those best qualified by education, experience, technical knowledge and skill, and pedagogical knowledge and skill should be assigned to instructor duties. The accomplishment of the training mission and the achievement of training objectives hang in the balance.

For this reason, a carefully selected list of instructor prerequisites must be developed for each training system operated by an enterprise. Such a listing will provide a firm basis for identifying potential instructors, screening records, interviewing and evaluating nominees and applicants, and making final selection decisions.

SOURCES OF PREREQUISITES

Prerequisites for instructors are identified by analyzing the training system from two perspectives: subject-matter content and instructional strategy. The type, level, and difficulty of the subject matter determine the kind and amount of technical expertise the instructor must possess. The instructional strategy determines the professional knowledge and teaching skills required by trainers. Therefore, the training objectives, the content of the training program, and the instructional strategies are the source of instructor prerequisites. These elements are found in the program of instruction.

Trainer prerequisites must be established initially by judgmental procedures. Study of the program of instruction in the light of past experience provides indicators of success in teaching which can be translated into prerequisites. During the validation phase of system design, prerequisites should be checked empirically and revised as necessary.

FACTORS IN INSTRUCTION

Competence in the performance of instructional duties is a function of four basic factors: subject-matter expertise, pedagogical knowledge and skills, communication skills, and personal traits and qualities.

Subject-matter expertise. An instructor cannot teach what he does not know. For this reason, a first consideration in the identification of potential instructors is to locate personnel who possess the technical knowledge and skills that are required by the job to be taught. The knowledge and skills needed for acceptable performance as an instructor fall into three categories: knowledge of the enterprise, job knowledge, and job skills. This subject-matter expertise is the product of education, training, and on-the-job experience.

Enterprise knowledge. The successful trainer needs to know the formal and informal organization structure, the lines of communication and authority, and the relationships among the various subdivisions of the enterprise. He needs to know organization policies, rules and regulations. He needs to know the roles of line supervisors and managers and the functions of staff offices. He needs a broad knowledge of the industry of which his organization is a part. And, finally, as a trainer he needs to know the resources available to him and his trainees as well as the relationship of the training activity to other organizational elements.

Job knowledge. If instructors are to be successful in planning and guiding learning experiences, they must possess a wealth of job knowledge. They must know the history, background, and operations of the jobs they teach and of all related jobs. They must know the common difficulties and emergencies that occur on the job. They must know the mistakes that personnel commonly make. They must be intimately familiar with standard operating procedures and standards of acceptable job performance. These items, too, are products of education, training, and on-the-job experience.

Job skills. All jobs contain a cluster of basic skills. These are described in the lists of duties and tasks contained in job analysis reports. Instructors must be highly skilled in the jobs, crafts, technologies, functions, and techniques they teach. They must also be able to use the tools, working aids, machines, equipment, references, and materials associated with the jobs, processes, or functions for which they provide instruction.

Professional knowledge and skills. Knowledge of subject matter and skill in the performance of job tasks represent only one side of the instructional picture. Subject-matter expertise alone does not make for quality instruction. Although it is impossible to teach what one does not know, it is possible for someone to know a subject and not be able to teach it. The missing ingredient in the latter case is professional knowledge and skills.

Professional knowledge. Instructors need adequate preparation in the organization and presentation of the content of the subject matter they teach. They must know sources of information on developments in education and training and the application of instructional technology to their areas of expertise. Finally, they must know principles of learning and teaching as they apply to adult learners.

Professional skills. Knowing and doing are quite different things, particularly in teaching. There are many identifiable skills and abilities associated with instructional duties. Among the most important are the skill needed to select and use a variety of instructional methods, techniques, and aids; the skill to deal with individual differences among trainees; the skill to motivate, guide, and counsel; and the skill to construct, use, and interpret evaluative instruments.

Communication skills. Basically, instruction is a communication problem. The efficient instructor, therefore, must be a skilled communicator both orally and in writing. Most of the basic methods used in instruction (lecture, demonstration, and conference); many of the techniques of instruction (questioning, explaining, and illustrating); and many of the media (training aids and devices) require high-level oral communication skills. In addition, highly developed written communication skills are necessary for such instructional tasks as writing lesson plans, instruction sheets, job sheets, and handouts; for preparing charts and other visuals; and for developing tests and quizzes.

Personal qualities. Although the variation in personality, temperament, and personal qualities among successful instructors is considerable, certain traits and qualities seem to be essential. Competent instructors are above average in intelligence, physically fit, emotionally stable, poised and self-confident, patient and understanding, and open-minded and receptive to change. In addition, they are people who like to work with others; they are fair and ethical in their relationships; and they enjoy their jobs.

Elements of Instructor Prerequisites

There are five elements to consider in establishing instructor prerequisites. These elements are as follows.

Administrative. This section contains items relating to enterprise rules, regulations, and policies. It includes:

1. Status requirement; for example, technician or supervisor, line manager or staff training specialist, military or civilian.
2. Length of service with the organization or length of service upon assignment.
3. Pay grade; for example, colonel; first sergeant, E-8; GS-9.
4. Security clearance requirements.

Educational. This section includes any educational or training requirements.

1. Minimum level of formal education; for example, master's degree with a major in systems analysis.
2. Special training; for example, formal training in automatic data processing.

Subject-matter expertise. This section identifies specific areas of knowledge required.

1. Enterprise knowledge; for example, company personnel policies.
2. Job knowledge and skills; for example, photo-finishing processes and quality control.

Experience. This element lists experience requirements.

1. Work experience; for example, teacher, salesman, or interviewer.
2. Military experience.

Personal qualities. Here are listed personal traits and qualities considered essential to success as an instructor.

1. Intelligence.
2. Interests.
3. Temperament.

Examples of prerequisites listings are shown in Figures 12-1 and 12-2.

Figure 12-1.   A list of prerequisites for a machine shop instructor.

Title: Instructor, machine shop

Administrative requirements
   Operative employee
   Minimum of three years' service with the company

Educational requirements
   High school, trade school, or vocational school graduate
   Formal machine shop training
   An instructor training course

Subject-matter expertise
   Hand tools: micrometer, scale, center punch, dividers, scriber, hammers,
      calipers, and compass
   Machine tools: lathe, milling machine, shaper, boring mill, drill press,
      electric drill, power saw, cutters, surface grinder, and flexible shaft wire
      brush
   Materials: iron, brass, copper, aluminum, and steel
   Other: layout work, blueprints, and trade drawing

Experience requirements
   Minimum of three years' experience as a machinist
   Conducted on-the-job training and coaching

Personal qualities
   Intelligent
   Mature
   Patient
   Desires to instruct

SOURCES OF INSTRUCTORS

There are several sources of personnel for staff instructor positions in enterprise training and development. Some are to be found out of enterprise; most will be found on the company payroll. Trained educators, operative and technical employees, staff training specialists, line supervisors and managers, and outside experts are the main sources of instructional staff.

TRAINED EDUCATORS

Managers of training and development activities have the option of employing graduates of teachers colleges and schools of education (or

Figure 12-2. *An abbreviated list of prerequisites for an instructor at the U.S. Army War College.*

Title: Instructor, management information studies

Administrative requirements
> Member of the active U.S. Army
> Grade of colonel or equivalent
> Minimum of three years of obligated service upon assignment
> Meets all requirements for a Top Secret security clearance

Educational requirements
> Graduate of a senior service college
> Master's degree with a major in business administration, economics, systems analysis, or related field
> Formal training in automatic data processing; for example, U.S. Department of Defense Computer Institute, the Adjutant General's School, or training in private or public agencies or institutions

Subject-matter expertise
> U.S. Department of Defense information requirements and systems
> Factors involved in the design, installation, and operation of management information systems, including automatic data-processing systems
> Computer hardware and software
> Computer applications in U.S. Department of Defense and U.S. Army (or other military department)

Experience
> Commanded group, brigade, regiment, or equivalent (for technical service officer)
> Staff experience at Headquarters, U.S. Army (or other military department), Office of the Secretary of Defense (or Secretaries of the military departments), and/or the Joint Chiefs of Staff (Joint Staff) in area of expertise
> Instructor experience in a service school, college, or university

---

Source: Charles A. Riegle, "Area of Expertise Analysis," *Areas of Expertise within the U.S. Army War College.* Carlisle Barracks, Pennsylvania; U.S. Army War College, June 19, 1967.

experienced college, technical school, and vocational school instructors) for service within the organization. Use of this option will insure that instructor personnel are well grounded in the professional knowledge and skills required for success in teaching.

The professional educator, however, seldom meets the subject-matter requirements of jobs in private enterprise. There are exceptions. For example, many of the skills taught in technical, trade, and vocational schools are applicable to industrial training. Instructors from these sources are immediately usable. For the remainder of the professional group, the problem is one of providing training in job skills and technologies before the educator can become productive. Some investment in training will be necessary for all recruits from the teaching profession. The great majority will lack knowledge of the enterprise, its organization, products, and services. This training must be provided before educators can be assigned to instructional duties.

OPERATIVE EMPLOYEES AND TECHNICIANS

The most promising source of instructors for orientation, trade and semiskills, and technical training is the operating units of the organization. Senior operative employees and technicians have potential as instructors. These employees have had firsthand experience with the job, craft, or technology they would be assigned to teach. If they also have had firsthand experience in on-the-job training or coaching, they have a running start on instructor qualification. At the very least, they have the subject-matter expertise and knowledge of the enterprise. Their limitation lies in their lack of knowledge of training methods and techniques and their lack of skill in instruction.

To convert operative employees and technicians to instructors requires an investment in either off-the-premises or in-house instructor training. Although attrition from such training is often high, the investment is usually worthwhile. Personnel so employed usually gain prestige and higher pay. These benefits help in recruiting instructors. Because operator and technical personnel have tenure, they are also likely to remain with the organization.

LINE SUPERVISORS AND MANAGERS

The use of line supervisors and managers as instructors is growing rapidly in both private and public enterprise. The reason for the increase is more than a matter of availability or economics. Particularly in pre-supervisory training and management development, line managers are replacing outside experts and staff training specialists. The primary reason for this is that line personnel are more credible than outside experts. Trainees show greater respect for operating managers, and they display less resistance to ideas and concepts presented. The appellations "It's good theory, but it won't work in practice," and "You don't know the realities of working in this organization" are no longer heard.

There are other advantages of using line managers as instructors. Teaching increases the competence of the manager. (The presentation of instruction often increases the understanding and skill of the instructor more than it does the trainees.) Line managers also display increased commitment to the concepts and ideas they have taught. Follow-through is infinitely improved. When the manager is back on the job, he becomes the actuator of his former students. Other side benefits include broadened experience for managers, reduced training expenses, and broadened experience for assistants who are given the opportunity to manage.

Of course there are disadvantages. Perhaps the major concern is the skill of the manager in instructing. However, if a manager possesses the technical and managerial competence required to manage, it should be possible to prepare him to conduct instruction with a minimum of training. A second disadvantage is loss of management time, since the manager is away from the duties for which he was primarily employed. Other disadvantages result from misapplication of the process. The best results are obtained when higher ranking managers are used as instructors. Too frequently, however, lesser lights are used because it is too difficult to release the top men. If lower ranking managers are used, they should be the "comers"—those with outstanding promotion potential.

When using line managers as instructors, there is a tendency to select those managers who can most easily be spared from their present responsibilities. This is a mistake because often these men are the least competent managers. Only fully qualified and completely competent managers should participate in a training program. Otherwise the program will be downgraded in both productivity and in the esteem in which it is held.

STAFF TRAINING SPECIALISTS

Most organizations today have at least a small corps of company trainers. Unquestionably, there are many training and development programs in which the talents of these specialists can be used to great advantage. They have the professional knowledge and skill; the enterprise knowledge; and in many cases, the subject-matter expertise required for success as an instructor. However, to use staff specialists primarily as instructors robs the enterprise of their potential contribution. The number of programs in which they can participate will be limited; and in most cases, the number of specialists available will fall far short of meeting all instructor requirements.

Staff training specialists can be more effectively used in staff support of training rather than in direct instruction. Their role should be primarily one of advice and assistance. Their task is to strengthen instructor skills among operative, technical, and line-manager instructors.

OUTSIDE EXPERTS

The final option is to use out-of-enterprise instructors. The main drawback to this option is usually assumed to be costs. True, fees for outside help are customarily high. But the main objection to the employment of outside experts is that they do not understand the organization and its peculiar problems. Their approach is often idealistic and academic, and their theories do not always fit the organization. They simply do not think like managers in the organization. As a consequence, resistance to their concepts and ideas is often high among trainees, and the graduates are apt to apply less of what they learn.

SKILLS REQUIRED BY DIFFERENT STRATEGIES

BASES FOR SELECTION

Analyses of training objectives and of outlines of content are essential to identify the professional competencies required to implement the program. But the content of a specific block of instruction and the instructional strategy chosen dictate the type of instructor required to handle the block. Although it must be assumed that all instructors have been exposed to instructor training in some form, their technical experience; their teaching experience, both in terms of kind and amount, their instructional skills, and their preferences for certain methods of instruction vary considerably. The objective in assigning instructor responsibility in a specific content area is to select the best qualified person both in terms of technical competency and instructional skills.

INSTRUCTOR COMPETENCIES

Different instructional strategies make varying demands on the instructor. Regardless of which strategy is used, the basic requirement is knowledge of the subject matter. An instructor, as noted earlier, cannot teach what he does not know. In addition to this primary consideration, there are instructor skills and abilities which are critical to the successful application of any strategy. These skills and abilities and related strategies are identified in the paragraphs that follow.

Lecture method. To use the lecture method well, the instructor must be able (1) to organize subject matter for effective oral presentation; (2) to speak clearly and forcefully; (3) to stimulate interest and enthusiasm and sell the importance of his subject; (4) to vary his presentation, in terms of vocabulary, sentence structure, and illustrations, according to his audience; (5) to select wisely and use skillfully a variety of training aids; and (6) to check the adequacy of his presentation through the effective use of on-the-spot techniques, such as questioning.

Conference method. To use the conference method well, the instructor must be able (1) to speak clearly and effectively; (2) to stimulate trainee interest and participation; (3) to maintain an informal atmosphere; (4) to provide the guidance required to keep the group continuously aware of desired teaching points and instructional objectives; (5) to keep the group aware of how well it is meeting its goals; and (6) to summarize discussion points quickly and clearly.

Demonstration method. In conducting demonstrations, the instructor must be able (1) to organize his demonstration to effect the most efficient learning; (2) to use tools, job aids, equipment, and training aids skillfully; (3) to speak clearly, forcefully, and effectively; (4) to adjust his commentary to the trainee group; and (5) to diagnose group difficulties and provide immediate remedial measures.

Performance method. In addition to the skills defined for the demonstration method, the instructor who uses the performance method must be able to diagnose individual trainee learning difficulties and function effectively as a tutor.

Programmed instruction. To use programmed instruction effectively, the instructor must be able (1) to diagnose *individual* trainee learning difficulties; (2) to conduct tutorial type remedial instruction; (3) to motivate, counsel, and guide each trainee; and (4) to determine the appropriate pace to be maintained by each trainee.

Combination instruction and team learning. To perform effectively using combination instruction or team learning, the instructor must be able to perform all the functions identified in the immediately preceding paragraphs.

Team teaching. For team teaching, the skills required of the instructor will vary with the position he occupies on the team. The team leader must be able to perform all the functions identified for the basic instructional methods. A team member, however, is not required to have the full range of instructor skills.

Special participative methods. Although there are differences in the mix of skills required of instructors using such participative methods as case studies, role playing, simulation, and management games, the major skill requirements apply to all these methods. Instructors must be able (1) to select appropriate materials, (2) to organize the trainee group for the learning experience, (3) to speak clearly and effectively, (4) to stimulate trainee interest and participation, (5) to keep the learning exercise on the track, and (6) to evaluate and critique *individual* and *group* performance effectively.

STANDARDS FOR DETERMINING INSTRUCTOR REQUIREMENTS

PHASES IN THE DEVELOPMENT OF STANDARDS

If instruction is to be conducted with optimum effectiveness, efficiency, and economy, scientific standards derived from experimental studies must be applied in determining instructor requirements. However, scientific standards cannot be developed overnight. It is suggested, therefore, that instructor standards be developed in three phases as follows:

Judgmental phase. The initial determination of instructor requirements is established largely by the application of judgment, supplemented by local experience and a review of standards used in similar training situations.

Experiential phase. Once judgmental standards have been established and put into use in a training system, experiential standards, based on observation and experience with the standards, are applied. That is, the judgmental standards are modified as a result of local experience with the initial standards.

Scientific phase. Lastly, experiential standards are subjected to rigorous and carefully controlled tryout. Analysis of the data resulting from controlled experimentation produces scientific standards for use in determining instructor requirements.

TYPES OF STANDARDS

All the steps completed up to this point in the development of the training system provide the data for determining how many instructors will be needed, what kind of instructors, and what skills they must have to operate the system. In addition, instructor requirements must be based upon careful consideration of equitable instructor workloads, reasonable and manageable instructor-trainee ratios, and realistic platform-to-preparation time ratios.

Maximum number of platform hours. A reasonable workload is essential if instruction is to be effective. Although it may be possible to schedule an instructor for eight consecutive hours of instruction, the quality of his performance is certain to deteriorate as the day progresses. In addition, to be effective, instructors must be well prepared. Time must be allotted for preparation. For these reasons, instructor workload during a single day and during a single week must be limited. Since certain types of instruction are more demanding both in terms of lesson preparation and delivery, different maximums must be set for each strategy. Recommended standards are shown in columns 2 and 3 of Figure 12-3.

Ratios of platform-to-preparation time. Different instructional strategies require varying amounts of preparation time. It should be evident that the original lesson or learning exercise requires considerably more preparation time than subsequent repetitions of the same lesson. The complexity of the content, the availability of reference materials, and the amount of research required are variables which may necessitate upward adjustments in the preparation time allowed. Suggested platform-to-preparation time ratios for various strategies are listed in columns 4 and 5 of Figure 12-3.

Platform-preparation factor. This factor represents the relationship between the number of hours an instructor can teach a specific block of instruction per day and the total number of teaching hours available per day. If it is determined that due to the complexity of the instructional material, an instructor can teach only two hours per day and there are eight hours available, the platform factor is 8 divided by 2, or 4.0. In determining the platform-preparation factor, the following items must be considered: (1) the complexity of the material to be presented, (2) the availability of reference materials, and (3) the amount of research and preparation required. Platform factors for each major instructional strategy are shown in column 6 of Figure 12-3.

Instructor-to-trainee ratios. The number of trainees that can be handled adequately by one instructor depends mainly on the strategy employed. At times, however, the content, particularly that which deals primarily with the development of manipulative and team skills, dictates larger instructor-trainee ratios. Other factors, such as limitations of content, room size, equipment, and the like may necessitate fewer trainees per instructor than would otherwise be needed. Recommended instructor-trainee ratios for different instructional strategies are listed in column 7 of Figure 12-3.

Figure 12-3. Interim standards for platform hours, platform-preparation time ratios, platform factors, and instructor-trainee ratios.

| Strategy | Number of platform hours | | Ratios of platform-to-preparation time | | Platform factors | Instructor-trainee ratios (Maximums) |
	Daily (Maximums)	Weekly (Maximums)	Initial (Minimums)	Succeeding (Maximums)		
1	2	3	4	5	6	7
Lecture method	4	12	1:24	1:1	2	1:100
Conference method	4	12	1:24	1:1	2	1:12
Demonstration method	4	12	1:24	1:1	2	1:12
Performance method (PE involving equipment)	6	24	1:8	3:1	1.3	1:6
Performance method (paper and pencil or problem-solving PE)	6	24	1:8	3:1	1.3	1:12
Combination lesson (PE and any other method)	6	24	1:8	1:1	1.3	1:24
Programmed instruction	6	24	3:1	3:1	1.3	1:24
Tutoring	2	10	1:2	1:1	4	1:4
Examination (paper and pencil)	6	24	3:1	3:1	1.3	1:30
Examination (performance)	4	16	1:2	3:1	2	1:6
Team teaching	4	12	1:24	1:2	2	1:100
Team learning	4	12	1:24	1:2	2	1:24
Closed-circuit television (including rehearsal and production time)	4	8	1:24			
Computer-based instructional systems	6	24	2:1	3:1	1.3	1:24

CALCULATING INSTRUCTOR REQUIREMENTS

DETERMINING THE NUMBER REQUIRED

The number of instructors required to conduct a course of instruction is determined by using the following factors:

1. The number of program of instruction (POI) hours of each type of instruction (for example, lecture, conference, or performance).
2. The instructor factor for each type of instruction.
3. The platform-preparation factor.
4. The number of classes taught per year.
5. A constant factor to cover supervision, vacations, sick leave, and the like.

Instructor factor. This factor represents the average number of instructor man-hours required to teach each hour of the POI in each primary method of instruction. The POI hours are separated according to the instructional strategy prescribed in the POI. In determining the number of instructors needed to apply a specific strategy, the following items must be considered: (1) the number of trainees in a class; (2) the number of trainee positions (seating and equipment) available in the classroom, shop, or laboratory; (3) the physical layout of the training facility; (4) safety requirements; (5) course content, particularly that which deals primarily with manipulative and team skills; and (6) any other special or limiting factors. A sample calculation of instructor factors is shown in Figure 12-4.

PROCEDURES

To calculate the number of instructors needed to conduct training, use Figure 12-5 along with the following steps.

Step 1. List all training systems in column 1.

Step 2. From the POI, determine the number of hours of lecture, conference, demonstration, performance, special participative methods, and examinations; and enter these numbers in column 2.

Step 3. Enter the instructor factors for each type of instruction in column 3.

Step 4. Multiply the instructor factor (column 3) by the POI hours (column 2), and enter the product in column 4 (platform hours per system).

Figure 12-4.   Sample calculation of instructor factors for a 368-hour program of instruction involving lecture, performance, training films, and examinations.

Example

Total hours in the program of instruction (POI): 368
Total lecture hours: 130
Total performance hours: 198
Total examination and training film hours: 40

Lecture: 130
  113 × 1   instructor man-hours = 113 man-hours
  17 × 3* instructor man-hours = 51 man-hours

                              164 man-hours
  164 ÷ 130 = 1.26 instructor factor

Performance hours: 198
  20 × 3   instructor man-hours = 60 man-hours
  178 × 5   instructor man-hours = 890 man-hours

                              950 man-hours
  950 ÷ 198 = 4.80 instructor factor

Examination and training film hours: 40
  2 × 1   instructor man-hours =   2 man-hours
  13 × 2   instructor man-hours = 26 man-hours
  25 × 3   instructor man-hours = 75 man-hours

                              103 man-hours
  103 ÷ 40 = 2.58 instructor factor

Instructor factors
  Lecture: 1.26
  Performance: 4.80
  Examination: 2.58

---

* There are 17 POI lecture hours that require the services of 3 instructors per POI hour.

Step 5. Enter the platform factors for each type of instruction in column 5, and multiply the platform hours per system (column 4) by the platform factor (column 5). Enter the product in the subtotal column (column 6).

Figure 12-5. Form for calculating the number of instructors required.

Organization _____ Location _____ Period covered _____ Date _____

Training system number and title 1	POI hours 2	Instructor factor 3	Platform hours per system 4	Platform factor 5	Subtotal 6	Man-hours per system 7	Number of classes 8	Man-hours per year 9	Total man-hours required 10	Item 10 × 0.000635 = number of instructors required 11	Remarks
	L,C,D*										
	P†										
	SPM‡										
	E§										
	L,C,D										
	P										
	SPM										
	E										
	L,C,D										
	P										
	SPM										
	E										
	L,C,D										
	P										
	SPM										
	E										

Total man-hours required

*L,C,D – Lecture, conference, demonstration.
‡SPM – Special participative methods.
† P – Performance.
§E – Examination.

Step 6. Sum the entries for each system by type of instruction (column 6), and enter the total man-hours per system in column 7.

Step 7. Enter the number of classes to be taught per year in column 8, and multiply by the total man-hours per system (column 7). Enter the product in column 9, man-hours per year.

Step 8. Sum the entries in column 9 to arrive at the total man-hour requirements. Enter this figure in box 10.

Step 9. Multiply the total man-hour requirements by the constant (0.000635) to arrive at the total number of instructors required, and enter this figure in box 11.

PROCEDURES FOR SELECTING INSTRUCTORS

The instructional skills required to conduct a specific block of instruction are implicit in the content to be presented and in the strategy selected to teach it. An earlier section of this chapter identifies the major skill requirements of each major strategy. The steps to be followed in reaching decisions about the types of instructors required for each block of instruction are as follows:

Step 1. From the POI determine the recommended primary and supporting strategy, and identify the instructor skills required.

Step 2. From the POI identify the technical content to be presented and its level of difficulty.

Step 3. Compare the requirements defined by steps 1 and 2 against the list of available instructor personnel, considering their technical or subject-matter knowledge and experience and their instructional skills.

Step 4. Select the best qualified instructor, and assign him responsibility for the block. Select the second best qualified instructor, and assign him as alternate, or backup, instructor for the block.

Step 5. If the desired combination of technical background and instructional competence cannot be obtained, select one of the following alternatives:

   a. Repeat steps 1 through 4 with the alternative strategy noted in the POI.
   b. Submit a request for the assignment of an instructor with the required qualifications when the missing element is subject-matter expertise.
   c. Train a technically qualified instructor in the strategy required if the missing skill is instructional.

CHECKLISTS

ESTABLISHING PREREQUISITES

1. Are lists of instructor prerequisites established for each training and development system operated by the organization?
2. Are interim prerequisites derived from analyses of the following:
   a. Job and task analysis data?
   b. Job descriptions?
   c. Training objectives?
   d. Outlines of content?
   e. Strategies listed in programs of instruction?
3. Do prerequisites listings include the following categories as a minimum?
   a. Administrative requirements?
   b. Educational requirements?
   c. Areas of subject-matter expertise?
   d. Experience?
   e. Personal qualities?
4. Are lists of prerequisites analyzed and revised on the basis of observation of the training system in operation? Is analysis based on review of reports of the following types:
   a. Observation and evaluation of instructors?
   b. Trainee interviews and surveys?
   c. Instructor interviews and surveys?
   d. Analysis of ratings and criterion test results?

DETERMINING INSTRUCTOR REQUIREMENTS

1. Have standards for determining instructor requirements been established and applied? Do they include standards of the following types:
   a. Maximum number of platform hours?
   b. Ratios of platform-to-preparation time?
   c. Instructor-trainee ratios?
2. Have instructor factors and platform-preparation factors been calculated for all training systems and for each major type of instruction?
3. Are these standards used in calculating instructor requirements?

SELECTING INSTRUCTORS

1. Are lists of prerequisites used to select instructors for assignment to the training activity?
2. Are the following sources tapped in staffing the training activity:
   a. Trained educators?
   b. Operative employees and technicians?
   c. Line supervisors and managers?

    d. Staff training specialists?

    e. Outside experts?

3. Does the instructional staff represent the full range of subject-matter expertise and teaching competence required by the training programs operated?

4. Are the numbers of instructors adequate for the training and development programs operated?

5. Are technical and instructional skill requirements of each block of instruction matched against available instructor resources?

6. Are facilities available for training instructors in required teaching skills?

7. Are primary and backup instructors designated for each instructional block in each training system?

SELECTED REFERENCES

Barr, A. S. *et al. Wisconsin Studies of the Measurement and Prediction of Teacher Effectiveness.* Madison, Wisc.: Dembar Publications, Inc., 1961.

Blake, Robert R., and Jane S. Mouton. "Using Line Instructors for Organization Development." *Training and Development Journal* (March 1966), 20:3: 28–35.

Broadwell, Martin M. "Training the Trainers." *Personnel* (September, October 1966), 43:5: 50–55.

————. "How to Train Trainers Better." *Training in Business and Industry* (May 1967), 4:5: 42–48.

Cenci, Louis. *Skill Training for the Job.* New York: Pitman Publishing Corporation, 1966, Chap. 2.

Daly, Andrew A. "Selecting and Organizing the Training Staff." In Robert L. Craig and Lester R. Bittel, eds. *Training and Development Handbook.* New York: McGraw-Hill Book Company, 1967, Chap. 27.

DePhillips, Frank A., William M. Berliner, and James J. Cribbin. *Management of Training Programs.* Homewood, Ill.: Richard D. Irwin, Inc., 1960, pp. 129–139.

Doyle, Robert J. "Instant Faculty for Supervisory Training." *Training and Development Journal* (March 1967), 21:3: 50–53.

Hall, Harry O. "Professional Preparation and Teacher Effectiveness." *The Journal of Teacher Education* (March 1964), 15:1: 72–76.

Jackson, Gene L. "Technical Instructors: What Are the Qualifications and Sources?" *Training and Development Journal* (August 1966), 20:7: 54–56.

Nordlie, David A. "The Competent Trainer." *Training and Development Journal* (May 1967), 21:5: 51–54.

Rose, Homer C. *The Development and Supervision of Training Programs.* New York: American Technical Society, 1964, Pt. I, Chaps. 1, 7; Pt. II, Chap. 1.

Tracey, William R. *Evaluating Training and Development Systems.* AMA, 1968, pp. 98–101, 104–106, 160–162.

13

Selecting Trainees

In the past aptitudes were considered special talents due exclusively to innate or hereditary differences among people. The current view, and a more accurate one, defines aptitude as a mixture of inborn potential and acquired abilities that have been enhanced by experience. It is important to keep in mind that different types of jobs require different combinations of ability and experience. Training and development resources will be wasted if personnel selected for training do not have the required aptitudes, traits, and basic abilities.

To be effective and efficient, training of any type must be provided only to employees who have been carefully screened and selected for suitability. The purpose of this chapter is to identify the principles and describe the procedures that should be followed in screening and selecting trainees for the various types of training and development programs operated by modern enterprise.

After completing the chapter, the reader should be able to perform as follows:

Behavior   Establish prerequisites for enrollment of employees in all the types of training and development programs operated or sponsored by his enterprise.

Conditions   Given: performance objectives and content outlines for each training program, job descriptions, the assistance of a psycometrist or psychologist, and opportunity to interview prospective trainees and their immediate supervisors.

Criterion In accordance with the standards and procedures defined in this chapter.

Behavior Screen and select trainees for enrollment in specific training and development programs.

Conditions Given: appropriate materials, applications, forms, recommendations, appraisals, records, and test results, lists of prerequisites; the assistance of a psychometrist or psychologist; and guides for interviewing and evaluating personnel.

Criterion In accordance with the standards and procedures defined in this chapter.

THE NEED FOR CAREFUL SELECTION

The effectiveness of training is determined by how well graduates of the training system do on the job. Theoretically, the individual who does well during training will do well on the job. But this goal—proficient performance of the job—can be achieved only if training is an integrated system that begins with the establishment of realistic prerequisites for entrance into the training program, continues with the application of valid screening and selection procedures and the provision of effective training, and ends with job effectiveness. The penalties for inadequate screening and selection procedures are heavy from both systems validation and systems operation perspectives.

SYSTEMS VALIDATION

During the validation phase of training system design, all subsystems are put together and tried out. One subsystem consists of the trainee input to the program. It is essential that trainees match input specifications. This does not mean that trainees will be identical in terms of aptitude, skills, prior education and training, and experience. There will always be a range or spread within the trainee group on all traits and abilities. It is critically important, however, that the range of trainee aptitude, education, experience, and the like be representative of the groups to be trained by the system in the future. Otherwise conclusions regarding the adequacy of the system will be invalid. Careful selection of trainees in accordance with preestablished specifications is therefore crucial to the validation of the system.

SYSTEMS OPERATION

Once a training or development system has been validated, screening and selection procedures continue to be important. From an operational perspective, screening and selection procedures are of concern for the following reasons:

1. The procedures used must insure an adequate supply of trained personnel for the jobs performed in the enterprise. Turnover of personnel is an enterprise fact of life. Although the rate of turnover will vary with the enterprise, the types of jobs, the geographical area, and the business environment, as well as many other factors, the need for replacement personnel is always present. In a growing organization, additional trained personnel are always required. Screening and selection of trainees will therefore be a continuing activity for operating managers and the training staff.

2. Waste of resources must be avoided or at least minimized. From the standpoint of screening and selection, the matter of waste may take several forms. If personnel selected for training possess skills, abilities, and other traits that exceed actual job requirements, the enterprise cannot maximize the potential contributions of these employees to the productivity or profit of the organization. Experience of many organizations shows that personnel trained for and assigned to jobs which do not challenge their abilities are likely to quit.

If, on the other hand, the aptitudes, abilities, and other traits of personnel selected for training do not match requirements, the employee will either fail to complete the training successfully or fail to perform at the required level on the job. In this instance, the investment of personnel, time, equipment, and other resources is lost. Attrition from the training program, then, must be minimized. A large part of the solution to the problem of attrition is to be found in the establishment of adequate prerequisites and in well-designed screening and selection procedures.

FACTORS IN SCREENING AND SELECTION

NUMBER OF TRAINEES

From a systems validation standpoint, the number of trainees is determined by the size of the sample required to arrive at reliable conclusions regarding the adequacy of the system. The sample must be large enough to insure a firm foundation for analyzing results. Since class size has implications for the selection of instructional strategy and the facilities and equipment needed to conduct the training, the number of trainees enrolled in pilot courses must be consistent with the size of future trainee groups. Otherwise, the adequacy of the other subsystems of the training program cannot be validly determined.

From a systems operation standpoint, the number of personnel selected for training is a function of short- and long-range projections of manpower needs for operative, supervisory, and managerial personnel. Basically, the number of trainees is determined by assessing data pertaining to the projected expansion or diversification of the enterprise in products and/or services and by using these forecasts to project personnel requirements. The actual numbers are calculated by projecting the number of new employees, the number of present employees who will leave their jobs, and the number of trainees who will fail to meet the requirements of the training program.

ATTRITION FROM TRAINING

During systems validation, the dimensions of the attrition problem must be ascertained. Ideally, a system should be so engineered that the attrition rate would be zero. However, this is just not possible. For one reason or another, trainees will fail to meet training system requirements and standards. Those enrolled in pilot classes during systems validation should not be dropped from the training program until it is absolutely clear that they cannot meet the standards. To prove this conclusively involves an investment of time and other resources far in excess of the amount allowable in a validated and operating training system. However, during systems validation it is a necessary expenditure in order to establish prerequisites, screening and selection standards, and procedures.

In an operating system, the matter of attrition becomes a different problem. Anticipated attrition must be added to the total system input to insure that the output meets the needs of the enterprise.

TRAINING AND DEVELOPMENT PERSONNEL

Again, from a systems validation point of view, the input to the training system must be compatible with available personnel resources in terms of number and kind of men and the skills they possess. If personnel selected for training and trainer personnel are incompatible in any respect, the validity of the system as designed cannot be determined.

In terms of systems operations, the number and kind of trainers and the skills they have must match the specifications of the training system and its strategy. If trainers are not technically and pedagogically qualified, or if there are too few of them, the output requirements of the system cannot be met.

SPACE AND FACILITIES

From a systems validation perspective, the space and facilities, in terms of kind, amount, and quality, must match the specifications developed by the systems designers if valid conclusions with respect to input are to be drawn.

Space and facilities are actually limiting factors when considered in relation to screening and selection. To select personnel in numbers greater than the space and facilities can efficiently handle results in waste of trainee time and backlogs of potential trainees awaiting enrollment. This is a primary consideration in an operating system.

THE NATURE OF PREREQUISITES

Prerequisites are the minimum qualifications a trainee must have prior to enrollment in an instructional system. Prerequisites represent a prediction of the aptitudes, knowledge, skills, experience, and values required for successful completion of training and effectiveness on the job. Prerequisites may be general or special. General prerequisites are often applicable to all enrollees for certain types or levels of training. Special prerequisites are applicable to specific instructional systems and are required of enrollees in addition to the general prerequisites. Prerequisites, then, are established to insure that the right people are enrolled in a training program.

USES OF PREQUISITES

Prerequisites are used to serve both administrative and instructional purposes. Prerequisites have utilitarian value in systems design. Systems designers must consider prerequisites when they formulate behavioral objectives, select and sequence content, prepare or select instructional materials, and choose instructional strategies. Decisions such as these hinge partly on the characteristics of the trainee input. That is, the aptitudes, abilities, and experiences of trainees have a direct bearing on the kinds of materials used and the nature of the learning experiences provided.

For example, the orientation and depth of a training program in economic analysis depends in great measure on the trainees' ability to deal with higher mathematics. Similarly, the success of a complex politico-military war game rests heavily upon the trainees' knowledge of, and experience with, political and military factors.

Administrative. The primary reason for establishing prerequisites is to insure that the right employees are selected for training. That is, prerequisites are set so as to increase the chances of satisfactory course completion by personnel selected for training. Therefore, prerequisites are used to establish and apply screening and selection instruments and procedures for assigning personnel to training systems. Specifically, prerequisites are used in the screening and selection process as follows:

Selecting or developing psychological tests and inventories. The selection or development of appropriate tests and inventories requires accurate and precise definition of skills, knowledge, aptitudes, temperament, and other traits required for successful completion of training. For example, if digital dexterity is identified as a prerequisite for training as an electronic equipment repairman, those responsible for screening and assigning personnel to repair courses must select (or devise) and administer a test of digital dexterity.

Screening applications and records. A list of prerequisites is essential for proper preliminary screening of applicants or nominees for course enrollment. Unsuitable personnel can be easily and quickly eliminated from consideration if a well-conceived list of prerequisites is available.

Interviewing applicants or nominees. If the personal interview is used as a part of the screening and selection process, a list of prerequisites can serve as the starting point for collecting data about applicants or nominees for training. Such a listing will insure that the information required for objective evaluation is obtained and that areas of particular interest are fully explored by the interviewer.

Instructional. Prerequisites can also serve instructional purposes. Two of the more important uses of prerequisites in instruction are as follows:

Lesson planning. Instructors can advantageously use prerequisite lists in planning their work and in developing instructional materials. The aptitudes, abilities, and experiences of the trainees have a direct bearing on the selection and development of appropriate instructional materials. To plan adequately, the instructor must have accurate information about the characteristics of the typical trainee. He needs to know what the trainee brings to the program in the way of skills, experience, and aptitudes.

Test construction. Trainee aptitudes and abilities must be considered in selecting or developing criterion measures and other evaluative instruments. A knowledge of the prerequisites of a training system is essential to the construction of appropriate achievement tests, particularly as they relate to the type of test, the directions to the trainee, the complexity of the sentence structure, and the vocabulary level.

SOURCES OF PREREQUISITES

Prerequisites must be derived from an analysis of the objectives and content of a training program. This approach is necessary because, without a clear view of what a training program attempts to accomplish, it is impossible to describe with any degree of precision the knowledge, skills, and experience required to participate successfully in the learning experiences provided by the system. That is, what the individual must *bring to* the program depends to a great extent on what he is expected to *get from* the program.

Initially, prerequisites must be selected on the bases of experience and judgment. Qualified systems designers, intimately familiar with the training program and its requirements and knowledgeable about the experiences, skills, and personal characteristics likely to be related to success in the program, establish interim standards for enrollment. Past experience with trainee groups may provide indicators of success in the program which can be translated into prerequisites. Analyses of surveys of graduates of similar or related training programs may provide useful leads.

During the validation stage of systems design, objective data are generated, which can be collected and analyzed. These data can then be used to determine the appropriateness and validity of the interim prerequisites and, if necessary, can be used to revise them. At this point, the establishment of prerequisites becomes empirical, hence more objective.

ELEMENTS OF PREREQUISITES

There are five elements to be considered in setting the prerequisites for any training or development system. These elements are as follows:

Administrative. This element contains items which insure compliance with enterprise rules, regulations, and policies. Administrative elements include:

1. Status requirements; for example, male or female, new or experienced employee, salesman or dealer, military or civilian, officer or enlisted.
2. Length of service with the organization or length of obligated service to the enterprise upon completion of training.
3. Pay grade; for example, Foreign Service Office, 2; sergeant, E-6; lieutenant colonel; general schedule, grade 12.
4. Security clearance requirements.

Physical. This element includes qualifications that will insure adequate physical capability to engage in the activities of the job for which the employee is to be trained. Examples are:

1. Physical profile categories.
2. Physical skills.
3. Special requirements; for example, height, weight, vision, hearing.

Educational. This element includes any educational or training considerations.

1. Minimum level of formal education; for example, high school graduate; college graduate; degree in electrical engineering.
2. Prior training; for example, PERT network diagramming; differential and integral calculus; basic combat training; IBM 360 console operation.

Experience and skills. This element includes any experience or skill considerations as follows:

1. Work experience; for example, foreman, instructor, salesman, typist, computer programmer.
2. Military experience.
3. Special skills or abilities; for example, licensed driver, pilot, linguist.

Interests and aptitudes. This element contains items pertaining to special interests or aptitudes as measured by psychological tests and inventories.

1. General scholastic aptitude.
2. Intelligence.
3. Special aptitudes.

4. Interests.
5. Personality and temperament.

Examples of prerequisite listings are shown in Figures 13-1 and 13-2.

Figure 13-1. An abbreviated list of prerequisites for electronic-equipment repair foreman trainees.

Administrative requirements
   Employed in an operating element of the company
   Three or more years of service with the company

Physical requirements
   Physical profile I or II
   Normal color vision

Educational requirements
   High school graduate
   Successfully completed one of the following training programs: basic electronics repair, recording systems repair, receiving systems repair

Experience requirements
   Minimum of two years of experience in electronic-equipment repair
   Served as a section leader

ESTABLISHING PREREQUISITES

Prerequisites must be established for each course based upon analysis of the job and the training program. The purpose of this section is to describe some general considerations which should be taken into account in establishing prerequisites for operative and presupervisory training and for middle- and upper-level management.

OPERATIVE TRAINING

Prerequisites for operative-type training are the simplest to establish and offer the greatest potential for substantial cost reductions. This is possible for three reasons: (1) the number of personnel to be trained is relatively large in most organizations; (2) job and task analyses are more definitive and objective; and (3) the jobs themselves are less complex than are those of any other job grouping.

Figure 13-2.   A hypothetical list of prerequisites for enrollment in a senior service college.

Administrative requirements
   Member of the military service, active or reserve
   Grade of colonel or lieutenant colonel or equivalent (U.S. Navy or Coast Guard captain or commander)
   Completed at least 15 but not more than 23 years of service
   Minimum of 2 years of obligated service upon completion of training
   Meets all requirements for a Top Secret security clearance

Physical requirements
   Physical profile I or II
   Possesses physical stamina and vitality

Educational requirements
   Graduate of the U.S. Army Command and General Staff College or equivalent
   Completed a minimum of 2 years of college or has established general educational development test (GED) equivalent

Experience requirements
   Served in a command position or managed a major staff section
   Participated in joint or combined exercises
   Well-developed skills in oral and written communication
   Analytical ability
   Possesses highly developed interpersonal skills

Interests and Aptitudes
   Interested in international affairs
   Achieved a minimum score of _____ on a test of general mental ability

Other requirements
   Minimum cumulative Officer Efficiency Index of _____
   Open-minded and receptive to change

In shop types of jobs, such as automotive stationized assembly, aircraft engine repair, and lathe operation; and in office-type jobs, such as stenographic and secretarial work, and computer operation, task analysis provides a relatively clear-cut list of requirements which can be readily translated into prerequisites.

PRESUPERVISORY TRAINING

The selection of personnel for training and ultimate advancement to first-line supervisory positions poses a much more difficult problem. Although the process of task analysis identifies the skills and job knowledge required for success in a particular supervisory job and offers leads to the identification of training and experience related to job proficiency, it does not provide all the answers. The problem is essentially one of identifying indicators of potential supervisory ability. Efficient selection of personnel to be trained can only be insured if the decision maker knows (1) the personal traits and qualities needed and the relative importance of each, and (2) how these required qualities can be identified in applicants and nominees.

Harold Koontz and Cyril O'Donnell in their recent book[1] suggest that the most important qualities to be sought in potential first-line supervisors are the desire to manage, intelligence, analytical ability, ability to communicate, and personal integrity.

In any event, the first task the systems designer faces in establishing prerequisites for presupervisory training is the selection of the traits and values to be required of enrollees. Then he must determine how these traits are to be evaluated in screening and selecting enrollees.

MIDDLE- AND UPPER-LEVEL MANAGEMENT DEVELOPMENT

Selection of middle managers and executive trainees poses an equally difficult but somewhat different problem than does selection of first-line supervisors. Although the functions performed by all managers are the same as those required of first-line supervisors, their relative importance is likely to be different. Therefore, in addition to identifying the skills, qualities, and abilities of managers, the systems designer is confronted with the problem of determining their proper mix.

Two other factors make the task of establishing prerequisites for management development even more critical. First, more risk is introduced into the selection process because of the impact that selection errors could have on the future of the organization. Second, at the time of selection it is difficult to predict the nature of management responsibilities ten to twenty years in the future and to identify the traits and abilities that will be needed at that time to perform managerial functions.

But the decision maker has one thing going for him—all candidates for development and promotion have had management experience. Most authorities in management development maintain that the most reliable predictor of a manager's success is his past accomplishment as a manager. For this reason, Koontz and O'Donnell suggest that the quality of each

[1] *Principles of Management*, pp. 422–424.

candidate's overall ability as well as his organizing, planning, controlling, staffing, and directing abilities should be evaluated.[2]

If these abilities are accepted as realistic requirements, the systems designer still must face the task of finding an objective means of evaluating these factors.

PROCEDURES

The following procedures should be used in establishing and revising prerequisites:

Step 1. Identify, list, and describe the interim prerequisites for each training system, giving particular attention to the following items contained in Job Analysis Reports, training objectives, content outlines, and follow-up reports:

    a. Summary description of the position.
    b. Details of duties and tasks.
    c. Knowledge and skill requirements.
    d. Aptitude and interest requirements.
    e. Special physical requirements.
    f. Knowledge supports as defined in the training objectives.
    g. Follow-up reports of similar or related jobs.
    h. The judgments of operating and staff supervisors and managers.
    i. The judgments of qualified instructors.

Step 2. Submit the list of prerequisites to other qualified systems designers for review and comment.

Step 3. Revise the prerequisites as necessary.

Step 4. Select personnel for enrollment in pilot courses in accordance with the interim prerequisites. Insure maximum variation in each variation in each category of prerequisites, but stay within the specified range.

Step 5. During the conduct of the pilot training course, collect data for later use in revising the prerequisites. The following sources of information should be tapped:

    a. Trainee interviews and surveys.
    b. Instructor interviews and surveys.
    c. Classroom, shop, or laboratory observation.
    d. Analysis of ratings and criterion measures, to include correlation and regression analyses and statistical analysis of the performance of failing and recycled trainees.

[2] *Ibid.*, pp. 425–426.

Step 6. Check the following items as a part of follow-up of graduates of the system upon their assignment to operating elements of the organization:

   a. The adequacy of interim prerequisites in providing an adequate supply of qualified personnel.

   b. The need for on-the-job training. (Are on-the-job training requirements excessive or acceptable?)

   c. The relationship between performance in training and performance on the job.

Step 7. Collate, review, and analyze all data pertaining to prerequisites; correlate scores or observations with the prerequisites.

Step 8. Revise the list of prerequisites in the light of the analysis.

Step 9. Use the resulting list of prerequisites to select personnel for the training or development system.

INFORMATION SOURCES FOR SELECTION

NOMINATIONS

Unquestionably, the best source of information about employees is their immediate supervisors. It is the responsibility of all management officials to insure that an opportunity to participate in training programs is provided to every employee who needs training and who meets established prerequisites and standards. Employees who have demonstrated a need for additional training or who have shown potential for higher-rated jobs should be nominated for training by their immediate supervisors.

Nominations for attendance should reflect consideration of the following factors:

1. The extent to which the employee needs the training.
2. The employee's potential for advancement.
3. The degree to which the employee desires the training.
4. The efforts the employee has made toward his own self-improvement.
5. The extent to which the employee is judged to be willing and able to apply the new skills upon return to the job or assignment to a new job.
6. The extent to which the employee's knowledge, skill, attitudes, or performance are likely to be improved by the training.
7. The degree to which the organizational element expects to benefit from the employee's new or improved knowledge and skill.

These considerations apply to the selection of personnel for training or development regardless of job grouping. In fact, the above factors are the justification for selection when personnel are nominated for training. They must be taken into account in selecting personnel for operative, sales, technical, presupervisory, and management training.

APPLICATIONS

Here the individual employee (or applicant for employment) requests assignment to a training program. Application forms for training and development should be designed to provide information that will aid in reaching selection decisions. Separate application forms for manual, clerical, technical, sales, supervisory, and managerial training programs are essential to insure that the information obtained is relevant to the selection task. In other words, application blanks should be tailor-made for each training program.

RECORDS

In most organizations the personnel department serves as the repository for employee records of most types. These records are a source of information essential to the proper screening and selection of personnel for training. A great deal of the information needed for preliminary screening of nominees, or applicants for training, regardless of whether the individual is new to the organization or an employee with considerable tenure, can be obtained from these records.

Four classes of data related to job success should be available in enterprise records.

Personal data. These include the employee's age, health, physical disabilities, length of service, prior work experience, education and training, test scores, rate of advancement, transfers within the organization, suggestions submitted, absenteeism, and accidents.

Production data. These include quantity of work products produced; time required to do specific jobs; number of rejects, reworks, or errors; amount of spoilage and waste; earnings and bonuses; and sales records.

Judgment of others. This includes performance ratings, rankings, peer ratings, recommendations, awards, and checklists.

Used with applications or nomination forms, company records provide the most efficient means of screening personnel for training. Personnel who are obviously unqualified for the training can be readily identified without going to the expense of applying more refined selection techniques.

TESTS

Psychological tests are not a panacea for all the problems of personnel selection. Nor do they provide cures for poor judgment. But, in spite of the fact that testing in public and private enterprise has been under continuing attack from many sources, psychological tests and inventories can and do serve important functions. They can be used in conjunction with other evaluative means to measure knowledge and skill, predict job performance, and analyze temperament and personality. All these functions are relevant to the task of selecting personnel for enrollment in training and development programs.

Psychological tests and inventories are commonly used to measure the following:

1. General mental abilities, as measured by such tests as the Wonderlic Personnel Test, the Adaptability Test, and the Wechsler Adult Intelligence Scale.

2. Specific mental abilities, as measured by the Differential Aptitude Test and the Army General Classification Battery.

3. Specific information, job knowledge, and trade knowledge, as measured by such tests as the Purdue Industrial Training Classification Test, the Purdue Vocational Tests, and the Purdue Personnel Tests.

4. Mechanical aptitude, as measured by such tests as Bennett's Test of Mechanical Comprehension, the Purdue Mechanical Adaptability Test, and the SRA Mechanical Aptitudes Test.

5. Spatial reasoning, as measured by such instruments as the Revised Minnesota Paper Form Board Test and the last four parts of the MacQuarrie Test for Mechanical Ability.

6. Psychomotor skills, as measured by the Minnesota Rate of Manipulation Test, the Stromberg Dexterity Test, and the Purdue Hand Precision Test.

7. Interests, as measured by such inventories as the Kuder Preference Record, the Strong Vocational Interest Blank, and the Purdue Job Preference Survey.

8. Personality and temperament, as measured by such instruments as Guilford's Inventories, the Minnesota Multiphasic Personality Inventory, the California Psychological Inventory, and the Gordon Personal Profile.

The foregoing list presents only a few of the literally hundreds of kinds of tests. Because no single test is a perfect predictor, or selector, test batteries are customarily used in evaluating applicants, or nominees, for training. The selection, administration, scoring, and interpretation of tests is a time-consuming and expensive process. Skill and experience are necessary for their proper interpretation, but the results are worth the investment.

When used to evaluate knowledge or skill, the major concern is that the competencies measured by the test are similar to those required by the job. When used to predict job performance, there must be statistical proof of the relationship between test scores and success on the job. And when used to analyze or assess temperament or personality, test results must be supplemented by professional psychological appraisal involving depth interviews, study of background information, self-reports, and records.

SELF-REPORTS

Biographical information has proved to be a good source of data with which to predict success in such areas as management and sales. These data also are good indicators of creativity. Essentially, self-reports are inventories of biographical information that have been systematically designed and statistically validated in much the same way as are tests.

Although the ways in which properly constructed and validated biographical inventories can be used are probably limitless, it is important to remember that they must be tailor-made by the user for each job. A comprehensive list of biographical items that may be useful in developing such inventories is available from the Business and Industrial Division of the American Psychological Association.

INTERVIEWS

The interview is probably the most frequently used method of collecting information and making decisions for enrollment in training and development programs. Operative employees are often chosen sight unseen by nominations, applications, or telephone calls; but when personnel are being considered for lengthy, expensive, or "high-risk" training programs, the interview will inevitably be a part of the screening and selection process.

The interview makes several unique contributions to the screening and selection process: (1) it affords the decision maker an opportunity to see the individual—to observe his personality in action; (2) it enables the decision maker to assess certain intangibles, such as attitudes, interests, motivation, initiative, judgment, and stability; and (3) it enables the decision maker to investigate in depth any item he wishes from the application or nomination forms, especially those items relating to job experience.

The reliability of data collected by means of interview and the quality of the judgments reached depend upon the skill of the interviewer. Interviewer biases and prejudices, likes and dislikes, and value judgments often get in the way of the facts. The tendency to talk too much and listen too little is another common fault in interviewing. In addition, the typical "guard-up" stance of the interviewee, as well as his lapses of memory; his tendency to screen information, and even to distort or deceive, often render the interview ineffective. In spite of these shortcomings, the interview remains an important source of information.

PROCEDURES FOR SCREENING AND SELECTING TRAINEES

The following sequence of steps should be used in screening and selecting trainees:

Step 1. Distribute the list of interim prerequisites for the training or development program. The objective is to locate a sufficient number of candidates to insure adequate but manageable variation on the predictive variables (prerequisites). Use the following means as appropriate:

a. Announcements to operating and staff elements.
b. Bulletin board notices.
c. Announcements in company bulletins and news media.
d. Application files.
e. Employment agencies.
f. College recruitment.
g. Personal contacts.

Step 2. Screen applications and nominations to eliminate obviously unqualified candidates for the training.

Step 3. Administer, score, and interpret appropriate tests and inventories; and record results.

Step 4. Analyze the complete records of personnel who have survived the screening measures applied up to this point. Eliminate those who do not meet the interim prerequisites. Consider the following:

a. Personal data.
b. Work records.
c. Production records.
d. Performance appraisals.
e. Test and inventory results.

Step 5. Interview the most promising candidates, and record a summary of observations and evaluations of each interviewee.

Step 6. Synthesize, review, and evaluate all data; and make the final selection of enrollees. Retain all data for later review and revision of prerequisites and screening and selection procedures.

CHECKLISTS

ESTABLISHING PREREQUISITES

1. Are lists of prerequisites established for each training and development system operated or sponsored by the organization?
2. Are interim prerequisites derived from analyses of the following:
   a. Job and task analysis data?
   b. Job descriptions?
   c. Training objectives?
   d. Outlines of content?
3. Are prerequisites listings complete? Do they include as a minimum, the following categories:
   a. Administrative?
   b. Physical?
   c. Educational?
   d. Experience and special skills?
   e. Interests and aptitudes?
4. Are prerequisites analyzed and revised on the basis of observation of the training system in operation and follow-up of graduates on the job? Is the analysis based on review of reports of the following types:
   a. Trainee interviews and surveys?
   b. Instructor interviews and surveys?
   c. Classroom, shop, or laboratory observation?
   d. Analysis of ratings and criterion test results?
   e. Follow-up of graduates on the job?

SCREENING AND SELECTING TRAINEES

1. Are lists of prerequisites used to screen and select personnel for enrollment in training programs?

2. Do trainees selected for training represent the full range of aptitude, education, and experience likely to be enrolled in the operating training system?
3. Is the number of trainees selected
    a. Sufficiently large to obtain reliable estimates of system effectiveness?
    b. Appropriate for available training personnel, space, equipment, and facilities?
4. Are the following sources used to collect information about potential trainees:
    a. Nominations of supervisory personnel?
    b. Applications?
    c. Personnel and production records?
    d. Psychological tests and inventories?
    e. Self-reports?
    f. Interviews?

SELECTED REFERENCES

Anastasi, Anne, ed. *Testing Problems in Perspective.* Washington, D.C.: American Council on Education, 1966, Chaps. 5, 11, 12.

Bassett, Glenn A. "Employment Interviewing: How to Plan Your Strategy." *Supervisory Management* (June 1965), 10:6: 19–23.

————. "Employment Interviewing: Does Your Approach Pay Off?" *Supervisory Management* (May 1965), 10:5: 4–8.

Buehler, Roy E. "Job-Related Behavior Rating Scale." *Training and Development Journal* (March 1969), 23:3: 14–20.

Calhoon, Richard P. *Managing Personnel.* New York: Harper & Row, Publisher, Incorporated, 1963, Chaps. 5, 6, 7.

Cook, Edward M. "Let's Be Realistic about Executive Development." *Training and Development Journal* (July 1968), 22:7: 50–52.

Davis, Frederick B. *Educational Measurements and Their Interpretation.* Belmont, Calif.: Wadsworth Publishing Company, Inc., 1964, Chaps. 6, 7.

DePhillips, Frank A., William M. Berliner, and James J. Cribbin. *Management of Training Programs.* Homewood, Ill.: Richard D. Irwin, Inc., 1960, Chap. 13.

Dooher, M. J., and Elizabeth Marting, eds. *Selection of Management Personnel.* AMA, 1957.

Equitable Life Assurance Society. "Which One Is Trainable?" *Training in Business and Industry* (February 1967), 4:2: 30–33.

Fleishman, Edwin A., ed. *Studies in Personnel and Industrial Psychology,* rev. ed. Homewood, Ill.: The Dorsey Press, 1967, Sections I, II.

Guion, Robert M. *Personnel Testing.* New York: McGraw-Hill Book Company, 1965.

Koontz, Harold and Cyril O'Donnell. *Principles of Management,* 3d ed. New York: McGraw-Hill Book Company, 1964, Chap. 21.

Lawshe, C. H., and Michael J. Balma. *Principles of Personnel Testing*, 2d ed. New York: McGraw-Hill Book Company, 1966.

Mahoney, Thomas A., Thomas H. Jerdee, and Allan N. Nash. *The Identification of Management Potential*. Dubuque, Iowa: Wm. C. Brown Company, Publishers, 1961.

Malone, Robert L. "Identifying and Developing In-House Personnel." *Training in Business and Industry* (October 1968), 5:10: 48–52ff.

Newman, William H. *Administrative Action*, 2d ed. Englewood Cliffs, N.J.: Prentice-Hall, Inc., 1963, Chap. 19.

Tracey, William R. *Evaluating Training and Development Systems*. AMA, 1968, p. 160.

14

Evaluating Training Systems

THE earlier chapters have focused on the design and development of the training system. Now the total system must be subjected to tryout and evaluation to determine its effectiveness and that of each of its components. Although conclusive proof of the adequacy of the system can be obtained only by follow-up and evaluation of graduates on the job, observation of the system in action can provide valuable data for improving all parts of the system. The purpose of this chapter is limited to identifying precisely *what* is to be evaluated, *who* should do the evaluating, and *when* and *how* the evaluation is to be done. It is in the next chapter that we take up the other means of evaluating the effectiveness of an ongoing training system: the administration and analysis of criterion measures.

After completing the chapter, the reader should be able to perform as follows:

Behavior Evaluate all components of an ongoing training or development system.
Conditions Given: appropriate guidelines for conducting observation, data-gathering instruments (rating scales, questionnaires, and schedules), an ongoing training or development system, access to trainees and instructors, and clerical assistance.
Criterion In accordance with the procedures defined in this chapter.

THE OBJECTIVES OF EVALUATION

PRIMARY OBJECTIVE

The primary and overriding objective of a program of internal evaluation is to collect data that will serve as a valid basis for improving the training or development system and maintaining quality control over its components. It must be emphasized that *all* components of the system and their interaction are the objects of scrutiny. The evaluation or rating of instructors separately and distinctly from other components of the system is not the objective. Instructors are evaluated only as one of the system components interacting with all the others.

SECONDARY OBJECTIVES

There are three secondary objectives which an internal evaluation system can serve. These are as follows:

1. To insure that instruction is conducted in a manner consistent with the system as planned and designed. There must be some means of insuring that the system as observed is the same as that planned; radical departures from the planned system cannot be tolerated because the validity and effectiveness of the system cannot be determined under such circumstances.

2. To provide a basis for instructor in-service training and upgrading. An effective in-service training or upgrading program for instructors cannot be based upon conjecture about deficiencies; it must be based upon observed needs. Data collected by qualified and trained observers can serve well as a means of identifying areas in which additional or remedial training for instructors can be planned and implemented.

3. To provide data which are usable in effecting revisions of the instructor training course. Objective evaluation often reveals common deficiencies among the instructor force which can be prevented by introducing changes to the instructor training program.

COMPONENTS TO BE EVALUATED

A learning situation involves trainees, instructors, course content, sequence, time allocations, instructional strategies, materials, equipment, and facilities. If any one of these components is substandard, the training or development program cannot be optimally effective in achieving the desired results.

TRAINEES

Regardless of the insight and skill with which a training system has been designed, it will fail to achieve the desired results unless the trainee input matches the target population of the system. All training and development systems have trainee prerequisites, although it must be noted that prerequisites are established initially on the basis of judgment and must be validated. If trainees do not possess the prerequisite aptitudes, skills, and backgrounds of training and experience (or if mistakes were made in establishing prerequisites), they are not ready for the system as designed. They will not be able to acquire the job skills the system aims to develop—at least not with the materials selected and within the established time limits. If it is discovered that the typical trainee does not measure up to the prerequisites set for a particular training system, changes must be made in the system to accommodate a lower quality input, or the prerequisites themselves must be changed. Close study and observation of the pilot groups are therefore necessary to determine the compatibility of the input and the training system as designed.

INSTRUCTORS

Even the best instructional strategy, facilities, equipment, and materials will fail to produce the required job skills if substandard instructors, or instructors without the required skills, implement the system. Again, it must be noted that prerequisite knowledge and skills were established by judgmental procedures and must be validated. The instructor is one of the key components of a training or development system. He must possess the required technical and pedagogical knowledge and skills, and be highly motivated, if he is to be successful in using the strategies, materials, and equipment selected or produced during the system planning phase. By observing instructors as they work with the other system components, it is possible to identify mistakes in establishing instructor prerequisites. At the very least it will be possible to identify instances where the faulty component is the instructor.

COURSE CONTENT

The selection of course content, as noted in an earlier chapter, is largely a judgmental procedure. Although in the final analysis, the adequacy of content taught, in terms of both kind and amount, can only be determined by evaluating the man on the job, much useful data can be gathered by observing as the content is presented. During the development of instructional materials, every effort should be made to avoid unnecessary duplication of content, gaps in content, and conflicts in concept. However, discrepancies are bound to occur, and these weaknesses must be identified and eliminated. Classroom observation is one means of doing this. The comments of instructors and trainees are another means of insuring that the content is appropriate. In addition, the appropriateness and level of the content presented can also be judged by observing the trainees and the instructor as they work with the materials.

SEQUENCE AND TIME ALLOCATIONS

The only practical way to determine the correctness of the sequence of instruction and the amount of time allotted to each block of instruction is to subject these system elements to actual trial. Trainees will quickly note blatant errors in sequencing because they will have difficulty with new material if they do not possess the knowledge and skills required to deal with it. Instructors will easily note cases of improper time allocation when they attempt to develop specific knowledge and skills. The comments of both trainees and instructors, as well as the observations of an outside evaluator, will provide the data needed to improve both sequencing and time allocations.

INSTRUCTIONAL STRATEGIES

The most reliable method of determining the optimum instructional strategy is to conduct experimental studies in which different strategies are compared. This is an expensive and time-consuming procedure. Nonetheless, some such studies should be conducted, but the number of controlled studies to be undertaken will be limited by personnel, time, and funds. For this reason, much of the initial data pertaining to the adequacy of particular instructional strategies must be obtained by observing the system in action. Along with observation, the judgments of all involved —trainees, instructors, and evaluators—must be recorded.

MATERIALS, EQUIPMENT, AND FACILITIES

Judgments about the adequacy of materials, equipment, and facilities can be made prior to the tryout of the system. However, valid judgments about the appropriateness of these system components, both in terms of kind and amount, require observation of the system in action and the comments of those directly involved. Part of the job of an evaluator is to note deficiencies in these areas, collect the judgment of trainees and instructors, and make recommendations for improvement.

PERSPECTIVES REQUIRED

COMMON DEFICIENCIES IN EVALUATION

A training and development system can be evaluated from several different but complementary perspectives. Unfortunately, in the great majority of training programs, only one or two of these perspectives are represented. The most common is the perspective of the training manager, with that of the trainee running a close second. The training manager is not directly involved in the training, although he must assume responsibility for its success or failure. His view, then, is that of an outsider to the learning situation. The trainee perspective, although frequently a matter of concern, is often haphazardly surveyed. The means of collecting the data are not sufficiently well planned, typically lack objectivity, usually deal with only the broader elements, and therefore rarely provide information that is usable for improving the system.

Even if these two perspectives are adequately represented and the data collected are usable, additional perspectives are needed. These include the observations and evaluations of instructors, trained evaluators, and line supervisors. With careful planning, training, and adequate controls, all these groups can provide information and recommendations of great value in improving and controlling the quality of a training or development system.

THE TRAINEE PERSPECTIVE

Trainees are often in the best possible position to provide insights into the operation of a training system. Full advantage of this source of feedback should be taken by periodically administering and analyzing trainee questionnaire surveys and by conducting interviews with trainees. Although it is true that trainee reactions, opinions, and judgments frequently lack objectivity and reliability, their perspective must be represented. Careful development of the data-gathering devices, skillful use and intelligent interpretation of findings will go a long way toward improving the objectivity and reliability of data collected by this means.

THE INSTRUCTOR PERSPECTIVE

The instructor, too, is an integral part of the learning system. For this reason, his observations and judgments are necessary inputs to an evaluation program. Furthermore, because of his training and experience, he can provide feedback to systems designers that is extremely valuable. Although bias is always a danger because of the instructor's desire to "look good," it is essential to collect and analyze the judgments of those who are—with the exception of the trainees—closest to the learning situation. The degree to which instructors can render objective judgments depends upon the area to be investigated and the means used to gather the data. Instructors can provide the best estimates of the adequacy of time allocations, sequence, strategy, equipment, and materials. Their judgments are equally reliable with regard to trainee input and the adequacy of facilities. Such information should be collected by having instructors complete rating scales and questionnaires, and by scheduling periodic interviews.

THE TRAINING EVALUATOR PERSPECTIVE

One of the best sources of valid and reliable data about the effectiveness of system components is the experienced training evaluator. He will be either an instructor or instructor-supervisor, hence he has the knowledge and skills essential to proper and complete evaluation. In addition, he is able to be more objective about the evaluation because he is not directly involved in the training system. By means of observation, rating, and interviewing, the evaluator collects data on the effectiveness and efficiency of various system components.

THE TRAINING MANAGER PERSPECTIVE

The training manager is ultimately accountable for the effectiveness and efficiency of training and development systems designed, developed, and operated in his enterprise. Although he has this "vested interest" in the success of the systems, his education, training, and experience in the design and conduct of training and development programs permit him to provide a professional appraisal of the effectiveness of systems components and their interaction. His special contribution must be exploited. The techniques he uses include observation, rating, and interviewing.

THE LINE SUPERVISOR PERSPECTIVE

Rarely is the line supervisor involved in internal evaluation of training or development programs. This is a mistake. The line supervisor not only has an interest in the kind of training his subordinates or potential subordinates receive, but he also has expertise in the job or skill being taught. He can render invaluable assistance to training systems designers by observing and reporting the adequacy of objectives, content, equipment, and materials. Although the line supervisor may not be qualified to comment on the strategies used or the effectiveness of other components of the learning system, his contributions to appraisal are invaluable and should be obtained.

PITFALLS IN EVALUATION

Too often, programs of evaluation based on the use of observation and evaluative instruments have failed. Mainly these failures can be attributed to inadequate planning, lack of objectivity, evaluation errors of one sort or another, improper interpretation of findings, and inappropriate use of results. Poor systems of evaluation produce anxiety, resentment, or efforts to sabotage the program. But what is of even greater importance, poor evaluation programs do not provide firm data for improving and controlling the quality of a training system. What follows are some of the most common pitfalls in evaluation.

POOR PLANNING

To be effective, a program of internal evaluation must be carefully planned. Some of the most common deficiencies in planning are these:

1. Failure to work out the details of the program, failure to include data-collection instruments, specific procedures to be followed, and the scheduling of observation, surveys, and interviews.
2. Failure to train evaluators in the principles and techniques of evaluation, which includes the use of data-gathering instruments.
3. Failure to make clear to all concerned the purposes of the evaluation program and the uses to be made of evaluations and recommendations.

LACK OF OBJECTIVITY

Although it is impossible to guarantee that evaluations will be completely objective, there are some steps that can be taken to make certain they will be more objective.

1. Select evaluators who are capable of making objective judgments.
2. Train evaluators.
3. Design appropriate data-gathering instruments.
4. Look at all the components of the learning situation as an integrated system.
5. Focus on important details—avoid "nit-picking."

EVALUATION ERRORS

When scales are used to evaluate quality of performance, traits, or materials, observers often differ in their ratings. These differences are called *evaluation errors,* although this may not be the most accurate term to use for all these disparities. Some errors are caused by faults in the design of the rating instrument; others, by the raters. Some errors occur only with certain groups of observers; and some occur only with individual observers. Other errors occur only when certain traits of individuals are rated. Some observers make errors when rating all persons; some when rating certain groups; and others when rating certain individuals.

Rating errors can be classified into four general categories: central tendency, standards, halo, and logical. All individuals are affected when they are rated by an individual subject to errors of central tendency or standards. Error of halo affects only certain persons in the group being rated. Logical error appears only when two or more traits of individuals are being rated. The effects of all these errors can be minimized, and some can be completely eliminated, by exercising great care in designing the instruments and in training observers.

Error of central tendency. Many evaluators are reluctant to assign either extremely high or extremely low ratings. Their ratings tend to cluster close to the middle of the scale. This error is most commonly made by inexperienced observers. However, even experienced raters can make this error when they rate personal qualities, or abilities, that are intangible; for example, leadership ability and teaching ability.

The tendency to give extreme ratings is the opposite of central tendency, but it is considered to be in the same category. Occasionally, an observer will place too many ratings at the extremes of the scale. Everyone is identified as either superior (error of generosity) or unsatisfactory (error of parsimony).

Error of standards. Some observers tend to overrate or underrate everyone in comparison to the ratings of other qualified judges. This is because their standards are either too high or too low. Experience with, and training in, the use of a particular rating scale usually results in similar distributions of scores by several raters, indicating that their standards are compatible.

When differences in standards are consistent and have enough stability to permit correction, the error is called *systematic*, or *constant, error*. Although this kind of error can be adjusted by adding or subtracting the same amount to all the scores of a given rater, a better solution is to provide further training to that rater so that he can correct his own error.

Error of halo. Some raters are unable to prevent a general impression they have of an individual from influencing their scoring of his performance or traits. Usually this impression that clouds their judgment is from prior observation or knowledge of the individual being rated. However, likes, dislikes, and prejudices may also cause errors of halo. A rater's reaction to physical features, race, or nationality can influence his general impression. It is important to note that halo error can be both favorable and unfavorable; therefore it can result in either a higher or lower score than the actual performance of the individual warrants.

It has been frequently observed that when a person rates a close friend, he tends to rate him higher than he should in all traits. This is called *error of leniency*. When halo error is traced to such sources as physical features, race, or nationality, it is called *error of stereotype*. Halo errors frequently go undetected; even when found, they are extremely difficult to correct.

Logical error. This type of error, sometimes called *error of ambiguity*, occurs when two or more traits or abilities are being rated. If the rater sees certain traits as related (although the relationship may be obscure or illogical to other qualified raters), similar ratings for the different traits or abilities will be given. For example, some people believe that a person who is intelligent is also creative, or that a person who is industrious is also efficient. Intelligent persons may be creative, but not necessarily. Similarly, industrious persons may or may not be efficient. Usually the person who exhibits logical error is not aware of his fault.

IMPROPER INTERPRETATION

The collection of data is one thing; interpreting the data is quite another. Here, the meaning and impact of the data are judged. If this step is not handled properly, the value of the information collected will be completely lost. Here are some of the main pitfalls in interpretation.

1. Assuming that consensus among one category of observers on a single system element guarantees a valid and accurate judgment.
2. Concluding that an observation or judgment made by only one observer is inaccurate or invalid.
3. Taking comments at face value, and not considering the nuances of language and the problems of semantics.
4. Failing to take into consideration the perspective of the individual making the observation.

Inappropriate Use of Results

When tabulated, data collected during internal evaluation have the aura of complete objectivity and truth. Sometimes the results of evaluation are used for purposes other than that originally intended. This is a major error. Some of the inappropriate uses to which evaluative data have been put are as follows:

1. Using ratings and reports of observation as the basis for disciplinary action.
2. Using ratings and reports designed for systems evaluation as a basis for denying or granting special privileges or promotion.
3. Using otherwise unsupported and unvalidated observations as a basis for causing significant changes to an instructional system to be made.

MEANS OF EVALUATION

The Evaluation Process

The first step in the evaluation process is to determine the specific aspects of the training and development system to be evaluated. Then the means and instruments to be used in collecting the data must be selected. After the data have been collected, they must be tabulated and summarized. Then they are both analyzed and interpreted, at which time recommendations are made and an improvement plan is drawn up and implemented. This section describes the most useful means of evaluating.

OBSERVATION

Observation is a method of determining the overt behavior of people as they act, interact, and express themselves in a situation selected to typify normal conditions. Observation is the most direct means of studying trainees, instructors, and the conditions that surround learning. It is the only way that certain aspects of a training system, notably the interaction of system components, can be studied.

Observation, in the context of training system evaluation, has certain characteristics:

1. *It is specific.* Observation is not just looking around or seeking general impressions. To be useful, there must be carefully defined things to look for.
2. *It is systematic.* Observation is not just dropping in on a training situation. The timing of observations, the length of the periods, and the number of observations must be carefully planned and scheduled.
3. *It is quantitative.* Insofar as is possible, measurable characteristics are the object of study in observation used for evaluation.
4. *It is recorded.* A record is made of observation either during or immediately following the visit to the classroom or training area. The results and findings are not entrusted to memory.
5. *It is expert.* Observation is conducted by fully qualified personnel who have been especially trained for the task.

As noted earlier, systematic observation of the learning system in operation is the most direct method of assessing the quality of formal training and of identifying deficiencies. The trained observer can readily identify strengths and weaknesses in the system by observing each of the components and their interaction.

During system validation, evaluators should observe as many classes as possible during each pilot course. Ideally, evaluators should be assigned so as to insure 100 percent coverage. As an absolute minimum, 25 percent of all scheduled instruction should be observed and evaluated.

In planning for observation, evaluators should insure that all *critical* points in the instructional sequence are observed and that an adequate sample of all other instruction is included. Critical points in the instruction are the times when trainees are introduced to important job tasks or skills and the times when they perform the job task or skill in a go, no-go situation. An adequate sample of other instruction is defined as observation of day-to-day instruction leading up to the critical performance. Figure 14-1 contains a sample observation report form which could be used to document and report these observations.

Figure 14-1.   A sample observation report form.

Course _____ Date _____

Instructional unit _____ Lesson plan title _____

Department _____ Division _____ Instructor _____

Directions: For each item listed below, circle the word which best describes
your evaluation of the system component or characteristic. Explain in the
"Remarks" section all items circled in columns 1 and 2.

Item	1	2	3
1. Students' aptitude for the instruction	Lacking	Questionable	Adequate
2. Students' readiness for the instruction, in terms of background and experience	Lacking	Questionable	Adequate
3. Students' motivation and interest	Lacking	Questionable	Adequate
4. Instructor's knowledge of subject matter	Inadequate	Questionable	Adequate
5. Instructor's teaching skills	Inadequate	Questionable	Adequate
6. Relationship between content and objectives	Inconsistent	Questionable	Adequate
7. Accuracy of content	Inaccurate	Questionable	Accurate
8. Level of instruction	Inappropriate	Questionable	Appropriate
9. Sequence of instruction	Inappropriate	Questionable	Appropriate
10. Time allocation	Improper	Questionable	Proper
11. Instructional strategy	Inappropriate	Questionable	Appropriate
12. Instructional materials	Unsuitable	Questionable	Suitable
13. Instructional equipment	Inadequate	Questionable	Adequate
14. Classroom facilities	Inadequate	Questionable	Adequate

Remarks

Item number	Description of deficiency	Recommendation

Evaluator_____

Personnel who perform observation should be fully qualified instructors, instructor-supervisors, training managers, or line supervisors. All must have received training in the techniques of observation and reporting.

RATINGS

Periodically during each pilot course, various elements of the training system should be rated independently by several qualified raters. These elements include trainees, instructors, equipment, materials, training aids, and facilities. A sample scale for rating a course or block by trainers is shown in Figure 14-2. Scales such as these should be prepared before the pilot courses begin.

Personnel using the rating scales must have received thorough training in the principles and procedures of rating, including some training in how to avoid rating errors, and should have had supervised practice in the use of these scales.

TRAINEE SURVEYS

As noted earlier, trainee judgments are valuable in determining the effectiveness of certain training system components. Although they may be less objective than the evaluations of others involved in the system, they should be surveyed. However, such surveys must be used in combination with other evaluative techniques to insure the reliability and validity of the judgments expressed.

At the conclusion of selected blocks of instruction and at the conclusion of the course, trainee questionnaire surveys should be administered to all members of the pilot classes. Instruments similar to the one shown in Figure 14-3 should be used for this purpose. Additional surveys may be administered as need for them becomes apparent; for example, when it is necessary to study smaller segments of the system.

TRAINEE INTERVIEWS

Personal interviews with trainees can provide information not available by any other means. With skillful questioning, the trainee can be encouraged to express himself fully and freely about the training program, his attitudes toward it, and its strengths and shortcomings. As with questionnaire surveys, interviews should not be used alone. The data they provide should be corroborated by other evaluative techniques.

Figure 14-2. A sample scale for rating trainers in a course or block of instruction.

Instructor _____ Course or block _____

Date _____ Location _____

Directions: Rate the course or block on each of the items listed. Place an X on each line at the place which seems to you to be the most appropriate. The highest possible rating for any item is 5, and the lowest is 1. To help you make your rating, three descriptions are given for each item. The one at the left identifies the highest rating, the one at the right identifies the lowest, and the one in the middle identifies the average rating.

Objectives

5	4	3	2	1

Crystal clear | | Reasonably clear | | Not at all clear

Importance of course or block to job

5	4	3	2	1

Critically important | | Of average importance | | Not important

Course or block organization

5	4	3	2	1

Exceptionally well organized | | Satisfactorily organized | | Poorly organized

Sequence of topics

5	4	3	2	1

Well sequenced, easy to follow | | Satisfactorily sequenced | | Poorly sequenced

Course requirements

5	4	3	2	1

Just right | | Reasonable | | Unreasonable

Methods and techniques

5	4	3	2	1
Varied and very effective		Occasionally inappropriate, more variety needed		One method used exclusively

Grading

5	4	3	2	1
Fair and impartial, appropriate evidence		Partial sometimes, based on limited evidence		Partial, no real evidence

Instructor's knowledge of subject

5	4	3	2	1
Broad, accurate, up to date		Somewhat limited, not always up to date		Seriously deficient, inaccurate, out of date

Level of trainee interest

5	4	3	2	1
Unusually high, completely attentive		Mildly interested and attentive		Disinterested, inattentive

General estimate of instructor

5	4	3	2	1
Superior		Average		Poor

General estimate of course or block

5	4	3	2	1
Very useful, effective		Average in usefulness, average in effectiveness		Extremely limited in usefulness, ineffective

Other comments

Figure 14-3.   A sample course or block evaluation questionnaire for trainees.

---

1. Did you get more or less out of the course or block than you expected? If less, what was missing?
2. What specific topics in the course or block should have been
   a. Omitted?
   b. Added?
   c. Emphasized more?
   d. Emphasized less?
3. Which techniques of instruction (lectures, demonstrations, discussions, practical exercises, case study, programmed instruction, etc.) did you get
   a. The most from?
   b. The least from?
4. Was the text helpful? If no, why not?

5. Were the handouts helpful? If no, why not?

6. What was your reaction to the tests and quizzes?

7. In what specific ways could the course or block be improved?

8. In what specific ways could the instructor improve his performance?

9. Would you recommend this course to your associates? If no, why not?

10. Please add any other comments you would like to make about any aspect of the course or block.

During the progress of each pilot course, evaluators should conduct interviews with a sample of at least 10 percent of the class. Standard schedules should have been designed prior to the start of the pilot course for this purpose.

Only personnel who have been thoroughly trained as interviewers should conduct these interviews. Personnel selected for this training should have demonstrated the following: (1) a knowledge of training principles and practices, (2) an understanding of the system as designed, (3) an ability to conceptualize and analyze, (4) an ability to formulate questions, (5) an ability to gain participant response, and (6) a capacity to withstand stress. Supervised practice in the conducting of interviews is the only means of insuring that personnel can meet these requirements. A nonstandardized interview form will be found in Figure 14-4.

Figure 14-4. Sample nonstandardized interview form (trainees or instructors).

Name _____ Date _____

Course _____ Instructional unit _____

Department _____ Division _____

Comments

    Student input:

    Instructors:

    Course content:

    Sequence and time allocations:

    Instructional strategies:

    Materials, equipment, and facilities:

_____
Interviewer

Figure 14-5. A sample questionnaire for instructors.

1. Were you satisfied with the performance of the group? What specifically
    were the shortfalls, if any?

2. What specific topics in the course/block should be

    a. Omitted? _____

    b. Added? _____

    c. Emphasized more? _____

    d. Emphasized less? _____

3. In terms of time allocations, what specific lessons

    a. Require more time? _____

    b. Require less time? _____

4. What changes, if any, do you recommend be made in the sequence?

5. What changes do you recommend in instructional strategies?

6. What materials should be

    a. Added? _____

    b. Eliminated? _____

    c. Revised? _____

7. What equipment should be

    a. Added? _____

    b. Eliminated? _____

8. What changes do you recommend in the evaluation strategy?

9. In what other ways could this course or block be made more effective?

INSTRUCTOR SURVEYS

Instructors, too, have much to contribute to the evaluation of a system in operation. Their observations and recommendations should be systematically collected to insure that the system is consistent with the needs of the implementers of the training.

Therefore, at the conclusion of each block of instruction and at the end of the course, questionnaires should be completed by all instructors. A standard questionnaire form similar to the one shown in Figure 14-5 may be used for this purpose.

INSTRUCTOR INTERVIEWS

Although instructors are usually less reluctant than trainees to make written judgments about a training system, their involvement is so direct that they may be hesitant to "tell it like it is." For this reason it is extremely profitable to interview instructors in order to draw out their true feelings and obtain their judgments about each major component of the learning system.

Therefore, at the conclusion of each block of instruction and at the end of the course, at least a sample of instructors should be interviewed in depth. Personnel with the same qualifications and training as those used for trainee interviews should conduct these interviews.

PROCEDURES FOR COLLECTING DATA

The collection of data involves the application of a number of evaluative techniques and devices including observation, rating, questionnaire, and interview. The most effective technique should be selected to collect the required information. Great skill is necessary if the data collected are to be pertinent, objective, and error free.

OBSERVATION

The following procedures should serve as guides to observation:

Step 1. Develop a plan for observation; this plan should indicate the number of observations, their length, and their spacing. In scheduling observation, observe these rules:

a. Include those activities which are truly typical of the system under study.
b. Include critical instruction.
c. Include enough day-to-day instruction to obtain a complete picture of the system in operation.

Step 2. Review the lesson plan and supporting materials prior to arrival in the classroom or the training area. Be sure that the objectives of the instruction are clear in your mind.

Step 3. Arrive in the classroom or training area before the instruction begins, and remain long enough to get a clear picture of the learning situation so that the objectives of the observation can be accomplished.

Step 4. Select your position in the training area carefully. Be sure that you can see and hear what is going on, but are not in the way.

Step 5. Make every effort to avoid being a distraction to either the instructor or the trainees. Obey these rules:

a. Be as quiet and unobtrusive as possible.
b. Refrain from commenting on content or procedures during the presentation.
c. Try to convey an attitude of interest, attention, and objectivity.
d. Guard against display of disagreement, displeasure, or boredom by facial expression, gestures, or posture.

Step 6. Focus your attention on each component of the learning situation, but pay particular attention to trainee reaction and performance.

Step 7. Complete the record of observation as soon as you leave the classroom or training area.

RATING

The following procedures should serve as guides to rating.

Step 1. Select the aspects of the training system to be rated.

Step 2. Establish a schedule for rating with dates, times, and raters indicated.

Step 3. Whenever possible use multiple ratings; that is, use several raters and average their ratings.

Step 4. Make certain that the use of the scale is understood by all raters. Points on the scale should have a common meaning for all users.

Step 5. Rate each member of a group or item in comparison with all others in the group. If only one person or item is being rated, compare him or the item mentally with others of the same level, type, class, occupation, or the like who are not being rated.

Step 6. Rate each person or item on one trait before going on to the next.

Step 7. Use all steps in the rating scale, even the extremes if they are deserved.

Step 8. Rate only after you have had enough time to observe the individual's performance.

Step 9. Do not rate individuals or traits for which you cannot cite specific evidence to support your rating. If you have no basis for judgment, do not rate that item. Mark it "no opportunity to observe."

QUESTIONNAIRES

The following guidelines should be followed in administering questionnaire surveys:

Step 1. Determine the purpose of the questionnaire.

Step 2. Develop a survey plan and schedule; include the who, when, and how.

Step 3. Select respondents by name.

Step 4. Distribute the questionnaires.

Step 5. Follow up if returns are not received within a reasonable time.

Step 6. Process and interpret the data.

Step 7. Compare the data with data from other sources.

Step 8. Prepare a summary report.

INTERVIEW

The following procedures should be followed in preparing for and conducting an interview:

Step 1. Determine the objectives of the interview; know specifically what it is that you are trying to find out.

Step 2. Select the interviewees by name.

Step 3. Learn as much as you can about each respondent in advance; study records, reports, test results, as well as reports of earlier interviews if any.

Step 4. Make an appointment for a mutually convenient time.

Step 5. Select a place for the interview that is comfortable, private, and free from the distractions of noise and interruptions.

Step 6. Conduct the interview. When interviewing, observe the following rules:

a. Explain the purpose of the interview and the use to which the findings will be put.

b. Establish a friendly, cooperative working relationship with the respondent before getting to the task at hand; put the interviewee at ease.

c. Begin with questions that are easy to answer and are not emotionally loaded.

d. Let the interviewee talk; let him feel free to express himself; do not dominate.

e. Deal with the interviewee in a forthright, sincere manner; do not be pedantic, and do not try to be shrewd or clever.

f. Avoid evidences of pressure, boredom, and irritation.

g. Give the interviewee an opportunity to qualify his answers.

h. Ask only one question at a time.

i. Avoid antagonizing, embarrassing, or hurrying the interviewee.

j. Do not push ahead too rapidly, but do not dawdle.

k. Keep control; do not allow the interviewee to go off on extended tangents.

l. Display an objective but not a disinterested attitude.

m. Be alert for leads; watch facial expression, gestures, and casual remarks.

n. Do not be perturbed by expressions of negative feelings, such as hostility and highly subjective criticism.

o. Encourage the interviewee to state his views completely without fear of censure or reprisal for honest criticism.

p. Raise questions to elicit responses about areas not covered in the interviewee's responses.

q. When the interview is over, summarize the main points to be certain that you have the facts as the interviewee presented them.

r. Record all data immediately.

TABULATING, INTERPRETING, AND USING EVALUATIVE DATA

Tabulating and Summarizing Data

The problems of tabulating and summarizing the results of observations, ratings, questionnaires, and interviews are numerous and varied. These difficulties apply whether the tabulating is done manually or by machine. Where the data are quantitative, the problems are relatively simple. However, some of the data collected for internal system evaluation is nonquantitative description. With these kinds of data the selection of appropriate summarizing categories is much more difficult. In any event, tabulating and summarizing data are slow and demanding tasks. Accuracy is the key word.

The steps to be followed in tabulating and summarizing data are as follows:

Step 1. Edit the completed forms and scales. Be sure that the responses on different parts of the same form or return are consistent and that they do not controvert *known* facts.

Step 2. Establish summarizing categories for both closed and open-end responses.

Step 3. Determine the mathematical treatment to be applied to each summarizing category; for example, mean, median, mode, percentage, range, rank order, percentile, or standard deviation.

Step 4. Make a preliminary list of responses under each summarizing category for the open-response type of item to determine the nature and range of responses.

Step 5. Establish a final list of responses for each summarizing category.

Step 6. Study each response on all returns (item 1 on all forms, then item 2, item 3, and so forth), and tabulate them in the proper category by placing a tally beside the item.

Step 7. Sum the tally marks in each category for each item and/or apply the mathematical function required.

Step 8. Prepare a summary report of significant items.

INTERPRETING DATA

The interpretation of data obtained from reports of observations, ratings, questionnaires, and interviews is not a simple routine procedure. On the contrary, it is the most demanding and the most crucial step in the whole evaluation process. In fact, in the strictest sense, interpretation of the data *is* evaluation.

This, then, is the stage that depends most heavily on the professional knowledge and the skills of the evaluator. If the data are complete and accurate, the skillful evaluator will be able to identify significant weaknesses (if any) and draw conclusions on which recommendations for improvement can be based.

Because of the almost infinite variety of ways of expressing the data, it is impossible to describe all the difficulties that may be encountered in the interpretation phase. An example must suffice.

The interpretation of frequency counts is a common requirement, and it presents immediate and formidable problems. For example, if 75 or even 80 percent of a group of trainees state that they believe a certain block of instruction should be eliminated, what does it mean? Are the trainees right or wrong? What should the evaluator conclude? On what basis should a recommendation for the retention or elimination of the block be made to the systems designers?

Although frequency of mention may very well be an element of importance in reaching a conclusion, it is only one element; and its significance must be evaluated by carefully analyzing its logical and functional contribution to the total picture.

Evaluative instruments are based on two fundamental assumptions. First, it is assumed that more objective judgments can be obtained about the *significant* aspects of a training or development system by focusing on one component or element at a time. The second assumption relates to instruments that yield a total or composite rating. It is usually assumed that total value can be calculated by summing the values assigned to the individual parts. As for the former, the question remains: are the items selected for evaluation the really critical ones? It is entirely possible that in designing the instruments certain crucial items were overlooked. And, as regards the second assumption, even if all significant elements have been included, can any mathematical function applied to the parts yield a *meaningful* total value?

For these reasons and others, evaluation based on the results of using a combination of appraisal instruments is likely to be more accurate, valid, and reliable than any single instrument. In interpreting data, the following steps should be followed:

Step 1. Analyze the summaries for each item in turn, and write a brief statement of their meaning and possible significance.

Step 2. Compare the statements derived from step 1 with the findings of other evaluative instruments dealing with the same category to determine areas of agreement and disagreement. Consider the nuances of language, the problem of semantics, and the perspectives of the respondents.

Step 3. Draw your conclusions, and state them in simple and concise language.

Step 4. Draft your recommendations.

USING RESULTS

The ultimate purpose of internal evaluation must be kept firmly in mind when the final product is to be put to use. Note that the purpose is to improve the training or development system as a whole by improving its components. The value of evaluation, then, depends upon what is done with the conclusions and recommendations that the evaluation system produces.

The steps to be followed in using the results of evaluation are as follows:

Step 1. Submit recommendations for system changes to the systems designers, the training manager, and the instructors for study.

Step 2. Schedule a meeting of the functionaries identified in step 1 to discuss the findings and recommendations.

Step 3. Establish a priority listing of changes.

Step 4. Determine the resources required to implement the changes.

Step 5. Submit the recommendations, priority listing, and required resources to the training manager for approval.

Step 6. Establish who should institute the changes, when they should be instituted, and how they will be accomplished.

Step 7. Acquire the needed resources, and institute the change.

Step 8. Follow up and reevaluate the changed component of the system.

SELECTED REFERENCES

Abbatiello, Aurelius A. "An Objective Evaluation of Attitude Change in Training." *Training and Development Journal* (November 1967), 21:11: 23–24.

Beckwith, Edward F. "Take the Guesswork Out of Performance Rating." *Supervisory Management* (June 1965), 10:6: 4–7.

Buohler, Roy E. "Job-related Behavior Rating Scale." *Training and Development Journal* (March 1969), 23:3: 14–20.

Catalanello, Ralph F., and Donald L. Kirkpatrick. "Evaluating Training Programs—The State of the Art." *Training and Development Journal* (May 1968), 22:5: 2–9.

Cronbach, Lee J. *Essentials of Psychological Testing*, 2d ed. New York: Harper & Brothers, 1960, Chap. 17.

DePhillips, Frank A., William M. Berliner, and James J. Cribbin. *Management of Training Programs*. Homewood, Ill.: Richard D. Irwin, Inc., 1960, Chap. 14.

Edwards, Allen L. *Techniques of Attitude Scale Construction*. New York: Appleton-Century-Crofts, Inc., 1957.

Ferguson, Wilburn C. "Quantitative Evaluation of Training Using Student Reaction." *Training and Development Journal* (November 1968), 22:11: 36–42.

House, Robert J. *Management Development: Design, Evaluation, and Imple-*

mentation. Ann Arbor: Bureau of Industrial Relations, Graduate School of Business Administration, The University of Michigan Press, 1967, Chap. 6.

Kirkpatrick, Donald L. "Evaluation of Training." In Robert L. Craig and Lester R. Bittel, eds. *Training and Development Handbook.* New York: McGraw-Hill Book Company, 1967, Chap. 5.

Noll, Victor H. *Introduction to Educational Measurement.* Boston: Houghton Mifflin Company, 1965, Chap. 13.

Rose, Homer C. "A Plan for Training Evaluation." *Training and Development Journal* (May 1968), 22:5: 38–51.

————. *The Development and Supervision of Training Programs.* New York: American Technical Society, 1964, Pt. I, Chap. 8.

Smith, Edward W., Stanley W. Krouse, Jr., and Mark M. Atkinson. *The Educator's Encyclopedia.* Englewood Cliffs, N.J.: Prentice-Hall, Inc., 1961, pp. 413–429.

Stufflebeam, Daniel L. "Toward A Science of Educational Evaluation." *Educational Technology* (July 1968), 8:14: 5–12.

Thorndike, Robert C., and Elizabeth Hagen. *Measurement and Evaluation in Psychology and Education.* New York: John Wiley & Sons, Inc., 1961, Chap. 13.

Tracey, William R. *Evaluating Training and Development Systems.* AMA, 1968.

Wohlking, Wallace. "Teaching Effectiveness and Feedback Mechanism." *Training and Development Journal* (June 1967), 21:6: 2–10.

Worthen, Blaine R. "Toward a Taxonomy of Evaluation Designs." *Educational Technology* (Aug. 15, 1968), 8:15: 3–9.

15

Administering and Analyzing Criterion Measures

I~N~ Chapter 6, the procedures for constructing criterion measures were described. The primary purposes of criterion measures are to validate the training or development system and to effect quality control of the operating system. However, criterion measures have secondary uses which are of considerable importance to trainees, trainers, training and operating managers, and to systems designers. These secondary uses include instructional uses (diagnosis of learning difficulties, providing feedback to instructors, and motivating and counseling trainees); administrative uses (eliminating trainees, grading and ranking, recycling, pretesting, assignment, selection for advanced training, and reporting to line managers); and experimental uses (pretesting system components, performing cost analyses, and establishing prerequisites). The purpose of this chapter is to describe the procedures to be used in administering and scoring criterion measures, and in analyzing and using test results to serve both primary and secondary uses. Upon completion of the chapter, the reader should be able to perform as follows:

Behavior   Administer and score internal and end-of-course criterion measures.

Conditions   Given: a validated criterion test; explicit directions for test administration and scoring; other required test materials, equipment, and facilities; and, when required, assistance of EAM/ADP (electrical accounting machine/automatic data processing equipment) operating personnel.

Criterion   Tests will be administered and scored in accordance with the standards defined in this chapter.

Behavior   Report the results of test administration and analysis to trainees, trainers, training and operating managers, and to training systems designers.

Conditions   Given: statistical analyses of tests, access to reports of analyses of other evaluative devices, and clerical assistance.

Criterion   In accordance with the standards defined in this chapter.

TESTING CONSIDERATIONS

Human behavior varies in many ways. For example, there is great variation in the speed and accuracy with which different people perform even the most simple tasks. Numerical values can be placed on a continuum which represents the full range of human behavior in any category. Discrete descriptions of behavior at any point along this continuum provide a standard against which observed behavior can be compared. Measurement is the use of numbers to compare observed behavior with such standards. Measurement is obtained by tests of one kind or another. A test is simply a means of observing how people perform in a specific, controlled situation. The test sets the tasks, and numerical values are used to depict how well the trainees perform the tasks.

TESTS AS TOOLS

Tests cannot stand alone from other elements of the training or development system. If they are to be truly effective, they must contribute directly, systematically, and continuously to the achievement of the objectives of the total system. Criterion tests, therefore, must be viewed as tools in a training or development program, as one means of achieving the training objectives, and not as an end in themselves.

ESSENTIAL CHARACTERISTICS OF A TEST

As indicated previously, criterion measures must meet certain standards. Specifically, every test must be valid, reliable, objective, standard, comprehensive, administrable, and economical. All tests meet these standards to some degree. But no test is completely valid or completely invalid, nor is any test completely reliable or completely unreliable. It is also important to remember that all the characteristics of a good test are closely related and that their effects are interwoven. Although all characteristics of a test are important, validity is the most critical feature because it is related to the purpose of the training.

PERFORMANCE TESTS

As pointed out earlier, most of the criterion measures used in training and development programs should be performance tests. These are instruments that require the trainee to demonstrate some operation or skill which is considered to be an essential part of a job. Usually, some kind of equipment or apparatus is involved. The performance of the trainee is observed and evaluated in accordance with some predetermined standard of performance or product of performance. These standards have been established as a result of carefully and scientifically collected and analyzed job data. Performance tests are much more likely to be valid than other tests because they consist of actual samples of behavior essential to the performance of jobs, duties, and tasks.

DEFICIENCIES IN CONVENTIONAL TESTING PROGRAMS

Job qualification at the conclusion of training is usually determined by one of two methods: relative standings (rank in class, standard scores, T-scores, or percentile scores) or by a percentage or letter grade cut (passing) score. Both these methods are unsatisfactory because, on the one hand, qualification is determined by comparing the performance of a man with his peers; and on the other hand, a score is set which may have little relationship to job performance requirements. But with data derived from job or task analysis, such grading practices are no longer necessary.

Because performance objectives have been derived from a detailed analysis of the job for which trainees are to be prepared, the nonessential but "nice-to-know" items have been eliminated. The criterion measure can consist of a test or series of tests which measure thoroughly every objective in terms of the behavior, conditions, and standards stated in the objectives themselves. To show that he has attained the objectives, the trainee must meet or exceed the level of performance required for each of the training objectives. Because all the objectives are essential, unsatisfactory performance on one part of the test cannot be compensated for by superior performance on other parts. Under these conditions, relative grades or standings become meaningless as indexes of job qualification, although they may be used to serve other purposes. Standards for criterion measures, therefore, can be set in terms of absolute grades, scores, or levels of performance which are acceptable as "minimum passing" or "minimum qualifying."

Ideally, every trainee who completes the training will achieve a perfect score on the criterion measure because it includes only those behaviors which have been determined to be relevant to the job. Practically, however, where a paper and pencil objective-type test is involved, a class average score of 90 percent, with a range from 80 to 100 percent, might be considered acceptable evidence that the objectives of the training have been achieved.

If 90 percent of the class achieve a score of 90 percent or higher, the trainees "learned" (met the criterion), and the instructional system is proved to be an effective one. If the trainees did not "learn" (fell short of the criterion), the system is ineffective.

In sum, the philosophy of criterion testing is completely different from conventional testing. Although a criterion measure can and does test the trainee, its primary purposes during the validation phase are to test the adequacy of the system, to identify weak elements in the system, and to provide data upon which to base modifications of the system.

TEST ADMINISTRATION

The most expertly constructed test is valueless unless it is properly administered. An improperly administered test will provide an inaccurate measure of the amount and quality of trainee learning and cannot serve the validation, quality control, or instructional purposes described in Chapter 6. Scores obtained under inappropriate testing conditions, with inadequate or misunderstood instructions, by cheating, or with improper assistance by the examiner will not serve the purposes of the testing program. Once an instrument is constructed, care must be taken to insure that the scores are obtained exactly as intended by the specialists who built the instrument.

IMPORTANCE OF TEST DIRECTIONS

As explained in Chapter 6, specific directions for the administration of all tests have been carefully prepared by the test developer. These directions are as much a part of the test as the test items or situations themselves. Directions include the exact wording of the instructions to the testees, the time limits, the way in which responses to test items should be recorded, the kind and amount of assistance the examiner may provide to the testees, and how the test is to be scored and critiqued. Departure from any of these directions can destroy the accuracy of measurement. For this reason, test directions must be followed strictly and without deviation of any kind by the examiner and the testees.

STANDARDIZED TEST CONDITIONS

The conditions under which tests are administered must be the same for every testee if reliable results are to be obtained. Procedures used for administering tests must be those which will enable every testee to do his best. The conditions which tend to encourage the best efforts of testees are as follows:

1. The testing area should be well lighted, well ventilated, and reasonably free from noise, movement, or other distractions.
2. Testees should be able to see and hear the examiner as he gives the test directions.
3. Testees should be seated or positioned as far apart as the room and facilities for testing permit to provide ample working space and to discourage collaboration.
4. Each testee must have a clear understanding of the requirements of the test, the rules of the testing situation, and what he is expected to do.
5. The directions for the test should be read to the testees exactly as written.

PROCEDURES FOR ADMINISTERING TESTS

Proper procedures for test administration include preparation, organization, and control. Although such details as seating the testees, distributing the materials, giving directions, and collecting the materials are subordinate to the primary activity of responding to test items and situations, the handling of these details enables the testing session to be either a smooth-running, organized activity or a confused affair. The key is *control*. If the examiner is well organized, if he has carefully planned the details of the testing period, and if he has prepared himself and his assistants adequately, the test will run smoothly and efficiently. Steps in the administration of criterion measures follow:

Step 1. Prepare for administration. The examiner should study the directions for administration to make certain that he knows the purpose of the test, the materials needed, and the problems he may encounter in administering the test. He should review the directions to be read aloud so that he will be able to read them in a conversational way. He should know the kind and amount of assistance that he may give the testees and how this assistance is to be rendered.

Step 2. Train assistant test administrators or proctors. If assistants or proctors are needed, the examiner should carefully brief them on their duties. Each assistant or proctor should be assigned responsibility for a specific number of testees and for a specific part of the testing area. Each should be required to check test materials, tools, and equipment to be sure that they are in good condition and are in sufficient quantity. Each should know how and when the materials are to be distributed and collected and how to patrol his assigned area.

Step 3. Assign testees to their seats or work stations. Allow enough space between testees to enable them to work without interference and to discourage collaboration.

Step 4. Explain simply and informally the purpose of the test. Tell trainees why it is important for them to do their best.

Step 5. Distribute the test materials (test booklets, answer sheets, pencils, tools, references, working aids, critique sheets, and the like). Double-check to be sure that each testee has everything he needs to take the test.

Step 6. Read aloud the directions from the manual for administration. Do not paraphrase, do not give directions from memory, and do not adapt instructions in any way. Directions are read verbatim and without additions. As a general rule, examiners may answer questions asked by testees prior to the beginning of the test. Most questions pertain to testing procedures, time limits, and the uses of test results. However, when the test is underway, examiners must be careful to avoid providing information that might interfere with proper evaluation of the individual. If a testee asks for help in interpreting an item or says that he does not understand a question, he should be told that providing this assistance would influence his response and result in an inaccurate evaluation. He should be encouraged to do the best he can with the question.

Step 7. Start the test. Immediately check to be sure that all testees are following directions correctly and understand what they are to do and how they are to do it. Be alert to detect incorrect methods of marking answer sheets when such devices are used.

Step 8. Monitor testees to be sure that each does his own work independently of his neighbors. Avoid distracting testees; move continuously but quietly among the testees.

Step 9. Strictly observe time limits for the complete test as well as for parts of the test. Use a stopwatch for this purpose. Inform the testees of time limitations by an oral announcement at the beginning of each part of the test, by a continuous reminder on the chalkboard, and by an oral announcement of the time remaining five minutes before the time is up. Chalkboard notices should appear as follows:

Starting time	1300:00
Time limit	50:00
Stopping time	1350:00

Step 10. Collect the test materials as quickly as possible after time is up. As soon as the stop signal has been given, instruct testees to bring all testing materials to the front of the room, and place each item (test booklet, answer sheet, scratch paper, critique sheets, and pencils) in the appropriate pile before leaving the testing area. Make sure that each testee has turned in all materials before he is permitted to leave. Testees who complete their work before the standard stopping time may be permitted to turn in their materials and leave the testing area.

Step 11. Report any unusual conditions surrounding the test to those who score and analyze. If errors are found in the test or associated materials, they should be reported to test construction personnel as well as to scorers and analysts.

SPECIAL PROVISIONS FOR ADMINISTERING PERFORMANCE TESTS

In addition to the steps just mentioned, there are some special considerations with respect to performance test administration, since these tests are scored as they are administered.

1. Only competent and carefully prepared instructors or test-construction specialists should be permitted to administer performance tests. The optimum examiner-testee ratio for performance tests is one to one. This is rarely practicable; however, one examiner cannot be expected to score more than six testees on the simplest of tasks with any degree of accuracy.

It is preferable to have someone other than the trainee's regular instructor administer performance tests. If this precaution is taken, the scoring will not be affected by previously formed opinions of the trainee's competence.

2. When administering performance tests, examiners must be especially careful to follow the written directions without deviation. If assistance is necessary to enable the testee to continue the test, the exact wording of the oral explanation should be read from the test directions. If the examiner is permitted to perform operations which the testee is unable to perform, but which are essential for the completion of the test, these operations should be completed as specified in the instructions.

SCORING TESTS

Even the most valid, reliable, objective, and comprehensive criterion test will yield meaningless results unless considerable thought has been given to the development of scoring procedures; these procedures must then be followed to the letter in scoring the tests. This section describes how test scores are obtained for multiple-choice and performance tests.

Regardless of how tests are scored, the procedure should be explained to all trainees at the time they take the test. If relative weights are assigned to various test parts or items, trainees should know these weights. If testees are to be penalized for guessing, they should be so informed. Only in this way can they know how to use the time available to best advantage.

Scoring is the process of comparing testees' responses with solutions determined by subject-matter experts (in advance of the administration of the test), to be the "correct" or "best" answers, the "correct" or "best" way of doing something, or an "acceptable" or "satisfactory" work product. A *raw score* on any test is a simple count of the correct responses.

METHODS OF SCORING

Paper and pencil tests may be either hand-scored or machine-scored. The decision is made before the test is administered on a regular basis to any group. Some tests require hand scoring either because the format of the test or the small number of testees does not warrant setting up a machine for scoring. Machine scoring has the advantages of speed and accuracy in marking large numbers of tests.

Hand scoring. To simplify, objectify, and reduce errors in scoring, scoring keys, or stencils, should be prepared. Strip keys may be used with tests in which the answer spaces are arranged along one side of the page in the test booklet or in vertical columns on an answer sheet. The keys are simply strips of heavy paper or cardboard containing the correct responses in a vertical column. They are used by being placed adjacent to the column of responses in the test booklet or answer sheet.

Window stencils may be used when the answers are scattered over the page in a test booklet or on an answer sheet. These stencils may be made of heavy paper or plastic in which holes have been cut. When the stencil is placed over the page of the test booklet or answer sheet, the correct answer spaces show through the holes. The scorer simply aligns the stencil and counts the number of responses that agree with the correct answers on the stencil. Heavy black guidelines connecting the "right-answer" holes may be placed on the stencil to guide the scorer's eye movements.

Machine scoring. Several devices for machine scoring answer sheets are now available. One of these is the IBM 1230 Optical Mark Scoring Reader. This is a fully automatic, solid-state machine for high-speed scoring of objective tests, surveys, or questionnaires. The machine will score up to 1,200 pencil-marked sheets per hour. Answer sheets are 8½ by 11 inches with 1,000 possible response positions for 400 two-part questions, 200 three- to five-part questions, or 100 six- to ten-part questions. For double capacity, both sides of a sheet may be used. The machine recognizes up to ten responses per question and digitally accumulates rights, wrongs, and omits (or optionally rights minus wrongs or rights minus fractional wrongs). The equipment rejects poorly marked or excessively erased sheets. Part and/or total scores are printed in the right-hand margin of the answer sheet. The IBM 534 Card Punch, Model 3, can be attached to the 1230 to provide punched-card output at the rate of up to 1,200 cards per hour. These cards can be used as input to a computer for statistical analysis of test results.

The National Computer Systems' Optical Mark Readers (OMR) 22-85 and 42-11 are general purpose, high speed, high volume units that read handwritten marks on a wide variety of input forms. The OMR reads both sides of a sheet with one pass and transmits the mark pattern directly to a general purpose computer for evaluation. The 22-85 reading rate, established by the processing capabilities of the associated computer, ranges from 2,000 to 5,000 documents per hour. The 42-11 model reads from 3,000 to 10,000 documents per hour. Output is in the form of magnetic tape, printed reports, or punched cards. The machines will accommodate a wide variety of document sizes and response patterns on answer sheets, questionnaires, or report forms up to 42 inches long. A total of 15,000 mark positions are available for use.

Another scoring machine, the OpScan 100 System, made by Optical Scanning Corporation, is an optical mark scanner which automatically reads and scores pencil-marked test answer sheets at the rate of 2,400 per hour. The system reads answer sheets in either of two basic 8½- by 11-inch matrices—the 805 matrix, containing 992 separate response positions, and the standard 1200 matrix, containing 1,488 response positions. Both sides of a sheet may be marked and scanned by making two passes through the system.

Feeding from an input stacker that takes up to 600 sheets, the unit scores rights or rights minus wrongs, comparing answers on the test form with correct answers stored in magnetic core memory. A separate score is computed for each test part, with up to seven test parts per sheet—plus total—printed in the right-hand margin. A dark-mark reading feature insures accuracy by selecting only the darkest mark, ignoring doodles and erasures.

The system can be programmed in minutes. Premarked control sheets are fed through the scanner, instructing the unit what to look for and where to scan on test answer sheets. Optical devices are available which make the unit capable of converting test data to computer input, transferring it automatically to punched card or magnetic tape.

The Grade-O-Mat Test Scoring Machine, made by Burgess Cellulose Company, is a portable, electronic scoring machine which scores standard, manually punched test answer cards. These answer cards are available in formats to accommodate 225 true-false questions or 150 three-choice, 112 four-choice, or 90 five-choice questions. Answer cards are punched by testees using a stylus and sponge. When placed on the carriage of the machine directly over a master or key card, the machine scores the card automatically in about 11½ seconds.

Port-A-Punch answer cards, standard-sized IBM cards with spaces for marking the answers to 80 multiple-choice items, can be used as input to a computer system for complete scoring, analysis, and reporting of test results. Additional cards can be used to increase the total number of test items to 160 (see Fig. 15-1).

Testees indicate their answers to test questions by circling the chosen alternative with a pencil. When the testee has completed the entire test, he uses a stylus and sponge to punch out his choices (see Fig. 15-2). However, before the punching operation, the testee may change his responses by putting an X in the circle he had originally marked and circling his new choice. There is no need to erase the pencil marks from the card. Care must be taken to avoid punching two responses to the same item. If a testee makes a mistake in punching, however, he can correct the error. He does this by wetting a punched-out bit of paper and replacing it in the erroneously punched hole. The punched cards are then processed by an IBM data-processing system. This equipment is programmed to score and analyze the test. It produces raw scores, stand-

Figure 15-1.   Answer cards 1 and 2.

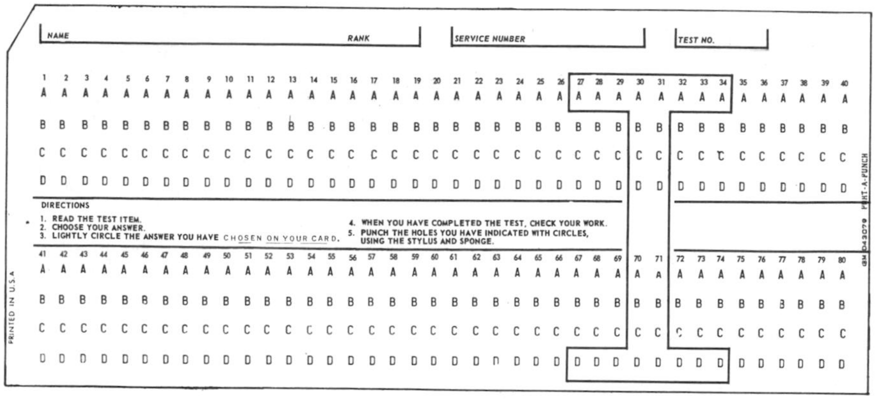

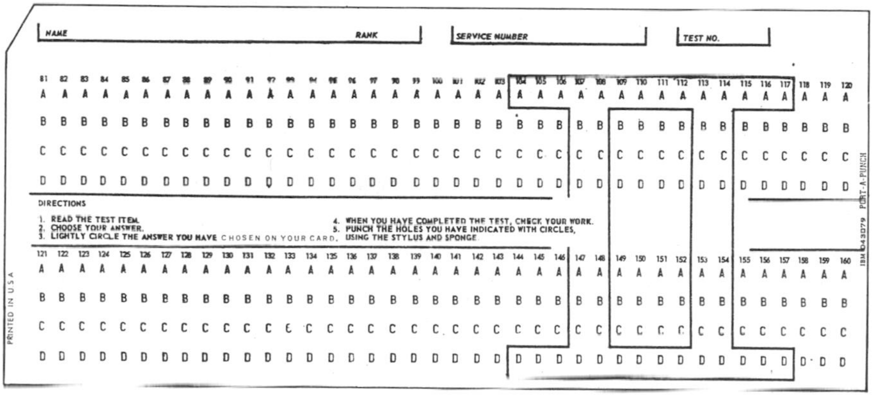

ard scores, percent scores, and ranks for each individual, by part and total test. It also produces the statistics pertaining to the test as a whole, test parts, and test items.

SCORING PERFORMANCE TESTS

Most performance tests are scored as they are administered. As emphasized earlier, directions for scoring each element of a performance test must be followed by examiners exactly and without deviation. As each segment of the job is performed by the testee, the examiner must observe carefully and objectively, match the performance against the criterion or standard, and enter the score in the appropriate space on the scoring form. If the test is divided into two or more parts, subscores

Figure 15-2.   Answer cards marked and punched.

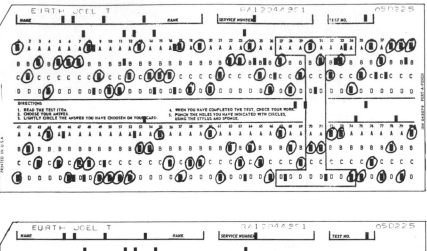

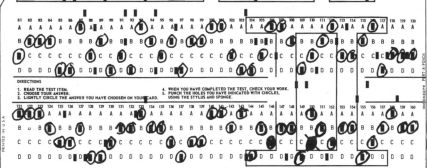

as well as total scores are entered as indicated in the instructions. With some performance tests, the product of the performance is scored. In such cases the scoring is done following the administration of the test. A product scale, scoring template, or standards for scoring are provided. These must be used exactly as the test constructor intended.

RECORDING SCORES

Regardless of the type of scoring system used, accuracy and legibility are the most important factors to be stressed in the process of recording scores. Every score copied from one document to another must be double-checked. Carelessness in computing and transcribing scores defeats the entire purpose of testing. All numbers must be typed or handwritten with extreme care. Reversals, omissions, repetitions, or switching of names and scores will result in damage to the individual, inaccurate estimates of the effectiveness of the instructional system, and a loss in confidence in the system by all concerned.

REPORTING TEST RESULTS

The numerical scores obtained from scoring a test or rating a performance are relatively meaningless for reporting and only slightly less meaningless for other evaluation purposes. The fact that a certain trainee received a rating of 36 for a certain performance and a score of 102 on a multiple-choice test has no significance in itself. Numerical raw scores must be translated into meaningful terms. This fact indicates that the form in which test scores are reported differs according to the user. Although it has been emphasized earlier that relative scores and certain types of absolute scores have no real utility in determining success or failure in a training program, such scores can and should serve other purposes.

TYPES OF SCORES

Test scores may be recorded and reported in any one or more of the following forms:

Adjectival scores. Terms like "outstanding," "above average," "average," "below average," and "unsatisfactory" are adjectival scores. At best they provide a gross index of performance, and often they fail to portray relative standing accurately. However, where a gross measure is adequate, scores of this type may be used. For example, in reporting performance to trainees, the use of adjectival scores may be helpful.

Raw numerical scores. A raw score is a simple count of the number of correct responses on a test. For a scoring system involving numbers, the determination of raw scores is a necessary first step. However, raw scores are meaningless in and of themselves. They must be converted to another type of score to be usable.

Rank order scores. Usually the next step in classifying and tabulating scores is to arrange the raw scores in order of size from highest to lowest. Simple ranking enables interpretations of each raw score as an indication of performance on the test in terms of best, next best, and so on, through to poorest. Columns 1 and 2 of Figure 15-3 show a collection of scores arranged by size and rank order.

It should be noted that such listings are long, unwieldy, and useless for making comparisons between large and small groups. For example, ranking nineteenth in a group of 25 is poorer than ranking nineteenth in a group of 75.

Frequency distributions. A list of scores can be made shorter by arranging the scores in a frequency distribution. The third and fourth columns of Figure 15-3 show the simplest form of frequency distribution.

Figure 15-3.   Raw scores arranged by size and rank order, and tabulated to the normal distribution curve.

		Tabulated	
Order of size	Rank order	Score	Frequency
1	2	3	4
102	1	102	1
100	2	100	1
97	3	97	1
95 ⎫	4.5	95	2
95 ⎬	4.5	90	1 ⎱ 12
90	6	87	1
87	7	85	3
85 ⎫	9	82	1
85 ⎬	9	80	1
85 ⎭	9	79	1 Midpoint of
82	11	76	1 frequencies
80	12	72	1
79	13	70	1
76	14	69	1
72	15	68	1
70	16	65	1
69	17	62	2 12
68	18	58	1
65	19	56	1
62 ⎫	20.5	50	1
62 ⎬	20.5	44	1
58	22		$N = 25$
56	23		
50	24		
44	25		
1914			

Scores are arranged in order of size, here from 102 to 44, and the number of times each score occurs is entered to the right of the score. Of the 25 frequencies in the figure, half are for scores 102 through 80; the other half are for scores 76 through 44. Therefore, the midpoint of the frequencies lies between 80 and 76, or at score 79.

If the midpoint fell between two actual scores (in the case of an even number of scores), the midpoint would be half the distance between them. For example, if there were 26 scores instead of 25 and the additional score were a 44, the midpoint would fall between the thirteenth and fourteenth scores (between 76 and 79); and the midpoint would be 77.5. The midpoint is the median score.

The *mean* (average) score is calculated by summing the individual scores and dividing by the number of scores. In Figure 15-3 the mean is 1,914/25 or 76.56.

For larger numbers of scores, some condensation of the frequency distribution should be made. This can be done by constructing a grouped frequency distribution. Procedures for doing this can be found in any good measurement book.

The range. The range is the difference between the highest and the lowest score plus one. For the scores shown in Figure 15-3, the range is 59 $[(102 - 44) + 1 = 58 + 1 = 59]$. The range is a crude measure of variability. Although with small numbers of cases the range tends to fluctuate from one group to another, it usually will suffice as a measure of variability of scores on a test.

Percentage scores. These scores are obtained by dividing the number of correct responses by the total number of items on the test. Percentage scores are difficult to interpret because they do not take into account the difficulty of a particular test or differences in the ability of the people taking the test. Setting a score of 70 (or any other score) as a passing and failing line is completely arbitrary. However, when considered in conjunction with other types of scores, or with tests of *known* difficulty for a specific group, percentage scores can be meaningful and useful.

Percentile ranks. A percentile rank is a point in the distribution of scores below which a stated percentage of all scores lies. Thus an individual at the sixtieth percentile has done as well or better than 60 percent of the testees and poorer than 40 percent. The median score is always the fiftieth percentile.

Percentile ranks portray relative standing on a test in terms of the percentage of the raw scores equaled or exceeded by any given raw score. They do *not* refer to the percent of questions answered correctly but to the percent of testees whose performance an individual testee has equaled or surpassed. Percentile ranks permit comparison of both individuals and groups; however, percentile ranks do not indicate *how much* better or poorer one man is than another in terms of raw scores. For example, a 5 percentile point difference for the higher scores may represent a difference of 15 raw score points, while a 5 percentile point difference for average scores may represent a difference of only 4 raw score points.

In sum, percentile ranks have certain advantages and disadvantages. On the plus side, they are easily calculated. They are readily understood even by those without statistical training, and they can be interpreted even when the distribution of scores is nonnormal. But they magnify small differences in scores near the mean which may not be significant. They reduce the apparent size of larger differences in scores near the tails of the distribution, and they cannot be used in many other statistical computations.

Percentile ranks may be calculated by arranging the raw scores in order of decreasing magnitude and finding for each score the number of scores equalling or lying below it. Each of these numbers is then divided by the total number of scores, and the quotient is multiplied by 100. This formula provides only approximate results. If more exact percentile ranks are required, other methods of computation can be found in any good measurement or statistics book.

Standard scores. A standard score is a derived score which takes into account the mean performance of a given group on a test and also the relative performance of all persons taking the test. If a test is neither too easy nor too difficult for the group tested, scores will be distributed normally, that is, they will be arranged similar to the normal probability curve shown in Figure 15-4.

Standard scores are calculated by dividing the deviations of testees' raw scores from the mean by the standard deviation of the group. The basic standard score formula (or z-score) is as follows:

$$z = \frac{\text{Raw score} - \text{mean}}{\text{Standard deviation}}$$

Because z-scores are often fractional and those below the mean are negative, it is helpful to set up a distribution of standard scores with a mean sufficiently greater than zero to avoid minuses and a standard deviation sufficiently greater than one to make decimals unnecessary. The result is a T-score. A T-score is calculated by converting the mean of the distribution to 50 and the standard deviation to 10 as follows:

$$\text{T-score} = \frac{10 \times \text{z-score}}{\text{Standard deviation}} + 50$$

or
$$\text{T-score} = \frac{10 \ (\text{Raw score} - \text{mean})}{\text{Standard deviation}} + 50$$

Standard scores have certain advantages. Differences in standard scores are proportional to differences in raw scores. Small differences in performance are clearly revealed. Individuals can be compared on performance. An individual's performance on several tests can be directly compared. Standard scores are mathematically convenient, which means that all arithmetic operations can be performed on these scores without damaging their integrity. The limitations of standard scores are that they

Figure 15-4. *Equivalent scoring systems and their relationships to the normal distribution curve.**

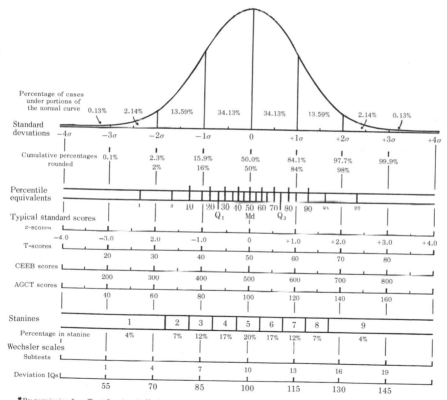

*By permission from *Test Service Bulletin* (January 1955), No. 48, p. 8, The Psychological Corporation, New York, N. Y.

NOTE: This chart cannot be used to equate scores on one test to scores on another test. For example, both 600 on the CEEB and 120 on the AGCT are 1 standard deviation above their respective means, but they do not represent "equal" standings because the scores were obtained from different groups.

cannot be interpreted readily when distributions are skewed, and untrained persons find them difficult to understand.

Stanine scores. Stanines are standard scores which divide the score distribution into nine groups. The mean of a set of stanines is 5, and its standard deviation is approximately 2. Each stanine represents a band of scores on the base line of the normal probability curve of one-half of a standard deviation. The entire range is divided into nine such bands. The middle stanine is the band including one-fourth of a standard deviation on each side of the mean. This is numbered the fifth stanine. On either side of this are four stanines; each is one-half a standard deviation. Those below the middle are numbered one to four and those above, six to nine. Stanines have all the advantages and disadvantages of standard scores. They are computed by the following formula:

$$\text{Stanine} = 5 + 2\left(\frac{\text{Raw-score} - \text{mean}}{\text{Standard deviation}}\right)$$

REPORTING TO INSTRUCTORS

Instructors need to have as much information about the performance of trainees as can be provided. The data given to instructors should be in a form and format that will facilitate use in diagnosing learning difficulties, from both individual trainee and group standpoints. These data will be an invaluable aid to the instructor when he is conducting examination critiques, counseling individual trainees, providing individual and group remedial instruction, and improving elements of the instructional system, such as instructional techniques and materials.

The data furnished instructors should include, but not be limited to, the following:

1. A roster of trainees, indicating their scores on the total test and each of its parts. Scores should be provided in all available types, including raw scores, percentage, percentile rank, standard (or T-scores) or stanine scores, and rank order. Figure 15-5 is an excerpt from a roster provided to instructors.

2. A frequency distribution of test scores for the total test and for each of its parts showing the mean, median, mode, and standard deviation. Figure 15-6 shows a portion of a report of this type.

3. In the case of a multiple-choice test, a graphic item count (GIC) with individual item difficulties identified. Figure 6-8 is an excerpt from a graphic item count.

4. A report of overall test characteristics, to include high and low scores, range, mean, standard deviation, mean difficulty, standard error

Figure 15-5. Excerpt from a test report to instructors.

Name	Number of items	Raw score	Percentage score	Percentile rank	Standard score	Rank
Anders, Maurice R.						
Total	137	87	63.5	62.3	104	9.5 of 15
Part 1	27	14	51.8	27.4	85	14 of 15
Part 2	27	13	48.1	51.9	95	10 of 15
Part 3	28	15	53.6	26.4	84	13 of 15
Part 4	55	45	81.8	100.0	136	1 of 15
Best, Lawrence						
Total	137	92	67.2	84.9	118	3.5 of 15
Part 1	27	19	70.4	90.6	123	8.5 of 15
Part 2	27	19	70.4	97.2	140	2 of 15
Part 3	28	17	60.7	55.7	97	8 of 15
Part 4	55	37	67.3	39.6	93	9 of 15
Hunt, Daniel E.						
Total	137	89	65.0	72.6	110	7.5 of 15
Part 1	27	20	74.1	94.3	130	6.5 of 15
Part 2	27	13	48.1	51.9	95	10 of 15
Part 3	28	18	64.3	67.9	104	4.5 of 15
Part 4	55	38	69.1	50.0	98	6.5 of 15
Mann, Dale D.						
Total	137	102	74.5	100.0	145	1 of 15
Part 1	27	24	88.9	100.0	160	1 of 15
Part 2	27	17	63.0	88.7	125	3.5 of 15
Part 3	28	21	75.0	88.7	124	1 of 15
Part 4	55	40	72.7	79.2	109	3 of 15

Figure 15-6. Sample frequency distribution of scores on a test of 137 items administered to 106 trainees.

Raw score	Percentage score	Standard score	Frequency	Cumulative frequency	Raw score	Percentage score	Standard score	Frequency	Cumulative frequency
102	74.4	145	2	106	84	61.3	96	2	39
101	73.7	142	1	104	83	60.5	94	3	37
100	72.9	139	2	103	82	59.8	91	1	34
99	72.2	137	2	101	81	59.1	88	4	33
98	71.5	134	0	99	80	58.3	85	6	29
97	70.8	131	2	99	79	57.6	83	2	23
96	70.0	128	0	97	78	56.9	80	5	21
95	69.3	126	1	97	77	56.2	77	4	16
94	68.6	123	1	96	76	55.4	75	3	12
93	67.8	120	5	95	75	54.7	72	0	9
92	67.1	118	4	90	74	54.0	69	1	9
91	66.4	115	3	86	73	53.2	67	2	8
90	65.6	112	6	83	72	52.5	64	1	6
89	64.9	110	6	77	71	51.8	61	2	5
88	64.2	107	5	71	70	51.0	59	1	3
87	63.5	104	7	66	69	50.3	56	1	2
86	62.7	102	10	59	68	49.6	53	1	1
85	62.0	99	10	49					

N = 106   K = 137   Mean = 85.41   Median = 85.90   Mode = 85.50   Standard deviation = 7.44

of the mean, standard error of measurement, and reliability. In the case of criterion measures that have been administered to earlier groups, the instructor should be provided a comparative picture of the performance of his class with other classes. Figure 15-7 shows a sample of this type of report.

REPORTING TO TRAINEES

If test results are to serve instructional and motivational purposes, they must be reported to trainees immediately. Experience with programmed instruction has conclusively demonstrated the importance of immediate feedback. Any delay in reporting results diminishes the value of the test to the trainee. Either he has moved on to another phase of the instruction, or he has been graduated.

The more detailed the information provided to a trainee about his performance, provided that it is in a readily understandable form, the more useful it is. The most important factors in reporting to trainees are that they know specifically how well they measured up to the established standard of performance, where they exceeded the standard, where they fell short of it, and what they need to do to raise all aspects of their performance up to, or above, the standard.

In the case of a performance test, each trainee should be individually critiqued in detail. The critique should be conducted by the examiner immediately following the administration of the test. Used in this way, the critique becomes a teaching device. The critique should cover the following points: (1) elements the trainee failed to perform; (2) elements performed incorrectly or out of sequence; (3) elements performed correctly but not in accordance with the standard; (4) elements performed above the standard; (5) other comments with respect to speed, accuracy, or the quality of the product.

For a paper and pencil multiple-choice test, the information provided to each trainee should include his raw score, percentage score, standard score, and rank in class on the total test as well as a picture of his performance on each part of the test. Figure 15-8 shows a sample report of this type.

Although formal reports of paper and pencil test results may take a day or so to prepare, trainees should be provided with immediate feedback on their performance. This can be done by giving testees critique copies of the test immediately following test administration. The critique copy of the test contains the correct answers or approved solutions. This technique enables the trainee to see the correct answers while the test items are fresh in his mind.

Figure 15-7. Report on test characteristics for a four-part, 137-item test.

Test T401C
Class TO50-01-70

	Number testees	Number test items	High score	Low score	Range	Mean score	Standard deviation	Mean difficulty	Standard error of measurement	Probable error of mean	Standard error of mean	Reliability
Current class	15	137	102	68	34	87.20	7.82	0.64	5.55	1.41	2.11	0.63
Past classes	91	137	102	69	33	85.11	7.34	0.62	5.65	0.51	0.77	0.62
Cumulative	106	137	102	68	34	85.41	7.44	0.62	5.73	0.48	0.72	0.62
Part 1	15	27				18.60	2.98	0.69	2.41	0.54	0.80	0.68
Part 2	15	27				14.67	2.77	0.54	2.60	0.50	0.74	0.54
Part 3	15	28				16.93	1.98	0.60	2.59	0.35	0.53	0.60
Part 4	15	55				37.00	4.34	0.67	3.52	0.78	1.17	0.67

Figure 15-8. *A sample report of a four-part test for trainees.*

Mix, Steven L.	80	58.3	85	13/15	T050	T401C
Name	Raw score	Percentage score	Standard score	Rank in class	Class	Test number

This is a report of your achievement on the examination you have taken.

In the chart to the right you will find a profile of your performance on the parts of the examination.

The range of scores shown for each part are standard scores.

If your score is below average for any examination part, you should ask for help.

Performance on test	Test part 1 2 3 4 5 6 7 8 9 0
Above 144	
135 – 144	
125 – 134	
115 – 124	
105 – 114	■
95 – 104	A V E R A G E
85 – 94	■
75 – 84	■
Below 75	

As soon as possible after a test has been scored, a group critique of the test should be conducted by the primary instructor. The reason for waiting until the test is scored is to make it possible to provide both the instructor and the trainees with data on individual and group performance. The delay also gives the instructor time to analyze the results, to study the comments and questions of trainees on the critique sheets, and to prepare himself for the conduct of the critique.

The primary purpose of the group critique is to improve trainee learning; it is a remedial technique. The secondary purpose is to improve the test. It should be noted that the instructor conducting the critique has data describing the performance of the group on the total test and on each of its parts. Each trainee knows how he performed on the test. It should be remembered also that during the test the testees were afforded an opportunity to note items they wished to have discussed or clarified during the critique. Questions that were not clear, that posed difficulty in terms of content or construction, have been identified. The instructor has had an opportunity to review these questions and comments. He also has the graphic item count and indexes of difficulty for each test item. These materials provide the instructor with information which will make the critique profitable. Items about which trainees have questions and items which posed difficulty for the group can be discussed in detail. Such discussion often reveals flaws in the test (as well as in the instruction) which can be reported to test-construction personnel for elimination from future versions of the test. The critique should be conducted as follows:

1. The instructor informs the group how well it performed on the test by identifying the range, mean, and median scores, and the number of testees exceeding the cut score.

2. Each item that posed difficulty for the group, or about which more than one or two trainees had comments or questions, is discussed. The reasons why each distractor (wrong answer alternative) is incorrect are identified as well as the justification for the correct answer.

3. Problems with individual items pointed out during the critique that indicate a needed revision are noted, and the information is forwarded to test-construction personnel for appropriate action.

4. The instructor makes changes in his approach and in his techniques. Remedial instruction is provided for the trainees that need it.

REPORTING TO SYSTEMS DESIGNERS AND THE TRAINING MANAGER

It will be recalled that the primary purposes of the administration of criterion measures is to validate the training or development system.

Systems designers need to know precisely where the system failed to produce the desired results so that they can make appropriate changes in the system. Test data reported to systems designers do not necessarily identify faulty system components. These faults can be identified only by careful and systematic analysis of test results together with evaluative data obtained by other means (observation, rating, questionnaire, and interview). But test results are a very important source of data. For this reason, systems designers should be provided the following information:

1. Frequency distributions of test results showing raw scores, percentage scores, standard scores, and the number of testees meeting and failing to meet the standard. If more than one group has taken the same test, comparative performance should be provided in a format similar to the one shown in Figure 15-9. If the tests are of the performance type, pictorial information, such as that shown in Figure 15-10, should be prepared.

2. A complete breakout of test characteristics to include the range, mean, median, standard deviation, mean difficulty, reliability, and standard error of measurement (see Fig. 15-7).

3. Information gathered as a result of the reports of test administrators, indicating such things as unusual testing conditions or errors in the test, and from critiques, indicating problem items and test situations, ambiguities, and errors.

This information should also be provided to the training manager because it represents a meaningful synopsis of the performance of the test and of the test population.

REPORTING TO THE ADMINISTRATIVE OR RECORDS OFFICE

Essentially the same information should be provided to the administrative or records office as is provided to the instructors. Class rosters with scores indicated should be forwarded for record purposes (see Fig. 15-5).

REPORTING TO LINE SUPERVISORS AND MANAGERS

Immediate supervisors should be provided with a copy of the report given to individual trainees (see Fig. 15-8). In addition, a synoptic report, written in narrative style and covering all aspects of the employee's performance, should be available to the immediate supervisor at the conclusion of training.

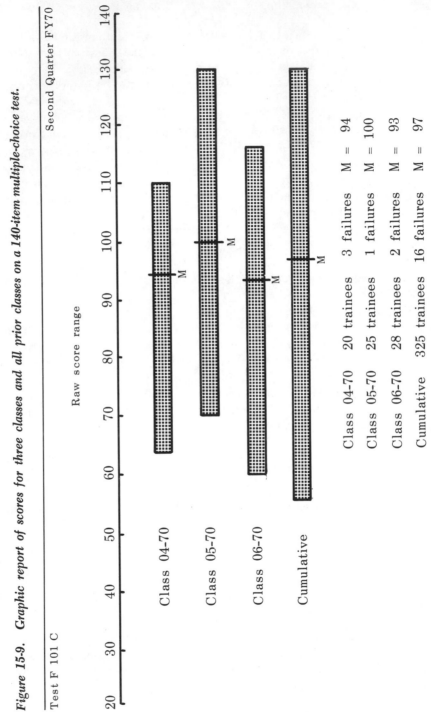

Figure 15-9. Graphic report of scores for three classes and all prior classes on a 140-item multiple-choice test.

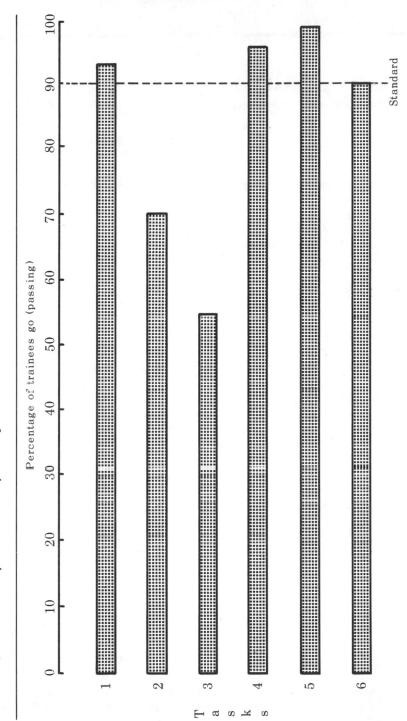

Figure 15-10. Performance of forty trainees on a series of performance tests for six tasks compared with a 90 percent system criterion.

CHECKLISTS

The following checklist may be used to determine the adequacy of test administration, scoring, analysis, reporting, and the use of test results.

TEST ADMINISTRATION AND SCORING

1. Are criterion tests administered in strict accordance with test directions?
2. Are the conditions under which tests are administered identical for all testees?
3. In the case of performance tests, are only competent instructors or test-construction personnel allowed to administer the tests?
4. Are scoring procedures carefully prepared in advance of test administration?
5. Are scoring procedures followed to the letter?
6. Are scores carefully recorded; are they checked for accuracy?

ANALYSIS AND REPORTING

1. Are critique copies of tests given to testees immediately following test administration?
2. Are performance tests critiqued immediately by the test administrator?
3. Are reports of test results prepared and distributed in a timely fashion? Are separate reports prepared for the following:
    a. Trainees?
    b. Instructors?
    c. Systems designers and the training manager?
    d. Administrative or records office?
    e. Line supervisors and managers?

USING TEST RESULTS

1. Are instructors provided with all materials required to conduct group critiques of tests?
2. Are group critiques conducted as soon as possible after test administration?
3. Are reports of unusual testing conditions, errors in the test, ambiguities, and other faults in the test reported to test-construction personnel following the critique?
4. Are test results used as a basis for remedial instruction?
5. Are test results used as a basis for recycling and drop actions?
6. Are tests revised on the basis of feedback from earlier administrations of the test?

7. Are appropriate changes in the instructional system made following analysis of test results in conjunction with analyses of complementary evaluative devices?

SELECTED REFERENCES

Adams, Georgia Sachs. *Measurement and Evaluation.* New York: Holt, Rinehart and Winston, Inc., 1964, Chaps. 2, 3, 4.

Anastasi, Anne, ed. *Testing Problems in Perspective.* Washington, D.C.: American Council on Education, 1966, Chap. 2.

Courts, Frederick A. *Psychological Statistics: An Introduction.* Homewood, Ill.: The Dorsey Press, 1966, Chaps. 3–5.

Cronbach, Lee J. *Essentials of Psychological Testing,* 2d ed. New York: Harper & Brothers, 1960, Chaps. 3 and 4.

Davis, Frederick B. *Educational Measurements and Their Interpretation.* Belmont, Calif.: Wadsworth Publishing Company, Inc., 1964, Chaps. 2, 4, 9; Appendixes A–M.

Diederich, Paul B. *Short-cut Statistics for Teacher-made Tests,* 2d ed. Princeton, N.J.: Educational Testing Service, 1964.

Ebel, Robert L. *Measuring Educational Achievement.* Englewood Cliffs: N.J.: Prentice-Hall, Inc., 1965, Chaps. 7 and 8.

Educational Testing Service. *Multiple-Choice Questions: A Close Look.* Princeton, N.J.: Educational Testing Service, 1963.

Educational Testing Service. *Selecting an Achievement Test,* 2d ed. Princeton, N.J.: Educational Testing Service, 1961.

Kolstoe, Ralph H. *Introduction to Statistics for the Behavioral Sciences.* Homewood, Ill.: The Dorsey Press, 1969, Chaps. 2, 4, 5, 9.

Noll, Victor H. *Introduction to Educational Measurement,* 2d ed. Boston: Houghton Mifflin Company, 1965, Chaps. 3, 14, 15.

Remmers, H. H., N. L. Gage, and J. Francis Rummel. *A Practical Introduction to Measurement and Evaluation.* New York: Harper & Row, Publishers, Incorporated, 1965, Chaps. 3, 6.

Smith, Robert G., Jr. *Controlling the Quality of Training,* Technical Report 65-6. Alexandria, Va.: George Washington University Human Resources Research Office, June 1965.

Stanley, Julian C. *Measurement in Today's Schools,* 4th ed. Englewood Cliffs, N.J.: Prentice-Hall, Inc., 1964, Chaps. 3, 10.

Stodola, Quentin, et al. *Making the Classroom Test,* 2d ed. Princeton, N.J.: Educational Testing Service, 1961, Chap. 15.

Tracey, William R. *Evaluating Training and Development Systems.* AMA, 1968, Chap. V.

Wood, Dorothy Adkins. *Test Construction.* Columbus, Ohio: Charles E. Merrill Books, Inc., 1961, Chaps. 8, 9.

Youmans, Charles V. "Testing for Training and Development." In Robert L. Craig and Lester R. Bittel, eds. *Training and Development Handbook.* New York: McGraw-Hill Book Company, 1967, Chap. 4.

16

Following Up Graduates

Up to this point, all efforts in the development of the instructional system have been directed toward the production of personnel qualified to perform specific jobs in the operating units of the enterprise. Although various evaluative techniques and devices have been constructed, used, and analyzed during and at the conclusion of the training program, the real proof of the system is the graduates' ability to perform satisfactorily on the job. To determine the effectiveness of the instructional system, and to provide a basis for updating and improving it, objective data pertaining to the on-the-job activities and performance of personnel exposed to the system must be collected and analyzed. The purpose of this chapter is to identify the kinds of data needed, the means to be used in collecting these data, and the specific procedures to be followed in gathering, analyzing, reporting, and using the data.

After completing the chapter, the reader should be able to perform as follows:

Behavior	Collect, tabulate, analyze, interpret, and report follow-up data.
Conditions	Given: data-collection forms, reports and questionnaires; access to graduates of the system and their supervisors; the assistance of trained follow-up personnel and clerical workers.
Criterion	In accordance with the procedures described in this chapter.

NATURE, OBJECTIVES, AND IMPORTANCE
OF FOLLOW-UP

THE MEANING OF FOLLOW-UP

Essentially an objective and systematic program of follow-up constitutes an external criterion against which the effectiveness of a training or development system can be measured. Such evaluation is not an integral part of the training program, but rather it is concerned with an evaluation of the *products* of the training program. It attempts to answer these very basic questions: Do the products of the system perform the duties and tasks of their jobs with acceptable proficiency? Does the system produce the results intended? Was it worth the investment? What changes have occurred in job duties, tasks, and elements since the job analysis data were collected? What changes should be made in the training system?

OBJECTIVES OF FOLLOW-UP

The primary objective of the follow-up program is to collect detailed information pertaining to the quality of the job performances of graduates of the training or development program. A secondary purpose is to update the job data to insure that the training system incorporates current requirements. In other words, follow-up methods should be designed to identify specific weaknesses of the products of the system so that these weaknesses can be remedied. Appropriate changes can then be made in the system, and the list of job duties, tasks, and elements gathered earlier by job analysis teams can be rechecked so that needed changes in objectives can be effected.

In summary, data collected by means of follow-up should be used (1) to validate the system; (2) to add to, substitute, delete, or modify training system objectives; (3) to make appropriate changes to system content and emphasis; and (4) to adapt the system to remedy deficiencies uncovered.

IMPORTANCE OF FOLLOW-UP

Without a well-conceived and well-handled follow-up program, no training system can be validated. In addition, no training system, regardless of quality, can continue to be responsive to changing operational requirements without a good follow-up program. Follow-up is critically important to five groups.

Trainees. A well-conceived follow-up program goes a long way toward insuring trainees that the training and development program truly meets their on-the-job needs. If trainees feel inadequate after training, they are certain to become frustrated and may even quit.

Instructors. Instructors need feedback on their effectiveness in preparing personnel for specific jobs. Without adequate feedback, instructors perform more or less in the dark, making changes in the program based upon conjecture. It is also reinforcing and rewarding for instructors to know that their efforts are producing the required product with the desired quality.

Systems designers. The follow-up program provides them with the most meaningful criterion of the effectiveness of the system they have designed. In addition, they must have an objective and reliable means of keeping the training system current.

Training manager. The quality of the training manager's performance must be measured in terms of the performances of the graduates. These products of the training systems that he manages are the ultimate indicator of the value of his unit and his services to the enterprise that employs him.

Line management. Supervisors, middle managers, and executives need objective data to assure them that the systems established to meet their training requirements do in fact meet enterprise needs. They also need assurance that the programs will continue to meet these needs— that they will be constantly updated. In addition, top executives need to have evidence that the investment of enterprise resources in training and development is paying off.

METHODS OF COLLECTING DATA

There are three complementary methods of collecting follow-up data: on-site follow-up, reports from operating supervisors, and questionnaire surveys. Although on-site follow-up should always be the primary method of collecting these data, reports and questionnaires should also be used as backup or as a confirmatory means of judging the effectiveness of programs. Full advantage must be taken of these data-collection opportunities.

On-site Follow-up

The most reliable sources of data on how well the products of an instructional system perform their duties are the graduate himself, his immediate supervisor, and other managerial personnel. Thus on-site follow-up should be used as the primary means of validating and updating training and development systems. Qualified observer-interviewer teams must be selected and trained to perform the on-site follow-up. They must be able to use standardized interview and observation procedures and techniques, and associated data-collection instruments. The follow-up involves observation and interview of the graduates of the training program on the job and interviews with supervisory and managerial personnel (foremen, supervisors, and, when appropriate, middle managers and executives). At least a sampling of graduates of all training and development systems should be followed up on the job.

Live follow-up has certain advantages. First and foremost, the data collected are more likely to be complete and reliable because personnel are often more willing to talk about things they would not commit to writing. Secondly, follow-up personnel interview both the graduate and his immediate supervisor. This offers an opportunity to identify discrepancies in reports and resolve them on the spot. Third, on-site follow-up insures standardization in the collection of data. Data-collection forms and procedures are developed in advance, and personnel are trained to use them as intended. Lastly, live follow-up enables evaluators to pursue leads, draw out information, obtain clarification, and double-check their findings by observation.

But live follow-up has limitations as well. The primary drawback is cost. The time involved in preparing follow-up materials, training personnel, and making arrangements is considerable. To these costs must be added travel expenses and the costs of time away from the job for operating managers and graduates while the follow-up is being conducted. The second major limitation is that the expertise of follow-up personnel directly affects the results. Unless they know their jobs and carry them out with skill, the findings will not be worth the investment. Follow-up personnel may even damage a good program by causing unnecessary or inappropriate changes to the training or development system.

REPORTS FROM THE OPERATING SUPERVISORS

A secondary means of evaluating the system and updating job data is the establishment of a schedule of reports by immediate supervisors of the products of the system. Since operating supervisors guide the activities of the graduates on a day-to-day basis, they are in an excellent position to provide data about the strengths and weaknesses of the graduates and to report changes in the duties and tasks the graduates are required to perform.

A schedule of reports can be established that will provide the data required by those directly involved in the design and conduct of training programs to insure that the system operates as intended; that modifications, substitutions, or deletions are made in objectives and content as required; and that appropriate changes are made in other components of the system.

It is, of course, important that specific procedures be developed and implemented to include who is to report; what is to be reported; and when, how, and where the reports are to be rendered. Such standing operating procedures should be published and distributed to all personnel who work with the graduates of the system. It is also important that these reports be kept as simple as possible so as not to add an unreasonable burden on supervisory personnel.

Two types of reports are needed: *spot reports* and *regular reports*. Spot reports are prepared by operating elements when items are identified that are likely to have a significant impact on training. For example, if changes in equipment, procedures, or manning levels are to be implemented, the training activity must be immediately notified so that plans can be initiated to modify the training program, its objectives and content, or its frequency, input, or prerequisites.

Regular reports should also be prepared by operating elements on the adequacy of the products of the programs. The frequency of these reports will depend upon the number of trainees assigned to the operating element and on the length of the time interval between graduation and assignment to the job. In any event, a report on the adequacy of every graduate received by an operating element should be submitted between two and three months after the trainee has been assigned to the job. This report should indicate, at least in adjectival terms, the ability of the graduate to perform all job tasks. It should also describe deficiencies and the probable reasons for them in enough detail to enable trainers to analyze and adjust their training systems.

Reports by operating elements have certain advantages: (1) These reports give trainers a meaningful estimate of their effectiveness in meeting the needs of line supervisory and managerial personnel for trained workers; (2) the reports provide data for reviewing and revising training and development programs in conjunction with other evaluative means; and the reports insure that the training activity is alerted to changes in operations which will have an impact on the programs.

But reports also have disadvantages: (1) decisions of line personnel on the adequacy of graduates are often subjective, based on overall estimates of subordinates rather than on the performance of specific job tasks; (2) line personnel may fail to render reports as required, or the reports may be incomplete; and (3) designing, conducting, and controlling a reporting system can be costly.

QUESTIONNAIRE SURVEYS

Questionnaires can be used to good advantage in supplementing data obtained by other means of follow-up. In addition, during periods of austerity and nonavailability of funds to support on-site follow-up, questionnaires may be used as an alternative means of collecting the required data.

Questionnaires can be designed to elicit information about the strengths and weaknesses of graduates of a training or development system and about changes in the duties and tasks of the job from the point of view of the graduates, their immediate supervisors, and other staff, supervisory, or managerial personnel.

Questionnaires may be of two types: *special* or *standard*. Special questionnaires may be prepared when a specific problem or deficiency is being studied. They are administered in response to a one-time problem. Regular questionnaires are standard forms prepared for distribution to all personnel trained or supervising graduates of a particular training system.

The advantages of the questionnaire method are as follows: (1) A 100 percent sample of the graduates and their supervisors can be obtained. (2) The questionnaire is less costly in terms of the expenditure of resources than is live follow-up. (3) It is an excellent means of validating data obtained by on-site methods and reports. However, the questionnaire method has several disadvantages: (1) returns may be incomplete, hence unusable; (2) questionnaires are difficult and time-consuming to construct; and (3) respondents may distort, deceive, or otherwise provide data which are inaccurate or misleading.

PROCEDURES FOR ON-SITE FOLLOW-UP

Follow-up requires detailed and complete planning if it is to provide usable results. In planning for on-site follow-up, the steps below should be taken:

Step 1. Select members of the follow-up team. Personnel selected to participate in on-site follow-up should be individuals who have demonstrated their objectivity and the ability to interview and observe. They should be qualified trainers, know the training system in intimate detail, and have more than a nodding acquaintance with the job to be surveyed.

Step 2. Train the members of the team. A formal training program for evaluators should be developed and conducted. This program should include a review of the techniques of observing and interviewing, the development and use of standard data-collection forms (see Figs. 16-1, 16-2, and 16-3), and a review of methods of evaluating and analyzing data.

Step 3. Identify the specific class or classes to be followed up. Ideally, all groups exposed to the training or development system should be followed up on site. However, where the output of a training program is very large, follow-up of all classes may be neither necessary nor practical. Timing is an important consideration. The time between graduation from the training system and follow-up on the job should be of sufficient length to enable the graduate to progress to the point where he is performing all job tasks but not so long that his proficiency is as much attributable to on-the-job training as it is to the formal training he received.

Step 4. Identify the specific operating elements to which graduates of the class or classes have been assigned. Usually this information is obtained before the graduates leave the training facility; however, a check must be made prior to follow-up to insure that the graduate has not resigned, been dismissed, or been reassigned to another unit.

Step 5. Select the operating elements to be visited and the graduates to be interviewed and observed by name. In selecting units or divisions, if less than a 100 percent sample of graduates is to be followed up, observe these rules:

    a. Select units that are representative in terms of enterprise organization and operations.

    b. Select units that reflect typical job requirements for the training or development system being studied.

    c. Select units that are representative in terms of geography, product, service, and environment.

Step 6. Develop a schedule for follow-up to include units, locations, dates, time of the visits, and the names of graduates.

Step 7. Notify the organization to be visited of the purpose, time, and duration of the visits, and, in general, who and what will be involved.

Step 8. Review documents pertaining to the organization to be visited and the jobs to be followed up. Include study of the following as a minimum:

    a. Mission and objectives.

    b. Organization chart.

(*text continues on page 398*)

Figure 16-1. Sample standard data-collection form for immediate supervisors.

Organization _____ Location _____

Interviewee _____ Position title _____

Name of graduate _____ Job _____

1. In comparison with other men in this job of the same grade and experience, how do you rate this graduate?

   Circle one: Outstanding   Above average   Average   Below average   Unsatisfactory

2. Rate this man's performance on each of the following tasks, and identify specific deficiencies in knowledge or skill.

Job tasks	Rating					Deficiencies
	E	G	F	P	N/A	
A.						
B.						
C.						
D.						
E.						
F.						
G.						

3. What additional tasks is the incumbent required to perform?

4. What can the training activity do to improve training for this job?

5. Other comments.

Interviewer _____

Figure 16-2. Sample standard data-collection form for graduates.

Organization _____ Location _____

Name of interviewee _____ Job title _____

Rank in graduating class _____ Supervisor's rating _____

1. How many weeks elapsed from the time you graduated and the date you reported for duty? _____ weeks.

2. How many days of on job training did you have before being placed on this job? _____ days.

3. How long have you been on this job? _____ weeks.

4. Rate yourself on each of the job tasks in this list.

Job tasks	Rating					Comments
	E	G	F	P	N/A	
A.						
B.						
C.						
D.						
E.						
F.						
G.						

5. What additional tasks are you required to perform?

6. With which aspects of your job do you have the most difficulty?

7. What can the training activity do to improve training in your job?

Interviewer _____

Figure 16-3. Sample standard data-collection form for higher level supervisory, managerial, and staff personnel.

Organization _____ Location _____

Interviewee _____ Position title _____

1. How do graduates of these training programs compare with graduates of earlier classes?

Training program	Number of graduates	Better	About the same	Poorer

2. In what specific ways are they better or poorer?

3. What was the level of job proficiency brought to your organization by graduates of these training programs?

Training program	Excellent	Good	Fair	Poor

4. What deficiencies in job knowledge and skills did graduates of these jobs display upon arrival at your unit?

Job	Deficiencies

Other comments:

Interviewer _____

   c. Organization and functions manual.
   d. Capabilities, products, and services in terms of both type and volume.
   e. Job descriptions of personnel to be interviewed or observed.
   f. The current training program.

Step 9. Prepare and rehearse separate but standard briefings for the operating manager and his staff, for line supervisors, and for graduates.

Step 10. Make travel arrangements, including transportation and housing.

CONDUCTING ON-SITE FOLLOW-UP

The following steps should be taken in conducting on-site follow-up:

Step 1. Brief the operating manager and his staff on the purposes, procedures, and requirements of the follow-up team. Include these items in the briefing:

   a. Why the follow-up is being performed.
   b. What the team requires in the way of assistance.
   c. How the team plans to conduct the follow-up.
   d. The approximate amount of time involved for each category of individual to be interviewed and observed.
   e. How the follow-up data will be used.

Step 2. Study the organization and functions of the operating unit. Pay particular attention to the following items:

   a. The accuracy of the organization charts and the organization and functions manual in reflecting the "real" operating structure.
   b. Local directives, instructions, and standing operating procedures pertaining to the jobs to be surveyed.

Step 3. Brief supervisory personnel on the purposes and procedures of the follow-up. Include the following information:

   a. All the information provided the operating manager and his staff.
   b. The specific kind and amount of assistance required by the team.
   c. A proposed schedule for interviewing and observing graduates and for interviewing supervisory personnel.

Step 4. Review the records of graduates to be interviewed, and note pertinent information on the follow-up forms.

Step 5. Brief each graduate on the purposes and procedures of the follow-up. Include these items:

a. Pertinent items from prior briefings of the operating manager and supervisors.
b. A proposed time for interview and observation.
c. Ask the graduate to do some preliminary thinking about his duties and how he performs them.

Step 6. Observe the graduate on the job. Follow these rules:

a. Observe long enough to see performance of the total job (if possible) and the environment in which it is performed. If observation of all job duties is not possible, stay long enough to observe performance of a major job task.
b. Ask questions only when absolutely necessary.
c. Make careful notes of observations.
d. Otherwise conduct the observation in accordance with the procedures defined in Chapter 14.

Step 7. Interview the graduate. Follow these procedures:

a. Allow at least one full hour for each interview.
b. Conduct the interview in accordance with the procedures defined in Chapter 14.
c. Use the job or task analysis techniques and forms described in Chapter 3 to record new tasks.
d. Cover all points on the follow-up form and make all required entries.
e. Orally summarize the main points to be sure that you have a clear and complete picture of the interviewee's observations and evaluations.

Step 8. Interview the graduate's immediate supervisor, and record the findings on the appropriate form. Conduct the interview in accordance with the rules presented in Chapter 14. In cases where the graduate and the supervisor disagree, attempt to resolve the discrepancy.

Step 9. Interview the personnel at the next higher level of supervision or management, using a standard interview form and the procedures defined in Chapter 14.

Step 10. Provide the operating manager of the unit with an oral summary of findings at an exit interview. Give him an opportunity to make additional comments.

POSTVISIT ACTIVITIES

If the on-site evaluation has been well thought out and conducted according to plan, the follow-up team should have, in readily usable form, a complete picture of the performance of the graduates of the training or development system under study. They should also have all data required to update the list of job duties, tasks, and elements. The following steps should be taken in tabulating, analyzing, and reporting the data:

Step 1. Tabulate the data provided by graduates, immediate supervisors, and other management personnel. This step should be relatively straightforward if the data-collection instruments have been well designed.

Step 2. Analyze the data from these standpoints:

a. What are the major deficiencies of graduates (if any), and to what may they be attributed?
b. What duties, tasks, and elements need to be added, deleted, or modified for the job under consideration?
c. What changes might remedy the deficiencies?

Step 3. Prepare a report and submit it for comment to the training manager, systems designers, and instructors. Include the following items in the report:

a. Major findings.
b. Recommendations for changes in the performance objectives of the training or development system.
c. Recommendations for changes in strategy, equipment, materials, documents, or any other pertinent component of the training system.

Step 4. Following coordination of the report and receipt of comments or concurrence, make required changes in the Performance Objectives Workcards using the procedures described in Chapter 4. Then initiate action to effect other system changes (criterion measures, course content, sequence, time allocations, instructional strategies, equipment, instructor requirements, course prerequisites, and instructional materials) in accordance with the procedures defined in the appropriate chapters of this book.

PROCEDURES FOR OBTAINING REPORTS FROM SUPERVISORY PERSONNEL

Designing Reports

If reports are to serve as a basis for effecting revisions to a training and development system, they must be designed with care. Factors which are most indicative of the success or failure, efficiency or inefficiency of the training and development system must be identified and used as the basis for the reporting system. The system must insure that reports are timely, accurate, objective, and usable. In terms of content and format, they must be appropriate for both the level of management receiving them and the uses to which they will be put. The reports must be sufficiently frequent to preclude wide deviations or significant degradation in the system before they are detected and yet not so frequent that an undue burden is placed upon reporting elements.

DESIGNING A REPORTING SYSTEM

The following steps should be taken in designing a reporting system:

Step 1. Determine the specific categories of information required and the source of each type of data. Consider:

a. Deficiencies in the output of the training or development system in terms of both skills and numbers (quality and quantity).
b. Changes in equipment, operations, staffing, or products and services.

Step 2. Design a simple report form that incorporates all required data, and prepare specific and detailed directions for completing the form.

Step 3. Submit the draft report form and directions to the training manager and other systems designers for comment and recommendations for changes.

Step 4. Revise the form and directions in accordance with the comments of the training manager and other systems designers.

ANALYZING AND USING REPORTS

The very nature of reports demands special handling. For one thing, the volume of reports received at any one time will vary considerably. Spot reports especially cannot be programmed since they are submitted when supervisory personnel identify a critical deficiency or a new training requirement. Below are the steps to be followed in analyzing and using reports:

Step 1. Establish a format, procedures, and time frame for tabulating and analyzing reports.

Step 2. Screen all reports upon receipt. If the nature of the report seems to indicate the urgency of an action, devise a plan for checking the item—this may involve the administration of a special questionnaire survey or on-site visit to the operating element to validate the new requirement.

Step 3. Tabulate routine recurring reports periodically. This may be done quarterly, semiannually, or annually.

Step 4. Analyze the data from these standpoints:

a. The major deficiencies of graduates and a tentative hypothesis as to what they can be attributed.
b. Changes in job duties and tasks and their impact on training resources.

Step 5. Prepare a consolidated report, and submit it to the training manager, other systems designers, and instructors for comment. In the report include conclusions and recommendations pertaining to

a. Changes in Performance Objective Workcards.
b. Changes in content, emphasis, and sequence.
c. Changes in any other component of the training or development system.

Step 6. Following receipt of comments or concurrence, make required changes in the system.

PROCEDURES FOR CONDUCTING
QUESTIONNAIRE FOLLOW-UP

CONSTRUCTING QUESTIONNAIRES

Questionnaires should be constructed for each training and development system operated by the training activity. Separate questionnaires should be designed for graduates of the system, their immediate supervisors, and the next higher echelon of supervision or management. The steps in constructing follow-up questionnaires are as follows:

Step 1. Determine the types and sources of information required. Include:

a. Evaluation of the job performance of individuals or groups.
b. Changes in job duties, tasks, and elements.

Step 2. Draft the questions.

Step 3. Assemble the questionnaire; design it in such a way as to permit machine tabulation where possible.

Step 4. Draft directions and cover letter to the respondent. Include:

a. The purpose of the questionnaire and the use to which data will be put.

b. The approximate amount of time required to complete the questionnaire.

c. When and how to return the completed form.

Step 5. Prepare a final draft and submit it to the training manager and other systems designers for criticism and comment.

Step 6. Revise the questionnaire.

Step 7. Determine the size of the sample to be obtained. (Usually it is desirable to survey 100 percent of the population.)

Step 8. Administer the questionnaire.

TABULATING, ANALYZING, AND USING QUESTIONNAIRE RETURNS

Essentially, the same procedures should be used in tabulating, analyzing, and using data from questionnaires as with the other means of follow-up. The main difference is that questionnaire returns are received at approximately the same time and can be tabulated in total. The steps follow:

Step 1. Tabulate all questionnaires.

Step 2. Analyze the data collected.

a. Identify deviations from established job performance standards, and hypothesize the reasons therefore.

b. Isolate the element of the process which is the possible cause for deviation.

c. Determine the direct cause of the deviation.

Step 3. Draft recommendations for adjusting or modifying the training system to remedy the deficiency.

Step 4. Submit recommendations to the training manager and other systems designers for comment.

Step 5. Upon receipt of comments or concurrence, make the required changes in the training or development system.

INTERPRETING DATA AND FORMULATING CONCLUSIONS AND RECOMMENDATIONS

The most difficult phase of follow-up, whether conducted on-site, by reports, by questionnaire, or a combination of all three means, is the interpretation and use of the data collected. Unless this part of follow-up is conducted with thoroughness and insight, the program will be a dismal failure. Personnel assigned to the tasks of interpreting data and formulating conclusions and recommendations must be handpicked for the job. They must be knowledgeable about both the job and the training system, dedicated to the task of providing the best training possible, cost conscious, and imaginative. In addition, they must follow a carefully sequenced series of steps in the process. These steps are defined below.

INTERPRETING DATA, DEVELOPING CONCLUSIONS, AND FORMULATING RECOMMENDATIONS

There are seven distinct steps in the analytical process of interpreting and using follow-up data. They are as follows:

Step 1. Define the problem. Data collected by means of observation, interview, report, and questionnaire do not directly identify training problems or system shortfalls. The real problem indicated by the data must be defined. The real problem is identified by:

a. Studying the facts collected and tabulated.
b. Examining all criticisms, suggestions, and complaints of respondents.
c. Judging the validity of each comment by checking it against other collection means.
d. Summarizing the situation or deficiency in simple terms so that anyone can grasp it.
e. Stating key facts that are *missing*, so that allowances can be made for the gap in identifying courses of action.
f. Examining every aspect of the situation to reveal organization, assignment, utilization, supervisory, or training weaknesses, and means of improvement.
g. Summarizing indicators of the problem in writing.

Step 2. Determine the cause of the problem or deficiency. Before a problem can be solved, it must be clearly defined and its underlying causes determined. The task here is to clarify the conditions that led to the problem or deficiency and that are sustaining it. Find answers to the following questions:

a. How long has the problem existed?
b. When and where did it start?
c. Is it widespread?
d. How was the deficiency noted?
e. What are the basic causes?

Step 3. Formulate criteria for judging the adequacy and practicality of the solution or remedy. Criteria for the solution must be identified and formulated before a solution is proposed. These criteria are essentially yardsticks against which alternative courses of action are measured. Criteria can be identified in terms of:

a. End results to be achieved, such as the acquisition of new skills, deletion of job tasks, or higher proficiency levels.
b. The time and other resources required or allowable to achieve these results.
c. Any other goals or limitations involved in reaching a workable solution.

Step 4. Select a solution or remedy. In step 3 the importance of formulating criteria for the solution was emphasized. These essentially provide standards against which to measure the adequacy or acceptability of alternative solutions. The procedure for finding a solution involves:

a. Canvassing all methods and procedures that could conceivably solve the problem.
b. Withholding judgment about the value of any solution until as many alternatives as possible have been identified.
c. Testing each alternative solution against the criteria developed in step 3.
d. Outlining the solution in broad terms for presentation to decision makers. Include: a list of the defects revealed by the follow-up; a picture of the proposed major changes to the system; the advantages and limitations of each proposal; the costs of the change in terms of the expenditure of time, materials, manpower, and other resources; and the steps required to place the new plan into effect.

Step 5. Get the solution or remedy approved in principle. The goal of the analyst is to develop a solution which will not only solve the problem but which will be implemented. Before working out the details of the solution, it is wise to get acceptance of the proposed solution in principle before going to the work of preparing detailed plans. For presentation to the decision maker, a complete summary of the proposal should be prepared as follows:

a. The subject and the scope of the study.
b. A definition of the problem deficiency and its causes.
c. The criteria to be met by the solution.
d. The proposed solution and its advantages and disadvantages.

Step 6. Develop the remedy or solution in detail. This step requires painstaking attention to detail. It is essential that the detailed solution be so clearly and carefully worked out that it will be understood and used by those who act on approved recommendations. Include the following items:

    a. What is to be done.
    b. Who is to do it.
    c. When it is to be done.
    d. How it is to be done.

Step 7. Install the changes and follow-up to insure that an effective solution or remedy has been provided. Develop a procedure and a schedule to evaluate all changes or recommendations approved and installed.

PREPARING A FOLLOW-UP REPORT

Every completed follow-up survey should be concluded by a report. This report should be written, and it should present the essentials of the follow-up evaluation clearly and concisely so that conclusions can be grasped quickly and easily. In addition, the report should include enough detail and discussion to insure correct interpretation of the findings.

A final written follow-up report serves the following purposes.

Communication. Reports are a means of informing the training manager, the trainers, operating executives, and other interested personnel of conclusions reached and the supporting facts. Also, when a follow-up has been carried out and is succeeded by a properly written report, recommendations which follow logically from the facts will be more readily understood and accepted by decision makers.

Record. Reports of follow-up serve as a concise, permanent record of findings. They will be a constant source of reference for training and other interested personnel.

Control. Reports facilitate the follow-up of accepted recommendations to insure their installation and evaluation.

FORMAT

A standard format should be used for all follow-up reports, but the format should be flexible enough to fit specific situations and problems. A workable format follows.

1. Introductory material. The following items precede the main body of the follow-up report:
    a. Letter of transmittal. This is used to forward the report to cognizant

authorities. It is frequently used by the training manager to express concurrence with the findings and approval or disapproval with all or certain recommendations found in the report.

b. Title page. This page identifies the job or jobs covered by the follow-up, the name of the organizational element conducting the follow-up, and the date.

c. Summary. Readers of a report want to know the findings immediately. Then, if they are interested, they can examine the evidence presented in support of the conclusions and recommendations. The summary, therefore, is presented first, although it is written last. It should be simple, clear, brief, and well organized, yet contain the key materials of the report. Usually, a summary contains three parts: (1) the background of the survey and a brief statement of the objectives or problem of the survey; (2) the method of data collection and analysis used; and (3) a résumé of the principal conclusions and recommendations.

d. Table of contents. All titles and subtitles in the text, all appendixes, and index, if prepared, are included in the table of contents.

e. List of tables and figures. If tables and figures are included in the report, they are listed immediately following the table of contents.

2. Body of the report. The main body of the report contains a discussion of the problem or problems requiring solution. Each problem should be presented as follows:

a. Statement of the problem. The statement of the problem is the basis of the entire report. The purpose and scope are defined. In simple terms, what needs to be accomplished is stated, such as describing a deficiency to be overcome. Assumptions are also identified or listed. Any information relating to priorities, need for emergency implementation, or other critical considerations should be included here.

b. Findings. Here are stated the facts that bear on the problem. Background material, references, and corroborating evidence should be included. Opinion should be used only when absolutely necessary and should be so identified. This section should also include definitions and information about the procedures used in the study. If the data are extremely detailed, tables or appendixes should be used to present them; however, their contents should be summarized in the body of the report.

c. Discussion. Here an analysis is made of the facts found by the follow-up survey. All results are stated, and relationships arising from the findings are explained. Next the criteria of the solution are described. The section also includes a listing of all alternative solutions or remedies considered as possible solutions of the problem together with their advantages and limitations. The purpose is to set the stage for reaching conclusions and recommendations.

d. Conclusions. The conclusions section contains statements describing the significance of findings relative to the solution of the problem. Where the findings and discussion disclose that the problem can be solved by only one of the alternative proposals, this section contains a careful evaluation of the proposal and describes its effects on the instructional system under consideration. The reasoning used should be explained. All inferences or deductions which bear on the final recommendation should be stated. Conclusions must follow from the facts presented.

   e. Recommendations. Here, recommendations are listed succinctly. These constitute a plan of action to solve the problem or remedy the deficiency. Each recommendation should include what is to be done, who is to do it, and when, where, and how it is to be done. Recommendations are derived from the statements made in the "findings," "discussion," and "conclusions" sections of the report.

3. Appendixes. Detailed or complex material or tables needed to support or verify portions of the body of the report should be placed in the appendix. This is done so that ideas may be developed clearly and without interference of too much detail in the body. However, as pointed out earlier, these details should be summarized or referred to in the body of the report.

4. Index. An index may be added to make longer reports more usable. This applies particularly to follow-up reports which deal with more than one job or training system.

CHECKLISTS

REVIEWING PLANS FOR ON-SITE FOLLOW-UP

1. Are the purposes of the follow-up clearly defined?
2. Have members of the follow-up team been carefully selected? Do they:
   a. Understand the purposes of the survey?
   b. Know the jobs to be surveyed?
   c. Know the current system of training for the job?
3. Have members of the team received training in the techniques of interviewing and observing?
4. Have appropriate data-collection forms been developed?
5. Have the specific units, classes, and individuals to be followed up been identified?
   a. Are they representative in terms of enterprise organization and operations?
   b. Do they reflect typical job requirements?
   c. Are they representative in terms of geography, product, service, and environment?
6. Is the timing of the follow-up visits appropriate (usually one to three months following completion of the training)?
7. Has a schedule of visits been developed, coordinated, and distributed to all concerned?

8. Have standard briefings been prepared and rehearsed for operating managers, line supervisors, and graduates?
9. Have organizational documents been reviewed by the team?
10. Have adequate transportation and housing arrangements been made for the team?

REVIEWING PLANS FOR FOLLOW-UP BY MEANS OF REPORTS FROM OPERATING ELEMENTS

1. Are the purposes of the reports clear to all concerned?
2. Are the reporting procedures and forms well designed?
   a. Are reports timely?
   b. Are they objective?
   c. Are they appropriate for the uses to which they will be put?
3. Do reports cover the following as a minimum:
   a. Deficiencies in knowledge or skills of graduates?
   b. Changes in staffing requirements?
   c. Changes in operations, equipment, techniques, products, or services?
4. Are directions for completing and returning reports clear?

REVIEWING PLANS FOR FOLLOW-UP BY MEANS OF QUESTIONNAIRE SURVEY

1. Are the purposes of the survey clear to all concerned?
2. Does the cover letter or instruction sheet to the respondent clearly define the purposes of the survey?
3. Have separate questionnaires been constructed for graduates, supervisory personnel, and line (or staff) managers?
4. Do the questionnaires provide for gathering data concerning the following:
   a. Proficiency of graduates?
   b. Deficiencies in knowledge or skill of the graduates?
   c. Needed changes in skills or job knowledge due to changes in the job or the work environment?
5. Is a 100 percent survey of graduates and their immediate supervisors planned?

SELECTED REFERENCES

Cenci, Louis. *Skill Training for the Job.* New York: Pitman Publishing Corporation, 1966, pp. 213–217.
Crumb, Charles V. "Training Followup." *Training in Business and Industry* (July, August 1965), 2:4: 39–40.

DePhillips, Frank A., William M. Berliner, and James J. Cribbin. *Management of Training Programs.* Homewood, Ill.: Richard D. Irwin, Inc., 1960, Chap. 15.

Kellogg, Marion S. "The Ethics of Employee Appraisal." *Personnel* (July, August 1965), 42:4: 33–39.

Kleinmuntz, Benjamin. *Personality Measurement: An Introduction.* Homewood, Ill.: The Dorsey Press, 1967, Chaps. 4–7.

Miller, Richard D. "A Systems Concept of Training." *Training and Development Journal* (April 1969), 23:4: 4–14.

Morrison, James H. "Planning and Scheduling." In Robert L. Craig and Lester R. Bittel, eds. New York: McGraw-Hill Book Company, 1967, pp. 583–588.

Rose, Homer C. "A Plan for Training Evaluation." *Training and Development Journal* (May 1968), 22:5: 38–51.

Tracey, William R. *Evaluating Training and Development Systems.* AMA, 1968, pp. 156–159.

Tracey, William R., Edward B. Flynn, Jr., and C. L. John Legere, "System Approach Gets Results." *Training in Business and Industry* (June 1967), 4:6: 17–21ff.

Tracey, William R., Edward B. Flynn, Jr., and C. L. John Legere, "Systems Thinking for Vocational Education." *Educate* (November 1968), 1:3: 18–24.

Appendix A

Cost Analysis Form

I. Direct costs

  A. Administration and supervision
    1. Director or coordinator
    2. Instructor supervisors   _____
    3. Clerk-typists   _____

  B. Instruction
    1. Instructors
    2. Assistant instructors   _____
    3. Projectionists   _____

  C. Instructional materials
    1. Course outlines or programs of instruction
      a. Preparation or drafting
      b. Typing   _____
      c. Proofing   _____
      d. Reproduction   _____
      e. Cost of materials   _____
      f. Distribution costs   _____
    2. Training aids (films, transparencies, posters, diagrams, maps, charts, models, mock-ups, placards)
      a. Cost for purchase
      and/or   _____
      b. Rental costs
      and/or   _____

    c. Development costs
       (1) Cost of materials   _____
       (2) Labor costs   _____
       (3) Processing costs   _____
    d. Distribution costs   _____
 3. Texts, programmed materials, handouts, supplies, and tests
    a. Commercial texts and workbooks, and programmed materials   _____
    b. Costs of contract development of texts, workbooks, programmed materials and tests   _____
    c. Costs of producing texts, workbooks, programmed materials and tests   _____
       (1) Planning
           (a) Job or task analyses   _____
           (b) Selecting and writing training objectives   _____
           (c) Constructing criterion measures   _____
       (2) Development
           (a) Design of materials   _____
           (b) Drafting or writing texts, workbooks, program frames, and test items   _____
           (c) Illustrations and artwork
                1. Labor   _____
                2. Materials   _____
                3. Processing   _____
           (d) Printing and typing costs
                1. Labor   _____
                2. Materials   _____
                3. Processing   _____
           (e) Editing and proofing   _____
           (f) Validating texts, programs, workbooks, tests
                1. Initial review   _____
                2. Individual testing
                    a. Writer or programmer   _____
                    b. Test population   _____
                3. Field testing
                    a. Instructor or administrator   _____
                    b. Test population   _____
                4. Tabulation and statistical analysis
                    a. Costs of EAM/ADP time   _____
                    b. Analyst time   _____
           (g) Revision of draft materials
                1. Rewriting   _____
                2. Review and editing   _____
                3. Illustrations and art work _____

    a. Labor   _____
    b. Materials or supplies   _____
    c. Processing   _____
   4. Publication costs
    a. Labor   _____
    b. Materials   _____
    c. Processing   _____
   5. Retesting
    a. Administrator   _____
    b. Test population   _____
  (h) Tabulation and statistical analysis
   1. EAM/ADP time   _____
   2. Analyst time   _____
  (i) Distribution costs   _____
 D. Training equipment
  1. Training aids equipment   _____
  2. Tools and test equipment   _____
  3. Operating gear   _____
  4. Supplies and spare parts   _____
II. Indirect costs
 A. Services
  1. Personnel
   a. Screening and selecting students _____
   b. Processing in and out   _____
  2. Consultation in developing and reviewing curriculum materials
   a. Subject-matter experts   _____
   b. Line supervisors   _____
  3. Maintenance (labor costs)
   a. Setting up classrooms, shops, and laboratories, including equipment _____
   b. Cleaning training areas and office space _____
  4. Equipment, facilities repair, supplies, and spare parts
   a. Training aids equipment _____
   b. Operational equipment   _____
   c. Tools and test equipment _____
   d. Furnishings   _____
   e. Electrical and heating equipment _____
 B. Utilities and facilities
  1. Electricity   _____
  2. Heat   _____
  3. Furnishings   _____
 C. Student costs
  1. Salary while in training
   or

Loss of productivity in regular assignments _____
  2. Travel and per diem
     a. Transportation to training area _____
     b. Per diem costs _____
  D. Instructor costs
     1. Recruiting costs _____
        a. Advertising _____
        b. Screening and selection _____
     2. Training costs
        a. Cost per instructor _____
        b. Travel _____
        c. Per diem _____
        d. Supplies _____
  E. Instructional materials
     1. Reviewing and selecting commercial materials _____
     2. Selecting contractors for development
        of materials _____
     3. Consultation fees _____
  F. Equipment
     1. Costs of moving equipment _____
     2. Estimated loss to production _____

Total cost _____

CALCULATION OF UNIT COSTS

1. Cost per trainee $= \dfrac{\text{Total cost of system}}{\text{Number of trainees per year}}$

2. Cost per hour $= \dfrac{\text{Total cost of system}}{\text{Number of hours instruction per year}}$

3. Cost per square foot $= \dfrac{\text{Total cost of system}}{\text{Number of square feet of floor space}}$

4. Equipment cost per trainee $= \dfrac{\text{Total cost of equipment}}{\text{Number of trainees in } X \text{ years}^{*}}$

5. Equipment cost per hour $= \dfrac{\text{Total cost of equipment}}{\text{Number of hours instruction in } X \text{ years}^{*}}$

6. Materials cost per trainee $= \dfrac{\text{Total cost of materials}}{\text{Number of trainees}}$

$^{*} X =$ projected life of equipment.

Appendix B

Evaluation of Proposals for Contract Training

Directions: Indicate the degree to which the contractor's proposal fulfills each requirement by entering one of the following numbers in the space provided.

6   Outstanding: a complete, clear, and exceptionally well-conceived response.
5   Superior: an extensive and detailed response.
4   Very good: a substantial response in clearly definable detail.
3   Good: a significant response that clearly meets requirements.
2   Fair: an acceptable response, but barely meets requirements.
1   Poor: a weak response; risky.
0   Nonresponsive.

Rating Elements	Rating

1. Understanding the problem.
   a. Knowledge of enterprise organization and operations. _____
   b. Understanding enterprise training and development goals, and policies. _____
   c. Familiarity with current training and development concepts and technology. _____
   d. Experience in solving similar or related training problems. _____
   e. Understanding the objectives of the proposed training program. _____
2. Proposed training system.
   a. Adequacy of objective statements (behavioral). _____
   b. Appropriateness of proposed methodology. _____
   c. Appropriateness of proposed media and materials. _____
   d. Appropriateness of proposed system of trainee and instructor organization. _____
   e. Adequacy of content and coverage. _____
   f. Appropriateness of criterion measures. _____
   g. Flexibility of proposed system. _____
   h. Efficiency and objectivity of proposed means of collecting, analyzing, evaluating, and validating the training system. _____
   i. Appropriateness of proposed sequence and scheduling. _____
   j. Appropriateness of proposed course length. _____
3. Organization, staffing, and capabilities of contractor force.
   a. Adequacy of the number of personnel to be assigned to the program. _____
   b. Adequacy of arrangements for supervision of personnel. _____
   c. Educational qualifications of personnel. _____
   d. Technical qualifications of personnel. _____
   e. Experience of personnel in preparing and conducting training programs. _____
   f. Stability of contractor personnel. _____
   g. Adequacy of contractor's training facilities. _____
   h. Adequacy of available trainee housing and subsistence facilities. _____

Total score _____

Index

absolute rating method, 114-119

acceptable performance, criterion of, 100

Adaptability Test, 327

adjectival scores, 371

adjustment tasks, 173

administrability, of tests, 137-138

administrative tasks, 173

aiming tasks, 172

applications, 326

appreciation, defined, 169

Army General Classification Battery, 327

Army War College, instructor prerequisites at, 299

assistant assignments, 32

attitude, defined, 168

attrition, from training, 316

auditory aids, in training, 240, 247-248

behavioral objectives, formulation of, 78

behavior standards, in writing objective, 98-99

Bennett's Test of Mechanical Comprehension, 327

brainstorming, as training strategy, 208-209

Burgess Cellulose Company, 368

buzz sessions, as training strategy, 209

California Psychological Inventory, 327

case study, as training strategy, 203-204

CCTV (closed-circuit television systems), 220-222, 237

central tendency, measures of, 158-159

change, training and, 21-22

checklist, in job analysis, 48-49

clerical and administrative tasks, 173

closed-circuit TV systems, 220-222, 237

closed-loop system, in systems analysis, 2, 5-6

coaching, as face-to-face counseling, 31

coding tasks, 173

combination instruction and team learning
  instructor in, 303
  as training strategy, 202-203

committees, 32
  in training strategy, 209-210

communication objectives, 79-80

communication skills, in instructor, 296

comprehensiveness, of tests, 138

computer-based instructional systems, 219-220

conference method
  advance preparation in, 195
  advantages of, 195
  directed discussion in, 194
  instructor and, 303
  seminar in, 194

objectivity in, 137
off-the-shelf or instructor-made, 135
optical scoring of, 367
oral objective, 144
paper-and-pencil, 144
paraphrasing in, 364
performance, 145-146, 361
planning of, 147
range of, 159
ratings and, 144-145
reliability coefficient for, 162-163
reliability in, 137, 162-163
scoring of, 366-371
   see also test scores
self-reports as, 328
stages in building of, 146-147
standardability of, 138
standard deviation of, 159-161
standard error of measurement in,
   163-164
standardized, 135
tailor-made, 134-135
as tools, 360
in trainee selection, 327-328
types of, 144-146
validity of, 136, 161-162
test administration
   criterion measures and, 362-366
   procedures for, 150-153, 363
test analysis, steps in, 155-156, 165
test conditions, standardized, 363
test construction, steps in, 149-150
test directions, importance of, 362-
   363
testing programs, deficiencies in, 361-
   362
test item characteristics, 164-165
test reliability, 137, 162-164
test results
   scoring of, 371-386
      see also test scores
   types of scores in, 371-376
test scores
   adjectival, 371
   checklists in, 386-387

comparison with system criterion,
   385
frequency distributions in, 372, 378
graphic report of, 384
IBM punched cards in, 368-370
percentage and percentile ranks in,
   373-374
probability distribution curves in,
   374-375
rank order in, 371
raw numerical, 371
recording of, 370
reporting to administrative or records office, 383
reporting to instructors, 376-379
reporting to line supervisors and
   managers, 383
reporting to systems designers and
   training manager, 383
reporting to trainee, 379-383
sample report in, 381
standard, 374-375
standard deviation in, 376
stanine scores and, 376
test characteristics in, 380
types of, 371-376
test tryout and analysis, steps in, 155-
   156
test validity, 161-162
T-group training, as training strategy,
   206
three-dimensional aids, 240, 244-245
time allocations
   in lesson-plan production, 270-272
   in training evaluation, 336
tools, test construction and, 150
tracking tasks, 172
trade training, 27
trainee(s)
   block evaluation questionnaire for,
      347
   evaluation of, 335
   number of per instructor, 305-306,
      315-316
   reporting of test scores to, 379-383